REANALYSIS IN SENTENCE PROCESSING

STUDIES IN THEORETICAL PSYCHOLINGUISTICS

VOLUME 21

The titles published in this series are listed at the end of this volume.

REANALYSIS IN SENTENCE PROCESSING

edited by

JANET DEAN FODOR

CUNY Graduate School and University Center, New York, U.S.A.

and

FERNANDA FERREIRA

Michigan State University, East Lansing, U.S.A.

KLUWER ACADEMIC PUBLISHERS

DORDRECHT / BOSTON / LONDON

A C.I.P. Catalogue record for this book is available from the Library of Congress.

ISBN 0-7923-5099-5

Published by Kluwer Academic Publishers,
P.O. Box 17, 3300 AA Dordrecht, The Netherlands.

Sold and distributed in North, Central and South America
by Kluwer Academic Publishers,
101 Philip Drive, Norwell, MA 02061, U.S.A.

In all other countries, sold and distributed
by Kluwer Academic Publishers,
P.O. Box 322, 3300 AH Dordrecht, The Netherlands.

Printed on acid-free paper

Printed in the Netherlands.

Contents

List of Contributors

Markus Bader: Institute of German Linguistics, Friedrich-Schiller-Universität Jena. Philosophische Fakultät; Ernst-Abbe-Platz 4; 07740 Jena; Germany.
xmk@rz.uni-jena.de

Charles Clifton, Jr.: Department of Psychology, University of Massachusetts, Amherst. South College; Box 37130; Amherst, MA 01003-7130.
cec@psych.umass.edu

Matthew W. Crocker: Centre for Cognitive Science, University of Edinburgh. 2 Buccleuch Place; Edinburgh EH8 9LW; Scotland, UK.
mcw@cogsci.ed.ac.uk

Marica De Vincenzi: Institute of Psychology of the National Research Council (CNR). Viale Marx, 15; 00137 Roma; Italy.
mkdv@kant.irmkant.rm.cnr.it

Fernanda Ferreira: Department of Psychology, Michigan State University. East Lansing, MI 48824-1117.
fernanda@pilot.msu.edu

Janet Dean Fodor: Program in Linguistics, CUNY Graduate School and University Center. 33 West 42nd Street; New York, NY 10036.
jfodor@email.gc.cuny.edu

Lyn Frazier: Department of Psychology, University of Massachusetts, Amherst. South College; Box 37130; Amherst, MA 01003-7130.

Angela D. Friederici: Max-Planck-Institute of Cognitive Neuroscience, Leizpig. Inselstraße 22-26; 04103 Leipzig; Germany.
angelafr@cns.mpg.de

Paul Gorrell: Max-Planck-Institute of Cognitive Neuroscience, Leizpig. Inselstraße 22-26; 04103 Leipzig; Germany.
gorrell@cns.mpg.de

John M. Henderson: Department of Psychology, Michigan State University. East Lansing, MI 48824-1117.
john@eyelab.msu.edu

Atsu Inoue: Department of Economics, Kantogakuin University. 4834 Mutsuura-Cho; Kanazawa-ku Yokohama 236; Japan.
71051.3021@compuserve.com

Richard L. Lewis: Department of Computer and Information Science, The Ohio State University. 2015 Neil Avenue; Columbus, OH 43210-1277.
rick@cis.ohio-state.edu

Vincenzo Lombardo: Dipartimento di Informatica, Centro di Scienza Cognitiva, Università di Torino. C.so Svizzera, 185; 10149 Torino; Italy.
vincenzo@di.unito.it

Suzanne Stevenson: Department of Computer Science and Center for Cognitive Science (RuCCS), Rutgers University. CoRE Building, Busch Campus; New Brunswick, NJ 08903.
suzanne@ruccs.rutgers.edu

Patrick Sturt: Centre for Cognitive Science, University of Edinburgh. 2 Buccleuch Place; Edinburgh EH8 9LW; Scotland, UK.
sturt@cogsci.ed.ac.uk

Preface

The topic addressed in this volume lies within the study of sentence processing, which is one of the major divisions of psycholinguistics. The goal has been to understand the structure and functioning of the mental mechanisms involved in sentence comprehension. Most of the experimental and theoretical work during the last twenty or thirty years has focused on 'first-pass parsing', the process of assigning structure to a sentence as its words are encountered, one at a time, 'from left to right'.

One important guiding idea has been to delineate the processing mechanisms by studying where they fail. For this purpose we identify types of sentences which perceivers have trouble assigning structure to. An important class of perceptually difficult sentences are those which contain temporary ambiguities. Since the parsing mechanism cannot tell what the intended structure is, it may make an incorrect guess. Then later on in the sentence, the structure assignment process breaks down, because the later words do not fit with the incorrect structural analysis. This is called a 'garden path' situation. When it occurs, the parsing mechanism must somehow correct itself, and find a different analysis which is compatible with the incoming words. This reanalysis process is the subject of the research reported here.

What defines the parser's reanalysis task is the nature of the first-pass analysis for the ambiguous word string, and its relation to the correct analysis. We need to start, then, with a clear view of which analyses are generally favored in the first-pass parse. (Note that we are presupposing here that the parser does not compute *all* analyses of an ambiguous string. Some partial parallel models of the human parsing routines have been proposed, but no current model assumes that the parser copes with ambiguity by pursuing all analyses simultaneously. Thus, at least some choices are made on-line, and reanalysis is sometimes needed.) Generalizations have been formulated to predict which analyses of an ambiguous sentence are favored by the parser and which are overlooked. The principles that have been proposed include Minimal Attachment, Late Closure, some more recent thematically based principles, and preferences based on the frequency of occurrence of structures in the language.

These models of first-pass processing have had considerable success. Yet relatively little attention has been given to the fact that parsing difficulty is not an all-or-none matter. Many kinds of garden-path occur, but they are not all equally severe. In some cases it is easy for the parser to shift from the initial wrong analysis to the alternative correct analysis. In other cases, it is remarkably difficult. An example of a garden path that is easy to recover from is *Sandra bumped into the busboy and the waiter told her to be careful.* When the phrase *and the waiter* is encountered, it could be part of the object of *bump into*. But when the verb *told* is reached, it shows that *the waiter* must be the subject of a new clause. The structure must therefore be rearranged, yet both experimental results and intuitive judgments confirm that this is not a difficult adjustment to make. By contrast, there are garden paths that are extremely difficult to recover from, as in *The daughter of the king's son admires himself.* Here, the preferred analysis of the subject phrase is [*the daughter of* [*the king's son*]], which is feminine and equivalent in meaning to *the daughter of the prince*. But this analysis is gender-incompatible with the reflexive pronoun *himself* that is encountered later in the sentence. So the first-pass analysis must be restructured into [[*the daughter of the king'*]*s son*], which means the same as *the princess' son*; since it is masculine it is compatible with the reflexive. In this case, very few perceivers arrive at the necessary analysis without explicit help or conscious deliberation.

Difficulty contrasts such as this are the bread and butter of research on reanalysis. They constitute the data base for developing and testing models of how the reanalysis mechanism is designed and how it operates moment by moment. From the data base we try to extract insights about what factors determine whether a misanalysis will persist or can be easily corrected.

Factors that might be relevant include: the semantic plausibility of the analysis that must be relinquished; how great the semantic distance is between the old analysis and the new one; whether or not the prosodic contour computed on the basis of the incorrect structure also needs to be modified; and how severely working memory is already taxed when the analysis breaks down and reanalysis must be undertaken. An important consideration is the distance over which the revision must occur. As Sturt & Crocker's chapter notes, the relevant distance might be between the point at which parsing breaks down and the earlier point at which the incorrect structure was chosen; or what matters might be the distance a phrase must move across the structural representation in order to correct the error. Structural relationships between these points could be at least as important as mere distance. And distance itself might be variously defined in terms of length in words (or syllables or morphemes), number of structural nodes, or processing time.

The methods used to establish which of these properties influence ease of reanalysis run the gamut from intuitive judgments of sentence difficulty, to high-technology methods such as measuring brain activity. In between, there are standard experimental paradigms for collecting judgments from subjects; for measuring reading times, eye movement patterns, and reaction times in secondary load tasks; and question-answering and sentence completion tasks to assess the interpretations that perceivers impose. Early work used exclusively visually presented materials, but it has become more practicable now to store and manipulate auditory stimuli, and there has been a growing interest in the study of spoken language. As yet, relatively few experimental studies of reanalysis have been conducted; intuitions tend to predominate in the early stages of research on a topic. But the current trend, as evidenced in this volume, is towards development of a pool of broadly accepted facts against which theories can be tested.

For example, one thread running through several chapters is that an adequate theory ought at least to be able to explain the well-established difference in revision difficulty between the constructions illustrated in (1) and (2).

(1) Mary forgot her husband needed a ride yesterday.

(2) Although Mary forgot her husband didn't seem very upset.

These particular examples are from the chapter by Lewis, but the same contrast clothed in different words is used as a yardstick by many of the contributors. In both examples, a noun phrase must be shifted from one clause to another one, but this shift is easy in (1) and difficult in (2). Other structures that readers will encounter in more than one chapter that follows include *wh*-movement questions, and subject and object relative clauses in German, as well as the venerable *The horse raced past the barn fell.*

In line with current interest in cross-linguistic comparisons, the work reported here addresses reanalysis in a range of languages: German, Italian, Japanese, and to a lesser extent Dutch, Hebrew, and Mandarin, in addition to English. To what extent the reanalysis routines are universal, as would be expected if the parsing mechanism is innate, is not known. But certainly the examples continue to have a familiar ring about them as we move from one language to another, and the same principles can often be seen at work.

Once we have some constraining data to work with, we need to devise a model incorporating a set of mechanisms that make sense of these facts. Several kinds of model are under investigation, with very different implications for the nature of the revision process, and hence of the parsing mechanism as a whole. For example, it has to established whether there exists a special-purpose reanalysis mechanism or whether the first-pass mechanisms are flexible enough to take on this task. One way in which they might do so is to revise an incorrect analysis by returning to the beginning of the sentence and re-parsing it, making a different structural choice at the point of ambiguity. Or it could be that the parser repeats as little of the existing analysis as possible. A parser may backtrack word by word through the current (incorrect) structure, considering alternatives as it goes, leaving earlier decisions intact. A more analytic revision mechanism would try to deduce what error was made on the first pass and how it can be corrected. It would implement the correction by repairing the structure previously assigned, presumably using routines distinct from the first-pass processes.

These are the sorts of issues that have recently taken center stage in current sentence processing research. The contributors to this volume approach the topic from different disciplinary traditions and so are able to bring to it a variety of methodologies and ways of thinking: computational, psychological, linguistic, and neurophysiological. Thus we converge on the theoretical and empirical problems with all the research tools that can be mustered.

We would like to express our thanks to the friends and colleagues who helped to put this volume together. We thank all our fellow authors for the superlative chapters they have contributed, and also for being wonderfully prompt and cooperative about practical matters. Our production editor Eva M. Fernández has earned the gratitude and admiration of everyone concerned with the preparation of the volume. Her fine editorial judgment has added value to the contents, and her calm and graceful efficiency has kept us on track for timely publication so that the ideas represented here will appear in print while they are still new and exciting. There are plans afoot to continue the debate begun in these pages, in a workshop and in further publications. The authors and editors would be pleased to hear from others who are working on this topic—or who are persuaded by this book that it would be good to do so.

1

Prosodic Influences on Reading Syntactically Ambiguous Sentences*

Markus Bader

Abstract

In this chapter, I will propose a new account for the question of why only some local syntactic ambiguities lead to strong garden-path effects whereas others do not. This account is based on the observation that readers do not only compute syntactic structures during reading but also prosodic structures. These prosodic structures are a product of the process of phonological coding which normally accompanies silent reading. Due to the lack of a one-to-one mapping between syntactic and prosodic structures, recovery from a syntactic misanalysis may be accompanied by the need to replace the original prosodic structure or not. According to the prosodic constraint on reanalysis, the need to revise the original prosodic structure makes recovery from a syntactic misanalysis difficult. Empirical evidence for this claim comes from a series of three self-paced reading experiments which investigated the German variant of the English *her*-ambiguity. These experiments manipulated the prosodic structure of sentences by inserting focus operators (focus particles, sentence adverbials) into locally ambiguous sentences. Thereby it became possible to independently determine the contributions of syntactic and prosodic factors to reanalysis. The results show that for the ambiguitiy examined, garden-path effects can be predicted on prosodic grounds but not on syntactic grounds. This finding supports the claim that for certain kinds of syntactic ambiguities reanalysis is prosodically constrained.

---

* The ideas presented in this chapter as well as Experiment 1A are from my dissertation, Bader (1994). This work was begun in 1993 at the University of Stuttgart and supported there by the Graduiertenkolleg Theoretische Grundlagen der Sprachverarbeitung. I am grateful to Josef Bayer, Anette Dralle, Christine Haag-Merz and Michael Meng for helpful discussions and comments. I would also like to thank Paul Gorrell and an anonymous reviewer for their comments.

J.D. Fodor and F. Ferreira (eds.), Reanalysis in Sentence Processing, 1–46.

1 Introduction

Local syntactic ambiguities and reading comprehension have been two cornerstones of research on the human parsing mechanism: most experiments investigating the human parser involve subjects reading syntactically ambiguous sentences (e.g., Frazier & Rayner, 1982; Stowe, 1986; Altmann & Steedman, 1988; cf. Mitchell, 1994, for a recent review). Despite its strong reliance on reading, research on syntactic ambiguity resolution has paid little attention to the question of whether processes confined to reading contribute anything special to human parsing. This paper will focus on *phonological coding*, a process that is found in reading but not in spoken language comprehension. Phonological coding is the process by which written language is paired with phonological representations. The result of phonological coding is the inner voice that we hear when reading something. In the case of syntactic ambiguity resolution, phonological coding might be important because it makes available a type of linguistic information that is lacking in written language, namely prosodic information. It has already been suggested before that one of the main roles of phonological coding for sentence comprehension consists in providing prosodic information (Slowiaczek & Clifton, 1980; Wilkenfeld, 1985), in contrast, or in addition, to the role that phonological coding might have for processes related to working memory (cf. Gathercole & Baddeley, 1993, for an overview of the latter position). For example, Slowiaczek & Clifton (1980) have proposed that phonological coding gives readers some way to compensate for the lack of prosody, since prosody is crucially needed for successful language comprehension.

The purpose of this chapter is to show that certain phenomena found in syntactic ambiguity resolution receive a natural explanation if one takes into consideration that readers do not only compute syntactic structures but also prosodic ones. The specific phenomenon that will be the focus of the following discussion is the problem of reanalysis. I will propose that reanalysis of an ambiguous sentence is difficult if not only the initial syntactic structure has to be revised but also the associated prosodic structure that has been computed via phonological coding (cf. Ferreira & Anes, 1994, for a similar proposal).

Seen from a broader perspective, the theory of reanalysis proposed here tries to derive certain properties of garden-path sentences directly from the architecture of the language comprehension system and how it is embedded within the architecture of general cognition. In particular, by making revisions of phonological representations responsible for certain garden-path effects, a new answer is provided for one of the questions posed by garden-path phenomena, namely, the question as to why certain garden-path effects lead to conscious difficulties while others do not. Since it is the phonological representation that gives rise to the conscious experience of an inner voice heard during reading, revising this representation will directly lead to some consciously detectable difficulties. Syntactic structures, in contrast, are related to the inner voice only indirectly via an intermediate phonological representation. Therefore, a syntactic reanalysis might go unnoticed if it can be accomplished completely within the parser, that is, without concomitant revision of the phonological structure, but not if it causes a revision of the associated phonological structure.

Experimental evidence for the hypothesis that phonological coding is one of the determinants of the ease with which a syntactic ambiguity can be disambiguated comes from self-paced reading experiments using German sentence material. In three experiments, the prosodic structures of sentences were manipulated using focus operators (focus particles and sentence adverbials). Focus operators allow for a direct control of the syntax-prosody mapping and thereby make it possible to tease apart syntactic and prosodic contributions to reanalysis.

2 Phonological Coding and Syntactic Ambiguity Resolution

The phenomenon of local syntactic ambiguity is illustrated in (1), taken from Frazier (1978). In the sentences in (1), the italicized phrase *the little boy* is locally ambiguous. It is the object of the purpose-clause verb *to help* in (1a) and the subject of the main-clause verb *put* in (1b). When reading a sentence like (1b), one is led down the garden path. The disambiguation in (1a), in contrast, is processed easily (for experimental evidence see Frazier & Rayner, 1982; Ferreira & Henderson, 1991).

(1) a. In order to help *the little boy* Jill put down the package she was carrying.
    b. In order to help *the little boy* put down the package he was carrying.

One way to explain the difference between (1a) and (1b) is by appealing to the notion of serial parsing (Frazier, 1987; Mitchell, 1994). Serial models of human parsing assume that the parser computes a single ongoing phrase-structural representation which is updated word by word. This ongoing representation is called the *current partial phrase marker* (CPPM). In the case of an ambiguity, where the CPPM can be expanded in more than one way, a serial parser opts for one of the possible expansions and pursues only this one. For the ambiguity in (1), the chosen structure is the one where the ambiguous NP is the object of *help*. If the CPPM computed at the point of ambiguity is compatible with further input, processing proceeds smoothly, as in (1a). If the CPPM initially computed is contradicted by following material, it has to be revised. This is necessary in (1b), where the disambiguating verb *put* requires the ambiguous NP to be reanalyzed as the subject of the main clause. According to serial parsing models, the need to reanalyze the original CPPM is responsible for the difficulty one experiences when reading *put* in (1b).

The initial computation of the CPPM is also termed *first-pass parsing*. Revising the original CPPM on encountering contradicting material is accordingly called *second-pass parsing*. Restricting our attention to ambiguities with two alternative readings, a serial parser will always process one reading easily while revision processes will have to be invoked for any other reading. One should therefore expect that all ambiguities pattern according to example (1) with respect to processing difficulties: one disambiguation should be processed without problems while the other should lead to trouble. This, however, does not seem to be the case. Some syntactic ambiguities do not exhibit a clear difference between their different disambiguations. An often cited example of such an ambiguity is given in (2), where the locally ambiguous NP *the answer* is the direct object of the main verb *knew* in (2a) and the subject of the embedded clause in (2b).

(2) a. Peter knew the answer immediately.
b. Peter knew the answer would be false.

Since the preferred structure for the ambiguity in (2) is the structure where the ambiguous NP is the object of *knew*, the original CPPM has to be revised on encountering the disambiguating auxiliary *would* in (2b). In contrast to (1b), the revision in (2b) is claimed to cause no consciously detectable difficulties (e.g., Gibson, 1991; Gorrell, 1995).

Ambiguities like the one in (2) pose a challenge to serial models of human parsing. Within the framework of serial parsing, any difference between two ambiguities with respect to ease of processing at the point of disambiguation must be attributed to the ease with which the original CPPM can be revised, i.e., to the process of reanalysis. Attributing the strength of a garden-path effect to ease of reanalysis raises an obvious question: why should reanalysis be difficult in some cases and easy in others? Recent answers to this question include Ferreira & Henderson (1991), Fodor & Inoue (1994), and Inoue & Fodor

(1995). Other researchers have abandoned serial parsing and proposed that contrasts like those between (1b) and (2b) should be explained in terms of parallel processing (e.g., Gibson, 1991) or in terms of minimal commitment parsing (e.g., Weinberg, 1993). For the purposes of this discussion I will assume that the human parser is a serial mechanism. This assumption has been argued for with evidence from German verb-final clauses in Bader (1994) (see also Bader & Lasser, 1994). As to why reanalysis is sometimes difficult and sometimes easy, I propose that, for a certain class of syntactic ambiguities, ease of reanalysis is dependent on the prosodic properties of the alternative syntactic structures. Prosody may have an influence on syntactic processing during reading—meaning normal, silent reading—due to the process of phonological coding already alluded to in the introduction. Processes of phonological coding pair written language with phonological representations. These representations lead to experiencing an inner voice that we can hear when reading. Phonological coding is a part of the more general phenomenon of *inner speech.* Inner speech comprises both the inner voice we hear when reading and the muscle movements of the speech organs that often accompany reading and that are called *subvocalizations.* According to Rayner & Pollatsek (1989), whose terminology I adopt here, phonological coding is the more pervasive phenomenon of the two components which make up inner speech. Therefore, I will restrict my attention to phonological coding in the rest of this discussion.

The inner voice which we hear during reading is not identical to the phonological structure computed during phonological coding. The phonological structure by itself cannot be consciously experienced, but it gives rise to the conscious hearing of an inner voice during reading. This is parallel to the relationship between the phonological code that is computed during auditory language comprehension and the experience of someone saying something (for a discussion of possible differences between phonological codes during reading and auditory language comprehension, see Rayner & Pollatsek, 1989).[1] The close relationship between phonological coding and inner voice becomes relevant for processes of reanalysis when one raises the issue of what kinds of local syntactic ambiguities lead to conscious garden-path effects and which do not. As explained below, taking prosodic properties of ambiguous sentences into account offers a new perspective for answering this question.

---

[1] I speak of prosodic structure here without going into the distinction between phonetic and phonological representations. Although this distinction will ultimately have to be taken into account when talking about phonological coding, it does not seem to be necessary for the present purposes (cf. Wilkenfeld, 1985).

During on-line reading comprehension, if readers compute not only syntactic structures but also prosodic structures, two situations can arise at the point where the CPPM encounters incompatible further input material. The reanalysis of the CPPM will make it necessary either to revise the associated prosodic structure as well as the syntactic structure or to alter only the syntactic structure while the prosodic structure is left intact. The claim to be defended in this chapter is that in the first situation, where both the syntactic and the prosodic structure have to be revised, processing difficulties will be experienced.

The existence of the two situations sketched above is due to the fact that the prosodic structure of a sentence is only partially determined by its syntactic structure. According to current theories of the syntax-phonology mapping, phrase-level prosody is comprised of three distinguishable aspects (cf., e.g., Selkirk, 1994; Dresher, 1996; Shattuck-Hufnagel & Turk, 1996): *prosodic phrasing*, the division of sentences into prosodic constituents; *sentence stress*, the location of the strongest stress in a sentence; and *phrasal rhythmic patterning*, the distribution of strong and weak syllables within phrases. For the examples in (1) and (2), it is prosodic phrasing that matters most. Intonation and phrasal rhythmic patterning will be introduced later, when I discuss examples where they will play a crucial role.

According to the theory of prosodic phonology (Nespor & Vogel, 1986), sentences are divided into prosodic units of increasing size. An important prosodic unit that is acknowledged in every theory of prosody is the intonational phrase (abbreviated as *I*). Intonational phrases are the domain of the intonational contours found in a given language, such as the declarative contour or the interrogative contour. The end of an intonational phrase is prosodically marked by boundary tones, and, optionally, by pausing and by lengthening phrase-final syllables. The end of an intonational phrase is thus associated with salient perceptual clues that are physically manifested in the pitch contour of an utterance. There is as yet no consensus as to the relation between intonational phrases and syntactic structures. According to Nespor & Vogel (1986), the basic intonational phrase corresponds to a root clause. From this basic case, various deviations are possible. For example, certain constituents of a sentence, like parenthetical expressions (3a) and nonrestrictive relative clauses (3b), always form intonational phrases of their own (examples from Nespor & Vogel, 1986).

(3) a. Lions ($_I$ as you know) are dangerous.
b. My brother, ($_I$ who absolutely loves animals), just bought himself an exotic tropical bird.

Preposed constituents also tend to form intonational phrases of their own. This can be seen when considering sentence pair (1) again. The default division of these sentences into intonational phrases is shown in (4).

(4) a. ($_{I}$ In order to help *the little boy*) ($_{I}$ Jill put down the package she was carrying).
b. ($_{I}$ In order to help) ($_{I}$ *the little boy* put down the package he was carrying).

In both (4a) and (4b), the whole sentence is made up of two intonational phrases. The first one comprises the fronted purpose clause and the second one the main clause. The ambiguous status of the NP *the little boy* is thus directly transferred from the syntactic to the prosodic level. In (4a), *the little boy* is both part of the purpose clause and the first intonational phrase. In (4b), it is both part of the main clause and the second intonational phrase. Given the prosodic structures shown in (4), the on-line process of reading sentence (1b) will proceed as follows. On encountering the ambiguous phrase *the little boy,* the parser will attach this phrase as the object of the verb *help.* In the syntactic structure there will be a clause boundary (CP) after the ambiguous NP, and in the prosodic structure there will be an intonational phrase (I) boundary. If the sentence then continues with the main verb *put*, the representations initially computed turn out to be wrong. Two revisions become necessary at this point, a syntactic one and a prosodic one. Both are shown schematically in (5). The syntactic reanalysis involves shifting the syntactic boundary from behind the ambiguous NP to the position in front of it. The revision of the prosodic structure involves a parallel shift of the prosodic boundary.

(5) a. ($_{I}$ [$_{CP}$ In order to help *the little boy*]) + put
⇒ b. ($_{I}$ [$_{CP}$ In order to help]) *the little boy* put…

Considered abstractly, the revision of the CPPM and the revision of the original prosodic structure both involve some kind of rebracketing. There is a crucial difference between these two rebracketings, however. Since material at the end of an intonational phrase is associated with certain intonational features, namely, boundary tones and lengthening of phrase final syllables, revising the original prosodic structure will make it necessary to destroy the original phonetic material and replace it by new phonetic material. First, the original boundary signals associated to *boy* in (5a) have to be deleted, and secondly, new boundary signals have to be attached to *help*, resulting in (5b). The claim that reanalysis is prosodically constrained means that the revision of the prosodic structure is the main determinant for (1b) eliciting a severe garden-path effect.

Under an approach that makes prosodic revisions responsible for garden-path effects, the processing of sentences like those in (2) looks rather different from the processing of sentences like (1). The respective prosodic structures for the two sentences in (2) are given in (6).

(6) a. ($_I$ Peter knew the answer immediately).
b. ($_I$ Peter knew the answer would be false).

Syntactically, sentence (2a) consists of a single clause, whereas sentence (2b) is made up of two clauses, a main clause and an embedded clause. Prosodically, however, both sentences consist of a single intonational phrase, at least under the default intonation assigned to sentences of this kind (Nespor & Vogel, 1986). For the processing of these sentences, this has the following consequence. On first-pass parsing, the ambiguous NP *the answer* will be attached as object to the main-clause verb *knew*. As soon as the auxiliary *would* is encountered, which disambiguates in favor of the non-preferred reading, second-pass parsing becomes necessary. This time, only the CPPM has to be altered, while the prosodic structure can be left intact. The hypothesis that prosodic revisions make reanalysis difficult therefore correctly predicts that the reanalysis necessary for (2b) is easier than the reanalysis that is needed for (1b).

The claim that reanalysis is prosodically constrained is captured in the *Prosodic Constraint on Reanalysis* (PCR) given in (7).

(7) *Prosodic Constraint on Reanalysis* (PCR): Revising a syntactic structure is difficult if it necessitates a concomitant reanalysis of the associated prosodic structure.

Before presenting experimental evidence for the PCR, two points should be clarified. First, the PCR does not claim that prosodic information is the only factor that contributes to the ease or difficulty of reanalysis. In particular, the PCR does not imply that all syntactic ambiguities where two alternative syntactic structures are associated with identical prosodic structures are easily processed. This will only hold if there is no additional source of reanalysis difficulty, like, e.g., the need to reaccess lexical representations (Ferreira & Henderson, 1991; Bader, 1996). This point will be discussed further in section 7. A second point to note about the PCR concerns the notion of difficulty of reanalysis and its relation to consciousness. The notion of difficulty in reanalysis is meant to capture the fact that garden-path effects vary in strength. In the literature, one can find two conceptualizations of garden-path strength. According to the first conceptualization, there is a broad spectrum of garden-path effects, ranging from very weak, barely detectable ones to very strong ones (e.g., Inoue & Fodor, 1995). According to the second conceptualization, garden-path effects fall into two classes, weak and strong: weak garden-path effects are not consciously noticed while strong garden-path effects are (e.g., Gibson, 1991; Weinberg, 1993). There seems to be no reason why these two conceptions should exclude each other. First of all, even a quick look at examples of conscious garden-path effects leads one to the impression that they are not all of equal strength. For example, the garden-path effect elicited by (8a) seems to be noticeably stronger than the one elicited by (8b) (Inoue & Fodor, 1995):

(8) a. They told the boy that the girl met the story.
 b. We saw the woman with the revolver.

There is also experimental evidence for graded garden-path effects. For example, Ferreira & Henderson (1991) show that sentences like (1b), which are generally claimed to elicit conscious garden-path effects (Gibson, 1991; Gorrell, 1995), differ in garden-path strength depending on the length and nature of the ambiguous region. They found that the garden-path effect becomes stronger with increasing distance between the verb of the initial clause and the head noun of the adjacent NP. Results such as these show that garden-path strength is not an all-or-none phenomenon (see Bader & Meng, 1997, for experimental evidence of graded garden-path effects in German). This is completely compatible with the PCR because it is to be expected that garden-path strength will vary with the amount of prosodic revisions that become necessary on disambiguation. However, this aspect of the PCR has not yet been explored due to the fact that research into prosodic effects on reanalysis is in a very preliminary stage. While the experiments to be reported below show that reanalysis is made difficult if the initial prosodic structure has to be revised, they allow no conclusion as to the actual strength of the observed garden-path effects. To address the latter issue, much more research is needed.

When saying that garden-path strength is a graded phenomenon there is no need to deny that certain garden-path effects are consciously detectable whereas others are not. While it might be a matter of dispute whether there are really garden-path effects which cannot be detected consciously, it seems to be indisputable that some garden-path effects are more easily detected consciously than others. With respect to the question of the conscious detectability of garden-path effects, the claim behind the PCR is that every revision of the original prosodic structure will lead to a garden-path effect that is consciously detectable (although the reverse might not hold, as pointed out). As already indicated above, the reason for this claim lies in the close connection between prosodic structure—as one aspect of the phonological representation computed during reading—and the perception of an inner voice while reading something. If readers assign prosodic structures to the sentences they read, and if these prosodic structures are automatically converted into the conscious perception of an inner voice, then any revision of the original prosodic structure will be detected consciously. This is in clear contrast to revisions of syntactic structures. Since syntactic structures are only indirectly connected to the inner voice—namely via the intermediate phonological structure—the revision of a syntactic structure will only affect our perception of an inner voice if it causes some revisions of the associated prosodic structure, and might otherwise go unnoticed.

The discussion of the ambiguities in (1) and (2) was meant to introduce the idea that syntactic reanalysis is prosodically constrained. With respect to why these particular ambiguities behave differently at the point of disambiguation, several alternative explanations that do not refer to prosodic information are available (e.g., Gibson, 1991; Fodor & Inoue, 1994; Weinberg, 1993). Furthermore, proponents of purely syntactic explanations of garden-path effects could argue that the involvement of prosodic processes in these examples is a pure epiphenomenon. Therefore, no strong point can be made in favor of the PCR by these particular examples. What is needed in order to justify a prosodically based reanalysis constraint is a local syntactic ambiguity that allows teasing apart syntactic from prosodic contributions to reanalysis. An ambiguity of this kind—which exists in both English and German—will be introduced in section 3. Its German variant will be experimentally tested in three reading experiments and an associated sentence completion study.

3 Focus Particles and Syntactic Ambiguity

The examples discussed in section 2 differed with respect to their phonological phrasing. Besides phonological phrasing, sentence stress—as part of the more general phenomenon of intonation—is an important determinant of the prosodic structure of a sentence. In this section, a syntactic ambiguity will be discussed that allows for a close control of sentence stress. This, in turn, will make it possible to clearly dissociate syntactic from prosodic influences on reanalysis. The ambiguity to be discussed in this section can be found in both English and German. The experimental evidence to be presented in the next sections stems from German. Consider first the English examples given in (9):

(9) a. Mary said that someone gave her money on her birthday.
    b. Mary said that someone gave her money to Peter.

The sentences in (9) contain a local syntactic ambiguity due the fact that the pronoun *her* is lexically ambiguous. It can function as either an object pronoun or a possessive pronoun. In (9a), *her* is the first object of the double-object verb *to give*. This reading will be called the *dative structure*. In (9b), *her* is a possessive pronoun modifying the noun *money*. This reading will be termed the *possessive structure*. The German counterpart to the ambiguity in (9) is illustrated in (10).

(10) a. Zu mir hat Maria gesagt, daß man ihr Geld anvertraut hat.
    to me has Maria said that one her money entrusted has
    'Maria said to me that someone entrusted money to her.'

   b. Zu mir hat Maria gesagt, daß man ihr Geld beschlagnahmt hat.
    to me has Maria said that one her money confiscated has
    'Maria said to me that someone confiscated her money.'

Despite important syntactic differences between German and English, the sentences in (10) are locally ambiguous in the same way as those in (9): the pronoun *ihr*, equivalent to the English pronoun *her*, can be either a dative pronoun or a possessive pronoun. Disambiguation in (10) is achieved by the subcategorization requirements of the respective verbs. The verb *anvertrauen* ('to entrust') obligatorily requires a dative object while the verb *beschlagnahmen* ('to confiscate') cannot be used with a dative object. In consequence, the sentences in (10) become unambiguous when the clause-final verbs are encountered. The ambiguity illustrated in (10) will henceforth be referred to as the *ihr*-ambiguity.

The main clauses in the English examples shown in (9) have the sole function of providing an antecedent for the pronoun *her*. For the German examples, there is a further reason for considering sentences made up of a main and a subordinate clause where the ambiguity of interest is contained in the subordinate clause. There are major syntactic differences between English and German with respect to the position of verbs. In contrast to the SVO word order of English, the base word order of German is SOV. In addition, German is a verb-second language, which means that in main clauses the finite verb is moved from its clause-final position to a position directly following the first constituent. Due to this characteristic, the SOV-nature of German can be seen directly only in subordinate clauses. As illustrated in (10), in a subordinate clause both the finite auxiliary (*hat*) and the nonfinite verbs (*anvertraut* or *beschlagnahmt*) follow the object(s).

The verb-second property of German, which shows up only in root clauses, is also visible in (10). In a root clause, the finite verb moves into the second position of the sentence (*hat* in (10)), and exactly one constituent moves in front of the finite verb (the PP *zu mir* in (10)). The processing of moved constituents falls outside the scope of this chapter; therefore, most of the ambiguities in the rest of the German examples discussed will be in subordinate clauses, which exhibit the underlying SOV word order transparently.[2] So long as nothing hinges on the content of the matrix clause, all subordinate clauses will be presented without an embedding matrix clause.

The two embedded clauses in (10), which contain the ambiguity under consideration, are phonologically identical up to the disambiguating verb. Therefore, the PCR predicts that these sentences should be easy to process. Intuitively, this is the case. Neither (10a) nor (10b) causes a perceivable garden-path effect. For the equivalent English sentences (9), the same has been reported (cf. Gibson, 1991; Inoue & Fodor, 1995). This picture changes if a focus particle is inserted in front of the ambiguous pronoun. The two sentences in (11), which are identical to the sentences in (10) besides containing the focus particle *sogar* (*even*) in front of the ambiguous pronoun *ihr*, are not equivalent prosodically.

(11) a. … daß man sogar ihr Geld anvertraut hat. Dative
that one even her money entrusted has
'… that someone entrusted money even to her.'

b. … daß man sogar ihr Geld beschlagnahmt hat. Possessive
that one even her money confiscated has
'… that someone confiscated even her money.'

In order to explain why (10a) and (10b) are equivalent with respect to their prosodic properties, whereas (11a) and (11b) are not, it is necessary to introduce

---

2 This does not mean that the effects to be reported are in any sense dependent on the word order of embedded clauses. The ihr-ambiguity is contained in the so-called middlefield, which is the portion of a sentence between C^0 (filled either by a complementizer or by the finite verb) and the clause final verb(s). There are no syntactic differences between the middlefield of an embedded clause and the middlefield of a root clause. Therefore, as long as the disambiguating verb is left in clause-final position, the distinction between root and embedded clauses should make no difference with respect to the processing of sentences containing the ihr-ambiguity.

some basic facts about sentence stress and its relation to syntactic structure. Consider the two utterances in (12), which differ only in their intonation (capitals indicate the presence of a pitch accent). In (12a), the word *Mary* carries sentence stress and is *focused.* (Focused phrases will be indicated by curly brackets subscripted with the focus feature *F*.) In (12b), it is *Peter* which is focused.

(12) a. Peter kissed $\{_F$ MARY$\}$.
b. $\{_F$ PETER$\}$ kissed Mary.

These two sentences have the same truth-conditional meaning but they are not equivalent. For example, one can answer the question *Who did Peter kiss*? with (12a) but not with (12b). On the other hand, (12b)—but not (12a)—can answer the question *Who kissed Mary?* This difference is due to a condition on question-answer pairs: the focused constituent in an appropriate answer to a *wh*-question must be the constituent corresponding to the *wh*-phrase in the question.

Sentence (12a) can answer not only the question *Who did Peter kiss?* but also the questions *What did Peter do?* and *What happened?* According to the constraint on question-answer pairs just mentioned, this means that in (12a) the focused constituent can be not only *Mary*, but also the VP *kissed Mary*, or even the entire sentence *Peter kissed Mary*. The phenomenon that a given pitch accent can license focused phrases of different sizes is called *focus projection.* Not every pitch accent licenses focus projection. Sentence (12b) is an appropriate answer only to *Who kissed Mary?* With a pitch accent on the subject no phrase can be focused other than the subject itself.[3] A further case where focus projection is prohibited is illustrated in (13). While an NP can be a focus if its head noun is accented, as in (13a), focus projection originating from a modifier is not possible. With an accent on the possessive pronoun *his*, only narrow focus on this pronoun is licit (cf. (13c)), while wide focus on the whole NP is barred (cf. (13b)).

(13) a.	What did Peter lose?		Peter lost $\{_F$ his WALLET$\}$.
b.	What did Peter lose?	*	Peter lost $\{_F$ HIS wallet$\}$.
c.	Whose wallet did Peter lose?		Peter lost $\{_F$ HIS$\}$ wallet.

The phenomenon of focus projection receives its importance for the current investigation from the possibility of defining the notion of unmarked or neutral

[3] This does not hold across the board. A certain class of verbs allow focus projection from their subjects. See Rochemont (1986) and Selkirk (1994).

intonation via the notion of focus projection. A definition of neutral intonation is given in (14), adopted from Jacobs (1992).

(14) An intonation pattern α of a constituent X is neutral iff X can be focused under α.

According to this definition, sentence (12a) exhibits neutral intonation while sentence (12b) does not. Similarly, the unmarked intonation for the NP *his wallet* is *his WALLET*, whereas *HIS wallet* is a marked intonation. Neutral intonation is the intonation appropriate for 'out of the blue' contexts, i.e., utterances without preceding context or with minimal context, utterances preceded by contexts like *What's new?* and *What happened?* In the experiments reported below, as in most other investigations of the human parsing mechanism, sentences will be presented without any context. For such sentences, it seems reasonable to assume that readers will assign neutral intonation, that is, the intonation that is appropriate under the given experimental circumstances.

The sentences in (12) and (13) illustrate what is called *free focus*. A focus is free as long as it is not bound by a focus-sensitive operator. Standard examples of focus-sensitive operators are focus particles like *only* or *even*. Consider the sentences in (15), where the respective foci are bound by the focus particle *only*.

(15) a. Peter only kissed $\{_F$ MARY$\}$.
b. Peter only $\{_F$ KISSED$\}$ Mary.

Due solely to the different positions of the pitch accent, (15a) and (15b) differ in truth-conditional meaning. While (15a) means that Peter kissed no one else other than Mary, (15b) means that Peter did nothing else to Mary other than kiss her. There are competing analyses for deriving the meaning contrasts in sentences like (15a) and (15b) which need not concern us here (for overviews see Bayer, 1996; Stechow, 1991). For our purposes, more important than the semantic impact of focus particles is the fact that a focusing particle must be associated with a focus, where certain grammatical restrictions hold for the structural relation between focus and focus particle.

Due to a particular restriction on the association of focus and focus particle, (11a) and (11b) (the *ihr*-ambiguity sentences, with focus particles) are prosodically not equivalent. Consider first the dative construction. A dative sentence containing a focus particle has only one prosodic structure. This is shown in (16a), where the pronoun is accented. If, as in (16b), the pronoun is left unaccented and the noun is accented, an ungrammatical sentence results. The pattern seen in the German sentences (16) holds in English too, as illustrated in (17).

(16) a. ... daß man sogar $\{_F$ IHR$\}$ Geld anvertraut hat.
b. * ... daß man sogar ihr $\{_F$ GELD$\}$ anvertraut hat.

(17) a. Mary gave even $\{_F$ HIM$\}$ pictures.
b. * Mary gave even him $\{_F$ PICTURES$\}$.

The grammaticality pattern seen in (16) and (17) is due to the requirement that the focus associated to a focus particle in the particular phrase-structural configuration of (16) and (17) must either be the phrase immediately following the focus particle or be contained within this phrase. In dative sentences, this condition can only be obeyed by focusing the dative pronoun. For possessive sentences, in contrast, this condition is fulfilled both by accenting the pronoun and by accenting the noun. This is shown in (18).[4] If the pronoun is accented, there is only one licit focus structure, namely the one shown in (18a). In case the noun is accented, either the noun alone, or the whole NP of which the accented noun is the head, is focused. For reasons of simplicity, only the former case is shown in (18b).

(18) a. ... daß man sogar $[_{NP}$ $\{_F$ IHR$\}$ Geld$]$ beschlagnahmt hat.
b. ... daß man sogar $[_{NP}$ ihr $\{_F$ GELD$\}]$ beschlagnahmt hat.

The pattern in the German sentences in (18) can be replicated in English, as the sentences in (19) demonstrate.

(19) a. Mary liked even $[_{NP}$ $\{_F$ HIS$\}$ pictures$]$.
b. Mary liked even $[_{NP}$ his $\{_F$ PICTURES$\}]$.

Comparing (16) with (18) shows why the sentences in (11a) and (11b) are not equivalent with respect to their prosodic properties: while the intonation *IHR Geld* is compatible with both the possessive and the dative structure, the intonation *ihr GELD* is only compatible with the possessive structure. It is now also possible to state more precisely the prosodic equivalence of sentences like (10), i.e., *ihr*-ambiguity sentences without focus particles. In sentences like

---

4 A third possibility would be to accent both the pronoun and the noun. This possibility will be disregarded here because it does not contribute anything new to the points developed with respect to the other two intonations.

(10), any word may bear sentential stress. There are no restrictions imposed by either of the two syntactic structures. In particular, both the dative structure and the possessive structure allow for sentential stress on the noun *Geld.* Furthermore, in both cases sentential stress on *Geld* is the neutral intonation for sentences of this kind, i.e., the intonation appropriate when these sentences are presented out of the blue.

Besides affecting the prosodic properties of the sentences under consideration, the introduction of a focus particle probably also alters the phrase-structural representation of the ambiguous region. In particular, one can argue that the focus particle forms a constituent with the phrase immediately following, thereby causing a phrase structural difference between sentences with and without focus particles. A test for constituenthood in German is provided by root clauses. As discussed in section 2, German root clauses are verb-second clauses. This means that exactly one constituent can precede the finite verb, which accordingly is in second-position. In order to test whether a string of words forms a constituent, one can put this string in front of the finite verb in a root clause. If the resulting sentence is grammatical, the string under consideration must be a constituent. As shown in (20), both *sogar ihr* and *sogar ihr Geld* can be fronted in root clauses.

(20) a. [Sogar ihr] hatte man Geld anvertraut.
even her had one money entrusted
'Someone entrusted money even to her.'

b. [Sogar ihr Geld] hatte man beschlagnahmt.
even her money had one confiscated
'Someone confiscated even her money.'

We may therefore assume that in sentences exhibiting the *ihr*-ambiguity, the focus particle and the following phrase form a constituent.[5] This yields (21) and (22) as the syntactic structures for sentences without and with focus particles, respectively (Bayer, 1996). As can be seen by comparing (21) with (22), introducing a focus particle requires introducing an additional node above the phrase immediately following the focus particle (circled in (22)).

---

[5] A different proposal has been made by Jacobs (1983), who contends that focus particles are to be treated syntactically on a par with sentence adverbials. As shown in the discussion of sentence adverbials in section 6 below, such an analysis would strengthen the point made in favor of the PCR.

(21)
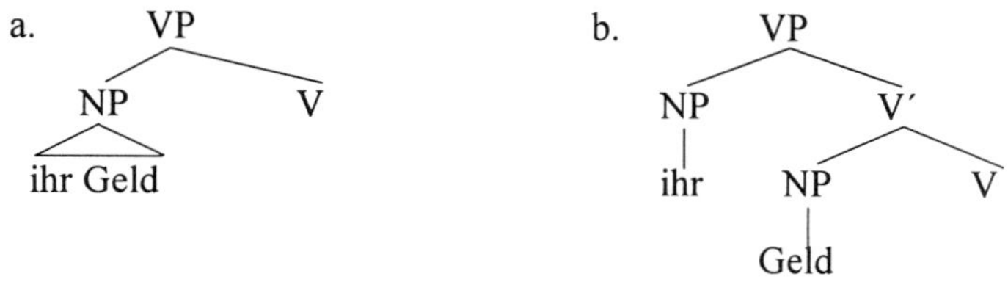

(22)
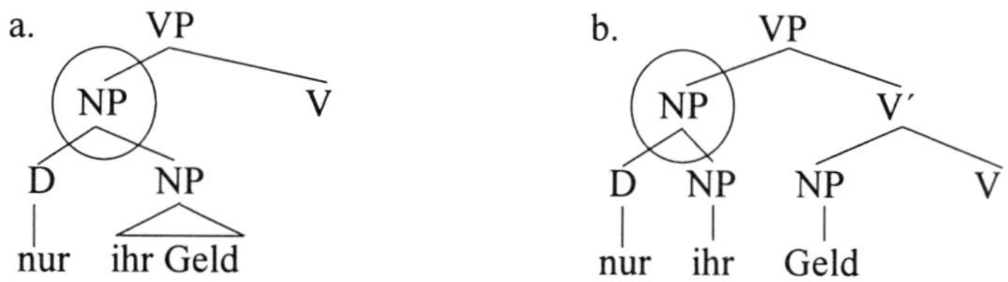

4 Experiment 1

Experiment 1 will compare the predictions that the PCR makes for the *ihr*-ambiguity with predictions made by syntactic theories of reanalysis. What predictions the PCR makes depends on which intonation readers initially assign to the ambiguous part of the sentences in question, i.e., to the string *daß (sogar) ihr Geld.* This, in turn, depends in part on the syntactic structure that is initially assigned to the ambiguous string. In anticipation of the results of a sentence completion study (cf. Experiment 1B), let us assume that readers prefer the possessive structure on encountering the string *ihr Geld.* Under the assumption that the default intonation assigned during reading is the neutral or unmarked intonation, readers will assign the intonation shown in (23) to sentences without focus particles. Under this intonation, where *Geld* bears sentence stress, the whole embedded sentence can be focused with an intonation appropriate for a sentence presented out of the blue.

(23) … $\{_F$ daß man $[_{NP}$ ihr GELD$]\}$…

If the possessive structure is the structure computed on the first pass, reanalysis becomes necessary if the sentence ends in a verb obligatorily requiring a dative object. As shown in (24), the syntactic structure has to be revised on encountering *anvertraut hat* but the prosodic structure can be left intact. Without a focus particle, the dative structure is fully compatible with the stress pattern *ihr GELD*, and, in fact, this stress pattern is also the one which allows focus projection up to the whole clause, as was the case with the possessive structure. Since no prosodic revision is necessary in (24), the PCR predicts that the reanalysis depicted in (24) is easy to accomplish.

(24) ... $\{_F$ daß man $[_{NP}$ ihr GELD$]\}$ + anvertraut hat
⇒ ... $\{_F$ daß man $[_{NP}$ ihr$]$ $[_{NP}$ GELD$]$ anvertraut hat$\}$

For sentences with focus particles, the situation is rather different. According to the above-mentioned constraint on the association of focus and focus particle, the focus associated to the focus particle in (11) must either be the phrase immediately following the focus particle or be contained within that phrase. If the syntactic structure initially assigned to the ambiguous string *ihr Geld* is the possessive structure, under this constraint both the possessive pronoun and the noun are possible targets for sentence stress. There are two reasons for expecting that the string *ihr Geld* will be read with the intonation *ihr GELD* and not with the intonation *IHR Geld*. First, for an NP like *ihr Geld*, the stress pattern *ihr GELD* is the neutral one. The second and probably more important reason lies in the fact that *ihr* is a closed-class function word whereas the following noun is an open-class content word. It is a well-known fact that function words (e.g., articles, complementizers, pronouns) differ prosodically from content words (e.g., nouns, verbs, adjectives), in that the former are prosodically less prominent than the latter. Function words also tend to be phonetically reduced in spoken language (Selkirk, 1984, 1995). An example for the different prosodic status of function and content words is provided by comparing sentences such as *Peter saw Mary* and *He saw her*. In the neutral case, where the whole sentence is focused, the most prominent element in *Peter saw Mary* is the object and the least prominent element the verb. In *He saw her*, on the other hand, the verb is more prominent than both the object and the subject. The difference between function and content words with respect to their phonological behavior holds in German as well as in English.

If readers obey the constraint that function words are stressless by default, they will assign an intonation like the one shown in (25) to sentences with focus particles.

(25) ... $\{_F$ daß man sogar $[_{NP}$ ihr GELD$]\}$...

Again, reanalysis will become necessary if the sentence turns out to end in a verb that obligatorily requires a dative object. This reanalysis, which is depicted in (26), will involve a revision of the original prosodic representation. This is due to the fact that for the dative structure, there is only one licit intonation, and that is the one where the dative pronoun gets accented. Therefore, the original prosodic structure shown in (25) has to be replaced by a prosodic structure where the pronoun is accented, thereby becoming the focus of the preceding focus particle.

(26) ... daß man sogar [$_{NP}$ {$_F$ ihr GELD}] + anvertraut hat.
⇒ ... daß man sogar [$_{NP}$ {$_F$ IHR}] [$_{NP}$ Geld] anvertraut hat.

Since the reanalysis depicted in (26) involves both a revision of the CPPM and a revision of the prosodic structure, the PCR predicts this reanalysis to be difficult. Intuitively, this is clearly the case. When reading the clause-final verb of sentences like (11a), one has the impression that an argument is missing, namely, the dative object that is required by the verb but that is not available since the only potential candidate, the ambiguous pronoun *ihr*, has been analyzed as a possessive pronoun both syntactically and prosodically. Only by reparsing the whole sentence and by stressing *ihr* is it possible to arrive at the appropriate syntactic structure. Experiment 1 tests whether the *ihr*-ambiguity without focus particles does in effect not lead to garden-path effects, and whether the introduction of a focus particles causes the possessive structure to become a garden-path sentence. In (27) I summarize the predictions developed so far. According to the PCR, subjects should have difficulties at the point of disambiguation when reading sentences like (27c), whereas (27a), (27b) and (27d) should be processed easily.

(27)	a.	... daß man [ihr$_{DAT}$] [Geld] anvertraut hat.	Easy
	b.	... daß man [ihr$_{POSS}$ Geld] beschlagnahmt hat.	Easy
	c.	... daß man sogar [ihr$_{DAT}$] [Geld] anvertraut hat.	Difficult
	d.	... daß man sogar [ihr$_{POSS}$ Geld] beschlagnahmt hat.	Easy

A different pattern of easy and difficult reanalysis is predicted by recent syntactic theories of reanalysis. For example, a deterministic theory of reanalysis like that of Weinberg (1993) or Marcus *et al.* (1983) would predict either that all four sentences are easy to process, or that, independently from the absence or presence of a focus particle, possessive sentences are difficult and dative sentences easy. The actual prediction depends on which structure is preferred on first-pass parsing. Since dominance statements can be added but not retracted by a deterministic parser, severe processing difficulties would be predicted in the case the possessive structure should be preferred on first-pass parsing. This is so because in order to switch from the possessive to the dative structure it would be necessary to delete a prior statement, namely, the statement that the NP dominating *Geld* also dominates the pronoun *ihr*. If, on the other hand, the dative structure were preferred, no difficulties would be predicted, since the dative structure could be converted to the possessive structure by adding a dominance statement, namely, that the NP dominating *Geld* also dominates the NP *ihr*. Indepedent from the question as to which structure is preferred on initial-pass parsing, a deterministic theory would predict that focus particles do not affect the processing of the sentences under consideration since the crucial dominance relations are not affected by the absence versus presence of a focus particle.[6]

Consider finally the parallel parsing theory of Gibson (1991). This theory would predict no severe processing difficulties in any of the sentences under consideration, and in particular no difference between sentences with and without focus particles. According to Gibson (1991), syntactic structures may be computed in parallel as long as they do not differ greatly in processing load. A main source of processing load is provided by NPs that have not yet received a thematic role within the ongoing syntactic structure. In our sentences, there will be two NPs without a theta-role before the point of disambiguation in the dative structure but only one such NP in the possessive structure (since *ihr* as a possessive pronoun receives the thematic role of possessor within the bigger NP consisting of *ihr* and the following noun). Syntactic structures that differ by such a small amount are pursued in parallel and are therefore still available at the point of disambiguation. Hence, neither structure should lead to severe processing difficulties. Since focus particles have no effect whatsoever on the assignment of thematic roles, this prediction holds both in the presence and absence of a focus particle.

Experiment 1 was designed to test the various predictions derived in this section. It has two parts. Experiment 1A used a self-paced reading task to test for garden-path effects in sentences exhibiting the *ihr*-ambiguity. Experiment 1B was a sentence completion task that looked for possible preferences in favor of either the dative or the possessive structure.

---

[6] This would also hold under the proposal by Marcus & Hindle (1990) who try to integrate certain prosodic properties into a deterministic theory of parsing. This is due to the fact that Marcus & Hindle are only concerned with prosodic boundaries but not with focus-related pitch accents. Therefore, their proposal does not apply to the sentences under consideration here.

4.1 Experiment 1A

4.1.1 Method

Subjects. Twenty-four students of the University of Stuttgart participated in Experiment 1A. All were native speakers of German and naive with respect to the purpose of the experiment.

Materials. Thirty-two experimental sentences were constructed, each sentence appearing in one of the four versions illustrated above in (27). All target sentences consisted of a main clause followed by an embedded clause. The ambiguity was always contained in the embedded clause. All embedded clauses were of the form shown in (27).

Half of the embedded clauses were active clauses that ended in a finite form of the perfect participle *haben* (cf. (27)). In these clauses, the clause-initial complementizer was immediately followed by an unambiguously nominative-marked subject, either the personal pronoun *er* ('he') or the indefinite pronoun *man* ('one'). The other half of the embedded clauses were passive clauses that ended in a finite form of the passive auxiliary *werden* ('become'). These sentences did not contain either *er* or *man* as subject. Instead, the noun following *ihr* functioned as subject in the dative structure (cf. (28a)). In the possessive structure, the whole NP made up of possessive pronoun and following noun acted as subject (cf. (28b)). Note that for German passive clauses the order indirect object followed by subject is the unmarked order. Moreover, for sentences like (28a), where the object is a pronoun and the subject a bare NP, reversing to the order subject before object is hardly possible. The reason for including passive clauses besides active clauses was that passive clauses allow for a wider range of nouns in the *ihr*-ambiguity.[7]

(28) a. ... daß $[\text{ihr}]_{DAT}$ $[\text{Vertrauen}]_{NOM}$ entgegengebracht wurde.
that her confidence shown was
'... that confidence in her was shown.'

---

[7] This is due to the agreement between possessive pronoun and head noun. In active clauses only neuter nouns can be used without losing the ambiguity (for example, the possessive pronoun for feminine nouns is not *ihr*, but *ihre*), whereas passive clauses allow both neuter and masculine nouns.

b. ... daß [ihr Vertrauen]$_{NOM}$ mißbraucht wurde.
that her confidence abused was
'... that her confidence was abused.'

Disambiguation was always achieved by using subcategorization properties of the main verb (participle). Since not enough verbs were found that either obligatorily require or obligatorily forbid a dative object, some verbs were used in more than one stimulus sentence. The two groups of verbs were matched with respect to length. The verbs requiring a dative object had a mean length of 10.31 letters whereas the verbs forbidding a dative object had a mean length of 10.06 letters.

All main clauses contained an antecedent for the ambiguous pronoun *ihr*. This antecedent was always a proper name except in two sentences in which the NPs *seine Schwester* ('his sister') and *seine Tochter* ('his daughter') were used, together with appropriate masculine antecedents for the possessive pronoun *sein* ('his'). For embedded clauses with the personal pronoun *er* as subject, the corresponding main clauses contained a further antecedent for this pronoun. All main clauses were unbiased with respect to the two alternative syntactic structures.

Yes/no comprehension questions were constructed for half of the experimental sentences. The questions were presented, all in one frame, immediately after subjects had read the last word of the sentence. The experimental sentences were divided into four lists. Only one version of each sentence was included within a given list. The experimental sentences were randomized individually for each subject. In addition to the experimental sentences, 80 filler sentences were created. All filler sentences had a main clause followed by an embedded clause. Half of the filler sentences were followed by a comprehension question.

Procedure. The stimuli were presented on an IBM-compatible PC. Subjects read sentences on a computer screen using a moving window display in which all nonspace characters of the sentence were initially replaced by underlines (Just *et al.* 1982). Subjects pressed a key to see each new word of the sentence. On each press of the key, a new word appeared and the previous word was replaced by underlines. The computer recorded the time between keypresses. The press of the key extinguishing the last word of the sentence either revealed the next sentence or a yes/no question which had to be answered by pushing the *j*-key for *ja* ('yes') or the *n*-key for *nein* ('no'). Subjects received no feedback for their answers.

4.1.2 Results

For each subject, reading times for words that fell more than 2.5 standard deviations away from his or her mean were replaced with the critical cut-off value (subject's mean plus 2.5 standard deviations). Less than 3.2% of the data were affected by this procedure. Preliminary analyses of the data revealed that the active-passive dimension had no significant effect on reading times. Since this dimension did not interact with any of the other factors, reading times were collapsed across this dimension. Figure 1 presents the reading times for the embedded clauses of Experiment 1. Separate two-way analyses of variance (structure (possessive versus dative) × focus particle (with versus without)) were conducted for each word's reading time with both subjects (F1) and items (F2) as random effects.

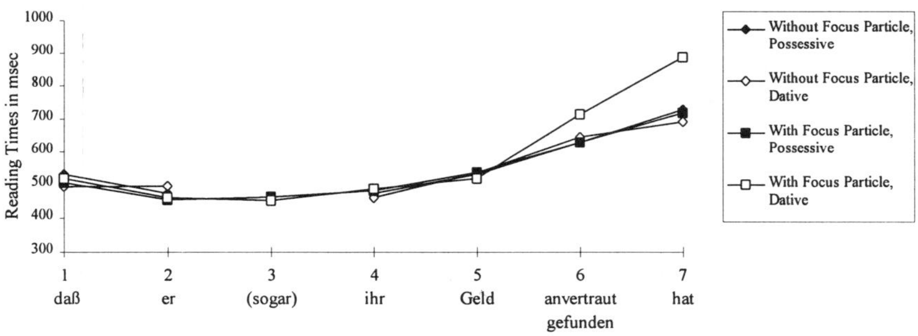

FIGURE 1: Reading times for the embedded clauses of Experiment 1A.

None of the positions preceding the participle (positions 1-5) showed any significant effects, with the exception of a spurious significant interaction at the complementizer (position 1). At the participle (position 6), there was a main effect of structure with dative sentences receiving longer reading times than possessive sentences (680 ms versus 628 ms; $F1(1,23) = 7.14$, $p < .05$; $F2(1,31) = 6.06$, $p < .05$). Sentences with focus particles took more time to read than sentences without focus particles, but the main effect of focus was only significant in the item analysis (637 ms versus 671 ms; $F1(1,23) = 2.45$, $p > .1$; $F2(1,31) = 5.84$, $p < .05$). Although reading times for possessive sentences did not differ depending on the absence or presence of a focus particle (629 ms versus 628 ms) whereas reading times for dative sentences did (645 ms versus 715 ms), the interaction of structure and focus was not significant in the subject analysis and only marginally so in the item analysis ($F1(1.23) = 2.52$, $p > .1$;

$F2(1,31) = 3.08$, $p < .1$). At the auxiliary (position 7), dative sentences had longer reading times than possessive sentences, resulting in a main effect of structure that was significant in the subject analysis but only marginally significant in the item analysis (790 ms versus 729 ms; $F1(1,23) = 6,81$, $p < .05$; $F2(1,31) = 3,13$, $p < .1$). Also at position 7, the main effect of focus was significant, with sentences containing a focus particle receiving longer reading times than sentences without a focus particle (894 ms versus 710 ms; $F1(1,23) = 6,03$, $p < .05$; $F2(1,31) = 17,17$, $p < .001$). These two main effects have to be qualified by the finding of a highly significant interaction of structure and focus ($F1(1.23) = 9,32$, $p < .01$ and $F2(1,31) = 17,59$, $p < .001$). This interaction is due to the fact that the insertion of a focus particle affected reading times for dative sentences (692 ms for dative sentences without a focus particle versus 888 ms for dative sentences with a focus particle) but had no effect on possessive sentences (729 ms for possessive sentences without a focus particle versus 719 ms for possessive sentences with a focus particle). Seen from a different perspective, this interaction can be described as resulting from the finding that dative and possessive sentences did not differ significantly from each other in the absence of a focus particle whereas in the presence of a focus particle the dative sentences took much more time to process than the possessive sentences.

4.1.3 Discussion

The results obtained in Experiment 1A confirm the predictions made by the PCR. For sentences without focus particles, there was no reading time difference between the possessive and the dative structure. For sentences with focus particle, a clear difference was obtained. Whereas possessive sentences with focus particles did not differ from sentences without focus particles, sentences with focus particles ending in a verb requiring a dative object showed a sizeable increase in reading times. That this increase was much stronger on the auxiliary than on the participle can be attributed to spill-over effects. Sentences of the kind tested in Experiment 1A might be especially prone to such effects because the participle and the auxiliary are syntactically closely connected, forming the so-called verbal complex, which is furthermore located in clause final position.

The results of Experiment 1A thus allow for two conclusions. (i) Sentences without focus particles do not lead to processing difficulties under either of the two possible interpretations. Therefore, syntactic reanalysis must be easy to accomplish for this kind of ambiguity. (ii) The finding of an increased processing load for the dative sentences containing a focus particle indicates that these sentences induced a garden-path effect, that is, that reanalysis is difficult for these sentences. This pattern is predicted if reanalysis is prosodically constrained, as claimed by the PCR. In contrast, this pattern is neither compatible with the deterministic theory of Weinberg (1993) nor with the parallel theory of Gibson (1991), since neither of these theories would predict any difference between sentences with and without focus particles. However, this does not mean that a syntactic explanation is completely impossible. As shown in (21) and (22), there is a phrase-structural difference between sentences with and without focus particles. Due to this phrase-structural difference, a syntactic explanation remains a possibility. For example, one might claim that reanalysis of the CPPM will be more complex for sentences with focus particles than for sentences without focus particles because the reanalysis from (21a) to (21b) will only involve breaking up a single NP whereas going from (22a) to (22b) involves breaking up both the lower and the upper NP. It will be the purpose of Experiment 2 to exclude this kind of explanation.

Another question left open by Experiment 1A is whether there is a general first-pass parsing preference in favor of either the dative or the possessive structure. This question will be addressed in Experiment 1B using a sentence completion task.

4.2 Experiment 1B

4.2.1 Method

Subjects. Thirty students of the University of Stuttgart and the University of Jena participated in Experiment 1B. All were native speakers of German and naive with respect to the purpose of the experiment.

Materials. In constructing the materials for Experiment 1B, 24 sentence quadruplets from Experiment 1A were selected. These 24 quadruplets were transformed into pairs of sentence fragments by replacing the participle and the auxiliary of the embedded clauses with a blank line. Since the possessive and the dative sentences only differed in the participle, this means that the factor of sentence structure (possessive versus dative) was eliminated. Half of the sentence fragments were derived from sentences containing embedded clauses in the active voice and half from sentences containing embedded clauses in the passive voice. However, after removing the clause final participle and auxiliary, it no longer makes sense to speak of active and passive sentences. Although the fragments derived from active sentences could only be completed by active verbs—due to restrictions on case marking—no such restriction held for fragments derived from passive sentences. These fragments could be completed with a verb either in the active or in the passive voice. Therefore, the former dimension active versus passive will be relabeled as 'with a separate subject' versus 'without a separate subject' for the purposes of Experiment 1B ('with subject' versus 'without subject', for short).

The experimental sentences were divided into two lists. Only one version of each sentence appeared on each list and both lists contained an equal number of sentences with and without focus particles. In addition to the experimental sentences, 16 filler sentence fragments were created. The filler fragments were also ambiguous but with structures unrelated to the ihr-ambiguity.

Procedure. Subjects received booklets containing the experimental and filler sentences randomly interspersed. The booklets included written instructions which told subjects that they should read each sentence fragment and then complete it immediately with some sensible continuation. The instructions also informed subjects that all sentences were ambiguous, and that they should choose the first completion that came to their mind. There was no time limit for completing the booklets.

4.2.2 Results

Subjects' completions were scored according to four categories: ambiguous responses that could not be classified as either possessive or dative; possessive responses; dative responses; and residual responses, including ungrammatical completions and omissions. There were less than 1.3% residual responses and less than 6.7% ambiguous responses. These responses are not considered in the following analysis of the results. Figure 2 shows the percentages of possessive completions.

Separate two-way analyses of variance (subject (with versus without) × focus particle (with versus without)) were conducted for the percentages of possessive responses with both subjects (F1) and items (F2) as random effects. There was a main effect of focus particle ($F1(1,29) = 5.87$, $p < .05$; $F2(1,22) = 6.01$, $p < .05$), with sentences containing a focus particle receiving more possessive completions than sentences containing no focus particle. The main effect of subject was significant in the subject analysis but only marginally significant in the item analysis ($F1(1,29) = 21,78$, $p < .01$; $F2(1,22) = 3.44$, $p < .1$). The interaction was also significant in the subject analysis and marginally significant in the item analysis ($F1(1,29) = 4.6$, $p < .05$; $F2(1,22) = 3.82$, $p < .1$). The reason for this interaction lies in the fact that the factor focus particle had no effect for sentences without subjects (89% for sentences without focus particles versus 90% for sentences with focus particles) but had an effect on sentences with subjects (80% for sentences without focus particles versus 67% for sentences with focus particles).

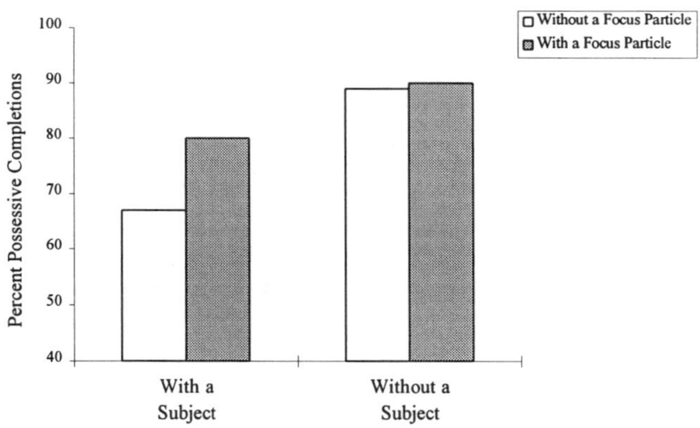

FIGURE 2: Percentage of possessive completions in Experiment 1B.

4.2.3 Discussion

The results of Experiment 1B show an overall advantage for possessive completions modulated by the factors subject and focus particle. In order to interpret this result, we have to take into account that the task of sentence completion is not only dependent on language comprehension processes but also on language production processes. First of all, there seems to be a moderate first-pass parsing preference in favor of the possessive structure. This is reflected in the results of the condition with subjects and without focus particles, where 67% of the completions were possessive constructions. That this moderate preference turned into a clear preference in the condition with subjects and with focus particles, and in both conditions containing no subjects, can be explained by (i) positing that focus particles have an effect on parsing preferences and (ii) noting that the experimental task of sentence completion involves processes of both language comprehension and language production.

Concerning the latter processes, the fact that sentences without a subject received more possessive responses than sentences with a subject, particularly in the condition without a focus particle, might simply be due to an asymmetry in the language with respect to possible continuations. An inspection of the possessive responses for sentences without subject showed that a large proportion of these responses were copular constructions. Fragments like *daß ihr Humor* ('that her humor') were often completed in the form of *daß ihr Humor eigenartig war* ('that her humor was strange'). Furthermore, the set of possible dative continuations is restricted to the subset of psych-verbs that take a dative object and to passivized verbs. Whereas the former set is rather small, the use of passivized verbs in language production seems to be associated with a general disadvantage when compared to active forms (cf. Ferreira, 1994). For sentence fragments containing a separate subject, on the other hand, a large range of possible continuations exists both for the possessive and the dative structure, namely, all transitive and ditransitive verbs, respectively, constrained only by the requirement of semantic appropriateness. Combined with some overall bias in favor of the possessive structure, this difference in the availability of dative and possessive continuations can be made responsible for the fact that a great majority of responses in the condition without subjects were possessive responses, whereas the advantage for possessive responses was much smaller in the condition of sentences with subjects, particularly in sentence fragments without focus particles.

A further finding, that sentences with focus particles elicited more possessive responses than sentences without sentence particles, can be explained as an effect of focus particles on first-pass parsing preferences. As was said above, *ihr* is a function word and as such unstressed by default. If *ihr* is read without stress both when it is preceded by a focus particle and when it is not, then it follows that a moderate preference for the possessive structure in the absence of a focus particle must turn into a strong preference in the presence of such a particle. The reason for this is that, without a focus particle, both the possessive and the dative structure are licit options for unstressed *ihr*, whereas with a focus particle, only the possessive structure is licit. Hence, by reading *ihr* unstressed one is forced by the grammar of the language to adopt the possessive structure.[8]

The finding of a preference in favor of the possessive structure poses a severe problem for deterministic theories of reanalysis since this preference means that these theories cannot even explain the processing of the simple sentences without focus particles. As explained above, under a deterministic account the revision from the possessive to the dative structure would involve the retraction of a prior dominance statement, namely the statement that the NP dominating the noun also dominates the preceding pronoun. Since it has been claimed that the retraction of a dominance statement causes severe processing difficulties (Weinberg, 1993; Marcus *et al.*, 1983), deterministic theories predict that sentences exhibiting the ihr-ambiguity should lead to a strong garden path under the dative disambiguation even in the absence of a focus particle. This is clearly not the case. The ihr-ambiguity is thus a clear counter-example to deterministic theories of reanalysis: it is easy to reanalyze although it involves raising a constituent out of the constituent in which it is embedded.

5 Experiment 2

While the results of Experiment 1 argue against particular syntactic approaches to reanalysis, they do not rule out any kind of syntactic explanation of the difference between sentences with and without focus particles. As pointed out above, this is due to the fact that the introduction of a focus particle affects the phrase-structural representation of the ambiguous region *ihr Geld*, at least under the syntactic assumptions outlined above. In order to exclude the possibility of a purely syntactic explanation, one would have to test sentences that display the same prosodic behavior as corresponding sentences with focus particles, but for which phrase-structural differences can be excluded. Sentences obeying these conditions can be obtained by replacing the focus particles with sentence adverbials like *tatsächlich* ('indeed') or *vielleicht* ('perhaps'). An example sentence pair is given in (29).

---

[8] An effect of focus particle on initial pass parsing has already been proposed in Bader (1994). In fact, in this work it has been assumed that, in the absence of a focus particle, there is no preference for either the dative or the possessive structure. This assumption was solely based on intuitive judgments. The reason for conducting the sentence completion study was that this assumption was sometimes questioned in discussions of the material presented in this paper.

(29) a. … daß man tatsächlich ihr Geld anvertraut hatte.
that one indeed her money entrusted had
'… that someone indeed entrusted money to her.'

b. … daß man tatsächlich ihr Geld beschlagnahmt hatte.
that one indeed her money confiscated had
'… that someone indeed confiscated her money.'

Two points have to be noted with respect to sentences like (29). First, the sentence adverbial cannot form a constituent together with the phrase following it. This can be demonstrated by transforming the embedded clauses in (29) into main clauses and fronting the string under consideration in front of the finite verb, where only a single constituent may be placed. As indicated in (30), the resulting sentences are ungrammatical.

(30) a. * [Tatsächlich ihr] hatte man Geld anvertraut.
b. * [Tatsächlich ihr Geld] hatte man beschlagnahmt.

Partial syntactic structures of sentences containing sentence adverbials are shown in (31); (31a) shows the possessive structure, (31b) the dative structure. Here, the sentence adverbial has been adjoined to VP. The important point is that the adjunction of a sentence adverbial does not affect the phrase-structural representation of the ambiguous region *ihr Geld*, as can be seen by a comparison of (31) and (21). A theory of reanalysis based exclusively on syntactic structure would therefore predict that sentences with sentence adverbials should pattern like sentences without any focus sensitive operators, and should not give rise to garden-path effects.

(31) a.
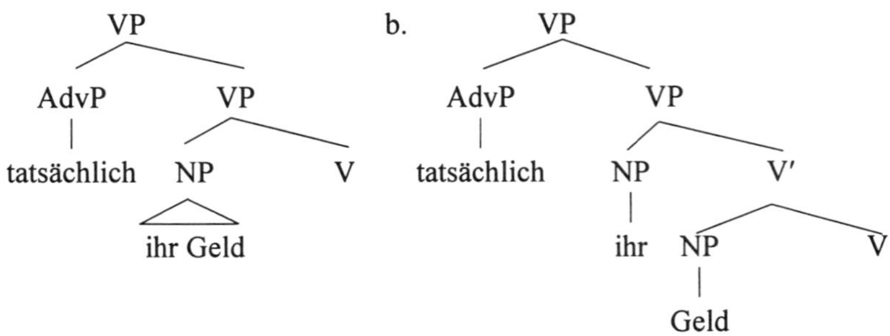

The second point to note with respect to the sentences in (29) is that they behave prosodically exactly like corresponding sentences with focus particles. A sentence adverbial in the position shown in (29) needs an associated focus. As with focus particles, this focus must be the phrase following the sentence adverbial or be contained in that phrase. For the dative structure in (29a), the dative pronoun is the only possible focus. For the possessive structure in (29b), there are again three possible foci, depending on which word is accented. Accenting the possessive pronoun leads to narrow focus on the possessive pronoun while accenting the noun is compatible with both focus on the NP *ihr Geld* as a whole and focus on the noun alone.

Since sentences like (29) behave identically to corresponding sentences with focus particles when compared with respect to their prosodic properties, the PCR predicts that the same results should be obtained if the focus particles in the materials used in Experiment 1 are replaced by appropriate sentence adverbials. This prediction was tested in Experiment 2, which had a slightly different design than Experiment 1. Whereas in Experiment 1 ambiguous sentences with and without focus particles were compared, Experiment 2 compared ambiguous sentences with sentence adverbials to unambiguous sentences with sentence adverbials. Unambiguous sentences are easily constructed by using the masculine counterparts to the ambiguous feminine pronoun *ihr*. For masculine third person pronouns, the dative form is *ihm* ('him') and the possessive form *sein* ('his'). The sentence fragments in (32) show the four versions that result from pairing the two factors: ambiguity (unambiguous versus ambiguous pronoun) and structure (dative versus possessive structure).

(32) a. … daß man tatsächlich [ihm_{DAT}] [Geld] anvertraut hatte. unambig.
b. … daß man tatsächlich [$\text{sein}_{\text{POSS}}$ Geld] beschlagnahmt hatte. unambig.
c. … daß man tatsächlich [ihr_{DAT}] [Geld] anvertraut hatte. ambig.
d. … daß man tatsächlich [ihr_{POSS} Geld] beschlagnahmt hatte. ambig.

The inclusion of unambiguous sentences allows to test a further prediction made by an approach that takes phonological coding into account. If the phonological effects induced by sentence adverbials are reflected in on-line measures, one should expect longer reading times for a stressed word than for an unstressed one. In particular, the unambiguous dative pronoun *ihm* must be stressed immediately following a sentence adverbial whereas the unambiguous possessive pronoun *sein* can be stressed or not. According to the assumption that readers do not stress function words unless they need to, a possessive pronoun will be read without stress. This difference between unambiguous dative and possessive pronouns should result in a greater processing load on the dative pronoun, which should be reflected in longer reading times on these pronouns.

5.1 Method

Subjects. Thirty-two students of the University of Jena participated in Experiment 2. All were native speakers of German and naive with respect to the purpose of the experiment.

Materials. The materials used in Experiment 2 were based on the materials used in Experiment 1. Twenty-eight of the original sentences of Experiment 1 were selected. These sentences were transformed to conform to the pattern shown in (32). First, all focus particles were replaced by sentence adverbials. Secondly, unambiguous sentences were constructed by replacing the feminine *ihr* with the masculine *ihm* in the dative condition and with the masculine *sein* in the possessive condition and by changing the antecedents in the main clauses accordingly. Thirdly, some of the main clauses were revised to make them sound more natural with a sentence adverbial instead of a focus particle appearing inside the embedded clause.

Half of the experimental sentences were followed by a yes/no comprehension question. The experimental sentences were again divided into four lists, with each list containing an equal number of sentences in each condition and only one version of a given sentence. The experimental sentences were randomized individually for each subject and interleaved with an additional 81 filler sentences.

Procedure. The same self-paced reading procedure was used as in Experiment 1A.

5.2 Results

As in Experiment 1, reading times for words that fell more than 2.5 standard deviations away from the mean were replaced with the critical cut-off value (subject's mean plus 2.5 standard deviations). Less than 4.1% of the data were affected by this procedure. Preliminary analyses of the data revealed that the active-passive dimension had no significant effect on reading times. Furthermore, this dimension did not interact with any of the other factors except at the clause final auxiliary, where the interaction of ambiguity and the factor active versus passive reached significance. This was due to the fact that unambiguous sentences without a subject took more reading time than unambiguous sentences with subject. Since this interaction does not affect the main point of Experiment 2, and since no other interaction involving the factor active versus passive reached significance, reading times at all positions were collapsed across the dimension active versus passive for all further analyses. The reading times for the embedded clauses of Experiment 2 are presented in Figure 3. Separate two-way analyses of variance (structure (possessive versus dative) × ambiguity (ambiguous versus unambiguous)) were conducted for each word's reading time.

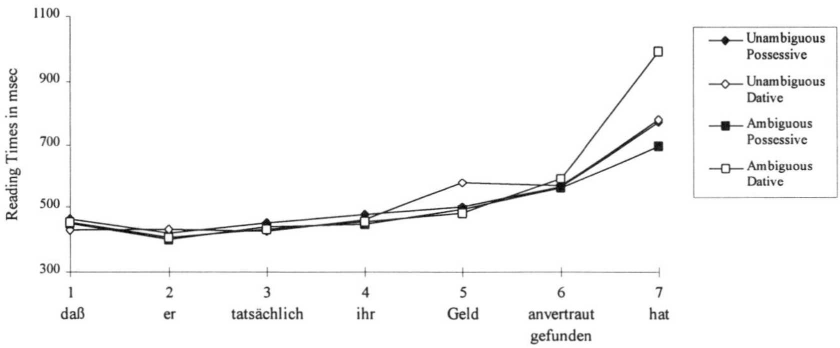

FIGURE 3: Reading times for the embedded clauses of Experiment 2.

No significant effects were found at positions 1 to 4. At the noun (position 5), nouns in unambiguous dative sentences received longer reading times (578 ms) than nouns in the other three conditions (490 ms). This difference resulted in a highly significant main effect of ambiguity ($F1(1,31) = 11.35$, $p < .01$; $F2(1,27) = 16.95$, $p < .001$), a main effect of structure that was significant in the subject analysis but not in the item analysis ($F1(1,31) = 4.68$, $p < .05$; $F2(1,27) = 2.62$, $p > .1$), and a significant interaction of ambiguity and structure ($F1(1,31) = 6,98$, $p < .05$; $F2(1,27) = 7.81$, $p < .01$). At the participle (position 6) no significant effect was found. At the auxiliary the same picture emerged as in Experiment 1a. The factor of ambiguity was significant, with reading times being longer for the ambiguous sentences than for the unambiguous sentences (844 ms versus 774 ms; $F1(1,31) = 4.94$, $p < .05$; $F2(1,27) = 4.20$, $p < .05$). Dative sentences took longer to read than possessive sentences, resulting in a highly significant main effect of structure (885 ms versus 733 ms; $F1(1,31) = 9.40$, $p < .01$; $F2(1,27) = 9.89$, $p > .01$). Again, the two main effects are to be qualified by the finding of a highly significant interaction of ambiguity and structure ($F1(1,31) = 11.80$, $p < .01$; $F2(1,27) = 17.72$, $p < .001$). This interaction is caused by the fact that unambiguous dative and possessive sentences did not differ from each other (778 ms versus 770 ms) but ambiguous dative sentences took much longer to read than ambiguous possessive sentences

(991 ms versus 696 ms). Post-hoc Scheffé tests revealed that reading times in the ambiguous dative condition differed significantly from reading times in the remaining three conditions, but that reading times in the remaining three conditions did not differ from each other.

5.3 Discussion

The results of Experiment 2 again show a garden-path effect for ambiguous sentences ending in a verb requiring a dative object. Since the addition of a sentence adverbial does not alter the syntactic structure of the ambiguous region, the garden-path effect found in Experiment 2 and the absence of such an effect for sentences without focus particles in Experiment 1 provide strong evidence for the claim that the processing of sentences exhibiting the ihr-noun ambiguity cannot be explained syntactically. Instead, sentences with sentence adverbials produced results similar to those of sentences with focus particles despite syntactic differences, but in accordance with the fact that sentences with sentence adverbials and sentences with focus particles behave alike prosodically, confirming the hypothesis that reanalysis is prosodically constrained.

Experiment 2 also provides evidence for an early influence of sentence adverbials on sentence processing. Unambiguous dative sentences showed increased reading times after the sentence adverbial. However, the exact nature of this influence is difficult to interpret, due to the fact that these increased reading times were not located on the pronoun which immediately followed the sentence adverbial but on the noun which followed the pronoun. One interpretation of this effect might be that readers accented the dative pronoun *ihm* as required by the grammar if this pronoun appears after a sentence adverbial, but that they did not accent the possessive pronoun *sein* since this is not required for the sentences under consideration. Phonetically, words bearing an accent are longer than words not bearing an accent. If this difference also shows up in the inner speech that accompanies reading, longer reading times for *ihm* in comparison to *sein* are predicted. The fact that longer reading times for stressed *ihm* in comparison to unstressed *sein* did not appear on the pronoun but on the immediately following noun might then be accounted for by assuming a spill-over effect.

6 Experiment 3

According to the PCR, garden-path effects can result from the need to revise a prosodic structure that has been computed via phonological coding. In particular, the parsing difficulties observed in this and the preceding experiment seem to be caused by the need to alter the prosodic status of the ambiguous pronoun *ihr*. Initially, *ihr* is read without stress but later has to be stressed as a result of second-pass parsing. This can be seen as a kind of 'prosodic garden-path effect': due to the local ambiguity in the syntax-prosody mapping, readers sometimes opt for an intonational structure that is contradicted by later input material. If this interpretation of our experimental results is correct, the garden-path effect observed for dative-sentences containing a focus particle should diminish if readers are given some reason to stress *ihr* on first encountering it. If such a reason could be given by merely manipulating prosodic properties while holding syntactic properties constant, this would be a further confirmation of the hypothesis that prosody influences the processing of certain syntactic ambiguities during reading.

A purely prosodic reason to stress *ihr* on initial encountering can be found in the rhythmic nature of natural languages. According to Nespor & Vogel (1989) "one of the generalizations that seems to hold true across most, if not all, languages is that the overall rhythmic pattern tends to be organized such that there is an alternation of strong and weak syllables" (p. 69). There are two ways that a string of words might deviate from the ideal of rhythmic alternation: clashes and lapses. A well-known clash arises in phrases such as *fourteen men*. Here, the stress on the second syllable of *fourteen* in isolation clashes with the stress on the word *men*, which bears phrasal stress in this phrase. In order to remedy this clash, the stress on the second syllable of *fourteen* is shifted to the first syllable, giving rise to the alternating pattern strong-weak-strong.

Lapses, the second kind of deviation from rhythmic alternation, are provided by long strings of unstressed syllables. This situation might arise, for example, by concatenating a long row of function words which are unstressed by default. Consider a sentence like *He must have been in bed.* This sentence contains five function words in a row. In order to avoid the long stretch of unstressed syllables in such a sentence, some of the function words receive stress. Two possible unmarked stress patterns for this sentence are shown in (33), where the function words receiving stress are in capital letters (cf. Giegerich, 1985, from whom this example has been taken).

(33) a. He MUST have been in bed.
b. He MUST have BEEN in bed.

For the ambiguous sentences under consideration, a lapse will arise if the pronoun *ihr* is preceded by a long focus particle like *ausschließlich* ('exclusively') or *ausgerechnet* ('of all people/things'). These focus particles consist of a first stressed syllable followed by two and three unstressed syllables, respectively (cf. Wiese, 1996). If one of these particles is followed by a further unstressed element, like the pronoun *ihr*, a relatively long string of unstressed syllables would emerge. If readers try to avoid long stretches of unstressed syllables, then they should put a stress onto *ihr* if *ihr* follows one of these long focus particles, as indicated in (34).

(34) … daß man ausschließlich IHR Geld…

Since the garden-path effects observed in the experiment reported above depend on *ihr* not being stressed, stressing *ihr* for rhythmic reasons should have the effect of reducing or eliminating the garden-path effect. If readers assign the stress pattern in (34) to ambiguous sentences with long focus particles, then no prosodic reanalysis will become necessary, independent of how the sentence continues, because both the dative and the possessive structure is compatible with stressed *ihr*.

Experiment 3 will test the prediction that the garden-path effect induced by focus particles diminishes in the presence of a long, initially stressed focus particle. A certain difficulty in testing this prediction lies in the fact that there are only very few focus particles that confirm to the given prosodic criteria. Hence it is not possible to test the factor short versus long focus particle with a random selection of short focus particles and a random selection of long focus particles. Experiment 3 will therefore contrast the two long focus particles *ausschließlich* and *ausgerechnet* with the two short focus particles *nur* and *sogar*. Furthermore, the experiment will also contain two conditions without focus particles, an ambiguous condition with the feminine pronoun *ihr* and an unambiguous condition with the masculine pronoun *ihm*. Only sentences ending in dative verbs will be tested, because Experiments 1 and 2 have already shown that sentences ending in verbs that enforce the possessive structure do not give rise to garden-path effects. To summarize, Experiment 3 will contrast the six conditions shown in (35).

(35)	a.	…daß man ihm Geld anvertraut hatte.	unambig., no part.
	b.	…daß man ihr Geld anvertraut hatte.	ambig., no part.
	c.	…daß man nur ihr Geld anvertraut hatte.	ambig., short part.
	d.	…daß man sogar ihr Geld anvertraut hatte.	ambig., short part.
	e.	…daß man ausschließlich ihr Geld anvertraut hatte.	ambig., long part.
	f.	…daß man ausgerechnet ihr Geld anvertraut hatte.	ambig., long part.

The selection of *ausgerechnet* and *ausschließlich* was dictated by prosodic criteria. Contrasting these particles with *nur* and *sogar* followed not only prosodic reasons but served also the exclusion of alternative interpretations of the possible outcome of Experiment 3. Semantically, *nur* is similar to *ausschließlich* whereas *sogar* is similar to *ausgerechnet.* Both *nur* and *ausschließlich* are restrictive particles. A sentence like *Peter only kissed MARY* claims that the referent of the focus, i.e., *Mary*, is the single element contained in the set of persons kissed by Peter. *Sogar* and *ausgerechnet*, on the other hand, are additive particles. A sentence like *Peter even kissed MARY* does not restrict the set of persons kissed by Peter, but adds the meaning component that it is in some way remarkable that Mary belongs to this set.

The classification of the four focus particles to be used in Experiment 3 according to semantic and prosodic criteria is summarized in (36). As can be seen, *sogar* patterns prosodically with *nur* and *ausschließlich* with *ausgerechnet*, whereas semantically *sogar* patterns with *ausgerechnet* and *nur* with *ausschließlich.*

(36)		*additive*	*restrictive*
	short	sogar	nur
	long	ausgerechnet	ausschließlich

If readers are sensitive to the rhythmic nature of language, the PCR predicts that the garden-path effects for dative sentences will diminish for the long focus particles.

6.1 Method

Subjects. Thirty-six students of the University of Jena participated in Experiment 3. All were native speakers of German and naive with respect to the purpose of the experiment.

Materials. The experimental materials of Experiment 3 were constructed based on the original materials constructed for Experiment 1A. Thirty of the original sentences were selected. All possessive sentences were removed and the remaining dative sentences transformed according to the model in (35). For half of the sentences, yes/no comprehension questions were created. The experimental sentences were divided into six lists. Each list contained exactly one version of each sentence and an equal number of sentences per condition. The experimental sentences were randomized individually for each subject. In addition to the experimental sentences, 88 filler sentences were constructed.

Procedure. The same self-paced reading procedure was used as in Experiment 1A and Experiment 2.

6.2 Results

Reading times for outliers (less than 3.6%) were replaced according to the same procedure used in the preceding experiments. The active versus passive dimension had no significant effect and there was no interaction involving this dimension. Collapsed reading times are shown in Figure 4. Separate six level, one-way analyses of variance (focus particle: no unambiguous versus no ambiguous versus ambiguous *nur* versus ambiguous *sogar* versus ambiguous *ausschließlich* versus ambiguous *ausgerechnet*) were conducted for each word's reading time.

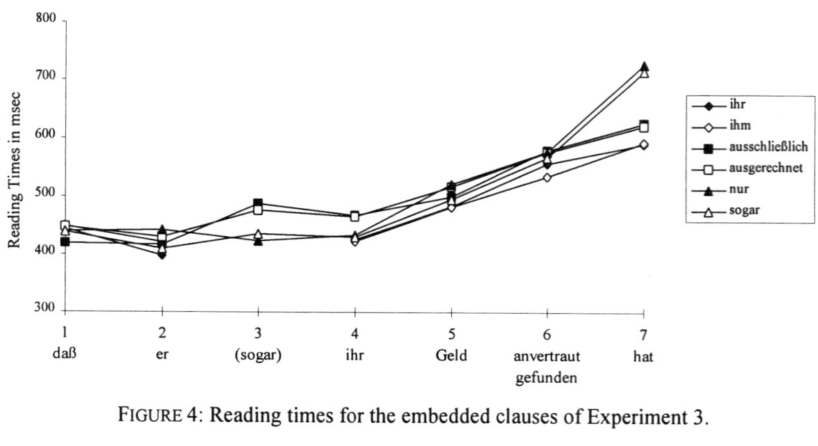

FIGURE 4: Reading times for the embedded clauses of Experiment 3.

There were no significant effects at the complementizer and the following subject. At the particle (position 3), where only the four sentence types with focus particles contributed to the analysis, long focus particles received longer reading times than short focus particles ($F1(3,105) = 9.57$, $p < .001$; $F2(3,87) = 4.93$, $p < .01$). At the following position of the pronoun (position 4), pronouns following long focus particles took more time to read than all other pronouns ($F1(5,175) = 4.31$, $p < .01$, $F2(5,145) = 3.28$, $p < .01$). At the position of the noun and the participle (positions 5 and 6), there were no significant differences. At the auxiliary, there was a highly significant effect of focus particle ($F1(5,175) = 3.92$, $p < .01$; $F2(5,145) = 4.15$, $p < .01$). Planned comparisons showed that sentences without focus particles (592 ms) did not differ significantly from sentences with long focus particles (624 ms), but that both sentences without focus particles and sentences with long focus particles differed significantly from sentences with short focus particles (721 ms).

6.3 Discussion

The results of Experiment 3 are a further confirmation of the claim that parsing processes during reading are subject to prosodic influences. First, Experiment 3 replicates the basic observation that ambiguous dative-sentences without focus particles are easy to process, whereas dative sentence containing certain focus particles lead to garden-path effects. Secondly, Experiment 3 shows that the garden-path effects induced by focus particles are diminished or eliminated if readers are given a reason to stress the ambiguous *ihr* on first encountering it. In sentences were ihr was preceded by a long focus particle like *ausschließlich* or *ausgerechnet*, *ihr* might be stressed in order to increase the alternation between stressed and unstressed syllables. If this actually happens, *ihr* is already stressed when the disambiguating dative verb is encountered and no prosodic reanalysis is necessary.

A further result of Experiment 3 was that *ihr* needed more reading time when following one of the long focus particles than in the other conditions. Since the long focus particles also needed longer reading times, increased reading times on *ihr* following long focus particles might be a simple spill-over effect. However, it might also be the case that the increased reading times on *ihr* reflect the stress given to this pronoun in the condition with long focus particles. This would be an explanation along the lines suggested for the unambiguous *ihm* of Experiment 2. A problem for this explanation is the difference between a result of Experiments 2 and 3, namely, in Experiment 2, increased reading times were not found on stressed *ihm* but on the following noun, whereas in Experiment 3 there was an immediate increase in reading times on *ihr*. The reason for this difference might be that, due to rhythmic factors, the long focus particles in Experiment 3 biased readers to stress the word immediately following the focus particle already before this word was encountered. This might account for the finding of prolonged reading times as early as the position of the stressed element. In contrast to the long focus particles, the sentence adverbials of Experiment 2 gave no indication that the next word should be stressed. The necessity of stressing *ihm* could only be figured out when encountering the unambiguous pronoun, which might explain why increased reading times were not found on the stressed element itself, as in Experiment 3, but one element later.

7 General Discussion

A series of three experiments has provided evidence for the claim that syntactic ambiguity resolution during reading is influenced by prosodic information. In many cases of phrase-structural ambiguity, syntactic and prosodic influences are confounded (cf. the above discussion of (1) and (2)). However, the particular structural ambiguity that was investigated in the preceding experiments allowed us to tease apart syntactic and prosodic contributions to reanalysis. One and the same phrase-structural ambiguity did not cause garden-path effects when the alternative syntactic structures were associated with identical prosodic structures but caused garden-path effects when prosodic differences were induced by the insertion of focus operators. As pointed out in connection with the discussion of sentence adverbials in section 5, a purely syntactic explanation seems rather improbable because the syntactic representation of the ambiguous region is not affected by the insertion of a sentence adverbial. Due to this lack of a syntactic difference between sentences with sentence adverbials and corresponding sentences without any focus-sensitive operators, there is no syntactic basis for predicting the parsing differences found for these sentences. Therefore, we can conclude that, at least for the ihr-ambiguity examined here, the ease of revising an initial structure is completely determined by prosodic factors.

This raises the obvious question as to whether the PCR can be applied to ambiguities others than the ihr-ambiguity. This seems indeed to be the case. Two examples were already given in section 2, namely, the examples in (1) and (2). A further example of a phrase-structural ambiguity that is amenable to the PCR is presented in (37) (from Frazier, 1978). The sentence pair in (37) illustrates the English her-ambiguity embedded within a preposed prepositional phrase. The simple her-ambiguity in English (cf. (9)) does not seem to elicit garden-path effects on either disambiguation (cf. Gibson, 1991; Gorrell, 1995), as for the German counterpart of this ambiguity, and can be explained in the same way. Of the two sentences in (37), in contrast, only (37a) is easy to process whereas (37b) elicits a strong garden-path effect.

(37) a. ($_I$ Without her contributions) ($_I$ the funds would be inadequate).

b. ($_I$ Without her) ($_I$ contributions would be inadequate).

This can be explained by the PCR by noting that sentence pair (37) is similar to sentence pair (1). The sentences in (37a) and (37b) contain preposed constituents, *without her contributions* and *without her*, respectively, that form intonational phrases of their own. The syntactic structure preferred on initial-pass parsing is the structure corresponding to (37a), which means that there is an intonational break after *contributions*. If the CPPM corresponding to the beginning of (37a) must be reanalyzed on encountering the disambiguating *would* of (37b), the associated prosodic structure must be altered, eliciting a strong garden-path effect.

As with the initial examples (1) and (2), several syntactic explanations are available for explaining the difference between the simple her-ambiguity and the prepositional variant of this ambiguity (e.g., Gibson, 1991; Weinberg, 1993). This points to a serious problem: how can we decide in cases where the processing of a particular ambiguity can be explained both syntactically and prosodically whether ease of reanalysis is determined by syntax, prosody, or both? One way to tackle this problem might be to look at whether ease of reanalysis for a given syntactic ambiguity is prone to prosodic influences. In particular, if it could be shown that a garden-path effect found in a certain structural configuration can be reduced merely by prosodic manipulations, this might point to the conclusion that revising prosodic structures might be more important for determining the ease of reanalysis than revising phrase-structures. An example for such a prosodic manipulation is provided by certain length-effects found for processing ambiguous sentences. In certain cases, reanalysis becomes easier if the disambiguating region is made longer. This can be illustrated by the examples in (38) from Frazier & Clifton (1996).

(38) a. ($_I$ John will explain to the kids) ($_I$ that their grandfather died tomorrow).

b. ($_I$ John will explain to the kids) ($_I$ that their grandfather died) ($_I$ after the operation they need).

In both sentences, the final temporal adverbial (*tomorrow* and *after the operation they need*, respectively) is initially attached low to the embedded clause but must finally end up attached high to the main clause. Reverting from the preferred low attachment to final high attachment is more difficult for (38a) than for (38b) (cf. Frazier & Clifton, 1996). This difference might be caused by the way these two sentences are grouped into prosodic units on first-pass parsing, as indicated in (38).

Assuming a first-pass preference for low attachment in both cases, *tomorrow* will be grouped together with the preceding embedded clause, whereas the temporal clause *after the operation they need* will form an intonational phrase of its own. Hence, on reanalysis, one has to break up an intonational phrase for (38a) in order to attach *tomorrow* to the main clause, whereas the phrasing in (38b) is already compatible with high attachment. This difference with respect to restructuring the prosodic structure derived by phonological coding might explain why (38b) is easier to process than (38a). According to such an explanation, revising prosodic structures would be a more important factor in explaining ease of reanalysis than revising phrase-structures. A deeper reason for this has already been given above: the prosodic structure computed during reading is part of the phenomenon of inner speech, which is what we consciously experience when reading something.

Lastly, let us come back to a point already mentioned when introducing the PCR, regarding the scope of the theory of prosodically constrained reanalysis proposed in this chapter. First of all, nothing said here precludes the possibility that factors other than prosodic ones may make reanalysis hard. Indeed, excluding this possibility would be clearly false. For example, Clifton (1995) has shown that thematic information can aid in recovery from syntactic misanalysis. A further example that shows that the PCR is only one of several determinants of ease of reanalysis is provided by subject-object ambiguities in German. These ambiguities provide a broad range of garden-path effects that cannot be explained by recourse to prosodic information. Two examples are shown in (39) and (40).

(39) a. Britta hat gesagt, daß sie gestern einige Studenten besucht hat.
Britta has said that she yesterday some students visited has
'Britta said that she visited some students yesterday.'

b. Britta hat gesagt, daß sie gestern einige Studenten besucht haben.
Britta has said hat sheyesterday some students visited have
'Britta said that some students visited her yesterday.'

(40) a. Niemand wußte, daß Uli letzte Woche ein Päckchen geschickt hat.
nobody knew that Uli last week a parcel sent has
'Nobody knew that Uli has sent a parcel last week.'

b. Niemand wußte, daß Uli letzte Woche ein Päckchen geschickt wurde.
nobody knew that Uli last week a parcel sent was
'Nobody knew that a parcel was sent to Uli last week.'

It has been demonstrated for sentences like those in both (39) and (40) that the order subject-before-object is preferred on initial-pass parsing. Consequently, when this order must be given up in favor of the non-preferred object-before-subject reading, as in (39b) and (40b), garden-path effects are observed. For (39b), these garden-path effects are rather strong whereas (40b) only elicits weak effects (cf. Bader, 1994, 1996). Neither the existence of garden-path effects in (39b) and (40b) nor the fact that these effects are much more severe for (39b) than for (40b) can be explained by prosodic differences between the subject-before-object and the object-before-subject reading. The reason is simply that there are no such differences between the (a) and (b) versions of these sentences. A sentence like (39a) differs from a sentence like (39b) neither with respect to prosodic phrasing nor with respect to sentence stress.

This situation equals the one found for sentences exhibiting the ihr-ambiguity and not containing a focus operator. We therefore have to ask why some ambiguities lead to garden-path effects in the absence of prosodic differences while others do not. At the moment, there seems to be no general answer to this question. However, as far as the contrast between the ihr-ambiguity and sentences of the kind in (39) and (40) is concerned, there is at least a suggestive syntactic difference: the ihr-ambiguity is a simple phrase-structure ambiguity, whereas the subject-object ambiguities in (39) and (40) are of a different nature. The example in (39) is an instance of a filler-gap ambiguity. Sentence (39a) with the subject preceding the object is base-generated whereas sentence (39b) with the reversed word order is derived by moving the object in front of the subject, leaving a trace behind between subject and verb. The example in (40) is probably neither a filler-gap nor a phrase-structure ambiguity, but an instance of what can be called a pure case-ambiguity (cf. Bader *et al.*, 1996, for a further example of a pure case ambiguity).

The evidence presently available indicates that overlooking a trace as in (39b) and the need to correct certain case features as in (40) can create difficulties independent both from phrase-structural and from prosodic factors (cf. Bader, 1996, for details). If this were indeed the case, it would lend some evidence to the assumption of specialized routines within the parser—routines for assigning phrase-structure and routines for creating filler-gap dependencies—as suggested by Frazier (1990). It would furthermore concur with the view proposed by Frazier & Clifton (this volume) that the strength of garden-path effects is governed by a variety of different factors and that no single mechanism can explain garden-path effects independently of the particular syntactic construction involved, as proposed for example by Gibson (1991) and Gibson *et al.* (1994).

Friedrich-Schiller-Universität Jena

References

Altmann, G. & Steedman, M. 1988. Interaction with context during human sentence processing. *Cognition*, 30, 191-238.

Bader, M. 1994. *Sprachverstehen: Syntax und Prosodie beim Lesen*. Unpublished doctoral dissertation, University of Stuttgart.

Bader, M. 1996. On Reanalysis: Evidence from German. Unpublished manuscript, Friedrich-Schiller-Universität Jena.

Bader, M., Bayer, J., Hopf, J.-M., & Meng, M. 1996. Case-Assignment in processing German verb-final clauses. *Proceedings of the NELS 26 Workshop on Sentence Processing, MIT Occasional Papers in Linguistics*, 9, 1-25.

Bader, M. & Lasser, I. 1994. German verb-final clauses and sentence processing: Evidence for immediate attachment. In C. Clifton, L. Frazier, & K. Rayner (eds.), *Perspectives on Sentence Processing*. Hillsdale, NJ: Lawrence Erlbaum, 225-242.

Bader, M. & Meng, M. 1997. Subject-object ambiguities in embedded clauses—An across the board comparison. Submitted for publication.

Bayer, J. 1996. *Directionality and Logical Form*. Dordrecht: Kluwer.

Clifton, C. 1995. Thematic roles in sentence parsing. In J.M. Henderson, M. Singer, & F. Ferreira (eds.), *Reading and Language Processing*. Mahwah, NJ: Lawrence Erlbaum, 94-118.

Dresher, B.E. 1996. Introduction to metrical and prosodic phonology. In J.L. Morgan & K. Demuth (eds.), *Signal to Syntax: Bootstrapping from Speech to Grammar in Early Acquisition*. Mahwah, NJ: Lawrence Erlbaum, 41-54.

Ferreira, F. & Henderson, J.M. 1991. Recovery from misanalysis of garden-path sentences. *Journal of Memory and Language*, 30, 725-745.

Ferreira, F. 1994. Choice of passive voice is affected by verb type and animacy. *Journal of Memory and Language*, 33, 715-736.

Ferreira, F. & Anes, M. 1994. Why study spoken language? In M.A. Gernsbacher (ed.), *Handbook of Psycholinguistics*. San Diego, CA: Academic Press, 33-56.

Fodor, J.D. & Inoue, A. 1994. The diagnosis and cure of garden paths. *Journal of Psycholinguistic Research*, 23, 407-434.

Frazier, L. 1978. *On Comprehending Sentences: Syntactic Parsing Strategies*. Unpublished doctoral dissertation, University of Conneticut, Storrs, CT. Distributed by the Indiana University Linguistics Club, Bloomington, IN.

Frazier, L. 1987. Sentence processing: A tutorial review. In M. Coltheart (ed.), *Attention and Performance XII. The Psychology of Reading*. Hillsdale, NJ: Lawrence Erlbaum, 559-586.

Frazier, L. 1990. Exploring the architecture of the language-processing system. In G.M. Altmann (ed.), *Cognitive Models of Speech Processing. Psycholinguistic and Computational Perspectives*. Cambridge, MA: MIT Press, 409-433.

Frazier, L. & Clifton, C. 1996. *Construal*. Cambridge, MA: MIT Press.

Frazier, L. & Clifton, C. (this volume). Sentence reanalysis and visibility.

Frazier, L. & Rayner, K. 1982. Making and correcting errors during sentence comprehension: Eye movements in the analysis of structurally ambiguous sentences. *Cognitive Psychology*, 14, 178-210.

Gathercole, S.E. & Baddeley, A.D. 1993. *Working Memory and Language*. Hillsdale, NJ: Lawrence Erlbaum.

Gibson, E.A.F. 1991. *A Computational Theory of Human Linguistic Processing*. Unpublished doctoral dissertation, Carnegie Mellon University, Pittsburgh, PA. Available as Center for Machine Translation Technical Report CMU-CMT-91-125.

Gibson, E., Hickok, G. & Schütze, C.T. 1994. Processing empty categories: A parallel approach. *Journal of Psycholinguistic Research*, 23, 381-405.

Giegerich, H.J. 1985. *Metrical Phonology and Phonological Structure. German and English*. Cambridge, UK: Cambridge University Press.

Gorrell, P. 1995. *Syntax and Parsing*. Cambridge, UK: Cambridge University Press.

Inoue, A. & Fodor, J.D. 1995. Information-paced parsing of Japanese In R. Mazuka & N. Nagai (eds.), *Japanese Sentence Processing*. Hillsdale, NJ: Lawrence Erlbaum, 9-63.

Jacobs, J. 1983. *Fokus und Skalen. Zur Syntax und Semantik der Gradpartikeln im Deutschen*. Tübingen: Niemeyer.

Jacobs, J. 1992. Neutral stress and the position of heads. In J. Jacobs (ed.), *Informationsstruktur und Grammatik. Linguistische Berichte Sonderheft*, 4, 220-244.

Just, M.A., Carpenter, P.A., & Wolley, J.D. 1982. Paradigms and processes in reading comprehension. *Journal of Experimental Psychology: General*, 111, 228-238.

Marcus, M., Hindle, D., & Fleck, M. 1983. D-theory: Talking about talking about trees. *Association for Computational Linguistics*, 21, 129-136.

Marcus, M. & Hindle, D. 1990. Description theory and intonation boundaries. In G.M. Altmann (ed.), *Cognitive Models of Speech Processing. Psycholinguistic and Computational Perspectives*. Cambridge, MA: MIT Press, 483-512.

Mitchell, D.C. 1994. Sentence parsing In M.A. Gernsbacher (ed.), *Handbook of Psycholinguistics*. San Diego, CA: Academic Press, 375-409.

Mitchell, D.C. & Holmes, V.M. 1985. The role of specific information about the verb in parsing sentences with local structural ambiguitiy. *Journal of Memory and Language*, 24, 542-559.

Nespor, M. & Vogel, I. 1986. *Prosodic phonology*. Dordrecht: Foris.

Nespor, M. & Vogel, I. 1989. On clashes and lapses. *Phonology*, 6, 69-116.

Patterson, K.L. & Coltheart, V. 1987. Phonological processes in reading. A tutorial review. In M. Coltheart (ed.), *Attention and Performance XII. The Psychology of Reading*. Hillsdale, NJ: Lawrence Erlbaum, 421-447.

Rayner, K. & Pollatsek, A. 1989. *The Psychology of Reading*. Englewood Cliffs, NJ: Prentice Hall.

Rochemont, M.S. 1986. *Focus in Generative Grammar*. Amsterdam: John Benjamins.

Shattuck-Hufnagel, S. & Turk, A.E. 1996. A prosody tutorial for investigators of auditory sentence processing. *Journal of Psycholinguistic Research*, 25, 193-247.

Selkirk, E. 1984. *Phonology and Syntax: The Relation between Sound and Structure*. Cambridge, MA: MIT Press.

Selkirk, E. 1994. Sentence prosody: Intonation, stress and phrasing. In J. Goldsmith (ed.), *Handbook of Phonological Theory*. Oxford: Basil Blackwell, 550-569.

Slowiaczek, M. L. & Clifton, C. 1980. Subvocalization and reading for meaning. *Journal of Verbal Learning and Verbal Behavior*, 19, 573-582.

Stechow, A. von 1991. Current issues in the theory of focus. In A. von Stechow & D. Wunderlich (eds.), *Semantik. Ein Internationales Handbuch der Zeitgenössischen Forschung*. Berlin: De Gruyter, 804-825.

Stowe, L.A. 1986. Parsing *Wh*-constructions: evidence for on-line gap location. *Language and Cognitive Processes*, 1, 227-245.

Weinberg, A. 1993. Parameters in the theory of sentence processing: Minimal commitment theory goes east. *Journal of Psycholinguistic Research*, 22, 338-364.

Wiese, R. 1996. *The Phonology of German*. Oxford: Oxford University Press.

Wilkenfeld, D.C. 1985. *Encoding Prosody in Silent Reading*. Unpublished doctoral dissertation, University of Connecticut, Storrs, Ct.

2

Reanalysis Aspects of Movements*

Marica De Vincenzi

Abstract

This chapter describes work focusing on the reanalysis of long-distance dependencies, specifically *wh*-questions, instead of phrase-structure reanalysis. It will show that holding all the above aspects constant, there is still a difference in reanalysis between WHO and WHICH dependencies. In particular, I will show that reanalyzing a strictly grammatical dependency is more costly than reanalyzing a coindexing relation. This difference will be attributed to the type of linguistic relation that WHO and WHICH enter into, namely an antecedent government chain (WHO) and a binding chain (WHICH). The finding has been motivated by experimental data on Italian (cf. De Vincenzi, in press), but it also accounts for some experimental data collected in English (cf. Carlson & Tanenhaus, 1988), therefore showing the cross-linguistic validity of such a difference in reanalysis.

1 Introduction

Several factors that affect the ease of reanalysis have been already identified in the psycholinguistic literature. Fodor & Inoue (1994) have demonstrated that the difficulty of recovery is related to the difficulty in diagnosing the initial error. Ferreira & Henderson (1991) have shown that the greater the distance between the head of the phrase and the disambiguating word (the point at which a reanalysis process can be initiated), the more difficult is the process of recovery. Pritchett (1988), Frazier & Clifton (1996), and De Vincenzi & Job (1995) have shown that reanalysis outside a thematic domain is more costly than

* I would like to thank Chuck Clifton, Janet Fodor, and Lyn Frazier for helpful and insightful comments.

J.D. Fodor and F. Ferreira (eds.), Reanalysis in Sentence Processing, 47–71.

reanalysis within a thematic domain. Gorrell (1995) has shown that revisions involving some syntactic operations, such as altering precedence relations, are more costly than structure addition operations.

We can think of many more factors that may affect ease of reanalysis: discourse constraints, semantic plausibility, frequency of use of alternative structure, just to name a few. In fact, the literature on reanalysis will probably mirror the literature on parsing preferences and the interesting theoretical questions that arise there, such as modular versus interactive accounts of the functioning of the language processor (cf. Fodor & Inoue, 1994). In short, the picture that emerges of the language processor is one in which limitations of memory and processing capacity, and sensitivity to fine linguistic distinctions, seem to be responsible for the parser's choices in the first pass as well as for the parser's recovery procedures.

The work on *wh*-dependencies that will be presented here will extend this picture of the language processor. We will see that holding constant several factors that have been shown to have an impact on reanalysis, there is still a difference in the way that syntactically distinct types of *wh*-dependencies are reanalyzed; in particular, we will see that this difference in reanalysis is due to the same factor that determine differences in initial analysis (cf. also Frazier, 1994). I will then show how this difference can account for some apparently irreconcilable findings concerning the processing of *wh*-dependencies in English.

2 Differences Between Types of *Wh-D*ependencies

In the linguistics literature, a considerable body of evidence demonstrates the existence of a distinction between types of *wh*-elements. Within the theory of Government and Binding, (Rizzi, 1990; Cinque, 1992; see also Engdahl, 1980; Pesetsky, 1987; Chung, 1994, for supporting evidence) the following distinction has been proposed: non-referential *wh*-elements, such as *who* and *what*, enter into *antecedent-government* chains. Referential *wh*-expressions (which can violate weak islands and can corefer with a lexically expressed variable, such as a resumptive pronoun) enter into *binding* relations. The difference between the two types of linguistic relations is the following: while antecedent government chains have to obey strict locality conditions, binding relations are simply a coindexation relation between two positions bearing the same referential index and one of which c-commands the other (cf. Cinque, 1992).

This linguistic analysis is corroborated by behavioral data from language impairment and language acquisition: Hickock & Avrutin (in press) studied two English-speaking aphasics who exhibit a processing dissociation between WHO and WHICH-N dependencies in a *wh*-question comprehension task. In an elicited production task, Thornton (1995) has found evidence that in long distance subject extraction, children treat WHICH-N questions differently from WHO questions: in WHO questions they produce a medial-*wh*, as if they had successive cyclic movement, while in WHICH-N questions the children use a resumptive pronoun, as expected if there were a long movement. The WHO/WHICH-N distinction is therefore present in linguistic data, in some aphasic impairments, and in language acquisition. The natural question to ask then is: what happens in normal adult language parsing?

In principle, there are several possible answers: one possibility is that the parser ignores the distinction and that whenever there is an element that can be identified as having moved from a sentence internal position, a so-called 'filler' in the psycholinguistic literature, then the parser adopts a unique strategy. The strategy could be to posit a *wh*-position as soon as possible (see the Gap as First Resort model of Crain & Fodor, 1985, or the Active Filler Hypothesis of Frazier, 1987), or the opposite strategy of positing a Gap as Second Resort (see Fodor, 1979). In either case, the parser operations would not be affected by the syntactic type of the *wh*-dependency. However, it would be difficult in this case to explain how the human language processor ignores this difference between *wh*-types in comprehension, but is still able to produce and to recognize as well formed different syntactic structures according to the type of *wh*-element they contain, and to explain why comprehension breakdown and acquisition show this distinction.[1]

Another answer we could give to avoid the objections just mentioned is to say that in fact the parser is directly sensitive to the linguistic distinction and that distinct filler-gap strategies apply to different types of *wh*-dependencies. We could therefore hypothesize that the Active Filler Hypothesis applies only to WHO-type dependencies and that Gap as Second Resort applies to WHICH-N-type dependencies.

---

1 It also seems to me that this move would entail to give up a mentalistic view of the grammar. However, up to now linguistic theories seem the best approximation to a mental grammar and a rich source of hypotheses about it (see also Fodor, 1989), and the positive results of most recent psycholinguistic research has shown this to be so.

However, unless otherwise motivated, the two strategies could apply exactly the other way around, i.e., the Active Filler Hypothesis could apply to WHICH-N-type dependencies and the Gap as Second Resort Principle could apply to WHO-type dependencies. This alternative is therefore unconvincing unless we find a principled way to account for the selective application of the two different filler gap strategies.

Another possible answer is to have a parsing strategy that is sensitive to the distinction between *wh*-types and that has a principled reason not only to detect such a distinction, but to process WHO and WHICH-N in different manners. This is what the Minimal Chain Parsing principle (MCP) tries to achieve: it hypothesizes that the parser is sensitive to syntactic complexity, in particular to the complexity of chains.[2] This entails that the parser tries to keep syntactic chains as simple as possible[3] and tries to complete them as soon as possible:

> *Minimal Chain Principle*: avoid postulating unnecessary chain members at Surface-structure, but do not delay required chain members (De Vincenzi, 1991).

What is the underlying motivation for the MCP? In particular, why does the parser exhibit this pressure to complete a chain? The answer lies in the fact that the ultimate reason to structure materials into a syntactic representation is to reach the semantic interpretation of each sentence. One essential task in arriving at a semantic interpretation of an NP[4] is to pair each NP with an argument position.[5] Since syntax pairs each argument with a structural position (such as subject, object), each NP must be paired with such a position. A chain ties together all the positions in a tree that an NP has moved through, and therefore contains all the information about which structural positions are

---

[2] A formal definition of chain (Rizzi, 1988) is a set of elements non-distinct in indices, with one thematic role and one case, where each element of the chain is in a relation of antecedent government with the next one.

[3] The strategy correctly accounts for the preferences in processing declaratives with a subject/object NP ambiguity in Russian (Sekerina, 1995) and in Italian (De Vincenzi, 1991) thereby showing that in declarative sentences with a chain ambiguity, the parser prefers the structure with fewer complex chains.

[4] The same reasoning applies to prepositional phrases. However, the experimental work that I discuss in this chapter focuses exclusively on NPs.

[5] Regarding adjuncts like *where* and *why*, or PPs like *near Bill*, or relative clauses, what is relevant for their semantic interpretation is the argument of which they are predicated. However, both adjunct and argument NPs need a position under the sentence node to be semantically interpretable.

available for that NP to assign theta roles and case. Therefore, the fastest way to have an NP ready for semantic interpretation is to attempt to construct the shortest possible chain.

In cases of NPs that are not in an argument position, like *wh*-elements, the pressure to do semantic interpretation will cause the parser to search for the shortest possible chain for the *wh*-element. The parser will attempt to link the *wh*-element to an NP position that receives a thematic role and case as soon as it can.

Given a parsing principle such as the MCP and given the above distinction among *wh*-elements, we can hypothesize that only non-referential *wh*-elements, such as WHO, should obey the MCP because they enter into the government chains relevant to the MCP.[6]

Why should WHICH-N type elements not fall under the MCP? An answer to this question comes from Cinque's (1992) observation that the class of quantifiers to which WHICH-N belongs is exactly the class of elements that are Discourse-linked, as defined by Pesetsky (1987). The intuitive idea of Discourse-linking is that an element refers to a group of object(s) pre-existing in the Discourse Representation.[7] The proposal I make is that WHICH-N *wh*-elements can start receiving an interpretation through their Discourse-linking properties, whereas WHO *wh*-elements can be interpreted in the discourse representation only when linked to the argument structure of a verb.

Let us examine in detail the predictions of parsing an Italian *wh*-question such as *Qui ha chiamato?* 'Who called?'.

---

6 The second part of the MCP only partly coincides with the Active Filler Hypothesis proposed by Frazier (1987). In fact, while the Active Filler Hypothesis predicts the same gap filling effect for any element identified as moved from an argument position, the MCP makes a distinction between types of moved elements.

7 It has been suggested (Crain & Steedman, 1985) that the relative definiteness of NPs, and not structural principles such as the MCP, governs sentence analysis. However, two questionnaire studies reported in De Vincenzi (1990) indicate that the *wh*-subject extraction preference and the WHO WHICH-N asymmetry persists whether the other candidate NP for subject position is a proper noun, a definite NP, or an indefinite NP. Therefore, a difference in terms of definiteness among quantifiers does not explain the present finding. Furthermore, the difference between WHO and WHICH-N cannot be properly characterized in terms of definiteness, but rather in terms of specificity (Enc, 1991).

(1)

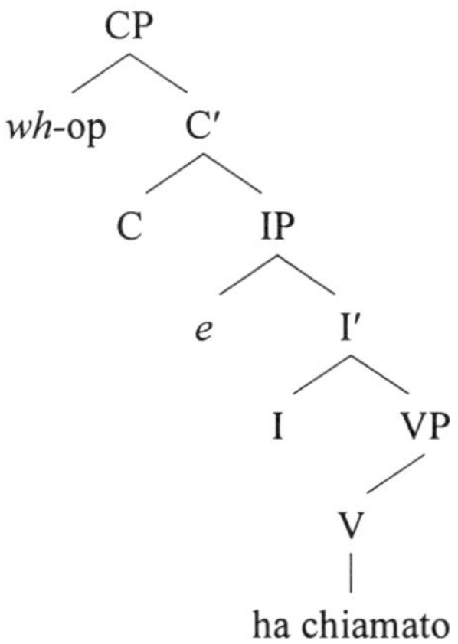

At the verb *ha chiamato* ('called') only the required syntactic structure (the IP and VP structures) will be projected. There is an obligatory argument (subject) position which is lexically empty. Given the MCP, and given that WHO falls under the MCP, WHO will immediately enter into an antecedent government chain with the subject position. This means that WHO will be immediately interpreted as subject; therefore a strong subject extraction preference for WHO is predicted.

In the case of parsing an Italian *wh*-question, such as *Quale N ha chiamato?* 'Which N called?', the quantifier can start receiving a partial interpretation through its Discourse-linking properties (see De Vincenzi, 1991, chapter 7, for a description). When the verb is read, the same syntactic structure can be projected as in (1), i.e., an IP and VP structure, with an obligatory argument (subject) position lexically empty.

This time the parser is not under any pressure to complete an antecedent government chain, given that there is a WHICH-N. It will instead evaluate what the possible options are for interpreting the available structure. The pre-verbal subject position could be interpreted as coindexed with a post-verbal lexical subject. This move should be excluded because it would require the postulation of additional unnecessary syntactic structure. The parser is then left with a lexically empty subject position and with a WHICH-N dependency, the latter already partially interpreted. To be fully interpreted, the WHICH-N requires an argument position (either empty or lexically filled by a resumptive pronoun) to be coindexed with. At this point, I assume that the decision about the coindexation of the WHICH-N and an argument position is taken by the coreference processor (cf. Nicol, 1988, 1993), given that the WHICH-N dependency is a binding relation, i.e., a relation of coreference similar to the one holding between a pronoun and an antecedent. I assume, following Nicol (1988), that the coreference processor "constitutes an intermediate stage between purely structural processes and interpretative processes" (p. 47).[8] Given that the subject position is a possible variable position to be coindexed with the WHICH-N, the coreference processor will do so, since this move will result in having a full interpretation for the WHICH-N.

Although both WHO and WHICH-N end up preferentially coindexed with the first argument (subject) position, the two coindexations are taken in different manners and for different reasons. This means that there is a difference in the initial analysis between the two types of quantifiers. In particular, I hypothesize that the WHICH-N initial coindexation is not done under the pressure of a syntactic parsing principle, but rather under a principle of interpretation. One prediction of this hypothesis is that WHICH-N relationships should be more sensitive to lexical properties of the verb, in that the coindexing decision is taken after on a syntactic representation already built.[9] We will see later in the exposition whether there is any evidence confirming this hypothesis.

---

[8] In particular, Nicol (1988) proposes that "the parser provides input to the coreference device. Thus, presented with a parse tree and applying information concerning valid coreference relations, the coreference device determines which referents are potential antecedents of a referentially dependent item, and accesses only those referents. This candidate set of referents may then be examined by higher level processes, and the most appopriate referent selected as the antecedent" (p. 124).

[9] Boland *et al.* (1995) have shown an effect of verb argument structure in processing WHICH-N questions. The experiments tested *wh*-questions containing either simple transitive verbs, or verbs (such as datives) that provide more than one potential gap site due to their subcategorization properties. The task was to press a button as soon as the sentence stopped making sense; the *wh*-fillers were either plausible or implausible with respect to the first gap position. The results show that in the case of simple transitive verbs there was a plausibility effect at the verb. The effect was absent when the verb provided multiple gap positions and the second gap was plausible for the filler.

(i) Which audience did the salesman show the movie to?

This result (as also pointed out by Gorrell, in preparation) is inconsistent with a parsing model which predicts a preference to fill the first available gap position, such as a radical version of the Active Filler Hypothesis. However, the result is consistent with the model proposed here: in the Boland *et al.* (1995) experiment, the MCP should not apply, because the WHICH-N cases are not antecedent government chains. Rather, they involve binding relations, in which we assume that it is the coreference processor which evaluates the possible argument positions for a coindexation of the WHICH-N phrase. If the direct object (theme) position is not a plausible position for coindexation, the coindexation will not be performed.

Let us then proceed to examine what happens when a post-verbal NP is reached. The post-verbal NP should be immediately attached as direct object (2), that is, in a position that requires the addition of the least syntactic structure.

(2)

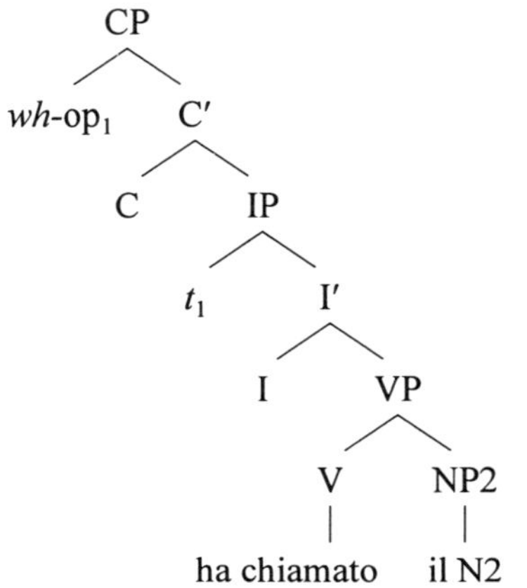

If this attachment has to be revised, there should be a renalysis cost for both types of *wh*-questions, because the post-verbal NP should be reanalyzed as post-verbal subject, in a chain with a pre-verbal position, as in (3).

(3)

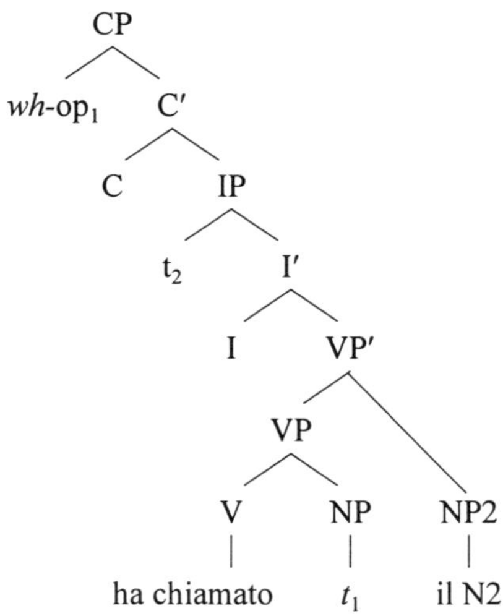

However, we predict a difference in reanalysis between WHO and WHICH-N, due to the different types of linguistic relations they enter into; in particular, we predict that the reanalysis of an antecedent government chain should be more costly than the reanalysis of a binding chain.

If we follow the linguistic analysis, an antecedent-government relation is a chain relation in which case and thematic role are transmitted from the variable to the operator. This means that for WHO, changing the analysis from subject to object extraction means changing the case and thematic role features both on the trace and on the *wh*-element. However, in the case of WHICH-N, changing a binding relation simply means that the referential index of the WHICH-N remains the same. What needs to be changed is simply the referential index, from being a variable in subject position to being a variable in object position (cf. Carlson & Tanenhaus, 1988, for a similar interpretation). It will be at some higher, discourse level interpretation that WHICH-N and its variable will be interpreted in much the same way as a pronoun and its antecedent are interpreted. The hypothesis is therefore that binding relations should be easier to revise than government relations.

These predictions regarding *wh*-dependencies have been tested in Italian (De Vincenzi, in press). In the following sections (3, 4, and 5) I will summarize the Italian data, and discuss their implications for processing theories of *wh*-movement in general and for aspects of movement in particular with regard to reanalysis.

3 The Italian Processing Data

The Italian experiments I will discuss below (see De Vincenzi, in press, for further details) manipulated the type of *wh*-element (WHO versus WHICH-N) and the extraction site (from a main or an embedded clause, with or without a lexical complementizer). The aim of these manipulations was to see whether processing reflects different types of movement and to analyze the interaction, if any, between types of movement and syntactic structure.

The experiments used sentences with a structural subject/object ambiguity pragmatically disambiguated on the post-verbal NP. The sentences had an equally plausible subject/object *wh*-extraction until the position of the verb. To avoid that the WHICH-N cases would bias an interpretation, the WHICH-N nouns were selected to be pragmatically neutral as either subject or object of the verb. All the disambiguation was carried by the post-verbal NP. In the *wh*-object extractions, the *wh*-expression was pragmatically implausible as direct object of the verb. (For example, in (4a′) and (4b′)—discussed below—an ‘owner’ cannot be 'fired'. The NP 'the owner' therefore has to be taken as subject of the verb 'fire'.)[10]

If the parser obeys the MCP in completing *wh*-dependencies, there are three general predictions. The first prediction is that for both types of *wh*-expressions, we should find a subject extraction preference, because in this structure the post-verbal NP is in a base-generated position, and therefore the overall structure of a *wh*-subject extraction (see (2)) has fewer (multi-member) chains than a *wh*-object extraction (see (3) above). The second prediction is that there should be a further advantage for the subject extraction of WHO, because the parser, following the MCP, tries to complete a chain immediately. Thus, WHO-subject extraction should be read and comprehended faster, compared to the other conditions. The third prediction is that reanalysis costs should be higher for antecedent-government chains (WHO) than for binding chains (WHICH-N).

The first experiment tested *wh*-extraction from a main clause. An example of the materials is given in (4) (forward slashes indicate segmentation):

(4) a. Chi / ha licenziato / il metalmeccanico / senza dare / il preavviso?
who fired the steel worker without give the notice

'Who fired the steel worker without notifying?'

a′. Chi / ha licenziato / il proprietario / senza dare / il preavviso?
who fired the owner without give the notice

'Who did the owner fire without giving notice?'

---

[10] Several factors were controlled in the preparation of the materials, including similar plausibility for subject and object extraction. This control was performed through a questionnaire study in which subjects were asked about the preferred interpretation of 30 quadruplets of *wh*-questions; for the experimental materials 28 of the quadruplets that were interpreted by these subjects in the intended meaning were chosen.

A further control ensured that the plausibility of the subject/object extractions was similar for the two types of *wh*-items. In fact, in the WHICH-N cases, the *wh*-phrase carries semantic content. This semantic information of the WHICH-N could help the reanalysis of the question. To control for this factor, questions were constructed with nouns and verbs that kept the same plausibility relations when combined with WHO and with WHICH-N. Then a rating study was run, asking subjects to rate, on a five-point scale, the naturalness of the presupposition of the sentence. Twenty-four quadruplets were chosen that got a plausibility rating in the subject/object extraction condition that was similar across WHO and WHICH-N.

(6) Chi$_i$ credi che *pro*$_i$ telefonerà t_i?
Who$_i$ do you think that *pro*$_i$ will telephone t_i?

If the parser obeys the MCP, in cases like (6) the subject extraction of a *wh*-element that enters into a chain (such as WHO/WHAT) should be penalized because it is more complex than a *wh*-object one.

In Experiment 3 the sentences were modified introducing the complementizer *che* ('that') after the upstairs verb, as shown in (7).

(7) Chi / pensi che / abbia licenziato / il metalmeccanico / senza preavviso?
who you think that fired the steel worker without notice
'Who do you think fired the steel worker without notifying?'

The results (see Table 3) showed that subject extraction cases were still facilitated relative to object extraction, as shown in the shorter reading times of the last segment and in the greater accuracy for the WHO subject condition. Again, this result is simply due to the fact that the post-verbal noun is in a base generated position.

TABLE 3: Average reading times (RTs) in Experiment 3, embedded clauses with lexical complementizer

segment # *who/which-N*	1 *you think that*	2 *fired*	3 *the NP*	4 *without*	5 *notifying?*	Comprehension Time	% Correct
WHO sub	636	695	810	**822**	**1002** >	2549	.90 >
WHO obj	628	672	789	**783**	**1062**	2565	.78
WHICH sub	887	760	858	**857**	**1081** >	2608	.89 >
WHICH obj	887	764	813	**872**	**1116**	2643	.75

Reading times after the disambiguation segment are in bold.
Arrows indicate significant differences between pairs of values.

However, unlike in Experiments 1 and 2, any further facilitation for the WHO subject extraction was lost. That is, the syntactic manipulation of introducing a

government is defined as follows: X properly governs Y iff X governs Y and X is either X° (a verb, a noun, a preposition) or NP$_i$, where Y = NP$_i$. *Government* is defined as follows: X governs Y iff Y is contained in the maximal X′-projection of X, X-max, and X-max is the smallest maximal projection containing Y, and X c-commands Y.

lexical complementizer selectively affected the *wh*-element that enters into antecedent-government chains.

4 Conclusions from the Italian Experiments

There are several conclusions that we can draw from the above experiments. First, the parser is sensitive to chain complexity. Second, the relevant notion of minimal chain refers not merely to the shortest linear distance between filler and gap, but additionally to the complexity of the chain (in terms of number of elements) between filler and gap. Third, there is a psychological reality of empty categories (cf. Sag & Fodor, 1995; Pickering & Barry, 1991), given that the parser is sensitive to manipulations that specifically concern empty categories (cf. discussion in De Vincenzi, in press)

In this section I will focus on some conclusions relevant to the processing of *wh*-questions. We have found that in fact there is an asymmetry in the processing of WHO and WHICH-N. In particular, as shown by Experiment 3, WHO has to move successively cyclically and therefore shows ECP effects in subject extraction across a lexical complementizer, while WHICH-N can move long distance, presumably coindexing with an empty pronominal subject, therefore avoiding ECP effects. This result strongly confirms the proposal of Cinque (1992) that, in fact, bare quantifiers only have the option of moving successively cyclically. But the result is also important for parsing theories, because it shows that the routines for processing filler-gap dependencies are sensitive to this linguistic distinction and do not just adopt a unique behavior for linguistically different dependencies.

With regard to reanalysis, it must be established whether or not a different mechanism exists for reanalyzing antecedent-government and binding relations. We could imagine that once the parser discovers that a wrong filler-gap assignment has been made, no matter how it has been made, the repair operations are the same. Although this possibility is perfectly legitimate, theoretically it would seem strange that limitations of memory and processing capacity, which are the driving motivations of parsing strategies such as the MCP (see discussion in section 1 above), would not play a role in the procedures the parser uses in its reanalysis routines.

However, we can discard this hypothesis empirically. If we consider the comprehension times in Experiments 1 and 2, that is, in those cases where the subject and object extraction were of identical complexity for WHO and WHICH

N, we find that a strong WHO/WHICH-N asymmetry showed up in comprehension (question-answering) time: the WHICH-N object extractions, which involve reanalysis, did not differ in comprehension time from the WHICH-N subject extractions. But the WHO object extractions, which involve reanalysis, strongly affected comprehension times in that they took longer than the WHO subject extractions. Notice that, given that WHICH-N has more semantic content to it than WHO, this difference precludes a simplistic hypothesis predicting more time for (or more cost associated with) revising a relation that involves more complex semantic elements.

This difference in reanalysis must therefore involve some other factor. Let us examine what specific steps are involved in the reanalysis of the *wh*-object extraction sentences of the Italian experiments. Pragmatic information signals an incongruity in the direct object analysis of the post-verbal NP. Then the parser starts a repair process which consists of several distinct operations. Specifically, it has to: (i) reanalyze the NP as an (inverted) subject; (ii) posit an empty NP category in object position; (iii) undo the coindexing of the *wh*-element with a variable in subject position; and (iv) coindex the *wh*-element with the empty category in object position. The first two operations do not involve *wh*-elements and have to be the same for both types of *wh*-dependencies. However, the third and fourth operations can differ between quantifier types.

As we suggested above, an antecedent-government relation is a chain relation in which case and thematic role are transmitted from the variable to the operator. This means that for WHO, changing the analysis from subject to object extraction means changing the case and thematic role features on the trace and transmitting them on the *wh*-element. However, in the case of WHICH-N, changing a binding relation simply means that the referential index of the WHICH-N remains the same. What needs to be changed is simply the referential index from being a variable in subject position to being a variable in object position. It will be at some higher discourse level interpretation that the WHICH-N and its variable will be related in much the same way as a pronoun and its antecedent are related.

The conclusion that we can draw is therefore that binding relations are easier to revise than government relations and that the parser is evidently sensitive to these different relations in reanalysis as well as in initial analysis. This conclusion offers a new perspective on the processing of *wh*-dependencies and, as I will try to show in the next section, it permits us to account for some psycholinguistic findings that are otherwise irreconcilable given previous processing models.

5 Some Evidence on Processing *Wh-Q*uestions in English

5.1 Some Conflicting Experimental Evidence

One question with regard to which the experimental work on comprehending *wh*-questions has focused is the role of lexical information, specifically verb transitivity preferences. One possibility illustrated by Fodor (1979) is the lexical expectation model, in which the parser posits an empty variable position following verbs that are typically used transitively, but not after verbs that are typically used intransitively. This model directly contrasts with the Gap as First Resort (or Active Filler) model which predicts that a gap will be initially posited at any grammatically legal position. The empirical evidence in support of the lexical expectation model is controversial and in the following I will examine it briefly and determine whether some conflicting evidence can be reconciled looking at the different types of *wh*-dependencies that have been used.

The experimental evidence in favor of lexical effects (i.e., verb transitivity) comes primarily form the work of Tanenhaus *et al.* (1985). In a grammaticality judgment task, Tanenhaus *et al.* asked subjects to judge sentences containing an embedded *wh*-question in which the *wh*-phrase was either the object of the verb (Early Gap condition) or the object of a preposition that followed the verb (Late Gap condition). The *wh*-phrases were either plausible or implausible as the object of the verb (Early Gap). Both plausible and implausible *wh*-phrases were equally plausible for the Late Gap sentences. So, plausibility effects with Late Gaps may be taken to mean that subjects initially filled the false Early Gap.

(8) Transitive preference verbs:

The district attorney found out which $\left\{\begin{matrix}\text{witness}\\\text{church}\end{matrix}\right\}$ the reporter ASKED ( ) about in the meeting. (Early Gap)

The district attorney found out which $\left\{\begin{matrix}\text{witness}\\\text{church}\end{matrix}\right\}$ the reporter ASKED anxiously about ( ). (Late Gap)

(9) Intransitive verbs:

The sheriff wasn't sure which $\left\{\begin{matrix}\text{horse}\\ \text{rock}\end{matrix}\right\}$ the cowboy RACED ( ) down the hill. (Early Gap)

The sheriff wasn't sure which $\left\{\begin{matrix}\text{horse}\\ \text{rock}\end{matrix}\right\}$ the cowboy RACED ( ) desperately past ( ). (Late Gap)

The dependent measures were the percentage of positive grammaticality judgements and the comprehension times for those sentences that were judged as making sense.

The results show that for preferably transitive verbs, there was an effect of plausibility with both Early and Late Gap sentences. However, with preferably intransitive verbs there was an effect of plausibility only with Early Gap sentences, suggesting that the parser does not posit a gap after an intransitive verb. The conclusion drawn by Tanenhaus *et al.* is that gaps are initially posited only following preferably transitive verbs, therefore supporting a lexical expectation model of filler-gap assignment.

However, there was another interesting aspect of the results, namely, for transitive preference verbs, Late Gap sentences were not more difficult to comprehend than Early Gap sentences, suggesting that there was little cost in reassigning a *wh*-filler from an Early to a Late Gap. Based on this observation, Carlson & Tanenhaus (1988) propose that *wh*-filler-gap assignment is not a syntactically driven process, but rather a process of thematic assignment, where "thematic assignment is an indexing and reindexing operation of the same general sort as reference assignment operations" (ms., p. 25).

However, Frazier & Clifton (1989) obtained an opposite pattern of results that does not support a lexical expectation model. Their materials (Frazier & Clifton, 1989, Experiment 2) consisted of *wh*-questions with intransitive verbs, as the sentences in (9) above. The task was self-paced reading and the dependent measure was the reading time on the parts of the sentence (forward slashes indicate segmentation). The logic of this experiment is similar to that in the preceding experiment: if readers assign a *wh*-element as object of the verb, then reading times should be slower when the preposition in the Late Gap sentences (*about* in example (10) below) is read, as compared to the Early Gap sentences.

(10) Intransitive preference verbs:

What did / the silly young man / whisper ( ) / to his fiancee / during the movie / last night? (Early Gap)

What did / the silly young man / whisper ( ) /to his fiancee about ( ) / during the movie / last night? (Late Gap)

Reading times on the critical segment were longer in the Late Gap condition than in the Early Gap condition, as if subjects had initially posited a gap after the verb also in the Late Gap condition. The conclusion drawn by Frazier & Clifton is therefore the opposite of that drawn by Carlson & Tanenhaus: gaps are posited not only after transitive expectation verbs, but also after intransitive expectation verbs; therefore filler-gap assignment is a filler-driven process, not a lexically-driven one.

Can these opposite findings be reconciled? The answer I propose is yes, if we look at the different properties of the type of *wh*-dependencies involved in the two sets of experiments. Let us start by addressing the use of lexical information that has been found by Tanenhaus *et al.*, but not by Frazier & Clifton. The experiments of Tanenhaus *et al.* used WHICH-N phrases, while those of Frazier & Clifton used WHO *wh*-elements. The hypothesis we have developed from the Italian experiments is that only WHICH-N elements can enter binding relations. Therefore they will not obey the second clause of the MCP principle, i.e., they will not elicit an active gap search. Rather, given that a binding relation is a structure co-indexing operation, as opposed to a structure building operation (see Berwick & Weinberg, 1984, for a similar distinction), the filler-gap assignment that involves a binding relation will be performed by the coreference processor in a moment successive to the building of the syntactic structure, when other types of linguistic information, such as lexical-semantic information, are also available. This entails that an element entering a binding relation should be more sensitive to lexical properties, which directly explains the conflicting evidence: Tanenhaus *et al.* found lexical preference effects because they used only quantified NPs; Frazier & Clifton did not find such effects because they used only bare *wh*-expressions, which enter antecedent government chains and, according to the MCP, should in fact elicit a top-down gap-search.

With regard to this distinction for movement dependencies, the second important finding of Tanenhaus *et al.* (no revision costs for *wh*-dependencies) can also be explained. In the Italian study it was found that reanalysis costs are stronger for WHO quantifiers and this asymmetry was attributed to the fact that reanalysis of antecedent government chains is more costly that the reanalysis of a binding relation. In fact, in comprehension time no reanalysis costs were associated with WHICH-type dependencies. This finding is very similar to the finding by Tanenhaus *et al.* that there is no cost in their Late Gap condition with transitive sentences, given that they used only WHICH-N types of quantifiers. I agree with the statement of Carlson & Tanenhaus (1988) that filler-gap assignment is a re-indexing operation, similar to the one occurring between a pronoun and its antecedent. However, the Italian data and the analysis described here restrict the validity of this statement only to WHICH-N type of quantifiers, that involve binding operations, because when WHO quantifiers were used a strong reanalysis cost was detected in comprehension times. Therefore, contrary to Carlson & Tanenhaus, I conclude that filler-gap assignment is always a syntactically driven process, rather than a process of thematic role assignment. It is the syntactic type of quantifier and consequent type of movement dependency that determines the differential application of processing strategies.

5.2 Some Conflicting Intuitive Evidence

Another dichotomy about models of *wh*-filler gap assignment is that between the Gap as First Resort or Active Filler model (Frazier, 1987), and Gap as Second Resort model (Fodor, 1979). The first model predicts that a gap will be postulated immediately following a possible transitive verb, before checking the lexical position after the verb; the second model predicts just the opposite, namely, that a gap will be postulated only when a mandatory argument is missing. The first model for filler-gap assignment has received empirical support from several experiments, most notably Crain & Fodor (1985), Stowe (1986), Frazier & Flores D'Arcais (1989), Frazier & Clifton (1989), Schriefers *et al.* (1995), Traxler & Pickering (in press).

However, there is one case where the preferred interpretation of *wh*-questions supports the Gap as Second Resort model. One prediction of Gap as Second Resort is that in the case of two adjacent phrases of the same syntactic category, extraction of the second one should always be more acceptable than extraction of the first. Fodor (1979) presents examples like (11) to support the prediction:

(11) Which patient did the nurse bring the doctor?

a. Which patient$_i$ did the nurse bring (to) the doctor e_i?
b. Which patient$_i$ did the nurse bring e_i the doctor?

The preferred interpretation of (11) is (11a), where the *wh*-expression is coindexed with the second of the two argument positions of the verb *bring*. This is predicted by Gap as Second Resort, if the processor initially prefers to fill an argument position with a lexically present item (*the doctor* in (11)), rather than with a *wh*-filler. This prefence goes against both the Gap as First Resort and the Active Filler models.

However Frazier (1987) pointed out that there are counter examples to the Gap as Second Resort preference, as in (12):

(12) Who$_i$ did Fred tell Mary left the country?

a. … tell Mary [e_i left…
b. … tell e_i [Mary left…

While Gap as Second Resort predicts that the preferred interpretation should be (12a), taking *who* as the subject of leaving, the preference seems instead to be for (12b), where *who* fills the object position of *tell*. This means that the parser, contrary to the prediction of Gap as Second Resort, prefers to postulate an early gap in (12), in accordance with the Active Filler Hypothesis.

Interestingly for the argument I am making, the examples supporting two alternative models use different types of quantifiers: the example supporting the Gap as Second Resort Principle has a *wh*-phrase, while the one supporting the Active Filler Hypothesis has a *wh*-word.[13] This difference is expected under the hypothesis that a *wh*-word enters antecedent-government chain, while a *wh*-phrase enters a binding chain, which has a very low reanalysis cost, undetectable by the end of the clause. Therefore in (12) WHO will be related to the first gap position and this preference is predicted to be harder to reanalyze and to persist until the end of the clause. Instead, for the WHICH-N element in (12) the assignment from the first gap position to another position can be easily reanalyzed with no noticeable cost, given that it is a binding relation.

[13] It would be interesting to see whether changing the type of *wh*-elements shifts the preferences.

(i) Who did the nurse bring the doctor?
(i′) Who$_i$ did the nurse bring e_i the doctor?
(ii) Which man did Fred tell Mary left the country?
(ii′) Which man$_i$ did Fred tell Mary [e_i left the country]?

5.3 Some Linguistic Remarks

In the analyses given so far, I have relied on the fact that there is a linguistic and processing difference between WHO and WHICH-N type of quantifiers. This difference holds in English as well as in Italian. However, there has not yet been a systematic processing comparison of WHO versus WHICH-N syntactic dependencies in English, except for the acquisition and aphasic data cited in the introduction. I will therefore give some examples that show how, in English as well, WHO and WHICH-N dependencies differ at the syntactic level, the level that should affect the syntactic parser.

One piece of evidence concerns the binding of resumptive pronouns. Resumptive pronouns in English are extremely infrequent. Nevertheless some contrasts can be found, as in (13) and (14).

(13) * Who were you wondering whether $\left\{\begin{matrix}\text{he}\\\text{they}\end{matrix}\right\}$ would come?

(14) ? Which girl were you wondering whether she would come?

According to English informants (Richard Kayne, p.c.), (14) is much more acceptable than (13). That is, while WHO can enter only antecedent government chains and can never bind a pronoun, WHICH-N may bind a pronoun in addition to being able to enter antecedent government chains.

Further, the contrast in (15) and (16) supports the same distinction. The constructions in (15) and (16) are parasitic-gap constructions, where the second gap (the 'parasitic' one) is filled by a resumptive pronoun:

(15) * What$_i$ did you file e_i without reading it$_i$?

(16) Which article$_i$ did you file e_i without reading it$_i$?

The contrasts in (13)-(14) and (15)-(16) show a difference in the ability to bind a resumptive pronoun between *wh*-words and *wh*-phrases. *Wh*-words seem to necessarily bind a variable at S-structure, while *wh*-phrases can also bind a resumptive pronoun. This distinction is exactly what Cinque (1992) suggests for Italian, identifying *wh*-words as belonging to the class of bare quantifiers that necessarily have to bind a variable, while *wh*-phrases belong to the class of quantified-NP, that can bind a resumptive pronoun.

6 Conclusions

We have examined some processing data from Italian which show that the parser in both initial analysis and reanalysis is affected by the same linguistic factors, namely type of *wh*-dependency. In particular, we have reduced the different parsing behavior to the operation of a unique processing principle, the MCP, which tries to complete antecedent government chains immediately, but does not apply to binding relations.

Further we have extended our analysis to some English data. We have shown some cases in which the lexical expectation versus the filler-gap model controversy can be resolved if we take into account the fact that dependencies entering into binding relations are more likely to show lexical effects, because they are performed on an already established syntactic structure. Further, we have noticed that, for both Italian and English data, WHICH-N dependency reanalysis is not costly. We have related this to the fact that the revision of a binding relation involves a simple coindexing operation; instead the revision of an antecedent government relation is a memory taxing process that involves more transmission operations.

The same arguments have been extended to reconcile some intuitive judgments on *wh*-dependencies that have been taken to support distinct parsing procedures, by showing that they can again be related to the operation of a unique principle, given that they involve different *wh*-dependencies.

The picture of the parser that emerges from this discussion is one that fully exploits linguistic differences and tries to minimize effort. An antecedent government chain is a relation where the parser has to hold a constituent (the *wh*-word) active in short term memory, while another constituent (the head of the chain) is processed and has to transmit grammatical information from the head to the *wh*-element. The parser will construct these chains only when obliged to do so, i.e., when a *wh*-element can enter only such a relation to be interpreted. However, when there is a *wh*-element that can enter other relations that can be temporarily interpreted, the parser does not construct such taxing chains; rather, it partially interprets the *wh*-element and continues analyzing the sentence in a bottom-up manner: the coreference processor will perform the coindexation operation. The same behavior is adopted in reanalysis, where binding relations seem to be revised with almost no effort, as if the parser were simply revising the local/head misassignment and later coindexing a new gap position with the referential *wh*-element. The parser thus seems to be subject to memory constraints also in reanalysis; to avoid unnecessary or memory taxing operations it fully exploits syntactic knowledge.

Institute of Psychology of the National Research Council (CNR)

References

Berwick, R. & Weinberg, A. 1984. *The Grammatical Basis of Linguistic Performance*. Cambridge, MA: MIT Press.

Boland, J., Tanenhaus, M., Garnsey, S., & Carlson, G. 1995. Verb argument structure in parsing and interpretation: Evidence from *wh*-questions. *Journal of Memory and Language*, 34, 774-806.

Chung, S. 1994. *Wh*-agreement and 'Referentiality' in Chamorro. *Linguistic Inquiry*, 25, 1-44.

Cinque, G. 1992. *Types of A' Dependencies*. Cambridge, MA: MIT Press.

Carlson, G. & Tanenhaus, M. 1988. Thematic roles and language comprehension. In W. Wilkins (ed), *Thematic Relations, Syntax and Semantics, Vol. 21*. New York, NY: Academic Press, 263-300.

Crain, S. & Fodor, J.D. 1985. How can grammars help parsers? In D. Dowty, L. Kartunnen, & A. Zwicky (eds.), *Natural Language Parsing*. Cambridge: Cambridge University Press, 94-128.

Crain, S. & Steedman, M. 1985. On not being led up the garden path: The use of context by the psychological parser. In D. Dowty, L. Kartunnen, & A. Zwicky (eds), *Natural Language Parsing*. Cambridge: Cambridge University Press, 320-358.

De Vincenzi, M. 1990. Processing of *wh*-dependencies in a null-subject language: Referential and non-referential *whs*. In B. Plunkett (ed.), *UMOP 15 Psycholinguistics*, 91-118.

De Vincenzi, M. 1991. *Syntactic Parsing Strategies in Italian*. Dordrecht: Kluwer Academic Publishers.

De Vincenzi, M. (in press). Syntactic analysis in sentence comprehension: Effects of dependency types and grammatical constraints. *Journal of Psycholinguistic Research*, 25, 1, 117-133.

De Vincenzi, M. & Job, R. 1995. An investigation of the Late Closure strategy: The role of syntax, thematic structure and pragmatics in initial and final interpretation. *Journal of Experimental Psychology: Learning, Memory and Cognition*, 21, 5, 1303-1321.

Enc, M. 1991. The semantics of specificity. *Linguistic Inquiry*, 22, 1, 1-25.

Engdahl, E. 1980. *Wh*-constructions in Swedish and the relevance of subjacency. *NELS*, 10, 89-108.

Ferreira, F. & Henderson, J. 1991. Recovery from misanalyses of garden-path sentences. *Journal of Memory and Language*, 30, 725-745.

Fodor, J.D. 1979. Superstrategy. In W.E. Cooper and E.C.T. Walker (eds.), *Sentence Processing*, Hillsdale, NJ: Erlbaum Press, 249-280.

Fodor, J.D. 1989. Empty categories in sentence processing. *Language and Cognitive Processes*, 4, 155-209.

Fodor, J.D. & Inoue, A. 1994. The diagnosis and cure of garden-paths. *Journal of Psycholinguistic Research*, 23, 407-434.

Frazier, L. 1987. Processing Syntactic Structures: Evidence from Dutch. *Natural Language and Linguistic Theory*, 5, 519-559.

Frazier, L. 1994. Sentence (Re-) Analysis. Paper presented at *Seventh CUNY Conference on Human Sentence Processing*, New York, NY.

Frazier, L. & Flores D'Arcais, G.B. 1989. Filler-driven parsing: A study of gap-filling in Dutch. *Journal of Memory and Language*, 28, 331-344.

Frazier, L. & Clifton, C. 1989. Successive cyclicity in the grammar and the parser. *Language and Cognitive Processes*, 4, 2, 93-126.

Frazier, L. & Clifton, C. 1996. *Construal*. Cambridge, MA: MIT Press.

Gorrell, P. 1995. *Syntax and Parsing*. Cambridge: Cambridge University Press.

Gorrell, P. (in preparation). The subject-before-object preference in German clauses. Unpublished Manuscript, Max Planck Institute for Cognitive Neuroscience.

Nicol, J.L. 1988. *Coreference Processing during Sentence Comprehension*. Unpublished doctoral dissertation, MIT, Cambridge, MA.

Nicol, J.L. 1993. Reconsidering reactivation. In G. Altmann & P. Shillcock (eds.), *Cognitive Models of Speech Processing*. Hillsdale, N.J.: Lawrence Erlbaum, 321-347.

Hickock, G. & Avrutin, S. (in press). Comprehension of *wh*-questions in two Broca's aphasics. *Brain and Language*.

Pesetsky, D. 1987. *Wh*-in-situ: Movement and unselective binding. In A. Ter Meulen & E. Reuland (eds.), *Representation of (In)definiteness*, Cambridge, MA: MIT Press, 98-129.

Pickering, M. & Barry, G. 1991. Sentence processing without empty categories. *Language and Cognitive Processes*, 6, 229-259.

Pritchett, B. 1988. Garden path phenomena and the grammatical basis of language processing. *Language*, 64, 539-576.

Rizzi, L. 1982. *Issues in Italian Syntax*. Dordrecht: Foris.

Rizzi, L. 1990. *Relativized Minimality*. Cambridge, MA: MIT Press.

Sag, I. & Fodor, J. 1995. Extraction without traces. In R. Aranovich, W. Byrne, S. Preuss, & M. Senturia (eds.), *Proceedings of the 13th West Coast Conference on Formal Linguistics*. Stanford, CA: Stanford Linguistics Association, 365-384.

Schriefers, H., Friederici, A., & Kuhn, K. 1995. The processing of locally ambiguous relative clauses in German. *Journal of Memory and Language*, 34, 227-246.

Sekerina, I. 1995. Ambiguity and scrambling in Russian syntactic processing. Poster presented at *Eighth CUNY Conference on Human Sentence Processing*, Tucson, AZ. Also to appear in the proceedings of the Fourth Annual Workshop on Formal Approaches to Slavic Linguistics, The Cornell Meeting, 1994.

Stowe, L. 1986. Parsing *wh*-constructions. *Language and Cognitive Processes*, 2, 227-246.

Traxler, M.J. & Pickering, M.J. (in press). Plausibility and the processing of unbounded dependencies: An eye-tracking study. *Journal of Memory and Language*.

Tanenhaus, M., Stowe, L., & Carlson, G. 1985. The interaction of lexical expectation and pragmatics in parsing filler-gap constructions. *Proceedings of Seventh Annual Cognitive Science Society Meetings*. Hillsdale, NJ: Lawrence Erlbaum, 361-365.

Thornton, R. 1995. Referentiality and *Wh*-movement in Child English: Juvenile D-Linkuency. *Language Acquisition*, 4, 139-175.

3

Syntactic Reanalysis, Thematic Processing, and Sentence Comprehension

Fernanda Ferreira & John M. Henderson

Abstract

This paper describes the current version of our model of reanalysis, which updates our earlier work to incorporate the critical notion of a thematic processing domain (TPD). This new model is motivated by the following experimental results: First, reanalysis processes are not tricked by the presence of a local NP that could potentially serve a critical disambiguating role. Second, reanalysis processes do not benefit from being able to save a particular thematic role label for a phrase; what matters is the relationship between thematic role and theta-assigner. Third, the presence of an object versus a subject relative clause in the ambiguous phrase of a garden-path sentence makes reanalysis difficult. Finally, this difficulty disappears when the verb in the main clause is passive. To explain these results, we developed a model of reanalysis that assumes the following: First, when assigners of thematic roles are encountered, all roles are made available in parallel. If roles from more than one theta-assigner must be dealt with simultaneously, processing difficulty results. If the thematic domains of two different theta-assigners must interact, even greater processing difficulty results. More precisely, processing cost results when: (i) a TPD is embedded inside another; (ii) two TPDs must interact; and (iii) two theta-assigners are adjacent. A sentence will be easy to comprehend when none of (i) through (iii) holds, harder if any one holds, harder yet if two hold, and most difficult if all three hold. Note that (i) and (iii) can hold even for non-garden-pathing sentences, including classic center-embedded sentences. Only (ii) is specifically about reanalysis of garden-path sentences. Interaction in our model refers to the construction of a TPD for one theta-assigner based on an incorrect syntactic analysis, which must then be changed to accommodate the new syntactic structure and to allow another theta-assigner to set up its TPD.

J.D. Fodor and F. Ferreira (eds.), Reanalysis in Sentence Processing, 73–100.

1 Introduction

Sentence comprehension is often described as easy and effortless; but sometimes it can be quite challenging. For example, if we were to encounter the sentence *The horse raced past the barn fell* (unlikely, unless we are participating in a discussion about parsing), we would almost certainly misanalyze the sequence *The horse raced past the barn* as an active main clause. The word *fell* cannot be incorporated into this syntactic structure, and so *The horse raced past the barn* must be reanalyzed into a large noun phrase containing a relative clause. According to numerous models of parsing, including the garden-path model (De Vincenzi, 1991; Frazier, 1978, 1987; Frazier & Clifton, this volume), the initial misanalysis is caused by the parser's adherence to a principle of syntactic economy: create the simplest grammatically permissible structure (Frazier's Minimal Attachment Principle). The active main clause reading of *the horse raced past the barn* is much simpler than the complex NP alternative, and so syntactic economy correctly predicts the misanalysis. In other models of parsing, the garden-path occurs because the main clause reading is more frequent than the altenative (MacDonald *et al.*, 1994; Trueswell & Tanenhaus, 1994). Thus, several models have been developed to explain the source of the misanalysis. The question that has received far less attention is: why is reanalysis so difficult?

As is attested by the existence of this volume, the study of reanalysis is now a growing concern (although still in its infancy). In this chapter, we will present the current version of our model of reanalysis. This model updates the one presented in our earlier work (Ferreira & Henderson, 1990, 1991a, 1991b) to incorporate the critical notion of a thematic processing domain (Frazier & Clifton, this volume). This model will assume the following: first, when assigners of thematic roles (typically verbs, but often prepositions and other syntactic categories; henceforth we will use the term theta-assigners) are encountered during comprehension, all thematic roles (agent, patient, theme, experiencer; see Jackendoff, 1990, and Parsons, 1990, for recent inventories of such roles) associated with that assigner are made available in parallel. If roles from more than one theta-assigner must be dealt with simultaneously, processing difficulty results. If the thematic domains of two different theta-assigners must interact, even greater processing difficulty results. In other words, this model attributes reanalysis difficulty to the effort involved in assigning thematic roles correctly to all the sentential entities that need them.

2 General Issues of Reanalysis

According to the most general version of the garden-path model of parsing, the parser incorporates material into the ongoing syntactic structure using as few syntactic nodes as possible. This Minimal Attachment principle is followed even when semantic and discourse-level information seem to indicate that a nonminimal interpretation is likely to be correct (Ferreira & Clifton, 1986; Mitchell *et al.*, 1992; Rayner *et al.*, 1983; Rayner *et al.*, 1992; for opposing views, see Altmann & Steedman, 1988; Pearlmutter & MacDonald, 1995; Sedivy & Spivey-Knowlton, 1994; Spivey-Knowlton & Sedivy, 1995; Taraban & McClelland, 1989). In the strongest version of the model, even some types of lexical information are ignored (Adams *et al.*, 1994; Ferreira & Henderson, 1990; Mitchell, 1989). For example, consider sentence (1):

(1) Mary knew Susan would leave.

Initially, the parser takes *Susan* to be the object of *knew* because that analysis is simpler than the correct alternative (subject of complement clause) (Ferreira & Henderson, 1990; for an opposing view, see Trueswell *et al.*, 1993). This analysis is attempted first even though the lexical entry for *know* specifies that the nonminimal structure is more frequent than the minimal structure (Connine *et al.*, 1984; Trueswell *et al.*, 1993). Thus, during initial syntactic processing, a very restricted range of information is consulted: information about lexical category, perhaps strict subcategorization (Ferreira & McClure, 1997; Frazier, 1987), and prosody (Ferreira *et al.*, 1996; Frazier & Clifton, this volume). Information about the relative frequency of different argument structures as well as constraints from semantic and discourse-based sources are ignored. Thematic roles are assigned to phrases as the syntactic structure is built. For example, in (1), *Mary* would be assigned the role of experiencer and *Susan* the role of theme, based on the minimal syntactic analysis. Notice, then, that reanalysis of this sentence will require not just syntactic revisions, but thematic revisions as well—*Susan* is not the theme of *know*, but rather is the agent of *leave* (the complement clause).

As argued by Frazier & Clifton (this volume), reanalysis difficulty cannot be based solely on structural factors in their terminology, reanalysis difficulty is based on sentence tokens, not sentence types. For (1) to be successfully reanalyzed, the parser must somehow recover the alternate syntactic structure in which *Susan* is the subject rather than the object of a new clause, and the alternative thematic structure in which *Susan* is an agent rather than a theme. Ease of reanalysis, then, is affected both by structural and thematic factors.

Intuitively, the ease with which this recovery can occur is influenced by the availability of the alternative structures and by how committed the parser is to the incorrect initial syntactic and thematic analyses. In our earlier model of reanalysis, we provided specific proposals detailing these points as well as empirical evidence for them. We will now turn to a discussion of that earlier model. From there, we will consider our updated model, as well as the data that have motivated this new version.

3 Ferreira & Henderson's (1991a, 1991b) Model of Reanalysis

To study reanalysis we have developed a paradigm in which we ask subjects about the grammaticality of sentences such as (2) (the subjects' mean responses for each sentence, from experiments described in more detail in Ferreira & Henderson, 1991a, are provided in parentheses):

(2) a. While the boy scratched the dog the girl yawned loudly. (82%)
b. While the boy scratched the dog yawned loudly. (69%)

The sentences are presented using Rapid Serial Visual Presentation (RSVP), with the words of the sentence presented alone on a computer monitor for 250 ms each. A single item is shown in only one version, but across stimulus items; each participant experiences all conditions of any given experiment. All experiments include filler sentences, half of which are clearly grammatical (e.g., *Too many raincoats are made of material that is not really waterproof*), and half of which are clearly ungrammatical (e.g., *The player hit the ball the man who saw it*). At the end of each sentence participants push a button to indicate their decision regarding its grammaticality. Decisions as well as decision times are automatically recorded, but we generally consider only the former, because the percentage of sentences judged to be grammatical is so low in some experimental conditions that analysis of the reaction time data is impossible. Thus, we compare the percentage of sentences judged to be grammatical across various conditions. For example, (2a) is judged to be grammatical more often than (2b) (e.g., 82% for (2a) and 69% for (2b) in Experiment 1 of Ferreira & Henderson, 1991a).

When using the grammaticality judgment task for studying reanalysis, it is important to be clear about the relationship between ease of reanalysis and participants' tendency to label a sentence as ungrammatical. We assume that each participant sets a subjective criterion for labeling a sentence as ungrammatical and that a number of factors affect where this criterion is set. If a sentence is 'objectively' ungrammatical (e.g., *Boy the danced those car*), participants will have no trouble categorizing it as such; similarly, participants will have little trouble with a simple grammatical sentence (e.g., *The boy danced all night*). However, not all sentences that are grammatical will be so categorized. In particular, garden-path sentences will sometimes be labelled as ungrammatical even though a legitimate analysis is possible for the string, because participants eventually terminate their search for a grammatical structure. To account for this time constraint, we also assume that participants set a limit on how long they are willing to spend trying to find the right syntactic structure. If that time limit passes without success, the sentence will be labelled ungrammatical. The more difficult reanalysis is, the more likely it is that the time limit will pass, and the more likely a participant is to label a sentence ungrammatical.

Applying this logic to the sentences in (2), we expect that participants given (2a) are not garden-pathed and therefore label the sentence grammatical most of the time. The NP following the first verb is initially taken to be the object, and that analysis turns out to be correct. This preference is consistent with both the Minimal Attachment Principle and Frazier's (1978) Late Closure Principle (incorporate material into the current constituent); to be consistent with our previous work we will call sentences such as (2a) 'Late Closure' and sentences such as (2b) (in which the NP after the first verb is the subject of the second clause) 'Early Closure' sentences. Interestingly, Late Closure sentences like (2a) are always rated grammatical less than 100% of the time (somewhere around 80% is typical), even though they do not garden-path the parser and therefore should not require reanalysis. In Ferreira & Henderson (1991a), we argued that this occurs for two reasons: first, the criterion comprehenders set for calling a sentence grammatical will change depending on the characteristics of the grammatical and ungrammatical fillers (this is a version of the argument given by Seidenberg *et al.* (1984)). Second, the RSVP technique requires comprehenders to hold the words of a sentence in memory and to construct a representation from those words. Comprehenders may occasionally fail to encode or remember a word and thus will be unable to recover a sensible interpretation of the corresponding sentence. For sentence (2b), we assume that when comprehenders encounter *yawned* they have to engage in syntactic reanalysis because they are are garden-pathed. Reanalysis is successful on only some of the trials, such that only about two-thirds of sentences like (2b) are considered grammatical. In other words, we infer from the difference between (2a) and (2b) that whatever difficulties are associated with the RSVP task and whatever influence comes from the fillers are equal for the two versions, but that (2b) has the additional source of difficulty caused by the garden-path and the need for reanalysis.

3.1 Effects of Lengthening the Ambiguous Region

The goal of the work presented in Ferreira & Henderson (1991a) was to examine how constituent length affected ease of reanalysis. Research conducted prior to our 1991a study had demonstrated that if the ambiguous region of garden-path sentences was lengthened, comprehension difficulty resulted (Frazier & Rayner, 1982; Warner & Glass, 1987). We replicated and clarified this result, and also tried to provide an explanation for it. We compared sentences such as (3). The (a) and (b) versions were Late Closure and the (c) and (d) versions were Early Closure. The (a) and (c) versions contained a short ambiguous region and the (b) and (d) versions contained a longer ambiguous region.

(3)
  a. After the Martians invaded the town the people were evacuated. (82%)
  b. After the Martians invaded the town that the city bordered the people were evacuated. (64%)
  c. After the Martians invaded the town was evacuated. (69%)
  d. After the Martians invaded the town that the city bordered was evacuated. (18%)

Consistent with previous work, we found that lengthening the ambiguous region of the Early Closure sentences caused comprehension difficulty (the huge 69% versus 18% difference). This result indicates that something about adding material to that region makes reanalysis difficult. However, lengthening the ambiguous region was costly for the Late Closure (i.e., non-garden-pathing) structures as well (the smaller but statistically reliable 82% versus 64% difference). We have obtained this latter result in every relevant experiment (by now, about ten) that we have conducted. The effect of lengthening the ambiguous region of the Late Closure sentences cannot be due to ease of reanalysis (these sentences do not cause a garden-path),[1] but we will argue

[1] It might seem that the Late Closure sentences cause the following syntactic misanalysis: perhaps in a sentence such as (3a) comprehenders are tempted to take *the people* as the second conjunct of a conjoined object of *invaded*, an analysis that would be disconfirmed upon receipt of *were*. However, this analysis should not be attempted according to Minimal Attachment. Specifically, if *the town* is analyzed as sister to the verb *invaded*, incorporation of *the people* as part of that object requires syntactic revisions as follows:

below in section 4 that the result can be explained by the difference in the thematic processing domains of (3a) versus (3b).

Having established that something about lengthening the ambiguous region causes reanalysis of garden-path sentences to become difficult, we then proceeded to try to determine precisely what it was that length was doing. One possibility was that it was not the addition of extra words per se that resulted in the additional difficulty, but rather the increase in syntactic complexity correlated with a greater number of words. To examine this hypothesis, we compared sentences such as (4):

(4) a. If the clerk forgets the customer typically yells. (63%)
    b. If the clerk forgets the customer that likes Bobby typically yells. (35%)
    c. If the clerk forgets the customer with turquoise shoes typically yells. (35%)

These are the Early Closure versions of this set of materials; the Late Closure versions were constructed by inserting an NP before the word *typically* (in this case, *the boss*). The critical comparison is between the (b) and (c) versions,

---

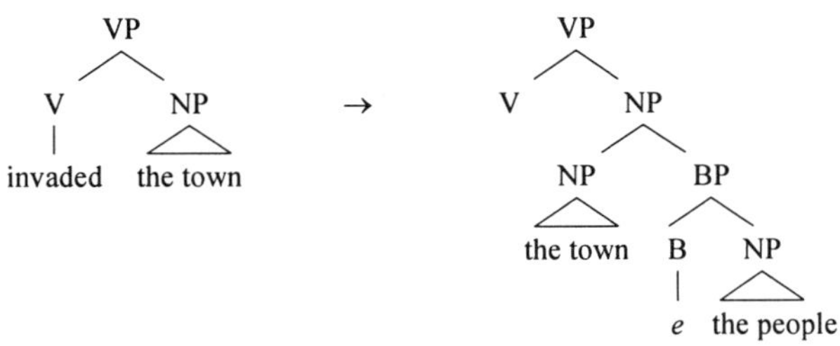

Here we have assumed Munn's (1993) analysis of coordinate phrases, according to which such phrases are Boolean Phrases (BPs), headed by the Boolean operator (B) which attaches into a larger NP. In the above structure, three nodes must be created to incorporate the NP *the people* as a conjunct. An empty boolean operator must be postulated as well. In contrast, for the subject-of-new-clause analysis, the phrase *the people* can be incorporated without changing the analysis of the town, and only an NP node for the subject and an IP node for the clause need be postulated. Thus, Late Closure sentences should not cause any type of garden-path.

It should be noted that other misanalyses of this sentence are also possible. One possibility is that comprehenders may take *bordered* to be part of a reduced relative clause and so interpret *the city bordered* in a way similar to *the horse raced* in the classic garden-path sentence. This analysis is disconfirmed upon enountering the next two words, *the people*. Yet another possible misanalysis involves taking *the people* as object of *bordered*, which also is disconfirmed later in the sentence. We bring up these misanalyses as well as the one involving coordinate phrases simply to point out that the sentences we are considering in our 'baseline' conditions actually contain numerous rather serious ambiguities. An important question—which unfortunately we cannot answer at this stage in our research—is whether these various analyses are considered by the syntactic processor.

which contain the same number of words but differ in syntactic complexity (more nodes are required to incorporate the material in (c) than in (b)). The percentage of sentences judged grammatical was the same in these two conditions (about 35%) and reliably less than in the short region condition (63%). (Again, we found a smaller but still significant drop for the Late Closure sentences: 81% in the short condition and about 69% in the two long conditions.) From this experiment, we concluded that the difficulty associated with lengthening the ambiguous region could not be attributed to syntactic complexity.

We then explored a further reason why lengthening the ambiguous region might cause reanalysis to become difficult. In the cases examined up to that point, lengthening the ambiguous region increased the distance between the head of the ambiguous phrase and the disambiguating word of the sentence—the word indicating that the analysis of the sentence constructed to that point was incorrect. To determine whether the effect of length was attributable to the distance between the head of the misanalyzed phrase and the disambiguating word, we compared conditions containing sentences such as those in (5):

(5) a. While the boy scratched the dog that Sally hates yawned loudly. (24%)
b. While the boy scratched the big and hairy dog yawned loudly. (51%)

(The short condition was also included—that is, containing just the phrase *the dog*. The Late Closure conditions were created by inserting the NP *the girl* before the word *yawned.*) The critical difference between these two conditions is that (5b) lengthens the ambiguous region but leaves the head of the ambiguous phrase and the disambiguating word adjacent; (5a), as in our previous stimuli, does not. In two different experiments, we found that sentences with an ambiguous phrase made long through the addition of prenominal adjectives (5b) were no more difficult than sentences with a short ambiguous phrase; sentences such as (5a), in contrast, were judged grammatical reliably less often. (Again, the pattern was the same but less exaggerated for the Late Closure sentences: equivalent percentage judgments for the short condition and the prenominal adjective condition, and significantly lower percentage judgments for the long relative clause condition.) From these results we concluded that reanalysis becomes difficult when the head of the misanalyzed phrase is distant from the sentence's disambiguating word.

In summary, the data from the Early Closure (garden-pathing) sentences demonstrated that reanalysis becomes more difficult as the error signal from the disambiguating word is separated from the head of the misanalyzed phrase. From this finding we concluded that thematic roles are assigned to phrases when their heads are encountered, and that reanalysis is more difficult the longer the sentence comprehension system has been committed to an incorrect syntactic and thematic analysis. Thus, in this model we attributed difficulty not to the accessing of thematic roles, nor to the assignment of thematic roles, but rather to the difficulty of revising an incorrect thematic role assignment. We also did not attempt to account for the finding that region length was costly for Late Closure sentences, although less costly than for garden-pathing structures. One goal of our updated model is to account for both results.

3.2 Effects of Argument Structure Frequency

In Ferreira & Henderson (1991b), we extended our model to account for the effects of biasing lexical information. As discussed above, it has long been known that a sentence is easier to comprehend when its ultimate form corresponds to the preferred biases of the lexical items comprising it. Thus, sentence (6a) is easier than (6b) because the ultimate form of the entire sentence is subject-verb-complement clause, and the verb *know* prefers this structure to the one where the second NP is a direct object. The matrix verb in sentence (6b) has the opposite bias, and so it is more difficult to comprehend.

(6) a. The woman knew the nervous man would leave.
    b. The woman saw the nervous man would leave.

In the garden-path model, including its more recent Construal version (Frazier & Clifton, this volume), the parser in both cases initially takes *the nervous man* to be the direct object of the matrix verb, and the overall difficulty of (6b) compared to (6a) is due to ease of reanalysis.

In Ferreira & Henderson (1991b), we accounted for the influence of verb bias on reanalysis as follows: we assumed that the parser initially creates syntactic structure according to Minimal Attachment and Late Closure. We assumed further that theta-assigners such as verbs make available all their possible argument structures in parallel as soon as they are encountered in the string. Finally, we assumed that these structures have activation levels proportional to their frequency of use. The processing of sentences such as (6) would then proceed as follows: *the woman* is made the subject of a main, active clause (by

Minimal Attachment); normally a thematic role would be assigned at *woman*, the head of the NP, but no theta-assigner has yet been encountered to make available thematic roles; the next word, the main verb, provides these roles. For (6a), *knew* makes available two argument structures:

<experiencer, theme>
<<experiencer, proposition>>

The second structure is more activated than the first due to its higher frequency. (We indicate the more activated, frequent structure by doubling the number of angled brackets.) The subject can now be assigned the role of experiencer. For (6b), the same two argument structures are activated, but the first more so than the second:

<<experiencer, theme>>
<experiencer, proposition>

As with (6a), the subject can be made experiencer. Next, the phrase *the nervous man* is parsed and, in accordance with Minimal Attachment, it is made a direct object. Crucially, this is true for both (6a) and (6b), that is, this takes place regardless of verb bias. Once the head (*man*) is encountered, it can be assigned a thematic role. For (6a), the role to be assigned to this object requires instantiating the lower frequency argument structure; for (6b), the opposite is true. We proposed in Ferreira & Henderson (1991b) that any argument structure not instantiated begins to decay. Now, the parser encounters the disambiguating word *would*. The syntactic rules of English state that any verb (including a modal) requires a subject, so at this point the parser's analysis breaks down. Now the processing of (6a) and the processing of (6b) diverge. For (6a), reanalysis will not be difficult because the argument structure that is ultimately correct is the one that had the higher activation level to begin with. Thus, even though the ultimately-correct structure began to decay once the other structure was (initially but incorrectly) instantiated, its level of activation is still reasonably high and so the structure can be retrieved relatively easily. For (6b), in contrast, the structure that is ultimately correct had a low activation level to begin with, and began to decay from that low level once its competitor was selected. Thus, the argument structure required for successful comprehension is one whose activation level is low and perhaps no longer accessible. As a result, reanalysis is more difficult for a sentence such as (6b) than for one such as (6a).

At this point, for both (6a) and (6b), the parser steals the NP *the nervous man* away from the previous verb and makes it the subject of a new clause, in order to maintain syntactic well-formedness. This step requires not only breaking the syntactic structure so that the NP is moved from the VP headed by *knew/saw* to the subject of an embedded clause, but also relinquishing the thematic analysis given to that same NP. *The nervous man* can no longer be a theme, but instead must be part of a proposition. Again, the more available the thematic structure in which a proposition occurs the easier that reassignment can be made, and thus in (6a) the reassignment is easy but in (6b) it is hard. Parsing of the rest of (6) then proceeds smoothly: *leave* is a theta-assigner and therefore its argument structures become activated; the role of agent is assigned to the NP *the nervous man* (once *man*, the head of the phrase, is encountered); as no other phrase is encountered, the intransitive argument structure for *leave* is instantiated. Comprehension (including initial and reanalysis) of (6) is now complete.

In Ferreira & Henderson (1991b), we described an experiment that provided evidence for this model. The stimuli varied on three dimensions: the sentences were ultimately Early or Late Closure; the ambiguous region was either short or long (a relative clause followed the head noun, distancing the head of the phrase from the disambiguating word); and the verb was either equally biased towards the Early or Late Closure structures (that is, it was equally transitive or intransitive) or it was biased towards the ultimately correct structure (intransitive for Early Closure and transitive for Late Closure). As before, the sentences were presented using RSVP at the rate of 250 ms per word, and participants judged each sentence for its grammaticality. The results were as follows: for the Early Closure sentences, the percentage of sentences judged grammatical was lower for sentences with a long rather than a short ambiguous region, but this difference was much smaller when the verb was biased rather than equi-biased (69% and 93% in the biased verb conditions versus 18% and 78% in the equi-biased verb conditions); in contrast, for the Late Closure sentences, there was a decrease in acceptability in the long region condition, but verb bias had no effect.

These results are just what the model of reanalysis we outlined above would predict. Consider the Early Closure sentences first. With a short region, the argument structure consistent with the ultimately correct structure could be retrieved more easily because it had had less time to decay. And the more biased the verb toward that ultimately correct structure, the less decay would have occurred. With a long region, the ultimately correct argument structure would have decayed more; with a neutral verb, the ultimately correct argument structure had such a low activation level to begin with that it might have decayed irretrievably by the time reanalysis processes were initiated. Now consider the Late Closure sentences. Verb bias had no effect, but length caused the familiar decrease in the percentage of sentences judged to be grammatical. Because reanalysis is not required for Late Closure sentences, there is nothing for verb bias to assist with. The effect of region length, though, was left unexplained in that work as in the work we discussed previously (Ferreira & Henderson, 1990), but it is remedied in our current model.

In summary, according to our earlier model of reanalysis, words are first syntactically analyzed according to the Minimal Attachment and Late Closure principles. When a theta-assigner is encountered, all argument structures associated with it are activated in parallel and in proportion to their frequencies. A thematic role is assigned to a phrase as soon as the head of that phrase is encountered. The initial assignment of thematic roles is to phrases constructed according to Minimal Attachment and Late Closure. If the syntactic analysis breaks down, syntactic and thematic reanalysis will occur. Ease of reanalysis is based on how easily the required argument structure can be retrieved. The less the initial activation level of an argument structure and the more it has decayed, the harder it is to retrieve, and the harder reanalysis turns out to be.

4 Our Current Model of Reanalysis

We recently conducted a number of experiments to examine reanalysis, and the results have led to a substantial revision of our earlier model. In the current version, difficulty of sentence comprehension is based on the ease of dealing with theta-assigners and assigning thematic roles. Rather than attempting to describe this model in detail at this point, we will instead proceed through the experimental evidence bit by bit, and slowly build up the case for this revised model. We will then describe the model, state how it differs from the previous version, and compare it to other proposals in the parsing literature.

4.1 New Experiments on Reanalysis

As described above, the experimental work reported in Ferreira & Henderson (1991a, 1991b) suggested that ease of reanalysis was affected by the distance from the head of a garden-path sentence's ambiguous phrase to the disambiguating word. From this result we concluded that thematic roles are assigned at the heads of phrases, and thematic analyses that are maintained for longer periods of time are more difficult to relinquish. To test this notion further, we conducted an experiment with the conditions illustrated by the following sentences:

(7) a. When the boy scratched the dog yawned loudly. (68%)
b. When the boy scratched the dog that hates Sally yawned loudly. (34%)
c. When the boy scratched the dog that seems furry yawned loudly. (38%)

(8) a. When the boy scratched the dog the girl yawned loudly. (81%)
b. When the boy scratched the dog that hates Sally the girl yawned loudly. (60%)
c. When the boy scratched the dog that seems furry the girl yawned loudly.(65%)

The sentences in (7) are Early Closure and those in (8) are Late Closure. The region manipulation is as follows: the (a) sentences exemplify the short region condition and the (b) and (c) sentences the two long region conditions. Notice that syntactic complexity and head location are the same for these (b) and (c) versions, but what differs is whether the verb inside the relative clause takes an NP or an adjectival phrase (AP) as its complement.

The reason for manipulating whether the long regions involve an NP or an AP complement is as follows: in our previous work, we considered only the thematic role assignments associated with the verb in the first preposed clause and the verb in the main clause; however, the inclusion of a relative clause in the ambiguous region of these sentences introduces an additional NP into the sentence, and right at a critical point. Perhaps the reason we saw reanalysis difficulty in our previous experiments when a relative clause or a PP was inserted into the ambiguous region was because relative clauses and PPs present the parser with a new potential NP (and an incorrect one) to serve as subject of the verb in the second clause. More specifically, consider the types of regions we contrasted in Ferreira & Henderson (1991a):

(9) a. When the men hunt the birds with bright plumage scatter. (difficult)
b. If the clerk forgets the customer that likes Bobby yells. (equally difficult)
c. While the boy scratched the big and hairy dog yawned loudly. (easier)

For (9a) and (9b), the parser has a potential NP to serve as subject of the new clause—*bright plumage* in (9a) and *Bobby* in (9b). Critically, in both cases, these NPs cannot ultimately serve as subjects of the second verb. That is, if the parser attempts to use these NPs as subjects, it will encounter yet another error signal from the result—the sentences in (10) are not ultimately acceptable.

(10) a. [When the men hunt the birds with] [bright plumage typically scatter]
b. [If the clerk forgets the customer that likes] [Bobby yells]

The parser would then have to reanalyze the sentences so that the larger NP (*the birds with bright plumage* and *the customer that likes Bobby*) is made the subject for the second verb. In contrast, (9c) causes no such reanalysis confusion: the closest NP to serve as subject of *yawned* is *the big and hairy dog*, and so the parser will hit on the right NP for reanalysis on its first reanalysis attempt.

The contrast in the present experiment between the conditions illustrated by (7b) and (7c) allows us to test this possibility. In (7b), *Sally* is a potential (and incorrect) subject for the parser to try as subject of the second verb in its first attempt at reanalysis; in (7c), *furry* provides no such potential subject and so the parser should correctly try to make the entire NP *the dog that seems furry* the subject of the second verb. The same paradigm was used in this experiment as in the previous ones: sentences were presented RSVP for 250 ms per word, and at the end of each sentence participants made their grammaticality judgment.

The results from this experiment are shown with the stimuli in (7) and (8) above. Both the effects of closure and the effects of region were significant, as was the interaction between the two variables. Based on the error term for that interaction, a difference of about 9% is required for statistical significance. As can be seen, the two critical region types ((b) and (c)) do not differ reliably from each other. Thus, it does not appear that the hypothesis described above is correct: the parser does not encounter extra reanalysis difficulty due to trying to make a local NP the subject for the second verb. We conclude that our original model was not challenged by this experiment: it still appears that what is critical for ease of reanalysis is the distance from the head of the ambiguous NP to the disambiguating word. Note that we continue to replicate the pattern from our earlier experiments to an extraordinary degree: the cost associated with making the region long is incurred by both Early and Late Closure sentences, but is much larger for the former. Indeed, not just the pattern but even the absolute values are remarkably similar across experiments.

To further refine the results from our previous work, we conducted an experiment to examine whether ease of reanalysis would be affected by whether the relative clause inserted into the ambiguous region of the sentences contained a subject or an object gap. It has been reported in the sentence processing literature that even unambiguous subject-relatives (the term we will use to refer to relative clauses in which the gap occurs in subject position) are easier than object-relatives (relative clauses in which the gap occurs in the object position) (Holmes & O'Regan, 1981; King & Just, 1991). Thus, we expected that this source of processing difficulty would influence the ease with which the sentences we have examined in our experiments can be comprehended. Specifically, we assumed that the cost associated with the subject versus object-relative is separate from the costs associated with garden-pathing and reanalysis. Therefore, any penalty from the object-relative should be merely additive with the other factors we have manipulated. We predicted, then, that Early Closure sentences would be harder than Late Closure sentences, and sentences with long ambiguous regions would be more difficult than those with short regions (with the effect of region being much larger for the Early Closures); however, we assumed that the effect of subject- versus object-relative would be present for both Early and Late Closure sentences, and roughly equivalently, on the assumption that this source of difficulty was unrelated to the processes we had previously examined.

To test these predictions, we constructed stimuli such as the following:

(11) a. When the boy scratches the dog yawns loudly. (69%)
b. When the boy scratches the dog that hates Sally yawns loudly. (40%)
c. When the boy scratches the dog that Sally hates yawns loudly. (29%)

(12) a. When the boy scratches the dog the girl yawns loudly. (80%)
b. When the boy scratches the dog that hates Sally the girl yawns loudly. (61%)
c. When the boy scratches the dog that Sally hates the girl yawns loudly. (60%)

The critical manipulation involves simply switching the order of the NP illustrated here as *Sally* with the verb in the embedded clause (*hates* in this case). The examples shown in (b) are the subject-relatives and the ones shown in (c) are the object-relatives. Based on the error term for the statistically reliable interaction, a difference of about 7% is significant at $p < .05$. We did not obtain the results we expected—more precisely, we obtained about half of what we predicted. The object-relatives indeed increased processing difficulty for the Early Closure sentences (29% and 40% for the object- and subject-relatives respectively); however, they did not cause any increased difficulty for the Late Closure sentences (60% and 61% respectively).

Now we have a puzzle. If the data had turned out as expected (i.e., if the penalty for object-relatives had turned out to be equivalent for Early and Late Closure sentences), we could have left our reanalysis model intact: ease of reanalysis could have been seen as influenced by the distance of the head of the misanalyzed phrase from the disambiguating word, and the effect of subject- and object-relative within the ambiguous region could have been viewed as an additive, independent, and unrelated effect. Alternatively, if the subject- versus object-relative manipulation had had no effect, we could have left our model untouched as well: we would simply have concluded that for whatever reasons, subject-relatives were no easier than object-relatives in our experiment (it is not clear how robust the effect of subject/object relative really is; Gibson, in press). What we found, instead, was the most challenging result possible: the subject- versus object-relative manipulation interacted with whether the parser had been garden-pathed and had needed to engage in reanalysis. Therefore, our model has to be revised: something besides distance of the head of the ambiguous phrase from the disambiguating word influences ease of reanalysis.

Before turning to what that something might be, we must describe the results of one final experiment. At that point, we will have in hand all the relevant facts that need to be accounted for, and we can proceed to describe the model to account for these various facts. This last experiment was designed to determine whether ease of reanalysis might have something to do with whether the parser can salvage its thematic analysis from its initial analysis and use it during reanalysis. Consider (13):

(13) After the boy scratched the dog that hates Sally was bitten.

For the moment, let us set aside the issues surrounding the type of relative clause in the ambiguous region. Consider just what thematic roles are initially assigned and then reassigned during reanalysis. Initially, once *scratch* is encountered, the phrase *the boy* can be made its agent. Then *the dog that hates Sally* is assigned the role of patient (at the head *dog*; ignore for now the thematic assignments related to *hates*). When the parser encounters the word *was*, it must revise the syntactic structure and make *the dog that hates Sally* the subject. Notice, though, that thematic reanalysis is not required, at least in the sense that the label 'patient' does not have to be relinquished; *the dog that Sally hates* is indeed a patient, albeit for a different theta-assigner (for *bite*). Thus, if thematic roles can be salvaged in this way, then this sentence should actually be easier than one in which the verb in the main clause is active.

We tested this possibility using the following conditions:

(14) a. After the boy scratched the dog that hates Sally was bitten. (26%)
 b. After the boy scratched the dog that Sally hates was bitten. (23%)

(15) a. After the boy scratched the dog that hates Sally the girl was bitten. (48%)
 b. After the boy scratched the dog that Sally hates the girl was bitten. (44%)

We dropped the short conditions because we already had sufficient data about them from previous experiments. We included the subject- versus object-relative manipulation in order to examine further the issues we considered in the experiment we described immediately above. The only significant result we obtained (as is quite clear from the percentage data given in (14) and (15)) was a main effect of closure: The Early Closure sentences were judged grammatical less often than the Late Closure sentences. We certainly have no evidence that the thematic role assigned initially can be maintained: the sentences in (14) are at least as difficult as the comparable Early Closure sentences we examined previously. Another critical finding is that we do not see any evidence for increased difficulty associated with the object-relative clause.

This experiment demonstrates clearly that reanalysis processes gain nothing from being able to maintain a particular thematic role label. This finding makes sense when we consider that thematic roles are inherently relational: something is not just a patient, but rather is the patient of some action (Parsons, 1990). Therefore, it is not surprising that the thematic processor does not benefit from being able to continue to call *the dog that hates Sally / the dog that Sally hates* a patient even on reanalysis; what matters is that the new theta-assigner *bitten* has been encountered, and these NPs must be analyzed as patients of that theta-assigner. However, this experiment also throws a new and puzzling fact into the mix: we must now account for why the subject- / object-relative difference disappeared when the verb in the main clause was passive.

Let us now list what we have learned from these experiments. First, we know that reanalysis processes are not tricked by the presence of a potential local NP that may serve as subject of the main clause. Second, reanalysis processes do not benefit from being able to save a particular thematic role label for a phrase; what matters is the relationship between a thematic role and a theta-assigner. Third, it appears that the presence of an object versus a subject relative in the ambiguous phrase of a garden-path sentence makes reanalysis difficult. Finally, this difficulty disappears when the verb in the main clause is passive.

4.2 Motivating the New Model

In this section we will consider the different types of sentences we have examined in our entire series of experiments, and we will try to account for the ease or difficulty of processing by invoking the notions of theta-assigners and thematic processing domains (TPDs). Theta-assigners have already been defined as lexical items that assign thematic roles. A TPD is the sequence that includes the theta-assigner and all the arguments to which it assigns roles (Frazier & Clifton, this volume; Gibson, in press). When we reach the end of this exercise, we will be in a position to lay out the new model of reanalysis more specifically.

Let us begin by considering the sentence that serves as the 'baseline' for the other conditions usually examined in our experiments (and those of others), and that always has the highest level of grammaticality:

(16) When {the boy scratched the dog} [the girl yawned] loudly.

This sentence, of the Late Closure type with a short ambiguous region, contains two theta-assigners, *scratch* and *yawn*, and correspondingly two TPDs. The first TPD is *the boy scratched the dog*, and the second is *the girl yawned (loudly).* The critical feature of this sentence is that the two TPDs are entirely independent.

Next, consider the sentence type that in every one of our experiments is associated with processing difficulty but that we failed ever to incorporate into our model of processing difficulty. This type is the Late Closure sentence with a long ambiguous region, which is almost always judged grammatical about 10% less often (always a statistically reliable difference) than the version shown in (16) with a short region:

(17) When the boy scratched the dog that hates Sally the girl yawned loudly.

The difficulty of (17) compared to (16) cannot simply be attributed to the greater number of words in (17); that is, the difficulty of (17) is due to the characteristics of the ambiguous region and not just to its length (as with the

Early Closure sentences we have already discussed). This conclusion is based on the results obtained in Ferreira & Henderson (1991a), Experiment 4, where we found that a Late Closure sentence with a long ambiguous region made long through the addition of prenominal adjectives was no more difficult than the same Late Closure sentence with a short ambiguous region. Thus, it appears that some property of the ambiguous region besides its length must be responsible for the increase in processing difficulty of (17) relative to (16).

To begin to account for this difficulty, note first that (17) has three theta-assigners, *scratch*, *hate*, and *yawn*, and therefore three TPDs: the first is *the boy scratched the dog that Sally hates*, the second is *the girl yawned*, and the third is *Op hates Sally* (*Op* stands for Operator, a null element generally thought to be involved in relative clause formation, and considered somewhat analogous to a zero relative pronoun; Haegeman, 1991). The relation among these three TPDs is shown below:

(17′) When {the boy scratched the dog that (*Op* hates Sally)} [the girl yawned] loudly.

The TPDs based on *scratch* and *yawn* remain independent, as in (16), but the TPD based on *hate* is embedded inside the one based on *scratch*. Our suggestion is that whenever TPDs overlap in any way, processing difficulty results. The comprehension system must juggle two sets of thematic roles simultaneously, the two associated with the two theta-assigners *scratch* and *hate*. Evidence for this suggestion comes from the work of Shapiro and colleagues (Shapiro *et al.*, 1991; Shapiro *et al.*, 1987), who have shown with non-garden-pathing sentences that verbs with a greater number of argument structures are more complex than verbs with fewer argument structures. This work suggests that juggling argument structures is costly for the comprehension system. (Indeed, in a sentence such as (17), the comprehension system must deal with two theta-assigners but more than two argument structures, since both *scratch* and *hate* have more than one argument structure.) The work of Shapiro and colleagues makes the case for processing cost caused by having available more than one argument structure linked to a single theta-assigner; our work extends this to the (somewhat more obvious) case of multiple TPDs associated with multiple theta-assigners.

Our first conclusion, then, is that processing difficulty results whenever TPDs overlap; specifically, when one is embedded inside another. We will be using the term ‘overlap’ as the more general category concerning TPDs. Two TPDs overlap when any part of one is contained inside any part of another. The term 'embed' is more specific—TPD-1 is embedded inside TPD-2 if TPD-1 is entirely contained inside of TPD-2. Below we will describe another way in which TPDs may overlap—when two TPDs 'interact' with each other.

Next, let us consider the easiest Early Closure sentence, typically judged to be grammatical about 60% of the time:

(18) When the boy scratched the dog yawned.

This sentence has two theta-assigners: *scratch* and *yawn*. What about their TPDs? Because this is a garden-path sentence, and because reanalysis requires revision of both syntactic and thematic decisions, we must discuss the TPDs constructed initially separately from the ones constructed in reanalysis. Initially, the comprehension system takes *the boy scratched the dog* to be the TPD of *scratch*. However, *yawned* is encountered next, requiring a subject by virtue of the rules of syntactic well-formedness in English. Reanalysis must begin. Simultaneously, because *yawn* is a theta-assigner, thematic roles become available that must be assigned. *Yawn* assigns the role of experiencer to its subject, but no subject is available until syntactic reanalysis is complete. Thus, the eventual TPD for *yawn* is *the dog yawned.* The critical feature of this sentence, then, is that the two TPDs interactóthe phrase *the dog,* which is a patient in the TPD for *scratch,* must be changed so that it is an experiencer in the TPD for *yawned*. This is illustrated in (18′):

(18′) When [the boy scratched {the dog] yawned}

We will use the term 'interact' to refer to a situation in which a TPD is constructed for one theta-assigner based on an incorrect syntactic analysis, syntactic reanalysis occurs, and that TPD must be changed to accommodate the new syntactic structure so that another theta-assigner can set up its TPD. This situation obtains in (18)—the first TPD includes *the dog*, reanalysis must occur based on the ungrammaticality of *yawned*, and a new TPD must be created covering *the dog yawned.* In other words, interaction will occur whenever syntactic reanalysis is required.

Our second conclusion, then, is that processing difficulty results whenever TPDs overlap so that one TPD must interact with another. This source of processing difficulty is greater than the difficulty associated with merely embedded TPDs, as evidenced by the greater drop in grammaticality from (16) to (18)—from Late Closure with a short region to Early Closure also with a short region—than from (16) to (17)—Late Closure with a short region to Late Closure with a long region.

Supporting our second conclusion is the type of sentence shown below as (19):

(19) When the boy scratched the big and hairy dog yawned

This sentence works precisely like (18): There are two theta-assigners, *scratch* and *yawn*, and their TPDs overlap in precisely the same way as in (18)—that is, they must interact. We would expect, then, that a sentence like (19) would be judged grammatical about as often as one like (18), and that is precisely what was found in Ferreira & Henderson (1991a). These arguments imply that we now consider the crucial similarity between (18) and (19) to be not that for both the head of the ambiguous phrase is adjacent to the ambiguous word, but rather that both sentences have the same number of theta-assigners and their TPDs interact in precisely the same way.

Next, we will discuss the cases in which we have Early Closure sentences containing a relative clause inside the ambiguous region. We begin with subject-relatives:

(20) When the boy scratched the dog that hates Sally yawned loudly

This sentence contains three theta-assigners: *scratch*, *hate*, and *yawn*. The TPD for *scratch* is initially taken to be *the boy scratched the dog*, but then must be revised to be just *the boy scratched*; the theta-domain for *hate* is *Op hates Sally*; and the theta-domain for *yawn* is constructed after syntactic reanalysis to eventually include *the dog that hates Sally yawned.* The relations among the three TPDs are shown below:

(20′) When {the boy scratched} [the dog that (*Op* hates Sally) yawned] loudly.

This sentence should be even more difficult than the other Early Closure sentences we have discussed so far in this section because this sentence has two sources of processing difficulty: one TPD (*Op hates Sally*) is embedded inside another, and two TPDs interact—*the dog that hates Sally*, which is at first taken to be the patient of *scratch* must be eventually interpreted as experiencer of *yawn*. And as our data make clear repeatedly, this sentence is indeed more difficult than either (18) or (19).

The experiment we described earlier showed that a sentence like (20) is no more difficult than one like (21),

(21) When the boy scratched the dog that seems furry yawned loudly.

This result again follows from what we have argued. Sentence (21) has three theta-assigners and accordingly three TPDs. The three TPDs are in precisely the same relation as in (20), as shown in (21′):

(21′) When {the boy scratched} [the dog that (*t* seems furry) yawned] loudly.

One TPD (the one associated with *seem*) is embedded inside another (the one associated with *scratch* initially and *yawn* ultimately), and two TPDs must interact (the ones associated with *scratch* and with *yawn*). Therefore, this sentence should be precisely as difficult as (20), and that is the result we obtained.

Now let us consider a sentence type from Ferreira & Henderson (1991a) and see how the difficulty of comprehending it can be accommodated in our new reanalysis model:

(22) When the men hunt the birds with bright plumage scatter.

The critical finding is that this sentence is as difficult to comprehend as (20). This result led us to argue (Ferreira & Henderson, 1990) that what matters is the location of the head noun of the ambiguous phrase, because that is what is the same about (20) and (22) (even though syntactic complexity differs). Furthermore, we argued that head location is what distinguishes these two cases from the one in which the ambiguous region was made long by adding adjectives (cf. (19) above). However, we overlooked another respect in which (20) and (22) are similar and different from (19): (20) and (22) both involve three theta-assigners and three TPDs is in exactly the same relations; (19) (as discussed above) has only two theta-assigners and two TPDs. To see this, let us look at (22) more carefully: It contains the theta-assigners *hunt*, *scatter*, and *with* (*with* is a preposition that assigns a thematic role, in contrast to one such as *of*). The TPD for *with* is *with bright plumage*; the TPD for *hunt* is initially taken to be *the men hunt the birds with bright plumage* and then revised to be just *the men hunt*; and the TPD for *scatter* is eventually *the birds with bright plumage scatter*. Thus, the relations among TPDs are exactly the same in (22) as in (21) and (20), as shown below:

(22′) When {the men hunt} [the birds (with bright plumage) scatter].

Thus, we have a new explanation for the finding that garden-path sentences with ambiguous regions made long through the inclusion of prenominal adjectives are easier than either garden-path sentences with regions made long through the insertion of a relative clause or a prepositional phrase. Previously, we stated that what the latter two had in common was head position, in contrast to the prenominal case. However, we now see that the two also have in common both the number of TPDs and their exact relations to one another. Thus, we now attribute the behavior of these different sentence types to their thematic properties, rather than their head location properties. We believe this new account has the virtue of explaining far more data, including the cases we have discussed in (16) through (22), as well as cases we have yet to discuss in this section. In addition, our new model makes an interesting prediction, namely, that a sentence such as (22), in which a prepositional phrase follows a head noun will be easier when the prepositional phrase is headed by *of* rather than when it is headed by a role-assigning preposition such as *with*. A study is currently underway to examine this intriguing prediction in which the critical contrast involves sentences such as the following:

(23) a. When the student leaves the professor of history becomes angry.
b. When the student leaves the professor with a history becomes angry.

Unfortunately, we do not yet have supporting data on these constructions, but we consider it a virtue of our new model that it generated such an interesting prediction concerning ease of reanalysis.

We have three cases remaining to discuss, and they will bring us to our third major conclusion, which is that processing becomes difficult whenever two theta-assigners are encountered one immediately after another. First, recall examples such as (24):

(24) When the boy scratched the dog that Sally hates yawned loudly.

This sentence is even more difficult to understand than (20), which is identical except that in (20) the relative clause is a subject-relative rather than an object-relative. This result was impossible to explain with the model of reanalysis we had previously; however, we now can explain not only why this object-relative case is more difficult than (20), but also why object-relatives cause no processing cost for Late Closure sentences such as (25):

(25) When the boy scratched the dog that Sally hates the girl yawned loudly.

Recall that it was precisely this interaction that could not be explained under the old model. First, (24) and (20) have the same number of theta-assigners and TPDs, and in just the same relations. Thus, the problem with (24) cannot be attributed to processes related to theta-assignment. However, notice that in (24), the theta-assigner *hates* is encountered and then *yawned* is encountered immediately following. This situation causes problems for the sentence comprehension system because while it is still assigning roles based on *hates* it has to deal with another set of roles based on *yawned*. Not only does this result in high processing load at this point in the sentence, but crosstalk may also occur among the various thematic roles, causing possible confusion and further comprehension breakdown. This argument has recently been made by Gibson (in press), in his model of sentence processing based on memory load. He argues that the difficulty of center-embedded sentences such as *The man the boy saw laughed* is due to the cost of dealing with the two sets of thematic roles piled up right next to each other. We are borrowing this idea to explain our results, especially our finding that object-relatives are difficult, but only for Early Closure sentences. Our suggestion is that we obtained this result because the combination of the Early Closure and object-relative structures placed the two theta-assigners *hates* and *yawned* right next to each other. In contrast, in (25), the presence of the phrase *the girl* not only makes the sentence a Late Closure structure (compared to (24)), but also separates the two theta-assigners. As a result, the sentence should be easy to comprehend; more precisely, there should be no difference between the Late Closure sentence (25) with the object-relative and the same sentence with a subject-relative (e.g., (12b)), because in both cases theta-assigners are not adjacent.

Finally, this account explains why there was no subject- versus object-relative difference for the sentences in which the verb in the main clause was passive:

(26) a. When the boy scratched the dog that hates Sally was bitten.
b. When the boy scratched the dog that Sally hates was bitten.

Recall that this result was obtained for both Early Closure sentences such as (26) as well as their Late Closure counterparts ((15a) and (15b))—region type made no difference, and Early Closure sentences were judged grammatical less often than Late Closure sentences. The passive morphology places a form of *to be* between the theta-assigner *hate* in (26b) and the theta-assigner *bite*. As a result, the two theta-assigners are not adjacent, and so (26b) should be no more difficult than (26a) (in which the two theta-assigners are also non-adjacent). Of course, sentences such as (26) were more difficult overall than the same types of sentences containing an active verb in the main clause ((20) and (24)). However, this result is not surprising, given that passives are known to be more difficult to comprehend than actives (e.g., Frazier *et al.*, 1984). Recall that even the Late Closure sentences with a passive verb in the main clause ((15a) and (15b)) were judged grammatical only about 46% of the time, a much lower value than we saw in previous Late Closure sentences with the same long regions but with an active verb in the main clause. Thus, we would expect *overall* levels of acceptability to be lower for sentences with a passive verb in the main clause; what is critical is that the subject- / object-relative difference disappears with these sentences, while it is found in the comparable cases with active verbs.

5 Summary of the New Model

Our attempt to put together all the relevant data from our studies of reanalysis suggests that the following model is correct. Processing cost results when:

(a) a TPD is embedded inside another,

(b) two TPDs must interact, and/or

(c) two theta-assigners are adjacent.

In other words, a sentence will be easy to comprehend when none of (a) through (c) holds, harder if any one holds, harder yet if two hold, and most difficult if all three hold. Of course, we do not claim to have identified all factors that can make a sentence easy or difficult to comprehend; for example, sentences containing infrequent words are more difficult than those containing frequent words, and our model says nothing about that. The goal of our model is to explain comprehension difficulty that results from factors related to thematic processing. Indeed, only (b) is specifically about reanalysis, that is, about what happens when a misanalysis occurs and must be corrected: (a) can hold even of a non-garden-pathing sentence; for example, (16) above. The factor in (c) can also hold of a non-garden-pathing sentence; for example, ((15a) and (15b)), as well as classic center-embedded sentences. Only (b) is specifically about reanalysis, for interaction in our model means that a TPD is constructed for one theta-assigner based on an incorrect syntactic analysis, syntactic reanalysis occurs, and that TPD must be changed to accommodate the new syntactic structure so that another theta-assigner can set up its TPD.

Michigan State University

References

Adams, B.C., Clifton, C., & Mitchell, D.C. 1994. Lexical guidance in sentence processing: Further evidence for a filtering account. Manuscript, University of Massachusetts, Amherst, MA.

Altmann, G. & Steedman, M. 1988. Interaction with context during human sentence processing. *Cognition*, 30, 191-238.

Connine, C.M., Ferreira, F., Jones, C., Clifton, C.E., & Frazier, L. 1984. Verb frame preferences. *Journal of Psycholinguistic Research*, 13, 307-319.

De Vincenzi, M. 1991. *Syntactic Parsing Strategies in Italian*. Dordrecht: Kluwer Academic Publishers.

Ferreira, F., & Clifton, C.E. 1986. The independence of syntactic processing. *Journal of Memory and Language*, 25, 348-368.

Ferreira, F., & Henderson, J.M. 1990. The use of verb information in syntactic parsing: A comparison of evidence from eye movements and word-by-word self-paced reading. *Journal of Experimental Psychology: Learning, Memory, and Cognition*, 16, 555-568.

Ferreira, F., & Henderson, J.M. 1991a. Recovery from misanalyses of garden-path sentences. *Journal of Memory and Language*, 30, 725-745.

Ferreira, F., & Henderson, J.M. 1991b. How is verb information used during syntactic parsing? In G.B. Simpson (ed.), *Understanding Word and Sentence*. North-Holland: Elsevier Science Publishers, B.V., 305-330.

Ferreira, F., & McClure, K.K. 1997. Parsing with reciprocal verbs. *Language and Cognitive Processes*, in press.

Ferreira, F., Henderson, J.M., Anes, M.D., Weeks, P.A., & McFarlane, D.K. 1996. Effects of lexical frequency and syntactic complexity in spoken-language comprehension: Evidence from the Auditory Moving Window technique. *Journal of Experimental Psychology: Learning, Memory, and Cognition*, 22, 324-335.

Frazier, L. 1978. *On Comprehending Sentences: Syntactic Parsing Strategies*. Unpublished doctoral dissertation, University of Connecticut, Storrs, CT. Distributed by the Indiana University Linguistics Club, Bloomington, IN.

Frazier, L. 1987. Sentence processing: A tutorial review. In M. Coltheart (ed.), *Attention and Performance XII*. Hillsdale, NJ: Lawrence Erlbaum Associates, 559-587.

Frazier, L., & Clifton, C. (this volume). Sentence reanalysis and visibility.

Frazier, L., & Rayner, K. 1982. Making and correcting errors during sentence comprehension: Eye movements in the analysis of structurally ambiguous sentences. *Cognitive Psychology*, 14, 178-210.

Frazier, L., Taft, L., Roeper, T., Clifton, C., & Jones, C. 1984. Parallel structure: A source of facilitation in sentence comprehension. *Memory and Cognition*, 12, 421-430.

Gibson, E.A.F. (in press). *Memory Limitations and Linguistic Processing Breakdown*. Cambridge, MA: MIT Press.

Haegeman, L. 1991. *Government and Binding Theory*. Oxford: Blackwell Publishers.

Holmes, V.M., & O'Regan, J.K. 1981. Eye fixation patterns during the reading of relative clause sentences. *Journal of Verbal Learning and Verbal Behavior*, 20, 417-430.

Jackendoff, R.S. 1990. *Semantic Structures*. Cambridge, MA: MIT Press.

King, J., & Just, M.A. 1991. Individual differences in syntactic processing: The role of working memory. *Journal of Memory and Language*, 30, 580-602.

MacDonald, M.C., Pearlmutter, N.J., & Seidenberg, M.S. 1994. The lexical nature of syntactic ambiguity resolution. *Psychological Review*, 101, 676-703.

Mitchell, D.C. 1989. Verb-guidance and other lexical effects in parsing. *Language and Cognitive Processes*, 4, SI 123-154.

Mitchell, D.C., Cuetos, F., & Corley, M.M.B. 1992. Statistical versus linguistic determinants of parsing bias: Cross-linguistic evidence. Paper presented at *Fifth Annual CUNY Conference on Human Sentence Processing*, New York, NY.

Munn, A. 1993. *Topics in the Syntax and Semantics of Coordinate Structures*. Unpublished doctoral dissertation, University of Maryland, College Park, MD.

Parsons, T. 1990. *Events in the Semantics of English: A Study of Subatomic Semantics*. Cambridge, MA: MIT Press.

Pearlmutter, N.J., & MacDonald, M.C. 1995. Individual differences and probabalistic constraints in syntactic ambiguity resolution. *Journal of Memory and Language*, 34, 521-542.

Rayner, K., Carlson, M., & Frazier, L. 1983. The interaction of syntax and semantics during sentence processing: Eye movements in the analysis of semantically ambiguous sentences. *Journal of Verbal Learning and Verbal Behavior*, 22, 358-374.

Rayner, K., Garrod, S. & Perfetti, C.A. 1992. Discourse influences during parsing are delayed. *Cognition*, 45, 109-139.

Sedivy, J.C., & Spivey-Knowlton, M. 1994. The use of structural, lexical, and pragmatic information in parsing attachment ambiguities. In C. Clifton, K. Rayner, & L. Frazier (eds.), *Perspectives on Sentence Processing*. Hillsdale, NJ: Lawrence Erlbaum Associates, 389-413.

Seidenberg, M.S., Waters, G.S., Sanders, M., & Langer, P. 1984. Pre- and postlexical loci of contextual effects on word recognition. *Memory and Cognition*, 12, 315-328.

Shapiro, L.P., Brookins, B., Gordon, B., & Nagel, N. 1991. Verb effects during sentence processing. *Journal of Experimental Psychology: Learning, Memory, and Cognition*, 17, 983-996.

Shapiro, L.P., Zurif, E., & Grimshaw, J. 1987. Sentence processing and the mental representation of verbs. *Cognition*, 27, 219-246.

Spivey-Knowlton, M., & Sedivy, J.C. 1995. Resolving attachment ambiguities with multiple constraints. *Cognition*, 55, 227-267.

Taraban, R., & McClelland, J.L. 1989. Constituent attachment and thematic role assignment in sentence processing: Influences of content-based expectations. *Journal of Memory and Language*, 27, 597-632.

Trueswell, J.C., & Tanenhaus, M.K. 1994. Toward a lexicalist framework of constraint-based syntactic ambiguity resolution. In C. Clifton, K. Rayner, & L. Frazier (eds.), *Perspectives on Sentence Processing*. Hillsdale, NJ: Lawrence Erlbaum Associates, 155-179.

Trueswell, J.C., Tanenhaus, M.K., & Kello, C. 1993. Verb-specific constraints in sentence processing: Separating effects of lexical preference from garden-paths. *Journal of Experimental Psychology: Learning, Memory, and Cognition*, 19, 528-553.

Warner, J., & Glass, A. 1987. Context and distance-to-disambiguation effects in ambiguity resolution: Evidence from grammaticality judgments of garden path sentences. *Journal of Memory and Language*, 26, 714-738.

4

Attach Anyway*

Janet Dean Fodor & Atsu Inoue

Abstract

The diagnostic model of garden path recovery that we have advocated in previous work holds that no repair processes are intrinsically costly. Repair costs depend entirely on the difficulty of establishing what revisions to make. The diagnosis process does not require a special-purpose inference system as long as the parser abides by the *Attach Anyway* principle: when it encounters an input word that doesn't fit into the current structure, it attaches it in the least unacceptable way. The attachment creates a conflict internal to the phrase marker, which is then resolved in consultation with the grammar by a process we call *Adjust*. In this chapter we propose a principled constraint on the operations of *Adjust*: the *Grammatical Dependency Principle*. We show that this clarifies some previously noted phenomena such as the Thematic Overlay Effect and the differential difficulty of different types of steal operations. The examples we present show that neither raising repairs nor semantic revisions are difficult *per se*.

1 Background

A garden path occurs when the parser selects the wrong analysis at a point of ambiguity in an input sentence, and discovers later that subsequent words of the input do not fit into the structure it has been building. In previous work (Fodor & Inoue, 1994) we presented a model in which recovery from a garden path consists in repairing the incorrect sentence structure to make it compatible with the current input. A repair system contrasts with a reparsing system, which

---

* We are grateful to Paul Gorrell and Patrick Sturt for their perceptive comments on an earlier draft.

J.D. Fodor and F. Ferreira (eds.), Reanalysis in Sentence Processing, 101–141.

gives up the current structure, returns to some earlier point in the sentence, and tries parsing it in a different way. A repair system must have some way of deciding what structural alterations to make. We proposed that recovery costs are entirely attributable to the difficulty of this diagnostic process. If it can be defended, this is a very desirable assumption on grounds of parsimony, since there must be some such process in any repair system, and it seems clear that the ease of deducing what error has occurred and how it can be corrected is bound to differ from case to case. It would not be necessary, then, to assume greater costs of carrying out one kind of repair than another (e.g., raising a node versus lowering a node), or even a greater inherent cost for repairs than for any other parsing processes.

Central to the diagnostic process is the nature of the misfit between the current partial phrase marker (CPPM) and the input word that is incompatible with it. This is necessarily the starting point, the premise for deducing which prior parsing decision was the source of the current problem. If the relation between this mismatch and the prior error responsible for it is transparent, recovery is predicted to be easy; if the connection is obscure, recovery would be difficult or impossible. To go from this general idea to predictions about particular examples we must say more about what makes this relationship transparent or otherwise. In other words, we owe an account of the reasoning capabilities of the revision component of the parser. Different reasoning algorithms would exhibit different profiles of success or failure for different examples. More interestingly, turning this around the other way gives us our methodology: observed patterns of difficulty can be informative of the nature of the diagnostic mechanism.

On this basis, we argued in our earlier work (Fodor & Inoue, 1994) against the idea of a repair agent which stands back and studies the whole CPPM and tries to calculate what changes would allow the current input to be integrated with it. The data we considered suggested that the repair system has no insight into clever solutions and that it is unable to combine facts productively; rather, it is successful only where the necessary inference can be made in small steps quite mechanically. For this reason we proposed a repair system that does not reason abstractly about the problem, but just sets about altering the CPPM one step at a time, starting at the specific mismatch that presents itself at the point of breakdown. In the ideal case (but not in every case: not all garden paths are revisable) these successive small adjustments will lead the parser back to the site of the original error. The final revision will be at that point, and the parser will re-attach the item that was incorrectly attached on the first pass; all subsidiary adjustments consequent on that repair will have already been made en route to it.[1] This account of how diagnosis and cure are effected has the great advantage that it does not presuppose abstract reasoning capabilities or require postulation of special-purpose revision routines; it can in large part draw on simple practical mechanisms already in place for first-pass parsing. This is so, given one crucial assumption about how the CPPM and the input are made to confront each other by the parser at the very outset of the repair process. This assumption is stated in the parsing principle that we call *Attach Anyway*, discussed in section 2.

Attach Anyway is a close relation of *Attach*, the fundamental principle of first-pass parsing in a full-attachment (non-delay) parser:

(1) *Attach*: On receiving a word of the input sentence, connect it to the current partial phrase marker (CPPM) for the sentence in such a way that the resulting CPPM is syntactically well-formed though possibly incomplete at its right edge.[2]

This simply enjoins the parser to integrate each input item into the sentence structure as it is received. If there is more than one way of creating a new well-formed CPPM, we assume the parser adopts whichever one is computed most rapidly. This is the *First Analysis Constraint* of Frazier & Rayner (1988), and Frazier & Fodor (1978). We follow this earlier work also in assuming that the simplest possible attachment wins the race. The simplest attachment is one that obeys both *Minimal Attachment* (MA) and *Right Association* (RA) or *Late Closure* (LC). These principles are specific instantiations of the *Minimal Everything* principle, which embodies the basic assumption that the human sentence parsing mechanism is a least effort device. Borrowing from unpublished work by Fodor & Frazier (1983) we assume here that MA and RA are jointly satisfied by the shortest possible path of linking nodes between the rightmost terminal symbol $i-1$ and the input item i that is now being attached, where this path goes up from $i-1$ through existing nodes in the tree, and then

---

[1] As will become clear, this 'backtracking' to the source error is very different from the word by word backtracking of an ATN (Wanner & Maratsos, 1978). We note also that in addition to the adjustments leading back to the source error, there may be others that stem from those. There is an example in Fodor & Inoue (in press), but none in this chapter.

[2] Semantic and pragmatic acceptability might also be a condition on *Attach*, but this will not be discussed here. We also lack space to discuss repairs of errors signalled by pragmatic conflicts. See Fodor & Inoue (1994) for examples where pragmatic symptoms are ineffective as pointers to the site of the original error. See Ni *et al.* (submitted) for a suggestion as to how pragmatic anomaly can initiate appropriate repairs in some circumstances.

down through newly created nodes to *i*.[3] Minimizing the up-path satisfies RA; minimizing the down-path satisfies MA. (We called this the *Minimal Connections* principle. See Phillips, 1995, for a new proposal along similar lines.) We lack space here to give further details of *Attach*. Fortunately, exactly how it is implemented is not germane to our concerns in this paper, as long as the mechanism is such that the preference principles (i.e., *Minimal Everything* and its subsidiaries) follow from it naturally without stipulation.

Attach Anyway is similar to *Attach* but applies in garden path constructions when the parse has broken down. The parser discovers that the current input is incompatible with the CPPM, and cannot be legitimately attached into it. *Attach Anyway* requires the parser to continue functioning as much like normal as it can in these circumstances. It is not allowed to quit, but must attach the problematic input into the structure despite the ill-formedness of the new CPPM it thereby produces. Then the principle *Adjust* directs the parser to set about correcting this ill-formedness. In the next section we give a more detailed presentation of both *Attach Anyway* and *Adjust*. They account for a range of garden paths. We present here some new examples not previously noted in the literature. We also propose a linguistically motivated locality constraint on the operations of *Adjust*, and show that this permits interesting refinements of previously noted phenomena such as the Thematic Overlay Effect, and the differential difficulty of different types of steal operations. As we proceed we will relate this system, in which repair is driven by *Attach Anyway*, to other repair models, noting both similarities and differences. Despite the number of competing proposals that have been made in recent years, it seems that we may be moving towards a consensus on at least some of the questions about why garden paths differ as they do in ease of recovery, and how this might follow from the way in which needed repairs are identified and carried out.

---

[3] In left-branching languages such as Japanese, the path above $i - 1$ may have new nodes above old nodes. In the 1983 manuscript we considered the possibility (from Cooper & Paccia-Cooper, 1980) that new nodes are costlier than old ones. It could also be that clausal nodes (or verbal projections) on this path cost more than other nodes. This would account for the general preference for attachment within the lowest clause; see Igoa (1995) and discussion in Fodor & Inoue (in preparation a). Other aspects of the Minimal Connections model are not considered here (e.g., the assumption that the parser establishes the minimal connection between adjacent words before checking whether this is consistent with how word *i* is already configured in the CPPM).

2 Attach Anyway and Adjust

We claim that there are just two principles of repair parsing: *Attach Anyway* and *Adjust*. *Attach Anyway* applies when the parse runs into a problem and it appears that there is no way for it to continue. *Attach Anyway* forces the parser to keep going.

(2) *Attach Anyway*: Having established that there is no legitimate attachment site in the CPPM for the current input word,[4] attach the input word into the CPPM wherever it least severely violates the grammar, and subject to the usual preference principles that govern *Attach*.[5]

An attachment made by *Attach Anyway* necessarily creates an ill-formed subtree within the CPPM. In a typical case, one of the new nodes introduced to link the input word *i* into the tree conflicts with the properties of some other node already in the tree: its mother or its sister, or, as we shall see, a node with which it enters into a long-distance dependency. This conflict within the CPPM is then resolved by the parser under guidance by *Adjust*.[6,7]

---

4 *Attach Anyway* does not always wait for complete breakdown of the first-pass parse, though for simplicity we will assume here that it does. If it did, that would be equivalent to a strict Revision as Last Resort principle (Fodor & Frazier, 1980). But in Fodor & Inoue (in preparation a) we give examples which show that RALR is not an absolute constraint: the wellformedness requirement and the attachment preference principles interact in determining the attachment made. (See also Stevenson, this volume.) This would follow from the First Analysis Constraint if illegal attachments sometimes, but not always, take longer to compute than legal ones, and if *Attach* and *Attach Anyway* are folded into a single principle *Attach (Anyway)*, as we argue they must be.

5 Some evidence that *Attach Anyway* exhibits the same attachment preferences as first-pass *Attach* comes from examples presented by Sturt & Crocker (1996). For instance, in *I know the man who believes the countess killed himself* the first-pass analysis makes *the man who...* the direct object of *know*, and *the countess* the direct object of *believes*; then for the correct revision, the VP *killed himself* should steal the higher NP, but instead the parser opts to steal the lower one. We presume this is due to RA (LC), which strongly disfavors attachment above the current clause (cf. Igoa, 1995).

6 Lewis (1993, this volume) proposes a similar process of attachment despite illformedness, followed by adjustment processes. In this respect our repair model is closer to Lewis' than to any other model, though it differs from Lewis' model with respect to which adjustments are permitted; see Fodor & Inoue (in press) for discussion. Also closely related is Stevenson's competitive attachment parser (this volume), which juggles the claims of a number of potential attachments, not all of which are compatible with the CPPM.

(3) *Adjust*: When a grammatical conflict has been created between two nodes or features X and Y in the CPPM, by either *Attach Anyway* or *Adjust*, eliminate the problem by altering minimally (i.e., no more than is necessary for conflict resolution) whichever of X and Y was less recently acted on, without regard for grammatical conflicts thereby created between that node and other elements in the CPPM.

Some aspects of (3) should be noted. The requirement that the adjustment be minimal, though made explicit here, actually follows from the least effort principle *Minimal Everything* (see Frazier, 1990; Inoue & Fodor, 1995). It precludes, for example, detaching a node from its current position if it could have been reconciled with the context by changing just one of its feature values. Nothing in (3) requires that there be only one node that a new or newly adjusted node is incompatible with, but the Grammatical Dependency Principle discussed in section 3 below will normally single out a unique node for the adjustment process to work on. *Adjust* is defined recursively. One application of *Adjust* may restore the whole CPPM to well-formedness. Alternatively, it may cure one grammatical violation only by creating another one elsewhere. In that case, *Adjust* applies to the new violation, and to any violation which it thus creates, continuing until a fully grammatical equilibrium is achieved. A stable state is not always reached, however, because the necessary series of revisions may block at some point (for reasons outlined below) or possibly because time runs out before the necessary computations can be completed (see Konieczny *et al.*, 1994; Ferreira & Henderson, this volume).

To avoid unproductive repairs going around in small circles, *Adjust* includes the requirement that when a conflict has been created in the tree, the parser is to hold onto whatever it most recently did under the direction of *Attach Anyway* or *Adjust*, and alter the *other* end of the incompatible relationship.[8] This condition in (3) gives *Adjust* the courage of its convictions: the adjustment made to a node is often at odds with other aspects of the tree, but this must not scare the parser into giving up on it. Rather, the parser needs this new conflict to drive further

[7] There are some special cases in which *Attach Anyway* does not result in a specific conflict between elements in the tree (e.g., where the symptom is the absence of a needed constituent). These are discussed in Fodor & Inoue (in preparation b).

[8] Informally we call this the *Hold Tight On The Right* principle (HTOTR), though it could be the case that the most recently revised element in a dependency is on the left rather than the right. The only necessary truth about linear direction is that the source error must be to the left of the symptom. We note that even HTOTR does not exclude all circular revision sequences, though if necessary it could be strengthened to do so.

repairs. Holding tight to the most recent attachment is the main difference between revision and first-pass parsing. First-pass parsing is subject to the *Revision as Last Resort* principle (RALR, Fodor & Frazier, 1980) which requires the parser to hold on to already built structure and make new input conform to it; structure built at the right side of the tree is constrained by decisions made on the left. By contrast, *Adjust* requires the parser to hold on to its ungrammatical emergency attachment at the right frontier of the tree, and let this determine what must give way further to the left.

A reanalysis system governed by *Attach Anyway* and *Adjust* first makes an illegitimate attachment and then makes changes to the CPPM to legitimize it. The alternative would be to first change the CPPM, postponing attachment of the conflicting input until it can be attached legitimately. The two strategies may seem to differ only trivially, but in fact the difference is critical. The illegitimate attachment demanded by *Attach Anyway* plays a pivotal role in the repair process because it converts a mis-match between the CPPM and subsequent input into a mis-match internal to the CPPM. At that point the *grammar* can be called on to identify the nature of the problem. The grammar knows what is an acceptable tree and what isn't, and it knows what is wrong with unacceptable ones. But without *Attach Anyway*, the grammar's ability to detect ungrammaticalities could not be put to work here. Without *Attach Anyway*, the lack of a well-formed attachment for the current input word *i* would prevent *i* from being attached. The CPPM would therefore remain incomplete, but it would be perfectly well-formed in accord with the grammar. It would be an acceptable CPPM, just like any other; it would be 'incorrect' only in the sense that it is not the CPPM *for this input string*. Internally it could not be faulted, so the grammar could not get a grip on it. The repair mechanism would therefore need a special diagnostic routine to exploit the information in the grammar in a reasoning process quite unlike first-pass tree building.

By contrast, an *Attach Anyway* parser puts the grammar to work to identify the nature of the problem that presents itself in a garden-path sentence at the point at which the parse breaks down. In diagnostic terms: the grammar identifies the error signal or *symptom* of the garden-path. The grammar can also be used to track from this point to the source error (i.e., the original attachment error earlier in the parse which caused the garden path). The grammar shows the parser where to look for the source error. This is another advantage that comes from starting the repair with attachment of the problematic current word, as opposed to trying to put things right in the tree before making the current attachment. The error locus is unknown; finding it is the *goal* of diagnosis. But the site of *Attach Anyway* is known; so the grammar is targeted efficiently to just the right spot. The parser will fix whatever needs fixing there, then shift attention to the damage done by that repair and fix that up, and so forth. This is how it finds its way to the true source of the trouble.

This successive repair process must have a way of knowing, at each step, where to shift its attention next. This, too, is information that the grammar can provide. The grammar can tell the parser which other nodes in the tree stand in a grammatical dependency with the node *n* currently being attended to by the parser. Necessarily, these are all and only the nodes that *n* could be in conflict with. So they are all and only the nodes which must be checked to see whether or not there is a conflict, and which must be altered if it turns out that there is. Checking the existence and well-formedness of dependencies between nodes in the tree may seem to be an enormous amount of work, but it is something that the first-pass routines must do all the time. An input word *i* can be acceptably integrated into the CPPM only if every potential relationship that *i* would thereby enter into in the tree is checked and found to be acceptable. Thus, every parsing model must do this or something equivalent to it, even if normally no mention is made of it; it is a process that is usually buried in implementation routines left unspecified. (But see Abney, 1986.) How heavy the computational burden actually is depends on the extent to which Universal Grammar and the grammar of the language constrain the relations that can hold between nodes: the fewer possible relations there are, the fewer relations the parser needs to check. In any case, we know that in the normal course of first-pass parsing the grammar is continuously providing the parser with information about dependencies. So the fact that *Adjust* needs this same information in order to know which node to consider revising next imposes no additional burden.

To summarize: By converting the mis-match between the input and the CPPM into a mis-match internal to the CPPM, *Attach Anyway* delivers a number of valuable consequences. It converts garden-path diagnosis from an open-ended reasoning problem into the familiar and concrete task of ensuring that all sub-trees of a CPPM obey the grammar. Specifically, an *Attach Anyway* parser can rely on the grammar to direct it toward exactly that piece of the CPPM that the newly attached input is incompatible with. The parser modifies that element to resolve the inconsistency. If that creates a new problem, the grammar will once again show the parser where and what the trouble is. Thus diagnosis and cure are not separate activities but are intercalated. And diagnosis is practical rather than abstract; it is simply the parser looking for its next repair to attend to. In the next sections we illustrate these general points with some examples.

3 The Grammatical Dependency Principle

If the current input item *i* is attached forcibly by *Attach Anyway* rather than *Attach*, then necessarily one of the new nodes introduced in attaching *i* is incompatible with some property of the prior CPPM. In most cases (though not quite all, see fn. 7) the offending new node stands in an improper grammatical relation with a node in the prior CPPM: a relation of mis-agreement, or mis-selection, or mis-match with an antecedent, etc. As noted, a conflict between two nodes can exist only if they stand in a relationship that is regulated by the grammar. This is so both for the first conflict, involving a new node introduced in the emergency attachment, and for later steps in the adjustment process; the adjustment mechanism is the same in all cases. Many grammatical relationships are quite local (structurally, if not linearly), e.g., subject-verb agreement. So very often, when a node conflicts with some other element in the CPPM, the two are in the same local sub-tree. But there are also long-distance grammatical dependencies such as pronoun binding, antecedent government, parallel structure requirements as in Gapping, and so forth. The scope of these various linguistic phenomena determines the size of the steps by which the parser makes its backward progress from the error signal to the original error site. We make this point explicit in the *Grammatical Dependency Principle*.

(4) *The Grammatical Dependency Principle* (GDP): When a grammar violation has been created in the CPPM by an action on node *n* in accord with *Attach Anyway* or *Adjust*, attempt to eliminate the problem by acting on a node that is grammatically incompatible with *n*.

The GDP is supported by empirical observations, such as the difficulty of revision in examples like (6) and (9) discussed below, compared with others such as (7) and (13)-(18). It is also in keeping with our general working principle that the revision routines draw on independently needed parsing mechanisms as far as possible. Together, these strongly suggest that the parser in *Adjust* mode tracks from node to node along pathways defined by grammatical relationships, and does not roam freely around the tree altering nodes wherever it pleases.

The GDP is (almost) implicit in the statement of *Adjust*, but since it is not a necessary property of a repair system, it is worth spelling out separately. (See section 5 for a version of the GDP which points out good repair sites but does not absolutely prohibit other revisions.) The GDP does have some empirical bite. For instance, it limits the movement of items from one phrase into another that happens to be nearby in the terminal string, if the phrases are not related to each other by any kind of grammatical dependency. As we discuss in section 5 below, this rules out some kinds of stealing repairs, in which an element in the tree grabs a linearly adjacent but unrelated constituent. This kind of stealing we call 'theft'. As we will show, there are contexts in which the parser attempts it, but with unhappy consequences because it violates the GDP. The GDP also rules out the complementary operation of stuffing unwanted material from one constituent into an unrelated one nearby. But the effects of a ban against stuffing are less drastic because stuffing of an element *x* (unlike stealing of *x*) is propelled by unacceptability of *x* in its current position; so the effect of stuffing *x* into a constituent *c* can also result from expelling *x* from its current local tree and subsequently reattaching it beneath *c*. Stealing cannot be thus simulated by two GDP-compatible operations, because there would be motive only for re-attachment, not for the initial detachment step.[9]

The GDP is a locality principle of sorts, but it does not impose a narrow definition of locality in terms of minimal distance. It condones some quite wide-ranging shifts—in fact, exactly as wide-ranging as grammatical dependencies can be. How great the distances are depends to some extent on the theory of grammar that is assumed, which may entail that what looks like a long-distance dependency is made up of a number of shorter links. In Government Binding (GB) theory, for instance, a 'long-distance' *wh*-movement dependency may be mediated by several coindexed empty categories; each link in the chain must satisfy Subjacency, the ECP and perhaps other locality conditions, though there is no limit on the length of the total chain. In HPSG a *wh*-dependency is composed of even more local links, since the SLASH feature that links filler and gap must be present on every node that dominates the gap but not the filler. On the other hand, HPSG also admits unmediated binding relations, as between an anaphor and an antecedent which is several nodes distant in the tree. GB does likewise as far as overt syntax is concerned, though it imposes a strict locality requirement on anaphors at LF (see Cole & Wang, 1996). Exactly how constraints at LF (or the Conceptual-Intentional interface) affect the parsing of overt syntactic structure is not yet well understood; though it is important, we cannot address it here. Also, it will suffice in what follows to

[9] Stealing is thus a primitive revision operation, not composed of actions familiar from first-pass parsing. Expulsion, ousting, and other varieties of detachment are also specific to repair. Thus, as Paul Gorrell (p.c.) reminds us, it is not the case that repair needs no new mechanisms. We can claim only that diagnosis by *Adjust* borrows heavily from the first-pass routines for grammar application.

assume basic mechanisms of GB theory, though translation into the Minimalist Program and into non-transformational frameworks should be possible.

In (5) there is an antecedence dependency between the object *himself* and the subject *the king's son.* In the garden-path sentence (6), a similar dependency exhibits a grammatical conflict: the anaphor is masculine but the subject is misparsed as feminine (cf. Fodor & Inoue, 1994, example (5)).

(5) The king's son admires himself.

(6) The daughter of the king's son admires himself.

In the first-pass parsing of (6) the grammar alerts the parser to the ungrammaticality of attaching *himself* as the object. However, for lack of a better option, *Attach Anyway* adopts this attachment despite the improper anaphor binding dependency. The grammar then directs the parser towards the subject NP at the other end of the dependency. This is the site where repair must be made, as required by *Adjust* and the GDP. Thus in (6) the parser knows that *the daughter of the king's son* must somehow be transformed into a masculine NP.

This example is of special interest because, though the grammar can point the parser to the right neighborhood in the CPPM, and can tell it very precisely what the outcome of the revision must be, it cannot help the parser find a way of achieving that outcome. The repair trail leads, in accord with the GDP, from *himself* to the NP node over the subject, whose [–MASC] feature must be changed to [+MASC]. This in turn requires the N′ beneath it to change to [+MASC], again in accord with the GDP, following the lines of vertical relations within a syntactic projection. The next step is from the N′ to the N beneath it, the noun *daughter*. Its gender feature is changed from [–MASC] to [+MASC]. But when the parser checks the lexicon it finds that there is no item *daughter* [+MASC]. Therefore the repair path dead-ends here. In general, lexical specifications are non-negotiable; revision attempts are stopped short by contrary lexical facts. (Though see Konieczny *et al.*, 1994, and Fodor & Inoue, 1994, on cases where the parser may override the lexical input.) However, there is an alternative path to be explored in (6): the subject NP could become [+MASC] if *daughter* EITHER could become masculine, OR could abdicate its headship of the subject NP in favor of a masculine noun. Though the former is impossible, the latter is not. The offending noun *daughter* could be expelled from the structure. Assuming some housekeeping operations (see section 5.3), we may suppose that *daughter* would take *the* and *of* with it, leaving just *the king's son admires himself.* This would look like progress: the gender problem is thereby solved. But it creates a new problem: *the daughter of* must then be re-attached into the tree, and there is no obvious way to do so. The *Re-attach* operation, we assume, is exactly comparable to first-pass *Attach*. So if the parser tried to rejoin *the daughter of* and *the king's son*, the result would be [*the daughter of* [*the king's son*]], headed by *daughter* just as before. In some cases detaching and reattaching material brings about a useful reconfiguration of the tree (see Fodor & Inoue, 1994, fn. 17), but in this case it yields no gain.[10] An alternative way of achieving a masculine subject NP would be to promote either *king* or *son* to a position above *daughter*. In fact it is *son* that needs to be raised. But the GDP blocks this, because there is no grammar-defined route of dependencies leading to *son* from the anaphor (or from the current focus of *Adjust*). There is no selection relation between the two positions, or agreement relation, or case or theta assignment relation, or coreference requirement, etc. Because of this, the parser does not know to shift its focus to *son*; and the grammar offers no guidance to the parser on where else to look. Thus garden path recovery fails in (6), despite the very obvious feature mismatch that set the repair process going. The GDP predicts, correctly, that this is a very difficult garden path to recover from.

Example (6) contrasts with other cases of agreement feature mismatch in which revision is successful. Consider (7).

(7) The sick sheep cannot easily find food for themselves in the winter.

Here, a singular interpretation of *sheep* on the first pass prevents attachment of the plural anaphor. *Attach Anyway* will force the anaphor into the tree as the complement of *for* despite the number mismatch, since this at least violates no X-bar principles, case principles, etc. The grammar then directs attention to the subject position; the parser must find a plural NP there as antecedent for the anaphor. The parser runs down the N-projection path to the head noun *sheep*, changes its [–PLU] feature to [+PLU], consults the lexicon to see if there is such an item, discovers that there is, and so the revision goes through. Thus in this case there is no need for the parser to flounder around without GDP guidance looking for an alternative solution. Note that the ease with which (7) is

---

[10] Since *Re-attach* is governed by MA and LC, as *Attach* is (note that the GDP is not relevant), it might have been expected that *the daughter of* would reattach at the lowest site, to *the king* rather than *the king's son*, resulting in the correct analysis. However, we assume that the cliticization of the possessive *'s* onto *king* forms a surface word which cannot be split, so there is in fact no structural position between the node over *king* and that over *the king's son* that could host attachment of *the daughter of*.

reanalyzed demonstrates clearly that the leap from object to subject position is easy, and that it is the juggling of *daughter*, *king* and *son* within the subject NP that makes (6) hard. Evidently the distance across which the parser's attention must shift is not the primary determinant of difficulty. Thus the GDP is superior to a fixed distance restriction.

Though the comparison of (6) and (7) rules out a distance-based difficulty metric, it is not sufficient by itself to show that the GDP is the correct generalization. After all, (6) requires more extensive repairs than (7) does. Given just these examples, then, the generalization might be quite different, e.g., that the parser has the capacity to revise only one node or feature per garden path. We have no space to consider this possibility here, but in Fodor & Inoue (in press) we show that it is far from true. We present examples there which show that even extensive revisions requiring several tree changes and spanning considerable distances can be easy as long as they conform to the GDP.

4 The Thematic Overlay Effect

We now show that the GDP sheds light on the nature of stealing and its relation to the Thematic Overlay Effect. The Thematic Overlay Effect (TOE) is not a parsing principle but just a statement of the observation that "a thematic role once satisfied in a sentence will resist letting go of its syntactic realization" (Inoue & Fodor, 1995, p. 47). That is, once the parser has associated some input item(s) with a certain thematic role, it will resist any revision which re-assigns those words elsewhere without substituting others for them or eliminating the role entirely by overlaying a new argument structure over the old one. Why this should be so, we discuss below. In our earlier work we speculated that the parser may forget to erase the stolen argument from the initial representation of the sentence, resulting in confusion as one word string is illegitimately assigned two thematic roles;[11] but we will show later that this cannot be all that is going on.

[11] The reference to thematic roles would need to be reconsidered if TOE applies also to adjuncts. Whether or not it does has never been quite clear. An example such as *Because Ann wanted to study quietly in the kitchen was not a good place for her to sit* does not seem quite as difficult as examples like (8) and (9) below. If this is so, the proposals in section 5.3 offer an explanation: adjuncts are more labile because they are not required by other elements in the tree. But the revision of adjunct attachments deserves considerably more attention. On other differences between argument and adjunct processing, see Frazier & Clifton (1996).

Examples where TOE has been claimed to occur are shown in (8)-(11); (8) is from Frazier (1978), and (9) from Ferreira & Henderson (1991a); (10) and (11) are from Inoue & Fodor (1995).

(8) While Mary was mending the sock fell off her lap.

(9) While the boy scratched the big and hairy dog yawned loudly.

(10) John warned the children at the day care center were noisy.

(11) John promised the children at the day care center would be good.

We will concentrate on (8) and (9) here, and return to (10) and (11) in section 5.2. Examples (8) and (9) are Late Closure garden paths. In (9) the NP *the big and hairy dog* is initially attached as object of *scratched.* Then the disambiguating word *yawned* is encountered, and the impression is of a tug of war between *yawned*, which clearly needs the NP as its subject, and *scratched*, which does not want to let go of the NP as its object.[12] *Scratched* resists giving up the NP despite the fact that this verb can easily be parsed as intransitive in other contexts where it is not temporarily assigned an object. For instance, in (12) the transitive misanalysis is blocked by the adverb *yesterday*, and intransitive *scratched* is not effortful to process. (The adverb doesn't fully block a Heavy NP Shift analysis, but we doubt that the parser favors it.)

(12) While the boy scratched yesterday the big and hairy dog yawned loudly.

What has to be explained, then, is why this same verb *scratched* is unhappy about being converted from presumed transitive to intransitive during reanalysis in (9).

Many other kinds of argument structure revision are tolerated comfortably by the human parser. Thematic reanalyses as in (13)-(15) do not cause any noticeable difficulty. (See Carlson & Tanenhaus, 1988.)

(13) a. We brought the homeless children to the orphanage.
b. We brought the homeless children some candy.

---

[12] Stevenson (1993) has proposed a *competitive attachment* parsing model which exhibits a tug of war between the two verbs for essentially the same reason as TOE, i.e., if the first verb were to relinquish the NP it would have no object to satisfy its lexical selection feature. Like the original TOE, this account could be extended to account for (18) below, but apparently it mispredicts that the construction in (10) is as difficult to revise as that in (9).

(14) a. John loaded the truck with bricks.
b. John loaded the truck onto the ship.

(15) a. The old man pushed to the front of the crowd.
b. The old man pushed to the front of the crowd the little child clutching a fistful of flowers.

Clearly, the revision of meaning in general, or of thematic roles in particular, cannot be the major reason for the resistance to revision of examples like (8) and (9). One possibly significant differentiating factor is that the thematic shifts in (13)-(15) are within-clause, while in (8) and (9) the ambiguous NP shifts across clauses. We will return to this point below (section 5.1). Note, however, that not all shifts across a clause boundary are equally hard: there is a striking difference in difficulty between the stealing of the object to become the subject of another clause in (8) and (9), and the stealing of an object to become the subject of another clause in (16) and (17):

(16) The boy noticed the big and hairy dog limped badly.

(17) The host was expecting his best friends to refuse the invitation.

In these examples there is no undue persistence of the old argument structure. Even when the meaning encourages confidence in the first-pass simple NP object analysis, as in (17), the clausal complement analysis is easy to spot, and is stable once computed. By contrast, the misanalysis in examples like (8) and (9) is persistent. It varies in strength a little, but is generally quite robust. Ferreira & Henderson (1991a) have shown that it depends in part on the position of the head noun in the ambiguous NP: if the NP is head-final, revision is easier than if the head is several words prior to the disambiguation. We return to this interesting fact in section 5. Clifton (1993) and Pickering & Traxler (1994) have shown that revision of these constructions is faster if the ambiguously attached NP is semantically or pragmatically incompatible with the first verb. Also, the TOE is diminished in this construction if the first verb is an intransitive-preference verb (Ferreira & Henderson 1991b). The extreme case of this is a clause with a pure intransitive verb, as in the example *After the child sneezed the doctor prescribed a course of injections* from Mitchell (1987), where a spurious and fleeting transitive analysis is apparently computed. It is plausible to suppose that the parser gives in initially to the considerable pressures to attach the NP low on-line (see Phillips, 1995; Fodor & Inoue, in preparation a) but then sets about expelling the NP from object position if the NP violates the selection feature or the transitivity preference of the verb, or if it is implausible as object of the verb. This expulsion by the first verb (perhaps with energy and timing proportional to the degree of the violation) would reinforce the subsequent efforts of the matrix verb to steal the ambiguous NP from the first clause, and could thus make this stealing more successful than it otherwise would have been.

The contrast between examples like (9) and examples like (16) has attracted theoretical attention, and several explanations of it have been proposed besides TOE. Unlike TOE, most explanations focus on the fact that the stealing in (9) raises the NP in the tree structure, while the stealing in (16) lowers the NP. A long tradition in deterministic parsing inspired by the D(escription)-theoretic approach of Marcus *et al.* (1983) assumes that raising revisions are always costly, because they involve destruction of domination relations between nodes. The NP *the big and hairy dog* in (9) was dominated by the VP and IP nodes of the subordinate clause in the first-pass analysis but not in the revised analysis. By contrast, in (16) this NP was dominated by the VP, IP, and CP nodes of the main clause in the first-pass analysis, and still is in the revised analysis; it is also dominated now by the subordinate IP and CP, but addition of domination relations does not violate D-theoretic determinism. Gorrell (1995a, this volume) adopts a modified version of this approach, called Structural Determinism, in which both domination and precedence statements are indelible. Pritchett (1992) also prohibits raising a node, though for somewhat different reasons: his On Line Locality Constraint (OLLC) requires a revised node to be either governed or dominated by the position it occcupied in the first-pass analysis. Gibson's (1991) Recency Principle attributes the difficulty of examples like (9) to the fact that the matrix clause node was hypothesized earlier than the subordinate VP node, a fact that is partly correlated with the greater height of the matrix clause; the analysis with matrix attachment of the NP is therefore pruned from the set of analyses being computed in parallel, so that when the disambiguation requires it, it is unavailable.[13] Lewis (1993) ascribes responsibility not to the fact that the ambiguous NP must be raised, but to the fact that it is too distant structurally from the error signal to be acted on at all.[14]

---

[13] Gibson's (1991) model, like that of Pritchett (1992), is based largely on thematic rather than structural relations, but it cannot account for the difficulty of (9) exclusively in terms of theta assignment. In Gibson's semi-parallel system, alternative analyses are constructed at the choice point in the parse, not at the disambiguation point—in this case, at the point of NP attachment, not after receipt of the matrix verb. At that point, high attachment of the NP is not much less attractive thematically than low attachment is, so the high attachment analysis is not pruned. Hence the tree-sensitive Recency Principle is needed to eliminate it.

[14] The Semantic Cost Principle of Frazier & Clifton (this volume) entails that revisions which alter the meaning assigned to the sentence are costly. This is applicable to (9), but it does not in

(See Sturt & Crocker, this volume, for a classification of models that penalize certain types of repair operations.)

There are examples, however, which show very clearly that neither raising nor a locality violation is what inhibits revision in this construction. These examples provide dramatic support for the TOE generalization that loss of the lexical realization of an argument is at fault. Consider sentence (18), which is like Ferreira & Henderson's example (9) except that the ambiguously attached medial NP consists of two NPs coordinated.

(18) While the boy scratched the little cat and the big hairy dog yawned loudly.

The intuition here is very strong. The whole coordinate NP is initially construed as object of the first verb. Then stealing occurs. Unlike in (9), the steal goes through quite easily, but only the second NP conjunct is stolen. This results in an ungrammatical, or at least incomplete, sentence; the whole string has been analyzed as a *while*-clause with internal coordination, and the main clause is missing. This structure is shown in (19), which has roughly the same meaning as *While the boy scratched the little cat and while the big hairy dog yawned loudly, ...*; it would be acceptable only if the input contained another clause, as in (20). Sentence (20), since it has this preferred reanalysis, is not difficult to grasp despite its complexity.

(19) While [[the boy scratched the little cat] and [the big hairy dog yawned loudly]]...

(20) While [[the boy scratched the little cat] and [the big hairy dog yawned loudly]] Kim slept.

The first-pass analysis with parsing breakdown is shown in (21). The unattained target structure is (22).

---

general discriminate well between easy and difficult revisions. The cost is assumed to increase (though perhaps non-linearly) the longer the misinterpretation has persisted, and the role of an NP is assumed to be assigned only when its head is processed. Therefore the disambiguation in (9) occurs very soon after the semantic commitment is made, and the revision cost should be slight. Furthermore, the distance between semantic commitment and disambiguation is exactly comparable in (16), so the Semantic Cost Principle appears to mispredict that (9) and (16) are equally easy (or difficult) to repair. See also the discussion of the related proposal by Ferreira & Henderson (1991a) in section 5.1 below.

(21) [While the boy scratched [the little cat and the big hairy dog]] [yawned... !!!

(22) [While [the boy scratched]] [[the little cat and the big hairy dog] yawned loudly].

The parser goes from (21) to (19) and hangs up there without reaching (22). Clearly the secondary move to (22) from (19) is very difficult. (The reasons for this are not relevant to current concerns, but are quite straighforward.)[15] What matters for present purposes is that the change from (21) to (19) is *not* difficult. This has several important implications.

The ease with which the second NP of the coordinate structure is stolen by the new verb shows clearly that raising a constituent can be easy, as long as the circumstances are right. This is counter to the principles of determinism in all its variants, including D-theory and recent work in the same tradition such as Gorrell's Structural Determinism thesis. It also disqualifies Pritchett's OLLC, Gibson's Recency Principle and Lewis' locality principle since they too apply with equal force to *the big and hairy dog* in (9) and *the big hairy dog* in (18). But the facts are exactly as the TOE predicts. The contrast between (9) and (18) makes very clear what the parser does and does not like to do. It does not mind raising nodes; it does not mind altering the sentence structure, the sentence meaning, or the theta role assignments; but it does not like to deprive a predicate which has a theta role to assign, and which has successfully discharged that role onto a syntactic constituent, of the chance to discharge it onto *some* syntactic constituent, i.e., the parser does not like to demote a semantic argument role from overt (lexically realized) to implicit (unrealized).[16] In (18), the parser can avoid this by giving up only one conjunct, and retaining the other as object of the subordinate verb so that the verb can continue to discharge its theta role

---

[15] The necessary revision from (19) to (22) is like the difficult revision of (9) in that the *whole* NP object of the first verb must be stolen into the next clause, which will become the main clause. This leaves *scratched* intransitive. Furthermore, (19) (unlike (9)) has a null symptom, and null symptoms commonly fail to trigger reanalysis.

[16] An intriguing alternative is suggested by a recent proposal by Bader (this volume), who argues that revision is inhibited when the prosodic contour as well as the tree structure must be modified. As Bader notes, this could account for the contrast between the constructions that are exemplified here by (9) and (16). It might also explain the easy revision of (18) if there is a weaker prosodic liaison between the two conjoined NPs in (18) than there is between the verb and its object NP in either (9) or (18). (We thank Patrick Sturt for this suggestion.) The only other account of (9) that we know of which can accommodate the contrast with (18) is that of Ferreira & Henderson, discussed in section 5.1 below. Like ours, it attributes the difficulty of (9) to the need to change the argument structure feature of the first verb.

(though not to the same phrase as before). Then, as we see, the other NP conjunct is easy to entice upward.

This contrast between (9) and (18) strongly supports TOE as the right sort of description of the phenomenon. Related accounts are those of Stevenson (1993; see fn. 12), and Ferreira & Henderson (1991a; see section 5.1 below). However, (18) does not support our original explanation of TOE in terms of forgetting. We portrayed the squabble between the two verbs for possession of the NP as a problem of tidying up the sentence representation after stealing has taken place. It arises, we said, because the parser fails to erase the NP as argument of the first verb even while assigning it as argument of the second one; since the grammar knows this is improper, it resists, and confusion ensues. This is the linguistic counterpart of an 'impossible' visual figure in which one line contributes to two incompatible three-dimensional projections. (See also the example *I own the horse raced past the barn* in Gorrell, 1995a, p. 158.) However, if this were the correct explanation it should be so in (18) also. Failure to erase should create a tug-of-war over *the big hairy dog* in (18) just as much as in (9), and yet clearly there is no such effect; once the stealing of *the big hairy dog* is undertaken in (18), the NP snaps into place with no resistance from the lower clause.

The underlying idea can be preserved, however, if we make one small change: the spotlight should be not on tidying up the representation assigned to the sentence, but on tidying up the lexical selection feature of the first verb. Examples like (18) show that the CPPM (or the whole sentence representation, including its meaning) can undergo radical alteration quite painlessly (if it is adequately signalled). More particularly, the argument phrase assigned in the CPPM to *scratched* can be freely edited. But the lexical selection feature of the verb *scratch* cannot be freely edited. The verb was transitive before, and cannot easily be made intransitive now. Thus the contrast between (9) and (18) greatly narrows down the delineation of the TOE problem. The ease of revising structure (21) to structure (19) in the parsing of (18) rules out many conceivable explanations of the difficult revision in (9). It is not the case that all stealing is bad. It is not the case that all stealing upward or all raising is bad. It is not the case that meaning cannot be revised, even after the end of the clause or theta domain. The only thing that differentiates the difficult from the easy stealing is that the former requires a change in the selection properties of the first verb.[17]

---

[17] This may be too strong. As noted in fn. 16, the possibility that there is a prosodic difference between (9) and (18) that affects revisability should also be considered. We note also that there is a difference in the ultimate height of attachment of the incoming verb and the stolen NP, which could be relevant since the preference for lower clause attachment is strong. However, the parser

We must conclude that the difficulty is due to inaccessibility of an alternative argument structure feature for that verb.[18] *Secondarily*, this blocks alteration of the tree.

Note that there is one loophole in this lexical inaccessibility explanation of (9): it allows for recovery to be easy if it bypasses lexical revision. This could be why revision of (18) by splitting the conjoined structure is easy. In (18), unlike (9), the tree could be reconfigured (switching *and* from being a linker of NPs to being a linker of IPs) without changing a lexical feature. It may be argued that a coordinating conjunction like *and* does not take arguments regulated by a selection feature in the lexicon, as a verb does. It is a functional category whose distribution is regulated by a rule schema in Universal Grammar (comparable to the X-bar schemata). The UG schema for coordination stipulates that a conjunction word must be flanked by categories of the same type, but otherwise it permits all categories to be conjoined (subject to some language-specific parameterization, e.g., only phrasal categories in some languages). When the parser attaches *yawned* in (18) and steals the immediately preceding NP to be its subject, it is creating an IP to the right of *and*. If it can rely on the general UG schema to approve this IP-conjunction analysis, it does not need to access the lexicon to know that it is legitimate. The schema will approve it on condition that the parser find a left conjunct that is also IP. This is possible in (18), so the revision goes through. This account of the difference in revisability between (18) and (9) thus rests on the different linguistic status of conjunction words and verbs. We propose an alternative explanation in section 5.3, but before

---

does not seem to be in doubt that *yawned* in (9) is the matrix verb; thus it appears that the high verb attachment is not the major problem.

[18] The original statement of TOE claimed that difficulty arises only if the theta role assigned to the NP by the first verb persists when the NP itself is stolen away, i.e., if it becomes an implicit argument. But the lexical inaccessibility explanation proposed here for (9) predicts difficulty if *any* change in the verb's argument selection feature is needed. We have been unable to find convincing test cases in which an argument is *added* during a non-GDP-guided revision. But even for stealing, the two accounts make slightly different predictions. The lexical inaccessibility explanation should apply not only to (9) but also to examples like (i)-(iii), in which the intransitive form of the first verb has only one thematic role, overtly realized by the subject NP.

(i) Just as my mother looked up the flight number appeared on the departures board.
(ii) As the water in the pot heated up the potatoes began to sizzle in the frying pan.
(iii) When the photographer moved his camera crashed against the lamppost.

It is not clear to us that these examples are quite as difficult as (9). Pending an experimental test of properly matched examples it would be premature to offer an explanation. However, we note that (9), unlike (i)-(iii), is *also* subject to the 'mild TOE' phenomenon that we discuss below (section 5.2). Thus a slight advantage of these examples over (9) would be explicable.

presenting it we need to establish a more articulated theory of stealing. We do this in the next section.

To summarize: A closer look at TOE has led to a remarkable discovery which overturns most previous thinking about garden path recovery. Despite prior claims to the contrary, it appears that altering the (syntactic and/or semantic) structure that the parser has computed for a sentence carries very little psychological cost. Where major costs are observed, they must be due instead to inability to diagnose the problem or, as we now see, to some specific resistance to carrying out the cure. The lexical resistance that we have observed is actually misplaced—the parser is blind to lexical alternatives, and so it acts as if the current analysis were obligatory even when it is not. The essentially cost-free status of all types of repairs, as long as they are readily diagnosable, was a central claim of the diagnosis model of Fodor & Inoue (1994), but this discovery of lexical inflexibility is something of a surprise. The diagnosis model freely permits re-access of lexical entries, though it requires that, like all other adjustments, lexical re-access must be specifically prompted by a prior step in the diagnostic process. The parser takes actions as needed; it does not flail around at random trying out changes opportunistically. But even so, accessing the lexicon in (9) is an action needed, so why does it not happen? In the next section we address this interesting puzzle about when re-entry to the lexicon can occur and when it cannot.[19] The parser can find the intransitive specification for a verb like *scratched* in first-pass parsing. It can find alternative lexical specifications for verbs in other temporarily ambiguous contexts, like (13)-(15), in revision mode. Yet it cannot find the alternative lexical specification for *scratched* in revision mode in (9).

5 Capture and theft

Though lexical resistance can explain why the stealing of one conjunct in (18) is easier than the stealing of the whole NP, we actually lack an explanation of why any stealing is possible at all in this construction. At first sight, (18) appears to be a clear counterexample to the GDP. There is no grammatical relation between the stealer (the verb of the second clause) and the material stolen (part

[19] For expository simplicity here we have adopted the assumption that initial lexical access retrieves only one argument structure for a verb, and revision is blocked by inability to reaccess the lexicon. As discussed below (section 5.1), an alternative is to assume there is parallel lexical access of all the argument structures of a verb, and revision is blocked if the one that is needed has faded before the garden path is recognized. The explanation we propose goes through on either basis.

of the object NP of the first clause). There is also no relation between the subject position to which the stolen material must move, and the position of the NP that is to be stolen. Thus the GDP apparently prohibits stealing of the object NP or any part of it in both (9) and (18). Yet it is clear that stealing does occur in (18), and at least an *attempt* at stealing is made in (9)—this is the tug on one side of the tug of war between the two verbs. This is particularly clear by comparison with an example where there is no sense of any stealing being initiated at all, such as (23). In (23) the top clause ought to steal *in the library* from the lower clause, but it does not even try; see Fodor & Inoue (1994) for discussion.

(23) Susan put the book that she had been reading all afternoon in the library.

The facts thus seem to be insisting that in both (9) and (18) the parser *tries* to steal—in spite of the GDP—but it fails to make off with the booty when there is lexical resistance from the subordinate verb, as in (9). Why does the verb resist change? So far we have concluded that it must be because the parser cannot locate the lexical feature for *scratch* which says that it can be intransitive. And though there are alternatives, we have assumed that this is because the parser cannot make contact with the lexicon in the course of this repair (though it evidently can in the case of (13)-(17) and other examples). But *why* can the parser not re-access the lexicon while revising (9)? The fact that the stealing in (9) violates the GDP provides an explanation.

Because there is no grammatical dependency along which the parser can travel from the matrix to the lower clause, the parser is forbidden by the GDP to steal the object NP node or make any other *structural* change in the lower clause. But it could try stealing at a different level where access to structural facts is not at issue. That is, it could grab some nearby words in the word string to fill up the hole in the matrix clause where the subject ought to be. This is to steal linearly and very superficially from the word string, rather than structurally and legitimately from the tree.

As a parse proceeds, the words of the input string are assigned category labels and attached as the leaves of the tree. These terminal elements of the CPPM are what we assume superficial non-GDP repairs operate over, when the parser is denied access to the significant grammatical relations between nonterminal nodes. Note that though the stealing is superficial it is initiated by a structural fact. In (9) the finite verb needs a (nominative) NP as its subject. But if this structural need cannot be satisfied by *Adjust* under control of the GDP, it can be converted into a word string search. The grammar specifies that an NP has an obligatory noun head (at least normally; the noun might be phonologically empty, or the NP could be a pronoun). So the parser could hunt for a noun in the preceding terminal string. If it finds one, it will make off with it together with all the words that follow it. It may also need to drag along some preceding words (e.g., a determiner) to make a complete NP in the new position. (See discussion in section 5.3.)

This stealing of terminal elements is what we call *theft*. It contrasts with *capture*, which is the stealing of a structural node in the tree. Theft of a string of words (even if they add up to an NP) does not address the NP node, and so it does not set in motion the train of subsequent repair operations that would normally result when an NP node is removed. This differs from the capture of an NP node, as in (16) or (17). Because this is a tree structure revision, *Adjust* does tidy up after it; it makes all necessary further repairs (if it can) until the CPPM is fully grammatical again. The GDP directs *Adjust* toward positions grammatically related to the captured NP. In (16) one of these positions is the verb's argument structure feature. There is a dependency between this feature and the arguments actually present in the VP; if they don't match up, the sentence is ungrammatical. So when capture of the NP occurs in (16), the GDP prompts the parser to change the verb's argument structure feature. The lexicon is checked to see whether this is acceptable, and if it is, the revision is successful.

The GDP does not predict that the human parser engages in word theft. Indeed, the occurrence of theft indicates that the GDP is not an absolute law, but is more like a recommendation for orderly and successful revision. The repair system can break away from the grammar-guided *Adjust* mechanism (though we assume only if it has been tried and failed); but if it does, its actions are less well-motivated linguistically, and success is chancy. The assumption that *Adjust* normally respects the GDP predicts that there will be cases where structural adjustments are needed but cannot be made, thus creating a situation in which the parser is tempted to resort to word-level theft. Since word theft is not an instance of *Adjust*, it is not followed up by systematic further applications of *Adjust*. Among other things, it is not followed up by a return to the lexicon to ratify needed changes in selection features. This predicts exactly the three-way split between (9), (16), and (18) that we have observed. The CPPM resists tree alteration just in case it implicates lexical property alteration, in cases which do not conform to the GDP; that is, in cases like (9).

All that remains to account for is which cases of stealing are node capture and which are word theft. Why can *limped* capture *the big and hairy dog* in (16) while *yawned* can only commit theft in (9)? The examples are repeated here for comparison.

(16) The boy noticed the big and hairy dog limped badly. CAPTURE

(9) While the boy scratched the big and hairy dog yawned loudly. THEFT

The answer has to do with where the verb is placed in the CPPM by *Attach Anyway*, which is determined by the interplay of preference principles and degrees of ungrammaticality mentioned in section 2. Without entering into a full discussion here, we sketch what seems reasonable for these two constructions. In the NP-versus-clause garden path in (16), the CPPM contains no attachment site for the finite verb *limped* when it is encountered: there is no finite VP awaiting its verb. The parser must create a VP somewhere. It could try positing a higher VP, with the current clause as its subject; it could try a medium-height attachment in a VP conjoined to the *noticed*-VP; or it could try a low attachment in a clause subordinate to the current one, a complement or relative. Low attachment is the usual preference. In any case, if the higher sites were attempted the revision would subsequently fail. The only thing that will succeed in (16) is low attachment into a complement clause, so let us track it through. The finite verb *limped* projects a subject [SPEC,IP] position to its left which it needs to fill. It can achieve this by tucking in next to *the big and hairy dog* in the CPPM; the projected subject NP can unify with this NP in the CPPM, thereby importing the IP (and CP) projections also. Two things then need to be checked: that the preceding verb *noticed* can accept a complement clause and give up its object NP; and that *the big and hairy dog* can change its feature values appropriately now that it is governed by *limped*. Its case feature must change from ACC to NOM, and its agreement features would need checking also, though in this example they happen to be neutralized on the verb. In (16) all outcomes are positive so no further adjustments are required; the repair is satisfactory.

The stealing of the NP in (16) satisfies the GDP because the stealer (the incoming verb *limped*) was not previously in the tree; and when it attaches it does so right at the site of the NP it steals, and enters into a subject-predicate relation with it. So there is no question as to whether its position in the CPPM is appropriately related to the NP it needs to steal; the process of attachment makes it so. This is the classic case of capture: the current input item *i*, in process of being attached into the CPPM, steals a node X by attaching itself to X as its sister, beneath X's mother, with secondary adjustments as necessary (addition of dominating nodes, revision of features such as case, agreement and selection features). Now compare the stealing in (9). Here the incoming verb *yawned* attaches far from the NP it needs to steal. It cannot snuggle in right next to the NP. (It may try to, since this is a desirably low attachment site, but it will be rejected when the lexicon is checked, because *scratch* does not take a clausal complement.) So *yawned* cannot capture *the big and hairy dog* on-line. The only place for *yawned* to attach is in the anticipated structure of the matrix clause. This attachment site is less preferred because it is less low, and has the additional drawback that the subject projected by the verb is missing; there will be a dangling NP node that lacks lexical content. But this just means that the verb must steal some lexical content for it. Note, however, that the verb *yawned* is now attached some distance away in the tree from the NP it needs to steal, so it has to reach across the tree from one position to another. Reaching across to the NP in the subordinate clause is blocked by the GDP, however. The two positions are not grammatically related, hence no legal stealing can occur. The parser can only resort to superficial theft of words (which, as we have seen, does not go well in this example). To summarize: The essential fact that forces theft rather than capture in examples like (9) is that there are two separate stages: attachment somewhere, then reaching out to steal the NP from somewhere else. Unlike capture in (16), the attachment stage drags the parser's attention away from the NP to be stolen. If the parser can't get back to the NP with the blessing of the GDP, word-level theft is its only option.

It is unparsimonious to postulate two kinds of stealing. But the contrast between theft and capture that we have outlined explains several other noteworthy facts. It predicts the effect of head position discovered by Ferreira & Henderson (1991a). It explains what has long seemed a strange and suspicious variability in the strength of TOE across different construction types. And it offers an interesting explanation of why a coordinate NP may be stolen without resistance.

5.1 The Head-Position Effect

Ferreira & Henderson (1991a) presented sentences to subjects word by word centered on a screen at a rate of 250 msec a word, and subjects gave timed grammaticality judgments. Acceptance of a garden-path sentence as grammatical was taken as evidence that the perceiver had succeeded in revising the incorrect first-pass structure. The mean "grammatical" judgments for four types of sentence are given below with typical examples. It should be noted that these results are from a single series of experiments with similar procedures, but not from the same experiment; therefore comparison of the outcomes can only be approximate. Ferreira & Henderson's paper should be consulted for more precise information.

(24) While the boy scratched [the *dog*] yawned loudly. ("grammatical": 61%)

(25) While the boy scratched [the big and hairy *dog*] yawned loudly. (51%)

(26) While the boy scratched [the *dog* that Sally hates] yawned loudly. (24%)

(27) While the boy scratched [the *dog* that is hairy] yawned loudly. (29%)

The recovery rate is quite low even at best, but we will be concerned here primarily with differences across the sentence types. In (24) the ambiguous NP is short and the recovery rate is the highest. In (25) the ambiguous NP is long but recovery is almost equally easy. In (26) and (27) the NP is long and reanalysis is more difficult than in (25), even though (27) roughly matches (25) in meaning. Ferreira & Henderson propose the generalization that "head location affects ease of reanalysis... the greater the distance from the head of the misanalyzed phrase to the syntactically disambiguating word, the harder the process of reanalysis becomes" (1991a, pp. 741-742). (We have italicized the head noun of the misanalyzed NP in (24)-(27).)

This effect of head position is an important finding, not anticipated in investigations based on intuitive judgments of processing difficulty. It is explicable given the GDP prediction that only theft can supply the missing subject in this construction. The parser is focused on the second verb and is seeking a noun in the terminal string preceding it. When the relevant noun immediately precedes the verb it should be easier to spot than when it is further back. For capture operations the position of the noun within the NP should not matter, since in terms of tree structure the NP node immediately precedes the verb in all cases. Thus it is predicted that comparable manipulations of head position for a garden path cured by capture, such as (16), would have little or no effect on revisability. But theft must check backward through all the intervening terminals between the verb *yawned* and the noun *dog*, so the success of theft should decline as the distance in words increases, as Ferreira & Henderson discovered.[20]

[20] Though less reliable than capture, it seems we must admit that theft does often succeed (up to 60% of the time under ideal circumstances, if the acceptance rates in Ferreira & Henderson's study reflect accurate reanalyses; see discussion below). Success may be due to assistance from

The head position effect might be accounted for in a number of other ways (e.g., head-driven parsing as defined by Pritchett, 1991), but we will not review them here since most of them fail to account for the ease of stealing the second conjunct in (18). The only exception, besides the superficial theft explanation, is Ferreira & Henderson's own proposal. They suggested that the possible argument structures for a verb are accessed in parallel though only one is adopted, and that unadopted ones start to decay once theta roles have been assigned. Assuming that a theta role is assigned to a phrase only when its head is processed, the difficulty of revising the attachment of a phrase will begin to increase once its head and its theta-assigner have both been processed, though only for revisions that entail change in the argument structure feature of the verb. In (26) and (27) the noun is followed by several other words before the disambiguator, so the intransitive argument structure has time for significant decay and there is a high probability that it will have vanished entirely by the time it is needed. In (24) and (25) the NP is head-final so the intransitive argument structure has little time to decay before the disambiguating verb is encountered. Note that the initial decay rate must be assumed to be quite steep since the acceptance rate even in these cases of immediate disambiguation is only 50-60%; this is the basic TOE phenomenon, which an early head position simply exacerbates.

Like the GDP/theft explanation of the TOE, and unlike all others in the literature, this decay proposal implicates inaccessibility of the correct lexical argument structure feature for the verb rather than the cost of making alterations in the syntactic/semantic representation of the sentence. It is therefore fully compatible with our observation that raising an NP is easy if the verb is not thereby entirely deprived of an object. However, the decay explanation (unlike the GDP explanation) apparently predicts that examples like (13)-(17) should be as difficult as (9) if matched for distance between the head noun of the mis-assigned NP and the error signal. We believe this is incorrect. Though there are no experimental data bearing directly on this predicted comparison, intuitive judgments strongly suggest that these other constructions are much less resistant to revision than (9) is. If this proves to be so, the decay model is incorrect as it stands. It would need to invoke additional factors that could either exempt (13)-(17) or else magnify the effect for (9).

---

expulsion (see section 4), or to lucky word theft followed by a confirmatory reparse. These are compatible with the strong claim that word theft by itself never results in a stable reanalysis involving lexical revision. We think this may be correct, but at present we have no grounds for excluding the possibility that nodes which exclusively dominate thieved words are pied piped along with them, provoking the checking of selection features as in legitimate node stealing, so that if by good luck the right NP node is pied piped, the theft will be approved.

Ferreira & Henderson (this volume) have developed a different explanation of this set of facts, in order to accommodate some new experimental findings; but it is of interest nonetheless to consider whether a decay model could plausibly account for the presumed contrast between (13)-(17), and (9). One possible assumption would be that the decay of unadopted argument structure features accelerates sharply when the clause (the argument structure domain) is closed off. We don't know whether this is so, but it is plausible: the parser would not normally have any use for such features once there is no further possibility of finding arguments for the predicate. In (13)-(17) the revision occurs while the parser is processing one of the arguments of the relevant verb. That is, the garden-path symptom occurs prior to any word not in one of the verb's arguments, or to any other signal that the verb's argument domain is closed; and the symptom word itself is such that it keeps that argument domain open. In (16), for example, the symptom *limped* is such that it must attach within the clausal complement of *noticed.* But in (9) the symptom *yawned* is not part of any argument of the first verb; it can only be the matrix verb. So as *yawned* attaches, it closes off the domain of *scratched*, triggering a sharp drop in accessibility of alternative argument structures for *scratched.* Some such discontinuity in the decay rate would explain why, in this particular construction, recovery is difficult even with immediate disambiguation, as Ferreira & Henderson's data show. (The difference in argument domain closure between (16) and (9) is not unrelated to the fact that (16) has the clause order main-subordinate, while (9) has subordinate-main order: a main clause can contain a subordinate clause, but not vice versa. This is the remnant of truth, perhaps, in explanations that point to raising as the source of the problem in (9).)

With some such modification, the decay theory could handle all the examples under discussion. On present evidence we cannot tell whether it or the GDP account of the TOE is correct (though the decay theory makes what we believe to be overly strong predictions for left-branching languages such as Japanese). Though alike in pinning the blame on loss of lexical flexibility, the two accounts differ in other respects.[21] For example, revision by theft predicts that when the

---

[21] As presented here the two accounts differ with respect to whether lexical access puts all of a verb's selection features into the CPPM, or only one. But this difference may be unimportant. The account of (9) in terms of theft that we have proposed is compatible with either serial or parallel access of lexical features. Even if the intransitive specification of *scratch* were present in the tree in (9) when the disambiguation occurred, the parser would be unable to refer to it for much the same reason as given above: theft of terminal items does not target the NP node, so the GDP would not direct attention to the verb's selection feature (with which the NP stands in a dependency), so the parser would fail to recognize the possibility of switching to a different feature.

head noun is not final in the NP, the parser may be very sensitive to the presence of other superficially appealing items closer to the thieving verb, as in *While the boy scratched the puppies of the big hairy dog yawned loudly.* An incomplete revision might occur in such a case, giving the perceiver the impression of having recovered from the garden path but not in fact achieving the correct analysis.[22] This and other differentiating predictions of the two explanations need to be tested.

5.2 Two Strengths of TOE

The TOE phenomenon has always shown a puzzling variability in its strength. In (8) and (9) the verb strongly resists giving up its object, but in other examples such as (10) and (11), repeated here, the resistance is slight.

(10) John warned the children at the day care center were noisy.

(11) John promised the children at the day care center would be good.

Both types of construction involve loss of the lexical realization of a thematic role. Why should they differ as they do in recoverability? Let us consider (10).[23] The garden path followed by revision is noticeable here but not

---

[22] Ferreira & Henderson (this volume) found no significant effect of a 'decoy' noun close to the verb in sentences such as *When the boy scratched the dog that hates Sally yawned loudly* (34% grammatical judgments) as compared with *When the boy scratched the dog that seems furry yawned loudly* (38% grammatical judgments). This may mean that the theft account is wrong, or it could be that subjects sometimes thought they had succeeded in grasping the sentence structure (and so reported that it was grammatical) when in fact they had not. To check whether the judgements that subjects give are sometimes over-optimistic, it will be important to find out whether ungrammatical sentences such as **While the boy chased the dog barked loudly* are also sometimes 'successfully' reanalyzed. Also, the discussion in section 5.3 below implies that it could matter whether there is a natural 'break point' in the middle of the NP. For instance, with *the puppies of the big hairy dog* there may be a tendency to keep *the puppies* as object of the first clause, and steal *the big hairy dog* as subject of the main clause (but the *of* is an embarrassment that would have to be ignored).

[23] Some perceivers find (10) difficult to parse because *warn* is not fully grammatical when it has neither an indirect object nor a complementizer. But the points of concern to our discussion can be made equally well with (11), which is generally regarded as acceptable. The construction with *warn* was first noted by Pritchett (1987) who judged it much harder to revise than examples with verbs of the *know* class, such as (28) below. We believe that the difficulty of Pritchett's early *warn* examples was due to their marginal grammaticality, and also to the fact that their revision involved other complications, as in (i) where there is uncertainty between an analysis like (10) and an analysis in which the NP *her mother* has been broken into two NPs with recategorization of *her* from determiner to pronoun.

(i) Mary warned her mother hated her.

When these complications are avoided, as in (11), the difference in revisability between *warn/promise* and *know* constructions seems much reduced. However, Pritchett (1992) does not

devastating; repair is achievable. On a scale of difficulty running from (16) (easy) to (9) (difficult), (10) seems to be closer to the easy end. For more precision let us compare (10) with (28), which is the same construction as (16) but matched to (10) in lexical content.

(28) John knew the children at the day care center were noisy.

The verdict, though only informal and perhaps not universal, is that (10) is not much harder than (28), with the important consequence that (10) is significantly easier than (9). Thus we seem to observe the TOE phenomenon in two strengths: mild in (10) and severe in (9). We argue now that these are in fact two different phenomena, though they have important aspects in common.

An explanation for why (10) does not exhibit the TOE at full strength follows from the GDP and the distinction between capture and theft. Though (10) resembles (9) in that its first verb loses an overt argument, it resembles (28) in *how* it loses it. The stealing in (9) is theft, as discussed above, but in (10) it is capture, as it is in (28). We assume that the post-verbal NP in (10) first attaches as object (Goal) of *warned*. The disambiguating verb *were* is finite and plural, and ideally would attach to the right of a plural NP. It finds no pre-existing verb attachment site in the CPPM. Its least undesirable attachment is as sister to the preceding NP, with introduction of clausal nodes above them, i.e., it captures the object NP. Directed by the GDP, the parser adjusts the lexical properties of the matrix verb (*warn*) to suit this new clausal context, and checks the lexicon to make sure that this is acceptable, which it is. Thus *warn* can be flexible about the loss of syntactic realization of its Goal NP, since the GDP reminds the parser to fit the verb's selection feature to it. However, the loss of the NP does meet with some slight resistance in (10); the revision goes through, but it is not quite as painless as in (28). It seems that this mild TOE in (10) must be explained as in past proposals, such as Pritchett's (1987) Theta Reanalysis Constraint, or the original 'forgetting to erase' version of the TOE. In some way or other, the problem is that the bearer of the Goal role was specified in the first-pass analysis of (10) and after the repair it no longer is. Note that it is the *losing* of information that is discomforting; (10) is worse than (29) where the Goal is unidentified from the start.

---

agree with this judgement. He maintains (pp. 82-ff.) that sentences like *Rex warned the ugly little man feared him* and *The teacher promised the students could leave* are (a) well-formed and (b) "unprocessable". Since it is important to our discussion to distinguish between mild and severe TOE garden paths, we must set aside Pritchett's judgments, which do not seem to be representative.

(29) John warned there were some noisy children at the day care center.

Exactly why this loss bothers the parser is not crucial to our general theory of tree repair, but it is still an interesting question. We suggest, tentatively, a slight variation on our 1995 proposal, an account which implicates confusion though not forgetting. In (10) the parser thought it knew the identity of the Goal, but the revision leaves it uncertain. It is not even clear whether the original incumbent of the role can be retained once the role becomes implicit rather than explicit. The identity of the Goal *can* be changed, but must it be? The answer varies from case to case: it is not a matter of syntax but of semantics and plausibility. Who did John warn that the children were naughty? Probably not the children. Also not himself, so presumably some third party not mentioned. Who did John promise that the children would be good? Probably not the children. But if John promised the children would have cake for lunch, who did he promise? Probably the children. The comprehension system must evaluate the candidates in each case. This is so whether the issue arises on the first pass or in revision. But in revision the usual processes of evaluation could well be disrupted by the initial illusion of having had precise information based on syntax rather than pragmatic guesswork. This is not far from the original idea behind the TOE, but now it is clear how slight the effect is. In Inoue & Fodor (1995) we observed the same for Japanese; after extraneous complications in Pritchett's examples were cleared away, TOE was detectable but weak. In general, then: loss of identification of the bearer of a thematic role in the course of an otherwise successful revision has a detectable but small effect on processing difficulty. This is distinct from the severe TOE in constructions like (9), where with a high probability (see Ferreira & Henderson's data above) the repair process fails to retrieve the lexical material it wrongly assigned to a thematic role. Something else is needed to explain that, and we have given evidence above that it is due to perseveration of a lexical feature.

To summarize: The examples we have compared permit a separation of two aspects of the problem that we dubbed the TOE. One is a mild disappointment or confusion at losing a clear identification of the bearer of a thematic role, after that role has been brought into focus by the first-pass analysis. This is represented by the comparison of (10) with (28) and (29). The other is a persistent rebellion against giving up an overt argument due to the mistaken belief that it is obligatory, where the mistake is due to failure to access lexical alternatives. This is represented by the comparison of (8) or (9) with all other examples discussed here. The two phenomena are not totally dissimilar. In both cases "a thematic role once satisfied resists letting go of its syntactic realization" during a garden-path revision. The difference that we overlooked in our previous work is between resistance that prevents any argument structure substitution at all, and distress after substitution has occurred if the new argument structure leaves a thematic role unclothed without eliminating it entirely. With the distinction between capture and theft, we are now able to explain when and why each of these occurs. The severe TOE occurs in cases of theft, where failure to reaccess the lexicon blocks adoption of any new argument structure. The needed revision appears to the parser to be syntactically ill-formed. The mild TOE occurs in cases of capture, where revision of argument structure is possible.[24] If the revision overlays the role in question (e.g., (28)) it is easy; if it does not there is a mild TOE experience as the parser tries to sort out what effect that has on the sentence meaning.

5.3 Conjunction and Raising

The contrast between (9) and (18) shows that stealing an NP out of a conjunction is quite different from stealing an NP away from a verb. We repeat the examples here for convenience.

(9) While the boy scratched the big and hairy dog yawned loudly.

(18) While the boy scratched the little cat and the big hairy dog yawned loudly.

It is a familiar fact that revision of an NP conjunction into a clausal conjunction, as in (30) and (31), is not particularly difficult. The garden path is perceptible on-line but it does not persist.

(30) John was talking to Bill and the twins were talking to Jane.

(31) The boy scratched the little cat and the big hairy dog yawned loudly.

This revision involves raising the NP that follows *and*, with the elimination of several domination relations. The NP moves out of the argument domain of the first verb. The conjunction word tags along with the NP, and is raised from inside the first VP up to the root level. These are the kinds of revisions that on most theories would predict a severe garden path, but that is not what is observed. In examples like this we have long had evidence that not all raising

[24] Note that *both* phenomena apply to a 'severe TOE' construction like (9). That is, if the parser does spot the correct analysis of such a construction (see fn. 20), the successful revision would then create a mild TOE, adding to perceived difficulty.

repairs are difficult. (This is not to say there is no coordination garden path at all; see Hoeks *et al.*, 1997.) The only novelty of (18) is that a revisable coordinate structure is put into a context where raising material out of the first clause is notoriously troublesome; but raising a conjunct is found to be easy nevertheless. So far our interest in this has been in what it shows about the Late Closure garden path construction in (8) and (9). But we turn attention now to coordination structures and ask why they are more easily revisable than the internal structure of VP. We suggested in section 4 that this is because *and* needs no lexical subcategorization for the complements it takes; it can take conjuncts of any category as long as they come in matched pairs. However, now that we have distinguished between theft and capture, a more interesting explanation is possible.

Consider (31) at the point at which the verb *yawned* is encountered. It is finite and needs a subject. In principle the parser might build a second clause, attach *yawned* in it, and then steal a preceding NP as its subject. But in general the parser strongly favors low attachment sites, for *Attach Anyway* as well as *Attach*, as noted earlier. So the preference would be for *yawned* to attach low and capture a preceding NP there. It could capture the whole coordinate NP or just *the large hairy dog*. The latter would be favored by the preference for low attachment. (If the higher attachment were tried it would require a three-way coordination of clauses for lack of a conjunction word between the first two; but in any case it would not thrive since it would run into TOE trouble as in (9).) The IP resulting from capture of *the large hairy dog* by *yawned* becomes the complement of *and*, taking the place of the NP complement.[25] Let us assume, as is standard, that coordination is not symmetric but has the structure shown in (32a). (We use XP^{and} in (32) as an arbitrary label to distinguish an XP marked with a coordinating conjunction from a 'plain' XP.)

(32)
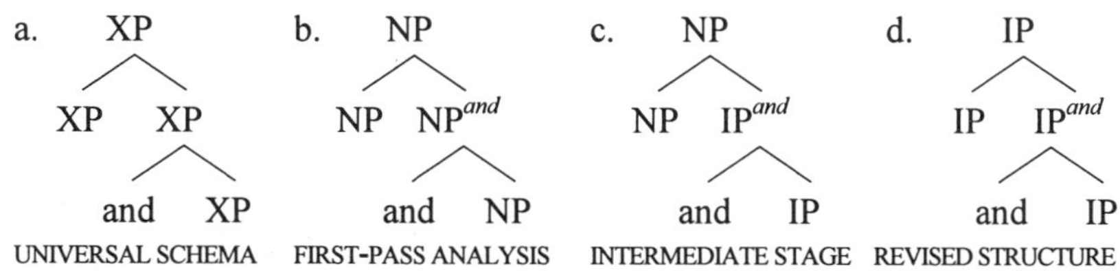

[25] There is a terminological problem here hiding a theoretical problem. To call the conjoined element the complement of *and* is to imply that *and* is the head of the coordinate structure. If that is so, the standard theory of phrasal projection needs to be refined, since with NP complements the structure has the properties of an NP, while with IP complements it has the properties of an IP, and so forth; see Kayne (1994). Whichever way this linguistic issue is eventually settled, the substance of our present claims should not be significantly affected.

Once IP is the sister of *and*, the NP^{and} node dominating them must be relabelled as IP^{and}, as shown in (32c). But this IP^{and} is incompatible with its NP sister and mother. The IP^{and} needs an IP left sister. The parser may try to convert the NP on the left into an IP somehow, but this will fail. It can't make *the little cat* into an IP; and there is no way to steal other constituents to combine with *the little cat* to make up an IP. So the IP^{and} does not fit with its context. The only thing the parser can do to continue this line of revision is to detach the IP^{and}. By good fortune this turns out to be just the right thing to do. The IP^{and} once free can find an IP on its left to join with. To do so it must rise up to the top of the CPPM, but evidently this is not costly. The revision is thus successful. Note that it is predicted to be easy whether *and* has a lexical entry of the standard kind or not.[26] If it does not have a standard lexical entry, the explanation goes through as in section 4; if it does, the fact that this repair started with a capture operation means that the lexical feature associated with *and* was changed accordingly, it was then checked against the lexical entry, and the revision was approved, subject to appropriate adjustment of the left conjunct. Thus the difference between stealing an NP from *and*, which is easy, and stealing an NP from a verb, which is difficult (at least in a structural context as in (9)), can be explained in terms of the difference between capture and theft.[27]

It is of interest that though revision of NP coordination to IP coordination is not painful, it is not always the preferred revision. Gorrell (1995b) has observed that when a coordinate NP is the ambiguous NP in an NP-versus-clausal-complement garden path, as in (33), the preferred revision retains the NP

---

[26] On balance, we are inclined to suppose that *and* and other coordinating conjunctions do have lexical entries containing selection features. Though part of the instantiation of a UG schema, they differ from each other in ways that the grammar must specify (e.g., *either/or* can take NP or IP complements while *neither/nor* can take NPs but not IPs).

[27] To forestall confusion we note that NP capture followed by expulsion and high re-attachment of the resulting clause is *not* possible in (9). We assume capture is tried in (9), and the selection feature of *scratched* in the CPPM is accordingly changed from selection of NP to selection of IP (or CP). But the lexicon then rejects this combination of *scratched* with an IP selection feature, so this line of revision can go no further. This is unlike the case of conjunction, where the feature change is approved by the lexicon and the repair process can proceed. The revision of (9) could continue along some other lines, but in fact there is no other legitimate action to be taken. The verb cannot expel the IP because there is no conflict between them; the conflict is internal to the verb. Reversion to the transitive verb feature would violate HTOTR (see fn. 8). The verb's selection feature cannot be erased to relieve the tension, because even an intransitive verb must have a selection feature. The lexicon cannot volunteer the information that *scratched* has an intransitive form, because each step in the repair process must have a specific trigger. The verb cannot be expelled along with the IP, as *and* can, because it is not now a licit lexical item; and in any case the first clause would not survive without it.

coordination structure and shifts it bodily from matrix object to complement subject position. Gorrell claims that (33) is preferentially reanalysed as in (34a) rather than (34b).

(33) John knew the men and the women were strangers.

(34) a. John knew [[the men and the women] were strangers]
b. [John knew the men] and [the women were strangers]

We agree with Gorrell's intuition about the preference here. It shows that the object-to-subject revision is less costly in this construction than breaking up the coordinate NP would be. This provides the valuable information that it is not the case that a coordinate NP always crumbles in the face of any parsing conflict. It splits easily in examples like (30) and (31), and it splits in (18) where the alternative revision meets lexical resistance, but it holds out against the alternative revision in (33). We may conclude that splitting a conjunction is harder than easy revisions but easier than hard ones. Though this is true as far as it goes, we can be more specific.

In Gorrell's example (33), a reanalysis like that sketched above for (31) is in competition with one in which the second verb captures the whole coordinate NP. The choice is between the verb *were* capturing the lower NP node over just the right conjunct, and its capturing the higher NP node over the conjoined structure. If it captures the higher NP, the lexical feature of *knew* must be adjusted (as in (16) and (28) above). If the lower NP is captured, the reanalysis continues with adjustment of the structure around *and*, as described for (31). To account for the observed preference for the analysis (34a) we must assume that the usual preference for low attachment is offset by the extra work involved in relabelling and reattaching the IP^{and} for (34b). This is in accord with the Minimal Revision principle (another instance of Minimal Everything; see Frazier, 1990; Frazier & Clifton, this volume; Inoue, 1991). Since all minimizing preferences are implicitly comparative, this carries the interesting suggestion, which we cannot pursue further here, that alternative repairs are undertaken in parallel, in a race, so that the first one that succeeds in resolving the problem wins. Though a lower attachment site is preferable to a higher one in general, attachment to the higher NP node gives a faster solution in (33) and so that is what the parser does.

In (18) the same choice presents itself except that here the higher attachment option is problematic. Just as for (9), the whole object NP cannot be captured because the verb *scratched* does not accept an IP. Stealing the object by reaching down from the matrix clause is theft and runs up against a severe TOE. Since high attachment is thus spoiled in (18), the option of capturing the lower NP is a clear winner. Finally, we may consider (9) again in light of these other examples ((31), (33), (18)). Here the stealing verb has no choice between lower and higher NPs. There is just one NP to steal; it cannot be captured, and theft is inhibited by the TOE, so the revision is difficult. The differing perceptual profiles of these four examples are thus accounted for by *Attach Anyway* and *Adjust* guided by the GDP.

Our claim has been that raising is as easy as any other repair, except where a construction has some specific property that makes raising difficult. Clearly there is no such factor at work in the coordinate structure revisions discussed here in which an IP^{and} is raised. This needs explaining also. Why can the IP^{and} in (18) and (31) float upward without restraint?[28] The answer we propose is that nothing is trying to hold the IP^{and} down. The NP to the left of *and* exerts no selection pressure on it. Selection is an asymmetric relation. A conjunction word needs its flanking XP conjuncts, but an XP does not need a following conjunction word. Thus the NP left sister to the IP^{and} does not protest the escape of the IP^{and}. Indeed it is glad to see it go, since it is a misfit where it is; the IP^{and} is expelled, rather than stolen by an external attractor. Thus there are two factors contributing to the ease of this revision, as compared with stealing an object away from a verb. One, noted above, is that the incoming verb can *capture* the preceding NP and does not have to attach high and resort to theft. The other is that the word *and* moves with the ambiguous NP, so that the constituent that raises is not attempting to escape from something which selects it and has an interest in retaining it. Indeed, the reason why the *and* raises along with the IP is that *and* does have an interest in retaining a constituent on its right (though it is flexible about its category). Given that *and* needs that constituent,

---

[28] The IP^{and} can even rise over two clauses as long as the symptom clearly signals it. Consider (i) and (ii).

(i) Susan thinks that Matthew had lunch with his sister and the twins did too.

(ii) Susan thinks that Matthew had lunch with his sister and the twins do too.

When the verb *did* captures *the twins* in (i), the resulting IP^{and} rises just far enough to take the lowest available IP as its left sister. But when *do* captures *the twins* in (ii), the IP^{and} rises one clause further. The effort is perceptible, perhaps, but the revision is successful (more successful, certainly, than NP raising in (9)). There is no resistance to the IP^{and} leaving its current position, and a good symptom (the tense and aspect of *do* in relation to the preceding verbs) indicates clearly where it should reattach. Under these circumstances there appears to be no limit imposed on how high it may rise. (We cannot, however, rule out the possibility that in (ii) the IP^{and} raises in two steps, trying out the lower clause attachment on the way.)

it has two options: it could block the raising of the constituent or it could raise with it. The first leads to a dead end in (18) and (31). The second is successful and painless, since nothing on the left complains when *and* moves.

This perspective on the 'pied piping' observed in some reanalyses offers clarification of an observation in section 4. We noted there that word theft (to the extent that it succeeds at all) may pull other words along with the targeted one. Since theft is a superficial operation, it seems odd that it should care about taking a complete well-formed phrase. But in fact we can see now that this could be due rather to the other words refusing to let go of the one being stolen. For instance: when a noun is stolen and a determiner goes along with it, this is not because the noun is dragging the determiner, but because the determiner is tagging along with the noun. Before the stealing, the determiner was already in the CPPM, so it was part of a structured tree reflecting grammatical constraints. When its noun is pulled away from it, those constraints set up a protest. The determiner's selection feature requires a noun complement (an overt one, except in special contexts). We assume this selection feature is present in the tree (as a verb's selection feature is), and is left unsatisfied if the complement is ripped away. (Note: this explanation goes through whether the determiner is analyzed as the specifier of NP or as the head of DP; only details differ.) As suggested above for conjunction, a determiner whose noun is the target of attempted theft has two options: it can try to prevent the noun from going, or it can go along with the noun. The latter may well be the easier course. How easy it is depends on whether there is something to the left of the determiner that cannot do without a DP to its right, such as a preposition. If there is, that will have to tag along too or it will block the whole process. For success in thieving there must be some point at which the word string can snap apart, i.e., a point at which the element on the left has no need of the element to its right. For a correct revision, this weak link must be at the point where the structure needs to be divided. In (31) the break to the left of *and* is perfect. In an example like *While John scratched the puppies of the hairy dog yawned loudly* there is a natural break to the left of the preposition *of*, but this is the wrong split from the point of view of the sentence structure, so revision is difficult. In (9) there is no natural snapping point at all (the verb won't let go of its object, the subject won't let go of the verb, the adverb *while* won't let go of the clause); so no reanalysis presents itself, not even a spurious one.

6 Conclusion

The data for a theory of garden path reanalysis are the differential costs of recovering from different kinds of garden paths. The goal is a model of the reanalysis process which explains those facts, i.e., a model which entails true generalizations about when recovery is easy and when it is difficult. In searching for these generalizations it is most reasonable to begin with simple strong hypotheses such as: revision is easy if and only if it does not alter the meaning assigned to the sentence; if it does not require erasure of domination statements; if it involves only local restructuring; etc. However, counterexamples to all of these hypotheses can be constructed. The diagnosis model that we have proposed is flexible enough to cope with the variety of examples observed.

A disadvantage of greater flexibility is that it may imply a more elaborate mechanism; but the diagnosis model, we claim, is exempt from this charge for two reasons. As we have noted previously, every repair model must have some machinery for calculating what repairs are possible in the case at hand and for selecting one repair to try out, as well as for effecting the appropriate changes in the tree. The diagnosis model assumes nothing more than this in order to predict reanalysis costs. But we have also tried to establish in this chapter that diagnosis does not require a rich reasoning component with open-ended deductive capabilities out of keeping with the dedicated modular design that we believe is characteristic of the first-pass routines. We have presented a practical reasoning machine that thinks by doing. It has no general powers of logic, but linguistically it is just as sophisticated as the first-pass parser, since it draws on the grammar in just the same way. It fails only where linguistic sophistication is of no benefit. Specifically, we have argued that the *Adjust* process fails if there is no linguistically motivated route, composed of grammatical dependency links, from the symptom back to the original error. There may be no such connecting path despite the fact that the original error was the cause of the apparent error that the parser is now confronted with. As in the examples discussed here, the original error may have used up some input words which really belong at a later position, a position structurally unrelated to it though necessarily linearly adjacent. In this way, an earlier choice may impinge on later options without there being any grammatical relation between the tree positions which *Adjust* could take advantage of. In such cases the adjustment process will blunder about and may fail to find the right revision, however obvious it might be to a general reasoning system.

CUNY Graduate School and University Center & Kantogakuin University

References

Abney, S. 1986. Licensing and parsing. In J. McDonough and B. Plunkett (eds.), *Proceedings of NELS*, 17, 1, 1-15.

Bader, M. (this volume). Prosodic influences on reading syntactically ambiguous sentences.

Carlson, G.N. & Tanenhaus, M.K. 1988. Thematic roles and language comprehension. In W. Wilkins (ed.), *Thematic Relations, Syntax and Semantics, Vol. 21*. New York, NY: Academic Press, 263-300.

Clifton, C. 1993. Thematic roles in sentence parsing. *Canadian Journal of Experimental Psychology*, 47, 2, 222-246.

Cole, P. & Wang, C. 1996. Antecedents and blockers of long-distance reflexives: The case of Chinese *ziji*. *Linguistic Inquiry*, 27, 3, 357-390.

Cooper, W.A. & Paccia-Cooper, J. 1980. *Syntax and Speech*. Cambridge, MA: Harvard University Press.

Ferreira, F. & Henderson, J.M. 1991a. Recovery from misanalyses of garden-path sentences. *Journal of Memory and Language*, 30, 725-745.

Ferreira, F. & Henderson, J.M. 1991b. How is verb information used during syntactic parsing? In G.B. Simpson (ed.), *Understanding Word and Sentence*. North Holland: Elsevier Science Publishers B.V., 305-330.

Ferreira, F. & Henderson, J.M. (this volume). Syntactic reanalysis, thematic processing, and sentence comprehension.

Fodor, J.D. & Frazier, L. 1980. Is the human sentence parsing mechanism an ATN? *Cognition*, 8, 417-459.

Fodor, J.D. & Frazier, L. 1983. Local attachment in a one-stage parser. Unpublished manuscript, University of Connecticut, Storrs, CT.

Fodor, J.D. & Inoue, A. 1994. The diagnosis and cure of garden paths. *Journal of Psycholinguistic Research*, 23, 407-434.

Fodor, J.D. & Inoue, A. (in press). Garden path recovery: The Grammatical Dependency Principle. To appear in *CUNYForum*, 20, Fall 1997.

Fodor, J.D. & Inoue, A. (in preparation a). The Diagnosis Model: Revision as Last Resort. To appear in M. De Vincenzi & V. Lombardo (eds.), *Cross Linguistic Perspectives on Sentence Processing*. Dordrecht: Kluwer Academic Publishers.

Fodor, J.D. & Inoue, A. (in preparation b). Null symptoms and empty categories. Manuscript, CUNY Graduate Center, New York, NY.

Frazier, L. 1978. *On Comprehending Sentences: Syntactic Parsing Strategies*. Unpublished doctoral dissertation, University of Connecticut, Storrs, CT. Distributed by the Indiana University Linguistics Club, Bloomington, IN.

Frazier, L. 1990. Identifying structure under X^0. In A. Jongman & A. Lahiri (eds.), *Yearbook of Morphology*, 3, 87-109.

Frazier, L. & Rayner, K. 1988. Parameterizing the language processing system: Left- vs. right-branching within and across languages. In J.A. Hawkins (ed.), *Explaining Language Universals*. Oxford, UK: Basil Blackwell, 247-279.

Frazier, L. & Fodor, J.D. 1978. The sausage machine: A new two-stage parsing model. *Cognition*, 6, 1-34.

Frazier, L. & Clifton, C. 1996. *Construal*. Cambridge, MA: MIT Press.

Frazier, L. & Clifton, C. (this volume). Sentence reanalysis, and visibility.

Gibson, E.A.F. 1991. *A Computational Theory of Human Linguistic Processing: Memory Limitations and Processing Breakdown*. Unpublished doctoral dissertation, Carnegie Mellon University, Pittsburgh, PA. Available as Center for Machine Translation Technical Report CMU-CMT-91-125.

Gorrell, P. (this volume). Syntactic analysis and reanalysis in sentence processing.

Gorrell, P. 1995a. *Syntax and Parsing*. Cambridge, UK: Cambridge University Press.

Gorrell, P. 1995b. Parsing theory and phrase-order variation in German V2 clauses. *Journal of Psycholinguistic Research*, 25, 135-156.

Hoeks, J., Vonk, W., Hagoort, P., & Brown, C. 1997. Processing coordination: Eye movements and ERPs. Poster presented at *Tenth Annual CUNY Conference on Human Sentence Processing*, Los Angeles, CA.

Igoa, J.M. 1995. Parsing decisions and the Construal hypothesis: Attachment preferences in primary phrases in Spanish. Paper presented at *Second Symposium on Psycholinguistics*, Tarragona, Spain.

Inoue, A. 1991. *A Comparative Study of Parsing in English and Japanese*. Unpublished doctoral dissertation, University of Connecticut, Storrs, CT.

Inoue, A. & Fodor, J.D. 1995. Information-paced parsing of Japanese. In R. Mazuka & N. Nagai (eds.), *Japanese Sentence Processing*. Hillsdale, NJ: Lawrence Erlbaum Associates, 9-63.

Kayne, R. 1994. *The Antisymmetry of Syntax*. Cambridge, MA: MIT Press.

Konieczny, L., Hemforth, B., & Scheepers, C. 1994. Reanalysis vs. internal repairs: Non-monotonic processes in sentence perception. In B. Hemforth, C. Scheepers, & G. Strube (eds.), *First Analysis, Reanalysis and Repair*. IIG-Berichte 8/94. Freiburg: Institut für Informatik und Gesellschaft, 1-23.

Lewis, R.L. 1993. *An Architecturally-Based Theory of Human Sentence Comprehension*, Unpublished doctoral dissertation, Carnegie Mellon University, Pittsburgh, PA. Available as Technical Report CMU-CS-93-226 from reports@cs.cmu.edu.

Lewis, R.L. (this volume). Reanalysis and limited repair parsing: Leaping off the garden path.

Marcus, M.P., Hindle, D., & Fleck, M.M. 1983. D-theory: Talking about talking about trees. *Association for Computational Linguistics*, 21, 129-136.

Mitchell, D.C. 1987. Lexical guidance in human parsing: Locus and processing characteristics. In M.Coltheart (ed.), *The Psychology of Reading, Attention and Performance, Vol. 12*. Hillsdale, NJ: Lawrence Erlbaum Associates, 601-681.

Ni, W., Fodor, J.D., Crain, S., & Shankweiler, D. (submitted). Anomaly detection: Eye movement patterns.

Phillips, C. 1995. Right Association: A single strategy for structural parsing. Paper presented at *NELS 26*, MIT, October 1995.

Pickering, M. & Traxler, M. 1996. Plausibility and recovery from garden paths: An eye-tracking study. Unpublished manuscript, University of Glasgow.

Pritchett, B.L. 1987. *Garden Path Phenomena and the Grammatical Basis of Language Processing*. Unpublished doctoral dissertation, Harvard University, Cambridge, MA.

Pritchett, B.L. 1991. Head position and parsing ambiguity. *Journal of Psycholinguistic Research*, 20, 3, 251-270.

Pritchett, B.L. 1992. *Grammatical competence and parsing performance*. Chicago, IL: University of Chicago Press.

Stevenson, S. 1993. A competition-based explanation of syntactic attachment preferences and garden path phenomena. *Association for Computational Linguistics*, 31, 266-273.

Stevenson, S. (this volume). Parsing as incremental restructuring.

Sturt, P. & Crocker, M.W. 1996. Monotonic syntactic processing: a cross-linguistic study of attachment and reanalysis. *Language and Cognitive Processes*, 11, 5, 449-494.

Sturt, P. & Crocker, M.W. (this volume). Generalized monotonicity for reanalysis models.

Wanner, E. & Maratsos, M. 1978. An ATN approach to comprehension. In M. Halle, J. Bresnan, & G.A. Miller (eds.), *Linguistic Theory and Psychological Reality*. Cambridge, MA: MIT Press, 119-161.

5

Sentence Reanalysis, and Visibility*

Lyn Frazier & Charles Clifton, Jr.

Abstract

Serial theories of sentence processing specify that the processor pursues just a single syntactic analysis of a sentence until that analysis becomes implausible or untenable, at which point revision of the first analysis occurs. Many theories of revision have been proposed in recent years. Here it is argued that revision cost cannot be calculated in purely structural terms: reanalysis complexity is a function of sentence token, not sentence type. It is also argued that a theory of revisions must include a Minimal Revisions principle. Finally, in revision and in first analysis, more recently postulated nodes provide preferred or more "visible" attachment sites than more distant nodes. Several types of evidence are used to support a Visibility principle which, it is suggested, may replace principles such as Late Closure (Frazier, 1978) or Recency (Gibson, 1991).

1 Introduction

Within structure-based theories of sentence processing, attention in recent years has shifted to the study of sentence reanalysis. A variety of proposals have been put forward. Reanalysis has been claimed to be easy if it involves reanalyzing a constituent to a position within the same thematic domain (Pritchett, 1988) or within the same government domain (Pritchett, 1992), if it involves only structure-addition (Suh, 1994) or lowering (Weinberg, 1995), or if it does not

* We are very grateful to Janet Fodor for extensive comments on this paper. We also wish to thank the students of Linguistics 712, Fall 1993, at the University of Massachusetts, Amherst, for discussion of the ideas reported here, as well as the audience at a talk at MIT in May, 1995, and the audience at the Seventh Annual CUNY Conference on Human Sentence Processing, 1994. This work was supported by NIH Grant HD-18708 to Charles Clifton, Jr., and Lyn Frazier and by NSF Grant #BNS9121375 to Keith Rayner and Lyn Frazier.

J.D. Fodor and F. Ferreira (eds.), Reanalysis in Sentence Processing, 143–176.

involve a revision of primary relations (domination or primacy) that have already been assigned (Gorrell, 1993).

Several proposals focus on differences between the processing of English and Japanese. Inoue & Fodor (1995) suggest that reanalysis is governed by the same principles as first analysis (Minimal Attachment, Late Closure, Minimal Chain Principle) in a system where choice points are flagged during the initial parse of a fragment. Revisions are typically cheaper in Japanese than in English, they propose, because Japanese perceivers must make more revisions and, therefore, are less confident of their initial choices. Sturt & Crocker (1995, 1996) suggest that reanalysis procedures are parameterized—they proceed bottom-up in English but top-down in Japanese.

Focusing primarily on English, Frazier & Rayner (1982) suggest that reanalysis is selective and depends on the informativeness of the error signal. Fodor & Inoue (1994) develop this approach, arguing for the 'diagnosis model', where revision difficulty arises when the move the parser should make appears to be incorrect: though the revision might remedy the error triggering reanalysis, it also creates a new problem. We think that this last sort of approach—selective reanalysis or 'diagnosis'—is the one best supported by the available evidence.

In the present paper, we will assume the existence of a depth-first modular syntactic processor and focus on three questions concerning sentence reanalysis procedures. First, can the cost of reanalysis be captured adequately in purely structural terms, as implied by several of the existing proposals, or is it necessary to take nonstructural factors into account? Second, which reanalysis does the parser prefer or attempt first? Third, are all attachment sites equally visible to the parser? We address each of these questions in turn.

2 Reanalysis Cost

Is the cost of reanalysis a function of sentence-type or sentence-token? We think this question is central, because many of the reanalysis models cited above (all except the error driven models) are purely structure-based. Of course, it is consistent with structure-based models for the complexity of reanalysis within a sentence-type to vary as a function of nonstructural information. However, if within the (predicted) easiest class of structures and within the (predicted) hardest class of structures it is possible to find complexity ranging from barely detectable complexity to conscious garden paths, one must question the validity of purely structure-based reanalysis proposals. So the question is whether structural and nonstructural factors interact in reanalysis, suggesting the need for reanalysis complexity to be based on sentence token. The alternative is that structural factors do reveal the basic story, and nonstructural sources of complexity can in fact simply be added on top, rendering viable a reanalysis theory based on sentence type.

2.1 Length

2.1.1 Length Increases Revision Cost

Considerable evidence suggests that the length of an ambiguous phrase may influence the difficulty of arriving at a correct analysis of a sentence. For example, in an eye movement study, Frazier & Rayner (1982) investigated sentences with short (1a) and long (1b) temporarily ambiguous regions. Longer reading times and larger disruption effects were found for sentences with long ambiguous phrases than for short ones. However, in this study, the short ambiguous phrases were not lengthened in a single systematic manner: in some sentences prenominal modifiers were added to produce the long ambiguous phrase and in others postnominal modifiers were added. The amount of material added to the short phrases to produce long phrases also differed considerably from one example to the next.

(1) a. Before the king rides his horse is always groomed.
    b. Before the king rides his beautiful white horse is always groomed.

In grammaticality judgment studies Warner & Glass (1987) also found longer judgment times for sentences with longer ambiguous phrases in examples like (2). They attributed the complexity of (2b) to the syntactic complexity of the longer ambiguous phrase and the consequent larger number of syntactic choice points available during reanalysis.

(2) a. Before the men kill the boy strikes. (short)
    b. If the horse kicks the boy the dog bites kills. (long)

In an on-line grammaticality judgment study, Ferreira & Henderson (1991) also provided evidence that the length of the ambiguous phrase influences reanalysis difficulty. Specifically they showed that what matters most is the length of the material intervening between the head of the ambiguous phrase and the disambiguating region of the sentence. However, the syntactic complexity of the intervening material does not influence reanalysis difficulty.

Grammaticality judgments for the unpreferred Early Closure cases (without the parenthesized material) are comparable when the ambiguous NP is modified by a relative clause (3b) and when it is modified by a simple PP (3c).

(3) a. When the men hunt the birds (the deer) typically scatter.
  b. When the men hunt the birds (the deer) that cheetahs eat typically scatter.
  c. When the men hunt the birds (the deer) with bright plumage typically scatter.

For the structurally-preferred Late Closure versions of the sentence (including the parenthesized phrase), the length of the ambiguous phrase did not make a difference. The absence of length effects for Late Closure sentences is expected if the effects of length in Early Closure sentences are due to the role length plays in delaying the arrival of disambiguating information which signals the need for a reanalysis of the structure assigned to preceding portions of the sentence.

The Warner & Glass (1987) and Ferreira & Henderson (1991) studies lengthened material between the head of the ambiguous phrase and the disambiguating material, with one exception. In one experiment, Ferreira & Henderson (1991) included a prenominal modifier in the ambiguous phrase and found no increase in revision times. Hence, they explicitly argued that it is the distance (or time) between the head of the ambiguous phrase and the onset of the disambiguation which is important. It must be asked, of course, why increasing this distance should complicate revision. Here it will simply be noted that the relation between length and revision cost follows if semantically interpreted decisions are more costly to revise than semantically uninterpreted decisions. With longer constituents the probability that an incorrect syntactic decision will have influenced some aspect of semantic interpretation increases, perhaps accounting for increased revision costs.[1] (See section 2.2 below for further discussion.)

Though many studies have observed an effect of lengthening the ambiguous region, as indicated above, it should perhaps be emphasized that the contrasts

---

[1] It remains unclear whether lengthening of the post-head material of an ambiguous phrase continues to contribute substantially to revision costs after the processor has completed its interpretation of the relation between the (head of) the phrase and its theta assigner. In other words, there may be limits to the length effect determined largely by how long it takes the processor to complete interpretation. An alternative position might focus on the life span of an analysis as a factor contributing to the processor's 'confidence' in its first analysis. More empirical work is needed to resolve this issue.

that have been studied have involved short and long phrases differing in length by several words or by a varying number of words. It is not known at present whether small differences in the length of the ambiguous phrase, e.g., involving the addition of only a single monosyllabic word, would also give rise to stable differences in the complexity of revising a structure. In short, more research on length effects (and on the timing of semantic interpretation) is needed before we know whether the length effect is 'quantal' or whether it is 'graded', with revision complexity more or less continuously modulated by the length of the ambiguous phrase.

2.1.2 Length Decreases Revision Costs

Under circumstances where the disambiguation occurs in the ambiguous phrase itself, it appears that lengthening the ambiguous phrase, especially after the point of disambiguation, facilitates the comprehension process. This follows if lengthening the ambiguous phrase allows revisions of the first decision to be accomplished before the end of the ambiguous phrase (or the end of the sentence) has been reached. For example, Frazier & Clifton (1996) found that a final adverbial phrase that cannot be incorporated into the current processing domain (e.g., the clause) results in ratings of lower comprehensibility with a short phrase like (4a) than with a long phrase like (4b).

(4) a. John will explain to the kids that their grandfather died *tomorrow.*
b. John will explain to the kids that their grandfather died *after the operation they need.*

It may be easier for the processor to revise decisions if the error, and the correct analysis, can be identified before the processor finishes processing the misanalyzed phrase and moves on to the processing of a new phrase or sentence. (In Frazier & Fodor, 1978, and section 3 of this chapter, other examples are discussed where lengthening a constituent decreases processing complexity. In some cases, a prosodic explanation of such examples seems possible.)

2.2 Semantic Effects

As was already discussed above, the effect of lengthening an ambiguous phrase is an increase in revision costs under circumstances where the disambiguating information follows the ambiguous phrase. Existing evidence seems compatible with an explanation of this effect relying on the following assumption.

(5) *Semantic Cost Principle*: Revising semantically interpreted (confirmed) decisions is more costly than revising semantically uninterpreted ones.

Assuming that the head of a phrase must be available in order to assign the phrase a thematic role, we may account for the finding (Ferreira & Henderson, 1991) that pre-head lengthening didn't contribute greatly to revision costs whereas post-head lengthening did. No thematic role will have been assigned in the case of the pre-head lengthening. Presumably the post-head lengthening of an ambiguous phrase supplies the processor with the time needed to complete thematic interpretation of the ambiguous phrase itself. Further, when the ambiguous phrase is itself at the end of an interpretive domain (e.g., a clause), the extra lengthening may also provide the processor with the time needed to fix the interpretation of other constituents in the sentence. (See recent studies of gap-filling including Goodluck *et al.*, 1992 and Pickering *et al.*, 1994.)[2]

In addition to examples like those above in (1)-(3), where both the correct and incorrect analyses are semantically viable, there are examples where the semantic interpretation of the incorrect analysis may signal the need for reanalysis. Reduced relative clause ambiguities, for example, show rather dramatic effects of semantic confirmation versus disconfirmation of an incorrect main clause analysis. Perhaps the most difficult garden path in English involves sentences like (6a), where perceivers follow the main clause analysis until the verb *fell* is encountered. At this point the analysis breaks down. Contrast (6a) with (6b), however.

(6) a. The horse raced past the barn fell.
    b. The letter sent on Monday arrived today.

In (6b) perceivers have no conscious awareness of having computed an incorrect structure, presumably because semantic information immediately disconfirms the main clause analysis of the verb *sent* (though see also Stevenson & Merlo, submitted).

Ambiguities concerning the analysis of a postverbal NP as direct object or as subject of the following clause are also easy to analyze when the direct object analysis is anomalous.

---

2 Goodluck *et al.* (1992) and Pickering *et al.* (1994) argue that filler-gap misanalyses are detectable only at the end of a potential sentence or clause.

(7) While Mary was mending the sky turned grey and dark.

Frazier (1978) showed that, although Early Closure sentences like (7) took longer numerically to comprehend than Late Closure sentences, they did not differ significantly from them, in contrast to sentences where the postverbal NP could semantically be analyzed as direct object of the preceding verb.

In a grammaticality judgment study, Stowe (1989) studied sentences like *After the truck/police stopped the Datsun disappeared into the night.* She found that postverbal NP (*the Datsun*) was easier to process when the subject of the first clause was inanimate (*truck*) than when it was animate (*police*). In two eye movement studies, Clifton (1993) investigated this type of sentence further to determine whether an inanimate subject prevents an incorrect direct object attachment of a postverbal NP, as Stowe (1989) suggested, or simply facilitates reanalysis, given that the direct object analysis was semantically odd or anomalous in Stowe's examples with inanimate subjects. In one study, sentences similar to Stowe's were used along with their disambiguated counterparts (8a) and (8b). In another study, materials were constructed where the direct object analysis was implausible even with the animate subject, as in (8c) and (8d).

(8) a. Before the $\left\{\begin{matrix}\text{police}\\ \text{truck}\end{matrix}\right\}$ stopped the Datsun disappeared into the night.

b. Before the $\left\{\begin{matrix}\text{police}\\ \text{truck}\end{matrix}\right\}$ stopped, the Datsun disappeared into the night.

c. Before the $\left\{\begin{matrix}\text{police}\\ \text{truck}\end{matrix}\right\}$ stopped the moon had risen over the ocean.

d. Before the $\left\{\begin{matrix}\text{police}\\ \text{truck}\end{matrix}\right\}$ stopped, the moon had risen over the ocean.

Like Stowe, Clifton (1993) found longer reading times in the disambiguating region of the ambiguous sentences for the animate subject condition compared to the inanimate subject condition. However, longer times for reading the ambiguous region itself in the ambiguous (no comma) inanimate subject condition suggested that readers attempted to incorrectly incorporate the postverbal NP as direct object and revised this analysis faster in the inanimate subject examples than in the corresponding animate subject examples. (This supports our assumption of a modular syntactic processor and the idea that a syntactic misanalysis is attempted even when semantic information could have precluded the misanalysis had the semantic information been consulted *before* a syntactic analysis was made.) On the syntactically disambiguating matrix verb, reading times were longer following the plausible object (8a) than following the implausible object (8c), suggesting that revision of the semantically confirmed decision was more difficult than revision of the semantically disconfirmed decision. In a similar study, Pickering & Traxler (1994) also showed that misanalysis of a postverbal NP is more costly to revise in (9a), where semantics confirms the direct object analysis, than in (9b), where it does not.

(9) a. Because the woman was editing the brand new sports magazine...
b. Because the woman was sailing the brand new sports magazine...

Consider next the example in (10), due to Inoue & Fodor (1995),

(10) The daughter of the king's son admired himself.

Extreme difficulty is noted by most perceivers at the point when *himself* is encountered. The problem is that *daughter* has been analyzed as the head of the subject NP. Since *daughter* is feminine there is no appropriate antecedent for the reflexive *himself*. Therefore reanalysis of the internal structure of the NP is required so that *son* is analyzed as the head (with *the daughter of the king's* as the genitive). Thus reanalysis of the structure of the NP is required only after *admire* has been processed, leaving time for a theta-role to be assigned to the subject before revision begins. Hence revision of a thematically interpreted phrase is required in the processing of (10).[3]

(11) The daughter of the king's son's butler admired herself.

(11′)

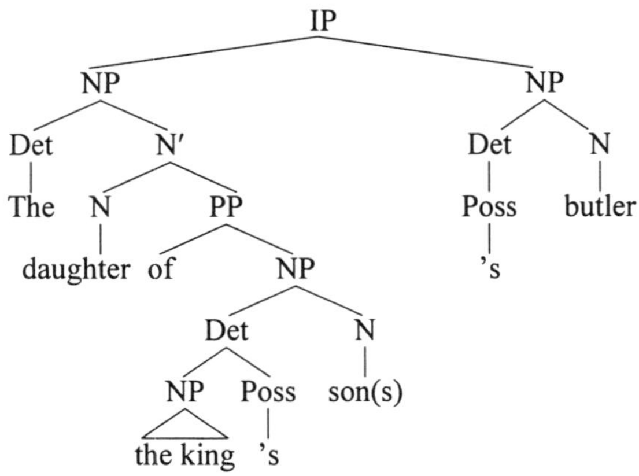

[3] The nature of the error signal is probably also important. The error signal involves a mismatch in gender between the reflexive and antecedent—either of which could be mistakenly marked. Our intuitions suggest that in (10) the processor entertains the hypothesis that *himself* is simply a speech error, with *herself* being the intended target.

By contrast, consider (11). The processor must revise an initial decision about the structure of (11), as shown in (11′). Nevertheless, the revision is not costly compared to the revision in (10). In fact, perceivers seem to correctly revise such sentences without excessive difficulty despite the need to restructure the lower NP, including assignment of *butler* as the new head of the complement to *of*. But in this case, unlike in (10), the subject NP has not yet been assigned a thematic role. Further, intuitions suggest that the processor has not yet finished interpretation of the string *the daughter of the king's son(s)* when the new item *butler* is encountered. Hence, the cheapness of the revision in (11), relative to (10), is plausibly attributed at least in part to the difference between revising a semantically uninterpreted decision versus revising an already semantically interpreted decision. In fact, Langendoen (1976) points out that phrases like (10) are not particularly difficult to comprehend if an error signal occurs within the NP itself, as in *the commander of the army's belt buckle*. The semantic anomaly of *the army's belt buckle* allows revision to occur before the erroneous structure is fully interpreted semantically.[4] We return to these structures later in section 3, where we examine this structure experimentally. For further

---

[4] Janet Fodor (p.c.) points out examples like those in (i), wondering why they contrast with Langendoen's (1976) *commander of the army's belt-buckle*.

(i) a. the daughter of the king's eyes
b. the children of the king's noses
c. the children of the king's nanny is poor
d. This woman is the children of the king's nanny.

One factor seems to be the length of the head noun. Our intuitions suggest that *the daughter of the King's eyeglasses* is much easier to process than (i-a). This is expected if the processor builds a structure and then rapidly evaluates that structure semantically rather than consulting syntax and semantics *before* building any structure. In examples with short head nouns like (i-a) or (i-b), by the time the processor has information allowing it to reject the low attachment analysis of the input, the end of the ambiguous phrase has already been reached. But lengthening the head noun (e.g., to *eyeglasses*) allows subsequent material to occur within the phrase after sufficient semantic information (from *eye*) is available to disconfirm the low attachment analysis. Examples (i-c) and (i-d) are different from (i-a) and (i-b): perceivers can analyze the ambiguous phrase with low attachment of *nanny* and this analysis is fine both syntactically and semantically until number agreement is taken into account. Hence, the intuition that (i-c) and (i-d) remain difficult even with number disambiguation suggests that number may be used as a filter on analysis, not guiding the identification of initial structural hypotheses. The role of agreement features in processing is a vast and interesting topic which goes beyond the scope of our present concerns. Some intuitions suggest that marked agreement features on the verb (plural, not singular) may be helpful in guiding processing in a way that the unmarked (singular) feature is not. For example, the example with a plural verb in (ii-a) seems to contrast with both (i-d) and (ii-b), being intuitively easier to process than either of the examples with a singular verb .

(ii) a. These are the daughter of the mayor's toys.
b. This is the daughter of the mayor's toy.

examples of semantic effects on reanalysis, see Carlson & Tanenhaus (1988), Clifton (1993), and Crain & Steedman (1985).

Inoue & Fodor (1995) argue that reanalysis in Japanese is less costly than in English. Instead, we suggest that the general ease of the Japanese revisions they discuss can be directly attributed to the fact that the incorrect structural decision could not have been fully semantically interpreted at the point when the decision was revised. Consider (12)—a Japanese sentence with a missing subject, an accusative-marked (-*o*) NP, and a verb.

(12)

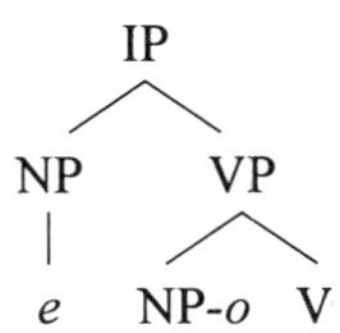

If this clause is followed by a nominal which is marked with -*ga* (nominative), then the phrase marker in (13) may be constructed. Here and throughout details of the phrase marker are suppressed if they are irrelevant to the discussion.

(13)

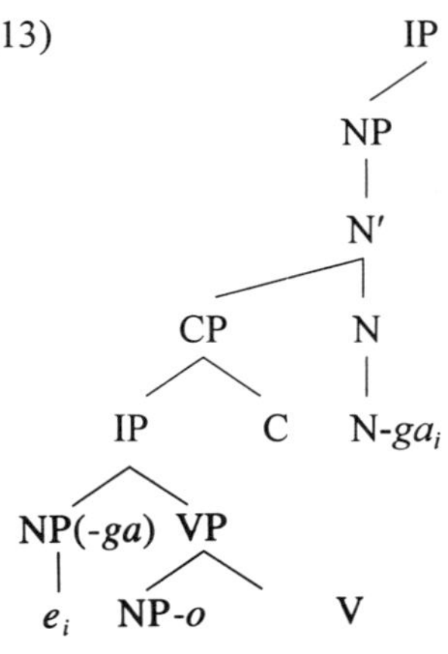

The new relationship between the already existing IP and the new head noun involves a revision or addition of structure, but no semantic revision is required (assuming that the null subject has not yet been interpreted). Of course the circumstance illustrated here is the simplest one. On other occasions the processor may have mistakenly analyzed an NP-*ga* from a higher clause as the subject of the relative clause, in which case a partial semantic interpretation may have been assigned to the misanalyzed subject. But, it is argued below, this circumstance—when a lexical phrase in an already interpreted clause must be reanalyzed outside that clause—results in revisions in Japanese which *are* intuitively costly, at least when more than one revision must be made (see (22) below) or when the error signal arrives long after the verb of the clause containing the misanalyzed constituent, as in the *kureru* examples Mazuka (1991) discusses.[5, 6]

---

[5] *Kureru* may be added to a verb with the resulting meaning 'someone did something for my/the speaker's benefit'. When *kureru* is added to the verb of a final matrix clause, it may require reanalysis of the thematic roles assigned to earlier NPs and may consequently require, for example, that a sentence-initial nominative be shifted out of a subordinate clause and analyzed instead as a main clause subject.

[6] Inoue & Fodor (1995) argue against a general Semantic Cost Principle, proposing instead a principle with a more limited scope, namely, the Thematic Overlay Effect:

(i) *Thematic Overlay Effect* (TOE): Revisions are costly when a lexical NP assigned to an already postulated thematic role is reassigned and the thematic role persists in the final representation but it is not assigned to a lexical NP.

Inoue & Fodor do not adopt a more general principle like (5) because they believe that it incorrectly predicts a greater cost than is observed in Japanese examples like (ii-b) (after Inoue & Fodor, 1995, example (8)).

(ii) a. Bob-ga Mary-ni ringo-o ageta.
Bob-NOM Mary-DAT apple-ACC gave
'Bob gave Mary the apple.'

b. Bob-ga Mary-ni [$_S$ ringo-o tabeta] inu-o ageta.
Bob-NOM Mary-DAT apple-ACC ate dog-ACC gave
'Bob gave Mary the dog that ate the apple.'

In processing (ii-b), apparently Japanese speakers initially assign the simple analysis appropriate for (ii-a) and "then they often report some sense of surprise, slight but detectable, at the verb *tabeta*" (Inoue & Fodor, 1995, p. 15). Inoue & Fodor seem to conclude from this and similar examples that recovering from Japanese garden paths is easier than recovering from English ones. If we understand this argument, a distinction is being drawn between the native Japanese speaker's sense of a 'slight but detectable' surprise in processing (ii-b) versus the native English speaker's sense of a garden-path in processing a comparable English sentence. For example, *lie* in (iii), like the verb *tabeta* in (ii-b), follows an ambiguous phrase and unambiguously warrants introduction of an S node above the preceding NP, rendering the preceding NP a constituent of the new clause.

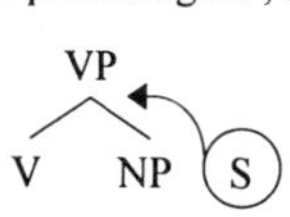

(iii) Mary knows boys lie.

Apparently the sense of surprise in Japanese (ii-b) is slighter than the sense of surprise in English (iii). At least this is what Inoue & Fodor need to maintain, namely, that in *comparable* examples, Japanese revision is easier than English revision. This may be the case, but we're skeptical and think that more evidence is required to support this distinction.

2.3 Frequency

The relative frequency of a verb's subcategorization frames seems to influence revision costs. Consider the sentences in (14), originally due to Fodor (1978), who was concerned with gap-location, not structural reanalysis. In (14) the processor must give up an already postulated filler-gap assignment when the obligatory prepositional-object gap is encountered.

(14) a. Which girl did the teacher walk (_) to the principal's office with _?
b. Which book did the teacher read (_) to the children from _?

Sentence (14a), where the processor must give up a lexically unpreferred gap following the preferred intransitive *walk*, is intuitively easier to process than (14b), where the processor must give up a gap corresponding to the most frequent subcategorization of the verb (*read*). Frazier & Clifton (1989) present experimental evidence showing that the processor initially detects even lexically unpreferred gaps corresponding to less frequent subcategorizations of a verb when a displaced constituent (a filler) has not yet been assigned to a gap. This evidence strongly suggests that the difficulty in (14a) is not due to the processor overlooking the gap (which corresponds to the less frequent subcategorization of *walk*) since it does not do so in other cases. Instead the difficulty is most likely due to the greater cost of revising the decision in (14b), where the processor must give up a more frequent subcategorization of *read* for a less

---

As far as intuitive evidence is concerned, we think it may be important to consider sentences with longer ambiguous phrases which often reveal intuitive difficulties obscured by examples with very short ambiguous phrases like (ii) and (iii). Experimental evidence would also be welcome, as we're sure Inoue & Fodor would agree.

Turning to the ease of revising (ii) relative to some of the difficult revisions in Japanese, we think this follows from a principle like (5). Though Japanese perceivers may assign some sort of interpretation in (ii-b) before *tabeta* is encountered (e.g., Agent-Goal-Theme), this interpretation may not be fixed or fully fleshed out before the theta-assigning verb is encountered. Hence the hypothesized ease of revision in many Japanese examples like (ii-b) may follow from the limited degree of semantic interpretation that is possible in these examples. Certainly we would expect examples like (ii-b) to be easier to reanalyze than examples where the theta-assigning verb was received before reanalysis takes place. See discussion of *kureru* sentences in footnote 5 above for examples with very late disambiguation. The correct analysis of those late disambiguation examples is described as 'difficult to obtain' (Mazuka and Itoh, 1995, p. 303).

In short, the 'slight surprise' in (ii-b) supports the idea that semantically interpreted decisions are more difficult to revise than uninterpreted ones. Thus (ii-b) shows that examples where full semantic interpretation (interpretation based on the actual theta-assigner) is not possible before the disambiguation arrives (because the theta-assigner follows the disambiguation) are easier to revise than examples where full interpretation may be assumed to have occurred.

frequent one, than in (14a) where it is the dispreferred subcategorization of *walk* that must be abandoned.

MacDonald *et al.* (1994) present evidence that in reduced relatives (e.g., *a prisoner captured...*) a higher frequency of past participle (versus past tense) usage of the verb was associated with higher plausibility ratings off-line. The normative data also predicted the comprehension difficulty in an on-line study by Pearlmutter & MacDonald (1995). This evidence might either be attributable to first pass parsing or it might be taken to suggest that the relative frequency of two lexical analyses of an input can influence revision costs. At present these two accounts are difficult to distinguish using data from structurally unpreferred sentences. Further, most of the current evidence concerning the frequency of lexical analyses seems to be confounded with semantic plausibility differences (see Kennison, 1995); for indications that subcategorization violations involve a semantic violation see Hagoort & Brown (1994).

In this section we have argued that reanalysis costs are not determined by structural factors alone. Depending on length, semantic, and frequency factors, reanalysis of a given sentence type can range from being conscious (a garden path) and/or experimentally detectable to being intuitively easy to process and possibly difficult or impossible to detect experimentally. We have presented substantial evidence that revising a semantically confirmed decision is more costly than revising the same structure either before it has been semantically interpreted or after semantic disconfirmation. This picture fits better with error-driven reanalysis models which predict token-based accounts of reanalysis difficulty than with reanalysis models based on sentence-type.

3 Reanalysis Preferences

When the initial analysis of a sentence becomes untenable, there is often more than one revision the processor could make. Which revision is preferred? In this section we argue that the processor's revisions are governed by the Minimal Revisions Principle in (15) (see Frazier, 1990).

(15) *Minimal Revisions*: Don't make an unnecessary revision. When revision is necessary, make the minimal revision consistent with the error signal, maintaining as much of the already assigned structure and interpretation as possible.

Consider first, the processing of *novel* English compounds, as in (16). When the first two nouns are encountered, the minimal analysis is that shown in (16a).

(16) a. b. c.

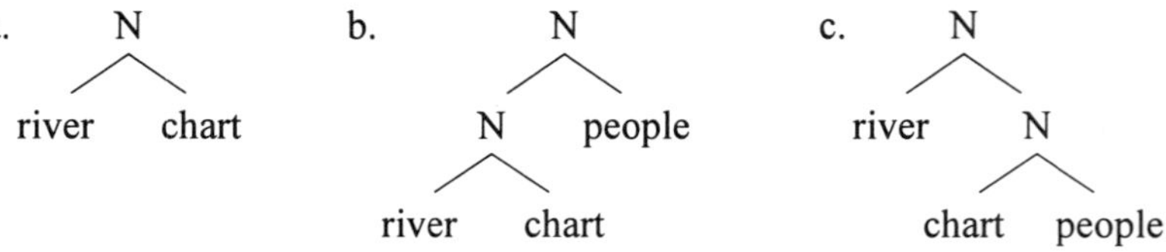

When the third noun is encountered, a revision is required. The processor may add a node high as in (16b) or low as in (16c). The minimal revision is the one shown in (16b) because it allows the already assigned structure and interpretation of the first two nouns to be preserved. This predicts a preference for a left-branching analysis of N-N-N compounds, as in (16b). Frazier (1990) presents evidence from a questionnaire study supporting this prediction in the interpretation assigned to ambiguous novel N-N-N sequences but not in that assigned to A-N-N sequences even for examples which are near paraphrases of each other (*city tax planning* versus *urban tax planning*) (see also Huitema *et al.*, in progress, for eye movement evidence in processing examples disambiguated to either the left- or right-branching structure.)

Notice that Minimal Attachment does not choose between these analyses since a single new node must be added to (16a) in either case. A principle favoring high revision might correctly predict the preference for (16b), but this is the opposite of what's usually claimed for English where low attachments or low revisions are generally favored.

Consider (17) next, where the first PP is initially analyzed as the locative argument of *put*. When the second PP arrives, some revision must be made: either the first PP must modify the preceding NP or the second PP must modify the NP preceding it (*the chest*).

(17) Brian put the silverware in the chest in the closet.

Adams (1990) shows that perceivers systematically prefer to make the latter revision. This is predicted by the Minimal Revisions principle because it allows the attachment and interpretation of the first PP to be maintained.[7] This

[7] Gorrell (this volume) claims that lowering is acceptable only if it doesn't erase precedence relations. Hence, considering only examples like (17), his model too could account for the data. Conceptually, however, we think that a model based on precedence is fundamentally flawed: precedence does not appear to play a basic role in the grammars of natural languages. Further, in

example shows that Minimal Revision does not always favor high attachments, as in (16). Taken together, the examples in (16) and (17) show that neither high nor low attachment/revision is consistently favored in English.

We turn now to a Japanese example first discussed by Inoue & Fodor (1995). The example will be of interest because the preferred revision cannot be attributed to Minimal Attachment but does follow from Minimal Revisions. Inoue & Fodor discuss the preferred interpretation of the Japanese prenominal adjective sequences, illustrated in (18).

(18)	toshitotta	takai	kutsu-no	shuurinin
	old (animate)	expensive	shoe-GEN	repairer

a. repairer of old expensive shoes
b. old expensive repairer of shoes
c. old repairer of expensive shoes

(19)

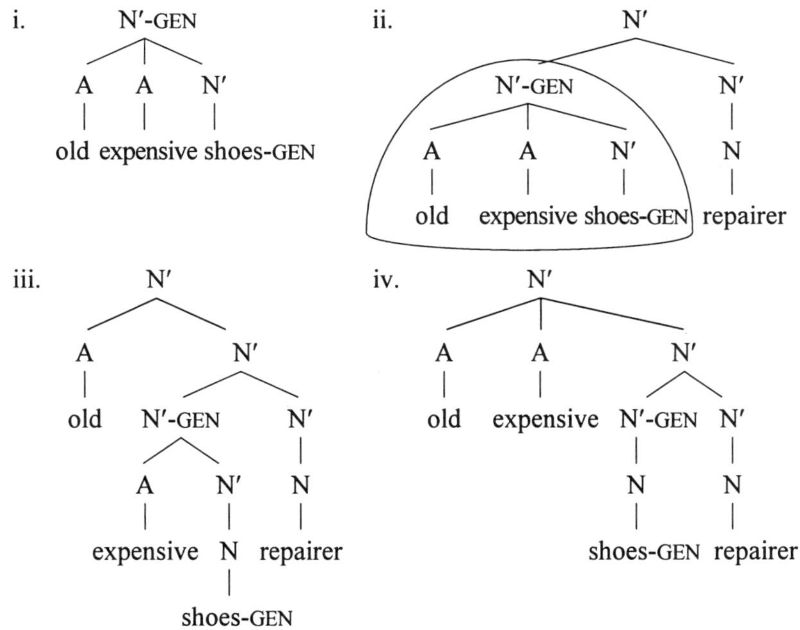

processing—e.g., in RSVP studies where the ordering of the input items is fragile at best—precedence does not act like a primitive relation. If precedence were a primitive relation, it should be available to order the input items in a string, predicting (counterfactually) that in RSVP the precedence relations between words should be the most available means of a structuring an input.

Assuming that syntactic analysis proceeds on-line roughly as each word is encountered, the initial sequence of (18) will be structured as shown in (19i) corresponding to the paraphrase in (18a). Inoue & Fodor note that intuitions suggest that (19i) is constructed initially despite the oddness of taking 'old (animate)' to apply to 'shoes,' and despite the fact that ultimately perceivers reject structures when 'old (animate)' modifies 'shoes'. When *shuurinin* is encountered, the minimal revision of (19i) is that shown in (19ii) where the structure and interpretation assigned in (19i) is preserved, as shown by the circled constituent in (19ii). According to Inoue & Fodor, this is indeed the preferred analysis. The alternative, where one adjective modifies 'shoes' and one modifies 'repairer' as in (18c), illustrated in (19iii), is disfavored by Minimal Revisions as well as by Minimal Attachment since the analysis entails an extra syntactic node (N′) not needed for the analysis in (19ii). (Here we are following the structure provided by Inoue & Fodor for these NPs. They make a standard assumption, namely, that N′ expands as A-N′, not A-N; the latter option is not recursive and would not allow an adjective to modify the entire N′ including (possibly) an already modified noun.) The alternative, where *both* adjectives modify 'repairer', does not require extra nodes to be postulated, as may be seen in (19iv). This analysis only requires more revisions than the one shown in (19ii) and thus it is correctly predicted to be disfavored only by the Minimal Revisions Principle.[8] (See Nagai, 1995, for another example which shows that an explicit account of Japanese parsing preferences requires the Minimal Revisions Principle.)

So far we have seen that the higher of two potential revisions was preferred in the English novel compound examples (16) and in the Japanese prenominal adjectives examples in (18) and (19), but the lower revision was preferred in the English *put* example in (17). The revision preferences discussed here already disconfirm Sturt & Crocker's (1995) proposal that English revisions proceed bottom-up resulting in low attachment preferences. They also disconfirm Inoue & Fodor's (1995) proposal that revisions are governed by the parser's first-pass parsing principles, including Late Closure which predicts a low attachment

[8] In examples like (19), Gorrell's model may or may not capture the preference for Minimal Revisions depending on the details of how case features are represented. If the genitive feature from *-no* has already literally percolated to N1 at the stage of processing depicted in (19i), then only (19ii) will be available as a cost-free revision in Gorrell's system. However, feature percolation may be implied by structure: if the head has a feature then its *eventual* projection in the final structure does too. In this case, (19iv) is a cost-free revision in Gorrell's system, because the lower N′ in (19i) may be lowered without erasing any precedence statements. In the resulting structure (19iv), the genitive feature will only percolate to the highest projection of 'shoes' and hence the highest N′ in (19iv) will not receive the genitive feature.

preference. Note, however, that two very recently postulated nodes are involved in the English example (16) where high revision is preferred. In section 4 below we will suggest that node visibility differs for recently postulated nodes versus nodes that were postulated less recently. This will result in a system very similar to those proposed by Inoue & Fodor and by Sturt & Crocker; however, it will differ from those systems when Minimal Revisions favors attachment to the higher of two recently postulated nodes. We return to this issue below where we introduce the Visibility Principle. Before turning to our proposal, however, we wish to show that the stipulation that top-down revisions are favored in Japanese is unnecessary—the preferred revisions follow automatically from Minimal Revisions.

Sturt & Crocker (1995) suggest that Japanese revisions proceed top-down, resulting in high revision preferences. In support of this proposal they present evidence from Mazuka & Itoh (1995) suggesting that revisions resulting in removal of one NP from a clause are easier than those resulting in removal of two NPs. Though top-down revision in Japanese could explain this observation, we will argue below that these data follow automatically from the Minimal Revisions principle without the need to parameterize reanalysis, stipulating that it is top-down in Japanese (and bottom-up in English, though see above for counterexamples to this part of their proposal).

Consider next the examples in (20), taken from Mazuka & Itoh (1995).

(20) a. Yoko-ga kodomo-o koosaten-de mikaketa takusii-ni noseta.
Yoko-NOM child-ACC intersection-LOC saw taxi-DAT put-on
'Yoko made the child ride the taxi she saw at the intersection.'

b. Yoko-ga kodomo-o koosaten-de mikaketa.
Yoko-NOM child-ACC intersection-LOC saw
'Yoko saw the child at the intersection.'

c. [Yoko$_i$-ga kodomo-o [O_i O_j koosaten-de mikaketa]
Yoko-NOM child-ACC intersection-LOC saw

takusii$_j$-ni noseta
taxi-DAT put-on

In (20a), the sentence may be taken as a simple clause until after 'taxi-DAT' is encountered, as in sentence (20b). When 'taxi-DAT' is processed, the simple clause analysis must be abandoned, making 'the taxi Yoko saw at the intersection' a relative clause, as indicated in (20c). The sentence in (20c) gives rise to a conscious garden path.

In (20c) both the subject and object of the initially postulated clause (headed by 'saw') end up outside the clause headed by 'saw'. In comparable examples where only the subject of the initially postulated clause ends up outside that clause, no conscious garden path is present, as in (21) from Mazuka & Itoh.

(21) [Yakuza-no kanbu-ga] [O_j wakai kobun-o sagasi-dasita
gang-GEN leader-NOM young member-ACC found

$otoko_j$-ni] rei-o itta.
man-DAT thanked

'The leader of the gang thanked the man who found the young member of the gang.'

Schematically the revisions involved can be seen in (22), where the circled nodes correspond to nodes added at the point of revision. (22a′) and (22b′) illustrate the consequence of making the revisions. (22a) corresponds to (21) and (22b) corresponds to (20). The revision in (22a) occurs at a higher node than the revision in (22b). But notice that the revision in (22a) is also more minimal than the revision in (22b) in terms of the number of new nodes added (only a subject gap in (22a), both a subject and object gap in (22b)) and in terms of the number of lexical phrases that get reanalyzed in that they end up outside of the clause in which they started out, i.e., outside the clause headed by V1.

(22) a. a′.

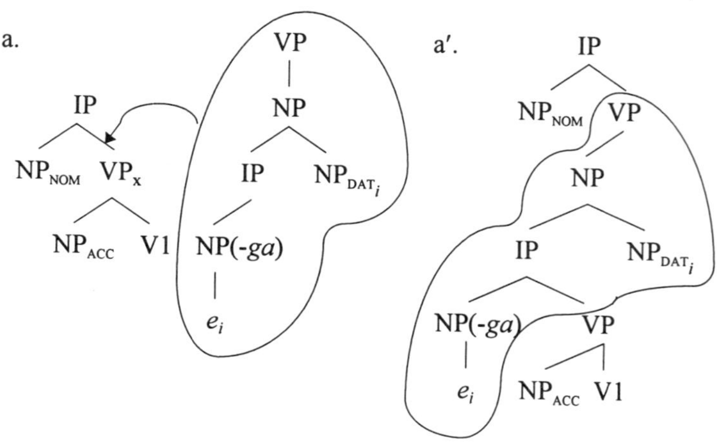

b.

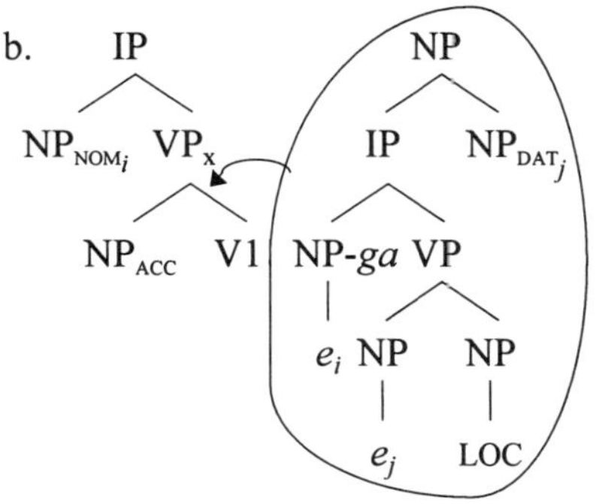

b′.

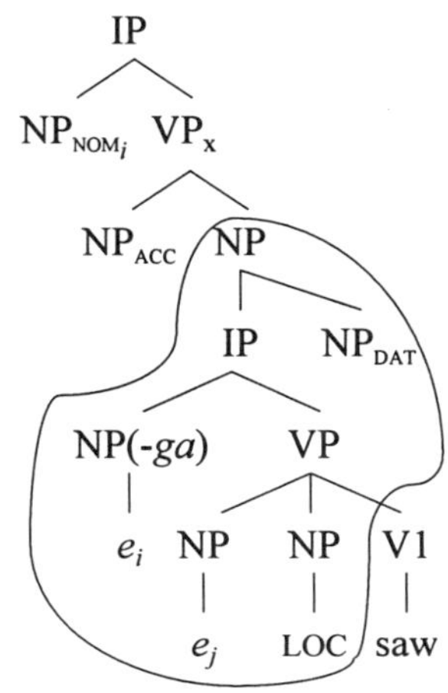

We have argued that the Minimal Revisions principle accounts for the Japanese evidence that Sturt & Crocker (1995) present. However, the Minimal Revisions principle does not account for an English example which they present. This example is the sentence in (23), where the preferred revision is the lower one, resulting in the analysis provided in (23a).

(23) I know the man who believes the count(ess) killed himself.

a. I know the man who believes [the count killed himself]$_{IP}$
b. I know [[the man who believes the count]$_{NP}$ killed himself]$_{IP}$

We agree with Sturt & Crocker's claim that the lower revision is preferred in this example. But this doesn't follow from anything we've said so far, since the lower (23a) and the higher (23b) revisions are equally minimal.

A similar example is presented by Phillips (1995).[9] He presents (24) as a counterexample to Minimal Attachment.

---

9 Phillips (1995) argues for the Generalized Right Association Principle given in (i):

(i) *Generalized Right Association* (GRA): For any pair of overt terminals X and Y, where X is the last terminal attached, attach Y such that the path from X to Y contains as few steps as possible.

We think GRA has many problems For example, it is inconsistent with English N-N-N compounds, with Japanese prenominal modifier examples, and with the Mazuka & Itoh (1995) examples discussed above.

(24) Whenever the class started to think the class had finished.

a. Whenever the class started to [$_{VP}$ think [$_{IP}$ the class had finished]]...
b. Whenever the class started to [$_{VP}$ think][$_{IP}$ the class had finished].

The NP *the class* may be attached as the subject of a sentential complement to *think* within the subordinate clause, as in (24a), or it could be attached as a subject of a following main clause, as in (24b). The lower attachment is preferred (though perhaps the difficulty of taking *think* as an intransitive verb contributes to the difficulty of taking *the class* as the main clause subject).

The examples in (23) and (24) are important because they show that Minimal Revisions does not by itself provide a satisfactory or complete characterization of sentence reanalysis. The examples reintroduce the problem motivating the sausage machine model of Frazier & Fodor (1978), namely, the problem that a generally preferred attachment is not necessarily preferred if it requires attachment to a distant node. It is to the issue of why distant attachments are dispreferred and why low attachments are preferred in examples like (23) and (24) that we will turn next. But first let us summarize the conclusions of section 3. We have argued that Minimal Revisions is needed to characterize sentence reanalysis. Minimal Attachment will not suffice: in English N-N-N compounds, given two equally minimal analyses, the processor favors the addition of a node high resulting in [[NN]N] because this allows the processor to maintain more of the already assigned structure and interpretation. Further, in Japanese, Minimal Attachment would not choose between (19ii), which keeps already assigned structure intact, over (19iv), which does not. A node-height principle will not suffice to characterize reanalysis either because, for example, English favors low attachment in many cases but high attachment/revision in the N-N-N compound cases. Minimal Attachment together with a node height principle (favoring high attachment/revision in Japanese but low attachment/revision in English) also flounders on the English compound examples. These examples show that, other things being equal, the processor favors an analysis that maintains an already assigned interpretation. This preference may force a high attachment/revision to be preferred when the two potential revision sites both involve nodes postulated very recently (assuming no intonational phrase boundary intervenes; see below). We have also suggested that Minimal Revisions automatically accounts for the evidence used to support the claim that top-down revision is preferred in Japanese.

4 Visibility

In this section we argue that it is difficult for the parser to come out of a deep right branch (as in (23b) or (24)) regardless of whether the attachment of the new constituent, the one to be attached high, is ambiguous or not (see Fodor & Frazier, 1980 for an early discussion based on intuitive evidence). We will argue that the difficulty of coming out of a deep right branch can be observed both in the parser's initial analysis and in reanalysis. We suspect that the reason for the difficulty is that the parser's attention is on the last node postulated, not ranging beyond the clause containing that node, and that nodes beyond the current visibility range of the parser can be accessed only with difficulty resulting in a measurable cost in terms of processing times.

We phrase the Visibility Hypothesis in (25) in a way that allows it to refer to both auditory and visual sentence processing. The Visibility principle is intended to apply in *both* first analysis and reanalysis. It applies, we will argue, in the processing of unambiguous as well as ambiguous sentences. The principle covers the examples that used to be covered by the Late Closure principle which was cast as an ambiguity resolution principle. Like Late Closure, it is intended to be a universal property of the human sentence processor. Below we report several experiments, some visual and some auditory, in support of the principle.

(25) *Visibility Hypothesis*: In first analysis and reanalysis, attachment to a visible node is less costly in terms of processing/attentional resources than attachment to a less visible node. (i) Node X is more visible than node Y if X was postulated later than Y. (ii) Nodes within a perceptually-given package (e.g., intermediate phonological phrase) are more visible than nodes outside the package (see Schafer, 1995).

Before turning to the first experiment, we must emphasize that the visibility of a node is continuous or graded, not an all-or-none property of a node. Since visibility is defined with respect to the timing of node postulation, not node-height, more visible nodes will not always be lower nodes, e.g., in left-branching structures. Moreover, because node-visibility is a notion admitting the existence of gradations, there is no expectation that visibility preferences should invariably override, or invariably be overridden by, preferences due to some other principle. In other words, visibility may appear to be an all-or-none factor but only if consideration is limited to the extremes, e.g., strictly the most visible node (the last one postulated) or the least visible node—one postulated so far back that it is long forgotten and not available at all. The above properties of visibility distinguish it from a Late Closure-like principle and from a bottom-up revision principle. Visibility is graded (like Gibson's Recency principle; see Gibson *et al.*, 1996), Late Closure is not. The interaction of visibility with node height automatically depends on the basic branching direction within a language; this need not be stipulated. The interaction of visibility with other parsing preference principles also distinguishes visibility from a preference principle, e.g., given two recently postulated nodes, other principles should 'win' over recency/visibility but not given a very distant/invisible node versus a less distant visible one. These differences are important to note because otherwise our arguments in section 3 against the Late Closure principle or bottom-up revision would also constitute arguments against our own proposal.

We have emphasized that visibility is determined by the recency of node postulation, not by absolute availability/nonavailability to the parser. In (26a), for example, there is a clear preference for the possessive marker *'s* to be attached low to the more visible node dominating *Sam* rather than to the higher less visible node dominating *the daughter of Sam*.[10]

(26) a. the daughter of Sam's son...
b. the daughter of Sam who...

But this cannot be attributed to the absolute invisibility of the higher node, as shown by the ease of processing (26b) which requires attachment of *who* to the higher node. In short, for reasonably visible nodes (typically those within the current clause), the relative visibility of nodes may influence attachment if no other factor is at play, as in (26a). However, if other factors are at play, as in the English novel compound examples, the Japanese prenominal modifier examples and the Mazuka & Itoh (1995) examples (where Minimal Revisions is at issue), then a relatively less visible attachment may be preferred. However, attachment to nodes not currently visible (very high in the structure, typically outside the

[10] We expect the genitive marker *'s* to be analyzed like other primary relations (Frazier & Clifton, 1996). One test for nonprimary relations is to omit an item (e.g., *'s*). If the resulting sentence is grammatical and all remaining constituents (i) receive the same interpretation they would have before the omission and (ii) all remaining items have as many arguments as they did in the original sentence, then the omitted material is non-primary. Clearly the *'s* in (26) fails this test (it is primary) whereas the relative clause passes it (and is nonprimary). Hence, in Frazier & Clifton's framework, *'s* will minimally attach to the most visible available node whereas *who* will associate to the most visible node, with the result that the entire complex NP (the extended projection of *daughter*) will be consistent with the initial syntactic commitment.

current clause) may be extremely difficult in ambiguous examples (see (23) and (24)) and time consuming even in unambiguous ones (as we show below).

We summarize the results of four experiments, one on the effect of the depth of a right branch on processing difficulty, two on the effects of prosody upon visibility, and one on the effect of phonological length (or weight) on perceptual packaging. These experiments must be considered as preliminary evidence suggesting the value of pursuing the Visibility Hypothesis further, not as full-fledged tests of the hypothesis.

4.1 Experiment 1: Depth of a Right Branch

In an eye movement study conducted with Michael Dickey, we investigated the processing of unambiguous sentences like (27).

(27) a. Unfortunately, [the space capsule everyone objected to] had been built by NASA *and cost* the taxpayers a fortune.
b. Unfortunately, [the space capsule everyone objected to after it was built by NASA] *had cost* the taxpayers a fortune.

In (27a), the subject of the main clause is modified by a relative clause that forms a right branch. Attaching the following constituents into the main clause involves coming out of a relatively shallow right branch. By contrast, in (27b), the relative clause contains an adjunct clause, *after it was built by NASA* and thus the relative clause is deeper than it is in (27a). This means that, at the point that *had cost* is encountered, the visibility of the main clause in (27b) (either the IP itself or the VP if the VP-node had been predicted in advance) is less than in (27a): many more recent nodes have been postulated in (27b) than in (27a). Thus the Visibility Hypothesis predicts that the predicate in (27a) should be easier to process than in (27b). Sentence (27b) should be particularly complex at the point where the processor must attach the input items high, outside the relative clause.

This prediction was supported. Thirty-six members of the University of Massachusetts community were tested in an eyetracking experiment in which they read 16 sentences like those in (27).[11] Standard eyetracking procedures

[11] Two additional forms were used in which a homophonous word—*capsule* in the example—was not disambiguated prior to its occurrence, as it is in (27). Subjects read four sentences in each of these four forms. These temporarily ambiguous forms showed the same effect reported in the

were used (Rayner *et al.*, 1989). A Dual-Purkinje Image eyetracker sampled eye fixation position every ms, with accuracy finer than a single character, while subjects read a sentence presented in its entirety on a computer-controlled video monitor. The total reading time for the critical (italicized) region (the sum of all fixation durations in that region, including time spent re-reading it) was shorter for the short right branch ones, like (27a), than for the long right branch sentences, like (27b): 39.7 versus 47.2 ms per character ($t(35) = 3.39$, $p < .01$). Similar results were found for other measures, including first pass times expressed in ms per character.

The results of the experiment support the Visibility Hypothesis in unambiguous sentences. This is informative because it suggests that Late Closure or similar principles are not the correct way of capturing recency or low attachment preferences. In other words, these preferences may be seen to follow from the visibility of the nodes in the phrase-marker, not from preference or ambiguity resolution principles. The results also disconfirm the Recency principle of (Gibson, 1991; Gibson *et al.*, 1996) which assigns a cost to distant attachments only if a more recent attachment is grammatical.

4.2 Experiments 2 and 3: Prosodic Effects

If the Visibility Hypothesis is correct, then the processor should need help in order to identify a very low visibility attachment site. Prosody might provide helpful evidence. In a pilot study of auditory comprehension conducted with Amy Schafer, listeners heard sentences like (28) with the instruction to pull a trigger as soon as they had understood a sentence.

(28) a. The journalists who noticed the strange employees at the factory stumbled.
b. The journalists who noticed the strange employees at the factory STUMBLED.

Sentence (28a) should be extremely difficult to process because the processor must come out of a deep right branch in order to attach the final word as the main predicate. The only evidence that *stumbled* must be attached as the main predicate is the fact that the sentence ends and there is as yet no predicate. Indeed, comprehension was only at 53% as indicated by answers to questions

---

body of the paper, but reading times were longer, reflecting the need to disambiguate the lexical ambiguity.

about *Who stumbled?* (see description below for details). Intuitively the predicted difficulty of (28a) also seems to be confirmed, as the reader may verify by comparing (28a) with (29), which seems intuitively to be much easier to process.

(29) The journalist who noticed Sam stumbled.

In (28b), however, *stumbled* is focused. In spoken English focus is conveyed by a prominent pitch accent (see Selkirk, 1984, 1995, for example). A pitch accent on *stumbled* should make processing the sentence easier for two reasons. First, focus is expected to occur in the main predicate. So the processor has additional evidence about the correct attachment site for *stumbled* in (28b). Second, the duration of a word carrying a prominent pitch accent is typically much longer than the same word when it does not receive a focal accent. Both the extra evidence and the extra time provided by the focal accent in (28b) should help the processor to identify the low visibility attachment site for *stumbled* resulting in faster and/or more accurate comprehension of (28b) relative to (28a). Intuitions support this prediction.

In the experiment with Schafer, 48 University of Massachusetts students heard 16 sentences, together with 60 sentences from unrelated studies and 32 filler sentences. Each sentence had four versions as illustrated in (30).

(30) a. The gardener who saw the general at the capitol sang.
b. The gardener who saw the general at the capitol SANG.
c. The gardener who saw the general at the capitol sang STARED.
d. The gardener who saw the general at the capitol SANG STARED.

Subjects were to indicate by pulling a response lever as quickly as possible after the end of the sentence whether or not they understood the sentence to their satisfaction. Standard counterbalancing procedures were used. 25% of the experimental items were followed by a question (*Who sang?*). Numerically, the percentage of sentences which the subjects indicated that they understood to their satisfaction was higher for sentences with an accented verb (62.5 for (30b), 42.2 for (30d)) than for sentences with an unaccented verb (53.1 for (30a), 25.0 for (30c)). However, neither this difference nor the difference between reaction times was significant. In a replication study where each sentence was followed by a question (*Who sang?* or *Who stared?*), accented forms were classed as 'comprehended' more often than unaccented forms (72.9 versus 79.1 for (30a) versus (30b), 28 versus 34.3 for (30c) versus (30d)) but again this difference was not significant. However, in the replication response times for 'comprehended' sentences differed significantly (1573 versus 1317 for (30a) versus (30b), $p < .06$ by subject, $p < .02$ by items). Response times for control forms did not differ (1158 versus 1043 for (30c) versus (30d)). To summarize, comprehension was relatively low in both studies and numerically lower for the unaccented (a-) form than for the accented (b-) form. In the replication, the difficulty of the a-forms was also observed in the response time measure where the a-form was significantly longer than the b-form. The results thus provide suggestive support for our claim that it is difficult for the processor to come out of a deep right-branch (see also Ferreira & Henderson, this volume).

We turn now to effects of phonologically optional intonational boundaries. The examples differ from the above examples in (28) and (29) because they do not involve coming out of deep right branches to attach a constituent to a low visibility node which is higher in the phrase structure. Instead, the examples suggest that the presence of an intonational phrase boundary (e.g., an 'intermediate' phrase boundary in the system of Beckman & Pierrehumbert, 1986) renders syntactic nodes preceding the boundary less visible, than they would have been without the intonational boundary.

We suspect that many of the examples discussed by Frazier & Fodor (1978) may have been influenced by covert manipulations of intermediate phrase boundaries that perceivers unconsciously supply in making judgments about sentences containing a long constituent. Frazier & Fodor argued that making a difficult attachment to a distant node is easier for the perceiver when the constituent to be attached is long. They examined two types of examples of particular relevance here, using intuitive evidence. One type involved examples like (31a) where a short constituent would minimally attach to the VP on the preferred analysis.

(31)	a.	NP V NP	short constituent
	b.	NP V [NP, NP and NP]	short final constituent
	c.	NP V [NP, NP and NP]	long final constituent

When the preceding constituent was lengthened by making it a conjoined phrase as in (31b), for example, the preference would switch to a preference for a local attachment, even resulting in an anomalous analysis as in *John threw the bat, the ball and the glove down* where one seems to attempt to make *glove down* a constituent. Lengthening the final constituent made the distant attachment intuitively easier, as in *John threw the bat, the ball and the glove down the stairs and out the door*. Perhaps a structurally clearer example (where no possible shift from a particle to a prepositional analysis of *down* arises) is *John sent a package, some newspapers, several magazines and a letter to Mary and the other women living in his old apartment.* There may be a strong temptation for perceivers to place an intonational boundary before the very long constituent (in (31c)) resulting in a less visible and less tempting local attachment site. Similarly in the multiply center-embedded examples Frazier & Fodor discuss, lengthening the VPs may in each instance increase the likelihood of inserting an intonational boundary before the VP, rendering less visible/tempting the VP node dominating the preceding material. Consequently lengthening the second and third VPs in a NP-NP-NP-VP-VP-VP sentence should help perceivers. Frazier & Fodor argued that in fact it does. (See the original article for details.)

The idea that an intonational boundary renders preceding nodes less visible was tested experimentally by Schafer. The same experiment described as Experiment 2 above included 16 sentences like those in (32) (see Schafer, 1995, for a fuller description). Schafer investigated the effect of optional prosodic boundaries during auditory sentence comprehension using sentences with a PP attachment ambiguity like those in (32).

(32)	a.	The bus driver angered the rider with a mean look.	(none)
	b.	The bus driver angered the rider # with a mean look.	(-PP)
	c.	The bus driver angered # the rider with a mean look.	(-NP)
	d.	The bus driver angered # the rider # with a mean look.	(both)

She created four versions of each sentence, as illustrated in (32) where # indicates the presence of an optional intermediate intonational phrase boundary. She hypothesized that an attachment site within the same intermediate intonational phrase as the new item should be more tempting or more visible than an attachment site outside the current intermediate intonational phrase. Thus she expected that the minimal (VP-) attachment would be preferred in (32a) and (32b), but that nonminimal, low (NP-) attachment would be preferred in (32c), where only the low potential attachment site occurred within the current intermediate phrase. Preferences in (32d) should be intermediate between the other conditions.

This is exactly what Schafer (1995) found. She played 48 University of Massachusetts students 16 sentences, four each of the four forms illustrated in (32). After each one, a video terminal presented a question like *Who had a mean look?* and the subject answered orally. The frequency of giving an answer consistent with the 'high' (minimal attachment) interpretation was high for sentences like (32a) and (32b), averaging 64%, but was a significantly lower 47% for sentences like (32c) (and an intermediate 57% for (32d)). Schafer claimed that listeners create full prosodic representations for sentences they hear, and they preferentially attach material to a node within the current intermediate phrase. We take her results as evidence that nodes within a perceptually-given package are more visible than nodes outside that package. We believe that a similar account may be applied in self-paced reading studies where effects of frame-segmentation have been demonstrated. This issue reappears below in our discussion of Experiment 4.

4.3 Experiment 4: Phonological Length

We have already discussed the processing of phrases like *the commander of the army's belt buckle*. When the possessive marker *'s* is encountered the processor must revise the structure in (33).

(33)

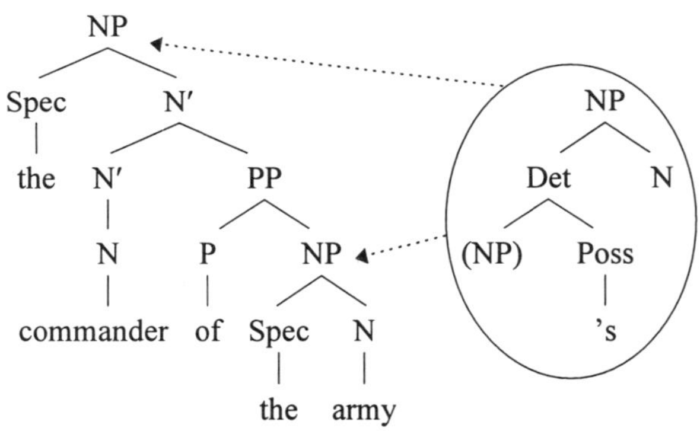

the commander of the army

The Minimal Revisions principle does not choose between revision at the level of the lower NP versus the higher NP. But the lower NP should be more visible, leading to a preference for the low revision. *Belt-buckle* semantically disconfirms the chosen (lower) analysis. Consequently, at this point, another revision is required in order to attach the possessive and *belt-buckle* high. Finding the higher attachment site should require time and effort. Furthermore, if the correct (high) attachment site is not in the preceding frame, reanalysis should be harder than if it is. This prediction was tested in a self-paced reading experiment investigating the processing of sentences like (34).

(34) a. The commander of the army's / belt / was not polished.
b. The commander of the army's / belt-buckle / was not polished.

c. The commander / of the army's / belt / was not polished.
d. The commander / of the army's / belt-buckle / was not polished.

Eight sentences were constructed with correct high attachment for a possessive marker *'s* and following noun. The noun was short in two forms, (34a) and (34c), and long in two forms, (34b) and (34d), to see if reanalysis is harder with short ambiguous phrase (when the ambiguous phrase carries the disambiguating information). Two forms, (34a) and (34b), were divided into three frames so that the entire *NP of NP's* string appeared as one frame; another two forms, (34c) and (34d), split this initial string into two frames. The latter, (34c) and (34d), were predicted to be especially difficult to reanalyze, because the correct attachment site is associated with (headed by) material two frames earlier than the ambiguous word (*belt*, *belt-buckle*).

As predicted, reading times averaged over the final two regions of the sentence (*belt* or *belt-buckle* and *was not polished*) were longer in the two-frame conditions than in the one-frame conditions ((34a) versus (34b), 1288 versus 1193 ms; $F(1,55) = 5.76$, $p < .02$). This supported the clearest prediction of the Visibility Principle. In addition, reading time was slower for sentences with long ambiguous words (*belt-buckle*) than for sentences with short ambiguous words (*belt*), but this is of little interest since the effect appeared only in the region being read, not in the following region (interactions of regions and length $F(1,55) = 4.90$, $p < .04$). Of more interest is the interaction between number of frames (one versus two frames) and length of ambiguous word (*belt* versus *belt-buckle*; $F(1,55) = 4.63$, $p < .04$). Reading time was long for the two-frame, long ambiguous item condition (1389 ms), compared to all other conditions (which ranged from 1186 to 1200 ms). Our analysis had led us to expect the most processing difficulty in (34c), with the short ambiguous item, not (as was actually observed) in (34d), with the long ambiguous item. We are currently conducting research to follow up this observation.

5 Why Visibility?

Various types of evidence indicate that it is difficult for the processor to come out of a deep right branch. These include intuitions about (23) and (24), as well as the experimental results described as Experiments 1 and 2. Further, the length effects characterized in Frazier & Fodor (1978) as well as Schafer's (1995) experimental results (Experiment 3) indicate that the presence of an intonational boundary decreases the visibility of nodes preceding the boundary. Experiment 4 suggests that visual segmentation effects may give rise to similar phenomenon. All these types of evidence suggest that nodes that are distant, because they were postulated long ago or because of an intervening intonational boundary, are less accessible to the processor than less distant nodes. Crucially the effects hold in extreme cases even for unambiguous sentences. This suggests that it is incorrect to characterize them with an ambiguity resolution principle—be it Late Closure, Right Association, Recency, or whatever.

We can imagine several reasons why distant nodes would become less visible to the processor. The (memory trace of) nodes might fade over time, for example. Alternatively, attentional mechanisms might be at work. The processor's attention may reside at the most recently postulated node.

We present (35) as intuitive evidence that the cost of low visibility attachments is likely due to the need to switch the focus of attention in the phrase marker and *not* due to nodes fading over time.

(35) I know the President will claim Bob Dole emphasized that the deficit will explode yesterday in order to scare the Senate into action.

a. I know the President will claim Bob Dole *emphasized it in order to* scare the Senate into action.
b. I know the President will *claim it in order to* scare the Senate into action.

After switching attention to the clause containing *emphasized* in order to make a legitimate attachment of *yesterday*, the *in order to* clause preferentially attaches into this same clause, as would be expected on an attention switching account of why it is difficult to travel long distances through the phrase marker. Though (35) is very difficult to process, our intuitions suggest that analysis (35a) is indeed preferred. The processor is required to switch attention to the past tense clause to attach *yesterday* in (35) and, once attention has switched to this (past tense) clause, the *in order to* clause may also attach within that clause.[12]

---

[12] Compare (34) to (i) where all clauses are future and the adverb *yesterday* has been deleted.

(i) I know the President will claim Bob Dole will emphasize that the deficit will explode in order to scare the Senate into action.

In (i), after an initial attempt to incorporate the *in order to* clause into the lowest clause, our intuitions suggest that, if anything, high attachment is preferred where the *in order to* clause is incorporated into the highest clause. This suggests that the preference in (34) results not from a

6 Conclusions

We have argued that purely structural revision theories are inadequate. Non-structural factors influence reanalysis ease dramatically. Specifically we argued that semantically confirmed decisions are costly to revise.

A variety of examples were used to support the Minimal Revisions principle as a characterization of the preferred reanalysis of a structure. Though we have not discussed the evidence indicating that the informativeness of the error signal matters (Fodor & Inoue, 1994; Frazier & Rayner, 1982), we see the Minimal Revisions principle as an elaboration of an error-driven or diagnosis-model revision procedure.

Finally we have proposed the Visibility Hypothesis and presented evidence that it applies in first analysis and reanalysis, in ambiguous and unambiguous sentences and in auditory and visual language comprehension. Visibility eliminates the need for a principle of Late Closure or Recency. Dealing with reasonably visible nodes (e.g., within the same clause as the current node), a more visible node is preferred (only) when no other principle comes into play which favors the relatively less visible node. Dealing with very low visibility nodes, only visible attachment sites seem, in the first instance, to be considered at all.

University of Massachusetts, Amherst

References

Adams, B.C. 1990. *Syntactically Motivated Parsing Repair: Consequences for Syntax and Semantics*. Unpublished doctoral dissertation, University of Pittsburgh, Pittsburgh, PA.

Beckman, M.E. & Pierrehumbert, J.B. 1986. Intonational structure in Japanese and English. *Phonology*, 3, 255-309.

Carlson, G. & Tanenhaus, M. 1988. Thematic roles and language comprehension. In W. Wilkins (ed.), *Syntax and Semantics, Thematic Relations, Vol. 21*. New York, NY: Academic Press, 263-300.

Clifton, C. 1993. Thematic roles in sentence parsing. *Canadian Journal of Experimental Psychology*, 47, 2, 222-246.

Crain, S. & Steedman, M. 1985. On not being led up the garden path: The use of context by the psychological parser. In D. Dowty, L. Karttunen, & A. Zwicky (eds.), *Natural Language Parsing*. Cambridge, UK: Cambridge University Press, 320-358.

---

low attachment preference but only from the attention switching required for attachment of *yesterday*.

Ferreira, F. & Henderson, J. (this volume). Syntactic reanalysis, thematic processing, and sentence comprehension.

Ferreira, F. & Henderson, J. 1991. Recovery from misanalyses of garden-path sentences. *Journal of Memory and Language*, 30, 725-745.

Fodor, J.D. 1978. Parsing strategies and constraints on transformations. *Linguistic Inquiry*, 9, 427-473.

Fodor, J.D. & Frazier, L. 1980. Is the Human Sentence Parsing Mechanism an ATN? *Cognition*, 8, 417-459.

Fodor, J.D. & Inoue, A. 1994. The diagnosis and cure of garden-path sentences. *Journal of Psycholinguistic Research*, 23, 407-434.

Frazier, L. & Fodor, J.D. 1978. The sausage machine: A new two-stage parsing model *Cognition*, 6, 1-34.

Frazier, L. 1978. *On Comprehending Sentences: Syntactic Parsing Strategies*. Unpublished doctoral dissertation, University of Connecticut, Storrs, CT. Distributed by the Indiana University Linguistics Club, Bloomington, IN.

Frazier, L. 1990. Identifying Structure under X^0. In A. Jongman & A. Lahiri (eds.), *Yearbook of Morphology*, 3, 87-109.

Frazier, L. & Clifton, C. 1989. Successive cyclicity in the grammar and the parser. *Language and Cognitive Processes*, 4, 2, 93-126.

Frazier, L. & Clifton, C. 1996. *Construal*. Cambridge, MA: MIT Press.

Frazier, L. & Rayner, K. 1982. Making and correcting errors during sentence comprehension: Eye movements in the analysis of structurally ambiguous sentences. *Cognitive Psychology*, 14, 178-210.

Gibson, E.A.F. 1991. *A Computational Theory of Human Linguistic Processing: Memory Limitations and Processing Breakdown*. Unpublished doctoral dissertation, Carnegie Mellon University, Pittsburgh, PA. Available as Center for Machine Translation Technical Report CMU-CMT-91-125.

Gibson, E.A.F., Pearlmutter, N., Canseco-González, E., & Hickok, G. 1996. Recency preference in the human sentence processing mechanism. *Cognition*, 59, 23-59.

Goodluck, H., Sedivy, J., & Finney, M. 1992. Sentence completeness and the understanding of long distance dependencies in natural language. *Proceedings of ECCOS*, Orsay, France, 99-108.

Gorrell, P. 1993. Incremental structure-building and the determinism hypothesis. Paper presented at *Sixth Annual CUNY Conference on Human Sentence Processing*, Amherst, MA.

Gorrell, P. (this volume). Syntactic analysis and reanalysis in sentence processing.

Hagoort, P. & Brown, C. 1994. Brain responses to lexical ambiguity resolution and parsing. In C. Clifton, L. Frazier, & K. Rayner (eds.), *Perspectives on Sentence Processing*. Hillsdale, NJ: Lawrence Erlbaum Associates, 45-80.

Huitema, J., Kennison, S., Schmauder, R., Frazier, L., & Clifton, C. (in progress). Head identification and the processing of novel compounds.

Inoue, A. & Fodor, J. 1995. Information-paced parsing of Japanese. In R. Mazuka & N. Nagai (eds.), *Japanese Sentence Processing*. Hillsdale, NJ: Lawrence Erlbaum, 9-64.

Kennison, S. 1995. The role of verb specific lexical information in syntactic resolution. Unpublished doctoral dissertation, University of Massachusetts, Amherst, MA.

Langendoen, D.T. 1976. A case of apparent ungrammaticality. In T.G. Bever, J.J. Katz, & D.T. Langendoen (eds.), *An Integrated Theory of Linguistic Ability*. New York, NY: Thomas Y. Crowell Company, 183-194.

Mazuka, R. 1991. Processing of empty categories in Japanese. *Journal of Psycholinguistic Research*, 20, 215-232.

Mazuka, R. & Itoh, K. 1995. Can Japanese speakers be led down the garden path? In R. Mazuka & N. Nagai (eds.), *Japanese Sentence Processing*. Hillsdale, NJ: Lawrence Erlbaum, 295-330.

MacDonald, M.C., Pearlmutter, N.J., & Seidenberg, M.S. 1994. The lexical nature of syntactic ambiguity resolution. *Psychological Review*, 101, 676-703.

Nagai, N. 1995. Constraints on topics: from a parsing perspective. In R. Mazuka & N. Nagai (eds.), *Japanese Sentence Processing*. Hillsdale, NJ: Lawrence Erlbaum, 77-104.

Pearlmuter, N.J. & MacDonald, M.C. 1995. Individual probabilistic constraints in syntactic ambiguity resolution. *Journal of Memory and Language*, 34, 4, 521-542.

Phillips, C. 1995. Right association in parsing and grammar. Unpublished manuscript, MIT, Cambridge, MA. (Poster presented at *Eighth Annual CUNY Conference on Human Sentence Processing*, Tucson, AZ.)

Pickering, M., Barton, S., & Shillcok, R. 1994. Unbounded dependencies, island constraints and processing complexity. In C.E. Clifton, L. Frazier, & K. Rayner (eds.), *Perspectives on Sentence Processing*. Hillsdale, NJ: Lawrence Erlbaum, 199-224.

Pickering, M. & Traxler, M. (1994) Plausibility and recovery from garden paths: An eye-tracking study. Manuscript, University of Glasgow.

Pritchett, B.L. 1988. Garden path phenomena and the grammatical basis of language processing. *Language*, 64, 539-576.

Pritchett, B.L. 1992. *Grammatical Competence and Parsing Performance*. Chicago: University of Chicago Press.

Rayner, K., Sereno, S.C., Morris, R.K., Schmauder, A.R., & Clifton, C. 1989. Eye movements and on-line language comprehension processes. *Language and Cognitive Processes*, 4, 21-49.

Schafer, A. 1995. The role of optional boundaries in disambiguation. Poster presented at *Eighth Annual CUNY Conference on Human Sentence Processing*.

Selkirk, E. 1984. *Phonology and Syntax: The Relation between Sound and Structure*. Cambridge, MA: MIT Press.

Selkirk, E. 1995. Sentence prosody: Intonation, stress and phrasing. In J. Goldsmith (ed.), *Handbook of Phonological Theory*. Oxford, UK: Blackwell.

Stevenson, S. & Merlo, P. (submitted) Lexical structure and processing complexity.

Stowe, L. 1989. Thematic structures and sentence comprehension. In G.N. Carlson & M.K. Tanenhaus (eds.), *Linguistic structure in language processing*. Dordrecht: Kluwer Academic Publishers, 319-357.

Sturt, P. & Crocker, M. 1995. Montonic parsing and reanalysis. Paper presented at *Eighth Annual CUNY Conference on Human Sentence Processing*, Tucson, AZ.

Sturt, P. & Crocker, M. 1996. Monotonic syntactic processing: A cross-linguistic study of attachment and reanalysis. *Language and Cognitive Processes*, 11, 449-494.

Suh, S. 1994. *The Syntax of Korean and Its Implications for Parsing Theory*. Unpublished doctoral dissertation, University of Maryland, College Park, MD.

Warner, J. & Glass, A.L. 1987. Context and distance-to-disambiguation effects in ambiguity resolution: Evidence from grammaticality judgments of garden-path sentences. *Journal of Memory and Language*, 26, 714-738.

Weinberg, A. 1995. Licensing constraints and the theory of grammar. In R. Mazuka & N. Nagai (eds.), *Japanese Sentence Processing*. Hillsdale, NJ: Lawrence Erlbaum, 235-256.

6

Diagnosis and Reanalysis: Two Processing Aspects the Brain May Differentiate

Angela D. Friederici

Abstract

A two stage parsing system is proposed in which the first stage is compatible with the initial stage of garden-path models held responsible for the build-up of the simplest structure justified by the input. The second stage consists of two subprocesses taking place once the initial structure has to be revised. The initial subprocess comprises the diagnosis of the need for reanalysis, the subsequent subprocess represents the actual reanalysis, i.e., the structural alterations necessary to recover from the structure that has been identified as being incorrect. On the basis of findings from studies using event-related brain potential measures it is hypothesized that these two subprocesses may be reflected in two different parameters of the positivity correlated with the processing of garden-path sentences, namely its onset latency and its duration.

1 Introduction

Several recent studies focus on the issue whether and under what circumstances the parser is forced to reanalyze a given language input. While advocates of the constraint-satisfaction-model (MacDonald, 1994; MacDonald *et al.*, 1994; Perlmutter & MacDonald, 1995; Trueswell *et al.*, 1994) claim that the frequency of lexical, syntactic, and probabilistic contextual constraints interacts continuously to govern possible sentence ambiguities, be they lexical or syntactic, proponents of the garden-path model (Frazier, 1978, 1987, 1990; Frazier & Flores d'Arcais, 1989; Frazier & Rayner, 1982) hold that the initial parse is independent of lexical and contextual information and that these information types only come into play during a second stage of parsing covering

J.D. Fodor and F. Ferreira (eds.), Reanalysis in Sentence Processing, 177–200.

thematic role assignment and, if necessary, reanalysis. The initial stage is described as a first-pass parse during which the simplest structure compatible with the input is constructed on the basis of word category information. This parsing principle, however, may not always lead to the correct structure as a given input may be compatible with more than one syntactic structure. Once the parser realizes that the incoming input is no longer compatible with the initial structure, reanalysis must take place. Although the initial stage of parsing is specified quite explicitly in this model and has triggered a large number of experimental studies, the process of reanalysis only moved into the psycholinguistic focus very recently.

From the different models it is not clear what the processes underlying structural revisions should be. Is it that the parser reconsiders the phrase level and reattaches phrases in the structural tree as assumed by garden-path models? Or is it that the parser does not reanalyze the structure in the proper sense but rather reactivates an initially nonpreferred though parsed structure? This latter view is held by the so-called parallel parsing models (Hickok, 1993; Gorrell, 1987). Although these models explain the processing of preferred versus nonpreferred structures by assuming different activation levels between these, they do not give a systematic account for the raising and lowering of the activation level for nonpreferred structures, which would allow clear predictions for the processing of different types of nonpreferred structures (but see Gibson (1991) for a proposal of this sort).

The ranked flagged serial model of Inoue & Fodor (1995) assumes that during first-pass parsing, alternatives to the preferred analysis are noted (flagged) and assigned a certain value (ranked), though these alternatives are not pursued further with respect to their structural details. If revision becomes necessary the parser looks back and selects a flag representing a good point to start reparsing from. It either finds an highly-ranked alternative leading to a reparse, or it might find alternatives which are rated extremely low, leading to the parser's decision of not going through the trouble of revising. In the latter case the parser may never escape the garden-path.

Yet another alternative is proposed by Fodor & Inoue (1994) in their diagnosis model. This model is not a reparsing model, but rather a repair model in that it proposes that the parser's ability to diagnose its initial error is the most important factor in recovery from first-pass misanalyses of ambiguous input. Once diagnosed, the correct sequence necessary for repairs available will be determined. The type of structural change required for reanalysis seems relevant only indirectly as it may influence the difficulty of finding the target sequence.

In contrast, Gorrell (1996), though acknowledging diagnosis as a factor, claims that the type of structural reanalysis does matter. According to this view, at least two types of ambiguity resolution can be differentiated: one that requires adding structure and another that calls for altering dominance and precedence relations. The former type of ambiguity resolution is assumed to be easier than the latter. This chapter presents empirical data from studies investigating the resolution of structural ambiguities. These data will be discussed against a processing-oriented view taking into account the temporal parameters of processes underlying initial parsing and reanalysis.

2 The Processing View of Revision

From a processing point of view we may consider the process of initial parsing and revision to encompass a number of different processes and subprocesses. In a two-stage garden-path model (Frazier, 1978, 1987; Gorrell, 1995) the parser is assumed to build, during the first processing stage, an initial structure which in case of structural ambiguity will be the simplest one justified by the input. This stage also represents the first processing step in the view advocated in this chapter.

In the garden-path model the second stage is assumed to encompass thematic role assignment and, if necessary, structural revision. We take the revision process as consisting of two subprocesses: diagnosis and reanalysis. If the initial structure is not supported by the subsequent input, the parser must diagnose the need and the possibility for reanalysis as a first step during this second stage. The ease with which the need for reanalysis can be diagnosed may contribute to the ease/difficulty of revision (Fodor & Inoue, 1994). If reanalysis is possible, it is carried out in a subsequent processing step. The type of structural changes required may also determine the difficulty of the revision process (Gorrell, 1996). Thus, the processing view holds that both aspects, namely the ease of diagnosis and the difficulty of the structural alterations, contribute to the ease/difficulty of the revision process.

Some empirical data in support of this view come from studies evaluating the processes of reanalysis of nonpreferred object fronted relative and complement clauses in German using event-related brain potentials (ERPs) as the dependent variable. This measurement permits the continuous tracking of the processes of parsing decisions and revisions as they unfold in time.

3 Language Processing in ERP

The event-related brain potential (ERP) is a transient series of recordable voltage oscillations in the brain that occur in response to discrete events. ERPs can provide a record on an individual's response to every word within a visually or auditorily presented sentence without the intrusive requirement of a manual or verbal response. Unlike reaction time measures, ERPs are multidimensional since ERP components can be distinguished by their amplitude, polarity, latency and scalp topography. Given that different brain systems are involved in language processing, as indicated by behavioral studies with patients suffering from brain lesions (e.g., Blumstein *et al.*, 1982; Friederici, 1983; Zurif *et al.*, 1993), one would expect ERP components to vary as a function of different aspects of language processing.

Three different ERP components have been identified as correlating with different aspects of language comprehension. One of these components, the N400, appears to reflect lexical-semantic aspects of language processing, particularly lexical integration. This component is a negativity which is present 400 ms after the onset of a critical word violating the lexical expectations (Kutas & Hillyard, 1983; Kutas & Van Petten, 1988; Van Petten & Kutas, 1991).

There are two components observed with syntactic aspects of processing: an 'early' left anterior negativity present between 200 to 400 ms after a critical element violating the phrase structure and a 'late' centro-parietal positivity present between 350 to 800 ms after a critical element which violates either a structural preference or a structural expectancy. This centro-parietal positivity can sometimes also be observed following an early left anterior negativity after a phrase structure violation. While the early left anterior negativity is taken to be associated to first-pass parsing processes, especially their failure, the late centro-parietal positivity is hypothesized to be correlated with aspects of structural reanalysis and repair processes, including those necessary when confronting ungrammaticalities from which the system can recover (Friederici, 1995). Phrase structure violations evoke a left anterior negativity (Friederici *et al.*, 1993; Münte *et al.*, 1993) sometimes followed by a centro-parietal positivity (Friederici *et al.*, 1996; Neville *et al.*, 1991). As the early left anterior negativity is observed, in particular, with violations of word category information disallowing phrase structure building, it is assumed to reflect central aspects of first-pass parsing. In contrast, violations of structural preferences requiring a reanalysis of the initial structure seem to generate a centro-parietal positivity only (Mecklinger *et al.*, 1995; Osterhout & Holcomb, 1992, 1993; Osterhout *et al.*, 1994).[1]

The positivity found in correlation with sentences requiring a reanalysis varies in amplitude (Osterhout *et al.*, 1994) and in latency (Mecklinger *et al.*, 1995; Friederici *et al.*, 1996). Osterhout *et al.* (1994) claim that the amplitude of the late positivity (P600) reflects the variation of the 'cost of processing', with higher processing costs being correlated with a higher amplitude. This was recently confirmed in a general sense in the study by Mecklinger *et al.* (1995) who found the reading of disambiguating elements in object-first relative clauses to be correlated with a positivity of higher amplitude than the positivity associated with reading the disambiguating element in subject-first relative clauses. However, the latency of this positivity (345 ms) was shorter than positivities observed in other studies investigating garden-path sentences (600 ms) (Osterhout *et al.*, 1994). The possibility has been raised that the difference in the positivity's latency may reflect the difficulty of reanalysis necessary to recover from a garden-path (Friederici, 1995; Friederici & Mecklinger, 1996). This was based on the observation that the revision process appeared to be particularly easy for those sentences used in the Mecklinger *et al.* (1995) study. Given the consideration of two subprocesses during revision, namely, diagnosis and reanalysis, these two subprocesses might be reflected in the different aspects of the centro-parietal positivity. The former subprocess may be reflected in the latency of the positivity whereas the latter may be reflected in the positivity's amplitude and/or duration.[2] As there is no processing theory specifying the number and type of processing steps needed for recovery from nonpreferred structures the present processing view of reanalysis and its assumed ERP correlates should be considered as a working hypothesis.

---

[1] It should be noted that a 'centro-parietal positivity only' pattern was also reported for subcategorization violations in one study (Hagoort *et al.*, 1993). However, this same error type was reported to correlated with a biphasic 'negativity-positivity' pattern in a different study (Rösler *et al.*, 1993). Moreover agreement violations were reported to elicit either a positivity (Hagoort *et al.*, 1993); a biphasic pattern, i.e., a negativity followed by a positivity (Gunter *et al.*, 1995); or an N400 (Osterhout & Mobley, 1995) depending on the particular type.

[2] Note that this hypothesis is independent of the notion of whether or not the centro-parietal positivity is a component specific to the process of reanalysis. It may well reflect processes of repair (after confrontation with ungrammatical sentences) as well. The hypothesis put forward here so far is only formulated with respect to those centro-parietal positivities observed in correlation with the processing of garden-path sentences.

4 Processing Subject-First and Object-First Structures

Previous behavioral studies on the initial structural analysis and the revision processes in temporarily ambiguous subject-first and object-first sentences, have shown a strong tendency to disambiguate these towards a subject interpretation in Dutch (Frazier, 1987; Frazier & Flores d'Arcais, 1989), in Italian (De Vincenzi, 1991) and in German (Schriefers *et al.*, 1995; Schlesewsky *et al.*, 1996; Bader & Lasser, 1994; Hemforth, 1993). Different linguistic and psycholinguistic explanations have been put forward for this subject-first preference (Frazier, 1987; Frazier & Flores d'Arcais, 1989; Gorrell, 1995, 1996; Schlesewsky *et al.*, 1996). Although we will not discuss them here in detail, we will briefly sketch each explanation. Two of the most general principles proposed to explain the subject-first preference are the Active Filler Strategy (Frazier, 1987; Frazier & Flores d'Arcais, 1989) and the Minimal Chain Principle (De Vincenzi, 1991). These principles specify that the displaced constituents are assigned to the first available position consistent with the grammar under analysis, predicting that object-first structures are harder to process than subject-first structures even in languages which do not have a strict word order, such as German. Gorrell (1996), subscribing to the principle of simplicity of structure building in general, notes that German shows only a weak subject-initial preference in parsing. Although there is a subject-initial preference for sentences which are totally ambiguous, revision processes seem easy for those sentences in which the first NP is ambiguous but the second NP is unambiguously case-marked with nominative case thus requiring an object-initial reading. His theoretical explanation for the observation is based on a particular analysis of the German verb-second clause (for details, see Gorrell, 1996, this volume). Important for the analysis is the proposal of Travis (1991) that preverbal subjects in German are in IP whereas preverbal objects (and *wh*-phrases) are in CP. Following the principle of simplicity, this proposal results in the preference to analyze preverbal NPs as subjects rather than preposed objects.

The empirical data presented here come from studies evaluating the revision processes for nonpreferred object-fronted relative and complement clauses in German. Different types of reanalysis, i.e., structural alterations, are assumed for the two clause types. The structural changes necessary to reconstruct an object relative clause from a subject relative clause are predicted to be easy as they only require re-coindexation of an already existing filler-gap relation (Figure 1). Reanalysis of an object-first complement clause is predicted to be difficult as it requires establishing a filler-gap relation in a structure where no such relation existed (Figure 2).

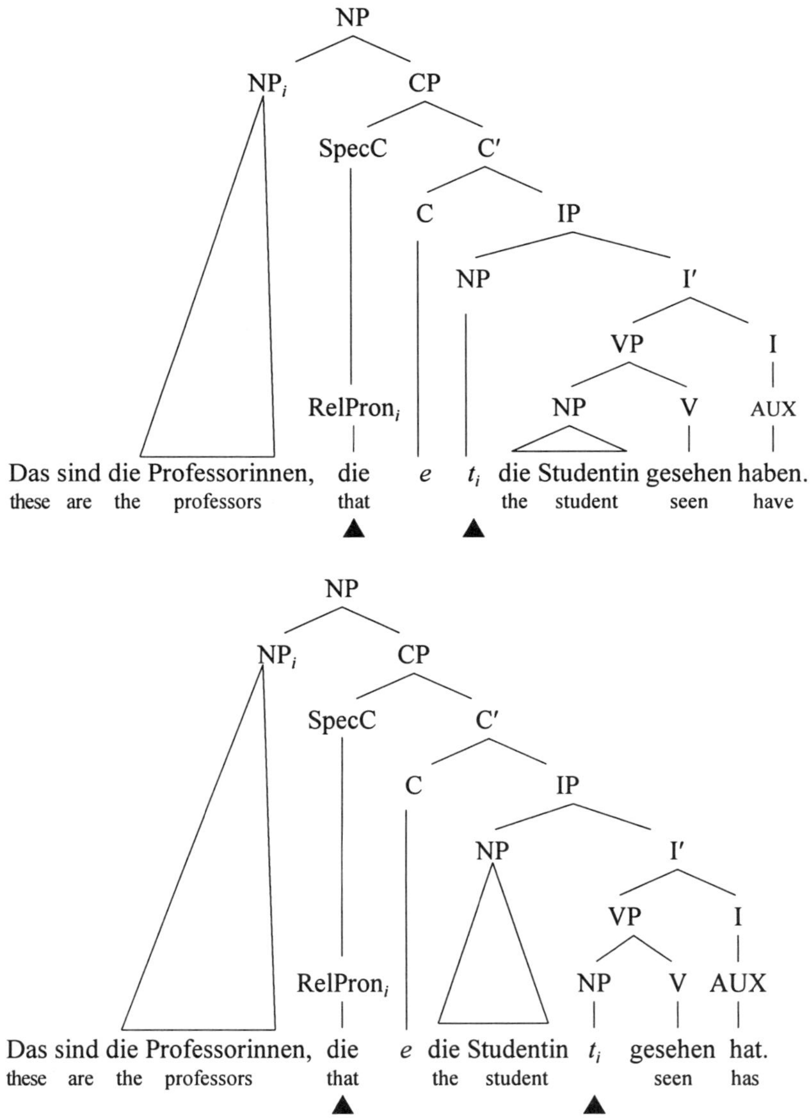

FIGURE 1: This figure displays the structural trees for German subject relative clauses (top) and object relative clauses (bottom). The filler-gap relation is marked by the filled triangles. Traces are indicated by t_i.

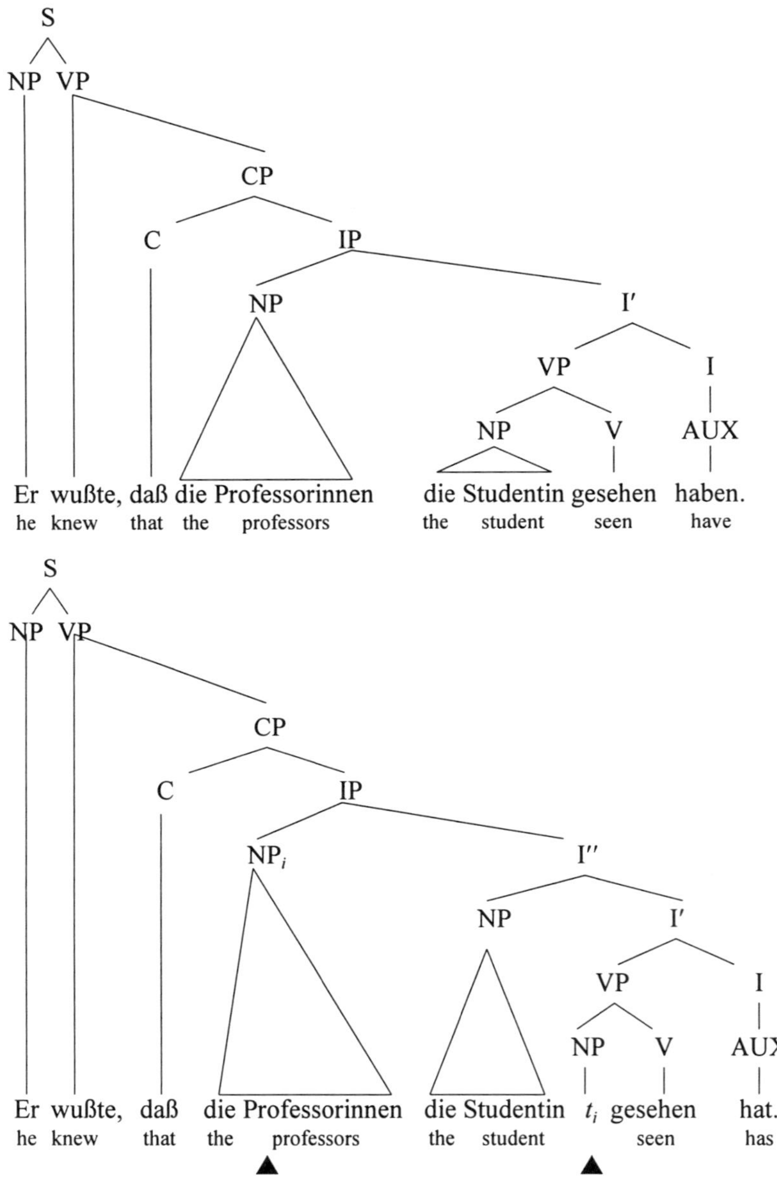

FIGURE 2: This figure displays the structural trees for German subject-first complement clauses (top) and object-first complement clauses (bottom). The filler-gap relation is marked by the filled triangles. Traces are indicated by t_i.

The predictions with respect to the aspect of diagnosis are less straightforward. Fodor & Inoue (1994) assume the ease of diagnosis depends on the effectiveness of the 'symptom', that is, the element signaling an error in a particular structure. In the sentences studied here, however, the identical element signaling the error appears in both clause types, (the relative clauses and the complement clauses). Thus, if the ease of diagnosis only depends on the particular element signaling the error independent of the structure in which it is embedded, it should be equally effective in both clause types. If, however, the effectiveness of the symptom not only depends on the element signaling the error, but also on the element in a particular structure, ease of diagnosis may vary as function of a diagnostic element in a given structure. If this is the case, the same element could have different effectiveness in different structures, while different elements could have different effectiveness in the same structure.[3] It will be shown that both the type of diagnostic element and the type of reanalysis are relevant for the immediacy and successfulness of the revision process.

5 The Data

5.1 Experiment 1

In a first experiment we investigated the processing of subject and object relative clause sentences which either contained a semantic bias for the particular structural interpretation, as in (1) and (2) below, or not, as in (3) and (4).

(1) *Subject relative, semantic bias:*
Das sind die Professorinnen, die die Studentin geprüft *haben.*
These are the professors that the student examined *have.*

[3] In the materials used in the present study different kinds of diagnostic elements (subject-verb agreement and case morphology) are used in two clause types which differ in syntactic structure (subject and object relative clauses as well as subject and object complement clauses) and thereby in the assumed type of reanalysis. Note that the relative clause and complement clause sentences used here, moreover, differ with respect to pragmatic aspects, namely with respect to their focus structure. Object-first complement sentences are rather heavily marked in the sense that in such sentences the subject must be narrowly focused. Marking is particularly strong if both the object and the subject are definite NPs. No such pragmatic constraints obtain for subject-first complement clauses or for relative clauses.

(2) *Object relative, semantic bias:*
Das sind die Studentinnen, die die Professorin geprüft *hat.*
These are the students that the professor examined *has.*

(3) *Subject relative, no semantic bias:*
Das sind die Professorinnen, die die Studentin gesehen *haben.*
These are the professors that the student seen *have.*

(4) *Object relative, no semantic bias:*
Das sind die Professorinnen, die die Studentin gesehen *hat.*
These are the professors that the student seen *has.*

These types of sentences are ambiguous up to the sentence final auxiliary. At this point number marking information disambiguates the sentences either towards a subject or an object relative clause interpretation.

As we have discussed the results from this study elsewhere in detail (Mecklinger *et al.*, 1995; Friederici & Mecklinger, 1996) we will only briefly report the major findings here. Using ERP registration while participants read these types of sentences, we observed a centro-parietal positivity peaking at 345 ms at the sentence final auxiliary for both the semantically neutral and the semantically biased sentences. The positivity with a higher amplitude for the object compared to the subject relative clauses was taken to reflect the revision process necessary to recover from an initially computed subject relative structure. The finding that this positivity was present independently of the semantic bias was taken as an indication that a sentence's initial structure is built independently of lexical-semantic aspects and not (necessarily) revised on the basis of lexical-semantic information alone. As the latency of the observed positivity was about 250 ms shorter than that found in other studies investigating the processing of garden-path sentences (Osterhout & Holcomb, 1992; Osterhout *et al.*, 1994), we hypothesized that the latency of the positivity may be a function of the type of revision process. This hypothesis was tested in a following experiment.

5.2 Experiment 2

In this experiment we varied the difficulty of the revision process by investigating the processing of semantically neutral sentences of different structures, namely subject and object relative clauses, examples (3) and (4) above, and subject and object-first complement clauses, examples (5) and (6) below (Friederici & Mecklinger, 1996).

(5) *Subject-first complement clause:*
Er wußte, daß die Professorinnen die Studentin gesehen *haben.*
He knew that the professors the student seen *have.*

(6) *Object-first complement clause:*
Er wußte, daß die Professorinnen die Studentin gesehen *hat.*
He knew that the professors the student seen *has.*

Sentences (3)-(6) are ambiguous with respect to case and are disambiguated by the number marking in the sentence final auxiliary. Case ambiguity is due to the fact that feminine NPs and pronouns have identical nominative and accusative forms (*die*). The processing of these sentences may be described as follows. Sentence (3) requires a subject relative reading whereas (4) requires an object relative reading. The parser, however, will only be able to apply the correct reading when encountering the number-marked sentence final auxiliary. If the parser initially computes the simplest structure justified by the input it will construct a subject relative structure identifying the relative pronoun *die* as the filler and giving it the grammatical function of the subject. In order to revise a subject relative clause to an object relative clause the parser may simply change the grammatical function of the already identified filler from subject to object without altering the structural tree as illustrated above in Figure 1. The processing of these relative clause sentences is compared to the processing of subject-first and object-first complement clauses, with the latter presumably requiring more difficult structural alterations during the revision process as they include the new positioning of a filler-trace relation. That is, in order to revise a subject-first complement clause (5) to an object-first reading (6) upon encountering the sentence final auxiliary, the parser has to posit a new filler-trace relation where a filler has not yet been identified. This operation, illustrated above in Figure 2, requires quite dramatic alterations in the tree structure. We assume that the difference in the difficulty of the revision process is reflected in the late centro-parietal positivity expected for the processing of the nonpreferred object-first structures.

The difference in the difficulty of the revision process could be due to the difficulty of the actual structural reanalysis as illustrated in Figures 1 and 2 alone and/or the ease with which the need for revision can be diagnosed (Fodor & Inoue, 1994; Gorrell, 1996). The latter aspect, however, can only predict differences for the particular sentences under evaluation if the original definition of the 'effectiveness of a symptom' (Fodor & Inoue, 1994) is extended to depend upon aspects beyond the diagnostic element signaling the misanalysis itself, as this element is the same in the relative clause sentences exemplified in

(3) and (4) and in the complement clause sentences exemplified in (5) and (6). It is not unlikely that the effectiveness of a given element as a symptom could be influenced by a number of aspects such as focus structure (marked versus unmarked) of a given sentence or frequency of occurrence of a given sentence structure (high versus low). Diagnosis of misanalysis may be harder in low frequency structures and in heavily marked focus structures. As object-first complement clauses are both more heavily marked and presumably less frequent than object-first relative clauses,[4] these two clause types may differ with respect to the ease of diagnosis in addition to the difficulty of the actual reanalysis to be carried out.

The aspect of difficulty of reanalysis as well as the aspect of ease of diagnosis may be reflected in different parameters of the centro-parietal positive ERP component such as its latency, amplitude and/or duration. Under the assumption that the revision process consists of two successive processing stages (diagnosis and reanalysis), and under the further assumption that the effectiveness of a symptom for diagnosis determines the ease with which the reanalysis itself can be initiated whereas the difficulty of the reanalysis is determined by the duration of the revision process, we hypothesized that the ease of diagnosis may be reflected in the latency, and that the difficulty of the actual reanalysis may be reflected in the duration and/or amplitude of the centro-parietal positivity observed in correlation with the processing of garden-path sentences.

The difference between the processing of object relative clauses and object-first complement clauses can certainly be characterized as a difference in the difficulty of the revision process. The revision of case ambiguous object relative clause sentences is assumed to be easy both on structural and processing grounds (Gorrell, 1996; Mecklinger *et al.*, 1995) whereas the revision process for object-first complement clause sentences requiring important structural alterations may be assumed to be more difficult (Friederici & Mecklinger, 1996). Thus we predict that the electrophysiological response elicited by the sentence final disambiguating element will differ in the duration and/or amplitude.

Moreover, if the revision process is triggered immediately by the element signaling the misanalysis we expect a late centro-parietal positive ERP component reflecting revision to be present at the element carrying the

---

4 Unfortunately no frequency count for structure is available for German.

disambiguating information.[5] As German is a case marking language we are able to test this additional aspect by using case-marked NPs in different positions in the sentence. For example, sentences (7)-(10) contain unambiguously case-marked pronouns and NPs in *clause-initial position* (first NP).

(7) *Subject relative clause, clause-initial disambiguation:*
Das ist der Professor, *der* die Sekretäre gesehen hat.
This is the (NOM sg) professor *that (NOM sg)* the secretaries seen has.

(8) *Object relative clause, clause-initial disambiguation:*
Das ist der Professor, *den* die Sekretäre gesehen haben.
This is the (NOM sg) professor *that (ACC sg)* the secretaries seen have.

(9) *Subject-first complement clause, clause-initial disambiguation:*
Sie wußte, daß *der* Sekretär die Professoren gesehen hat.
She knew that *the (NOM sg)* secretary the professors seen has.

(10) *Object-first complement clause, clause-initial disambiguation:*
Sie wußte, daß *den* Sekretär die Professoren gesehen haben.
She knew that *the (ACC sg)* secretary the professors seen have.

In the relative clause sentences the singular masculine relative pronoun carries an unambiguous marking for either nominative (7), indicating the functional role of subject, or accusative (8), indicating the functional role of object. In the subject-first and object-first complement clause sentences, disambiguation is possible at the first singular noun phrase when carrying nominative case marking indicating subject role (9), or accusative case marking indicating object role (10). Additional sentences contained the case-marked elements in *clause-medial position* (11)-(14) (second NP).

(11) *Subject relative clause, clause-medial disambiguation:*
Das sind die Sekretäre, die *den* Professor gesehen haben.
These are the secretaries that *the (ACC sg)* professsor seen have.

---

5 Although its presence should be independent of the position of the diagnostic element, its latency may not. However, no specific predictions were made with respect to the latency of the positivity expected for different positions of the diagnostic element in the clause.

(12) *Object relative clause, clause-medial disambiguation:*
Das sind die Sekretäre, die *der* Professor gesehen hat.
These are the secretaries that *the (NOM sg)* professor seen has.

(13) *Subject-first complement clause, clause-medial disambiguation:*
Sie wußte, daß die Professoren *den* Sekretär gesehen haben.
She knew that the professors *the (ACC sg)* secretary seen have.

(14) *Object-first complement clause, clause-medial disambiguation:*
Sie wußte, daß die Professoren *der* Sekretär gesehen hat.
She knew that the professors *the (NOM sg)* secretary seen has.

For these unambiguously marked sentences we predict a larger positivity (a positivity of higher amplitude) for the less preferred object-first sentences than for the subject-first sentences at the point of disambiguation, i.e., at the case-marked relative pronoun and the case-marked noun phrase. Furthermore, if structure assignment is made ultimately at the point of disambiguation no further effect should be observed for these sentences at the sentence final auxiliary.

The participants (N = 10) in this ERP study were presented with this type of sentences, visually displayed in six chunks of one word (or two, in the case of NPs). Presentation times (plus subsequent interstimulus intervals) for ERP-relevant chunks were 300 ms (+300 ms) for the relative pronoun, 550 ms (+550 ms) for the noun phrases (article plus noun), and 400 ms for the sentence final auxiliary. Two seconds after the offset of the auxiliary a yes/no question concerning the content of the preceding sentence (e.g., *Was the professor seen?*) was presented, to which the participant responded by pressing a button. The brain's electrophysiological activity was recorded from 11 electrode sites, including seven locations based on the International 10-20 System (Fz, Cz, Pz, F3, F4, O1, O2) and four nonstandard locations, (the Wernicke area (WL) and its right hemisphere homologue (WR), and the Broca area (BL) and its right hemisphere homologue (BR)).

5.3 Ambiguously Case-Marked Sentences

The ERPs during the interval from the onset of the disambiguating *clause final auxiliary* for case ambiguous relative clauses and case ambiguous complement clauses are displayed in Figure 3 and Figure 4. In each of the plots the ERPs from the subject-first and the object-first sentences are superimposed. For the relative clause sentences (Figure 3) we observed a first positivity between 300 and 400 ms after the onset of the auxiliary most evident at the three midline electrodes with a pronounced peak at 375 ms (indicated by the arrow). This was followed by a second, less pronounced positivity between 600 and 900 ms. The amplitude of both components was larger for object relatives than for subject relatives.

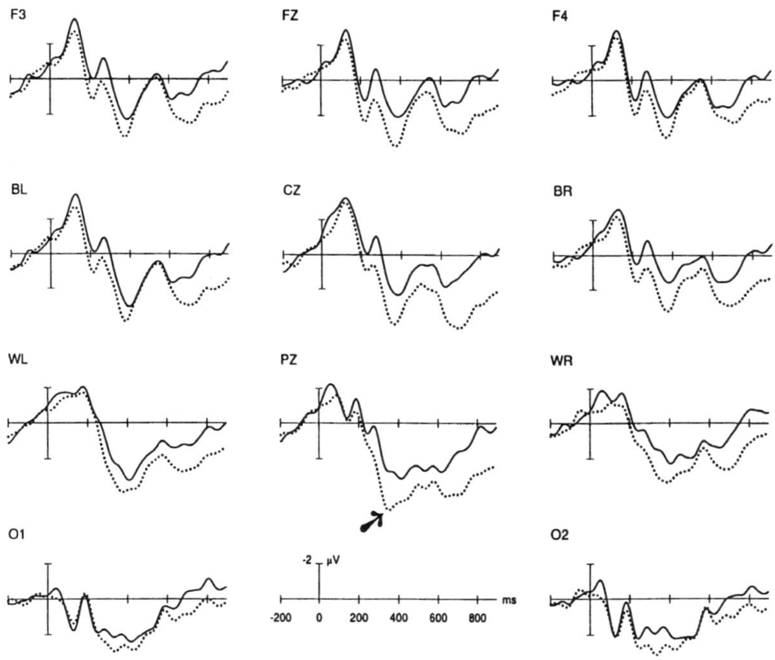

SR: —— Das ist die Professorin, die die Sekretärinnen gesehen HAT.
'This is the professor that the secretaries seen HAS.'

OR: ……… Das ist die Professorin, die die Sekretärinnen gesehen HABEN.
'This is the professor that the secretaries seen HAVE.'

FIGURE 3: This figure plots the average ERP wave forms elicited by the disambiguating sentence final auxiliary (*hat* versus *haben*) for the subject relative clauses (SR, solid lines) and the object relative clauses (OR, dotted lines) for selected electrodes over the left hemisphere (F3, BL, WL, O1), the right hemissphere (F4, BR, WR, O2), and over central recording sites (Fz, Cz, Pz). The arrow indicates the centro-parietal positivity for the object relative clauses (note that negativity is plotted up in this figure).

The first positivity observed here is consistent with previously reported results from a study investigating the same sentence types in German (Mecklinger *et al.*, 1995). The second positivity appears to be similar in both latency and distribution to the so-called P600, observed by Osterhout & Holcomb (1992) for the processing of other types of garden-path sentences. This additional second positivity may be due to the fact that the first experiment only presented relative clause sentences which were disambiguated at the end of the sentence, whereas the present experiment used not only relative clause sentences but also complement clause sentences, both varying the point of disambiguation.

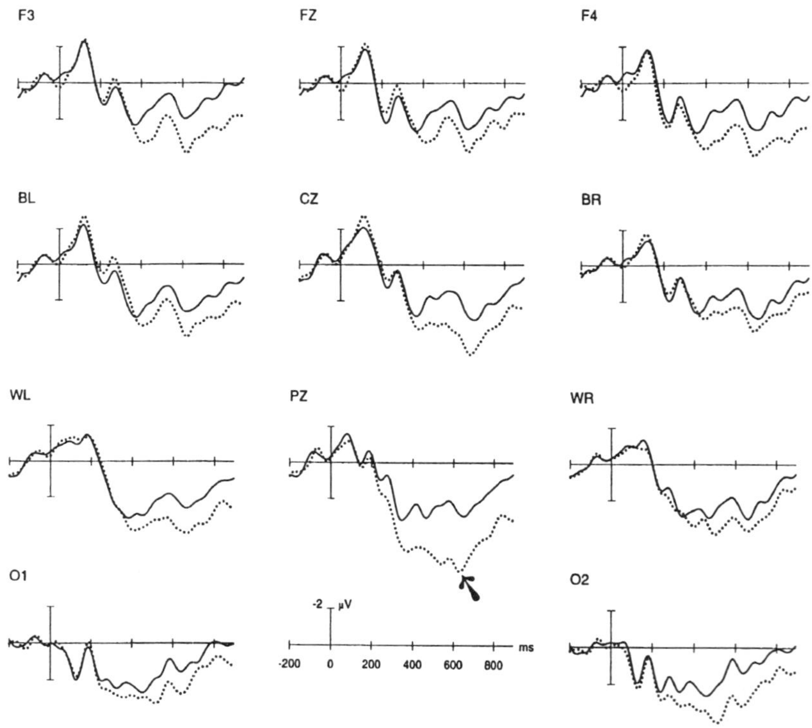

SC: —— Er wußte, daß die Professorin die Sekretärinnen gesehen HAT.
'He knew that the professor the secretaries seen HAS.'
OC: ········ Er wußte, daß die Professorin die Sekretärinnen gesehen HABEN.
'He knew that the professor the secretaries seen HAVE.

FIGURE 4: This figure plots the average ERP wave forms elicited by the disambiguating sentence final auxiliary (*hat* versus *haben*) for the subject-first complement clauses (SR, solid lines) and the object-first complement clauses (OR, dotted lines) for selected electrodes over the left hemisphere (F3, BL, WL, O1), the right hemisphere (F4, BR, WR, O2), and over central recording sites (Fz, Cz, Pz). The arrow indicates the centro-parietal positivity for the object-first complement clauses (note that negativity is plotted up in this figure).

In the ERPs for subject-first and object-first complement clauses (Figure 4), a positivity was building up at about 500 ms after the onset of the auxiliary for the object-first condition which peaked around 625 ms (indicated by the arrow) and was sustained until the end of the recording epoch. This pattern is similar to that reported by other studies in correlation with syntactic revision processes (Osterhout & Holcomb, 1992; Osterhout *et al.*, 1994).

The observation of an earlier positivity for the processing of object relative clauses and a later positivity for the processing of object-first complement clauses was confirmed by statistical analysis. The analysis evaluating the temporal course of the positivity in steps of 50 ms indicated that the positivity for the relative clause sentences was present as early as between 250-300 ms, not present between 400 and 650 ms, but present again in the time windows between 650 and 900 ms. For the complement clause sentences, the time course of the presence of the positivity showed a different pattern: it was not present until the time window of 500-550 ms in which it was marginally significant. It only became significant in the time window of 600-650 ms and remained significant in all time windows between 600 ms and 900 ms.

5.4 Unambiguously Case-Marked Sentences

Sentences containing morphological case markings can be disambiguated either at the clause-initial relative pronoun or at the clause-initial noun phrase, or in clause-medial position at the noun phrase following the pronoun or at the first full noun phrase. Nominative case in the relative pronoun of a relative clause or in the first NP in a complement clause requires a subject-first structure whereas accusative case requires an object-first structure. If structure assignment is ultimately made at the point of disambiguation, effects are to be expected for the disambiguating elements (i.e., the case-marked noun phrase or pronoun) and not at the sentence final auxiliary. ERP analyses were therefore calculated not only for the auxiliary, but also for the disambiguating clause-initial relative pronoun and the clause-initial noun phrase in the complement clauses as well as the clause-medial NP in both clause types.

As predicted, the ERPs from the onset of the sentence final auxiliary for the case unambiguous sentences with a clause-initial disambiguating element, (7)-(10), displayed no difference between the subject and object relative clauses, and no difference between subject-first and object-first complement clauses. This was confirmed by statistical analyses. This suggests that the sentence final auxiliary was processed in a similarly easy way across the four different sentence types.

The absence of any effect at the sentence final auxiliary supported our hypothesis that differences among the different conditions should occur at the disambiguating element itself, i.e., at the case-marked relative pronoun or noun phrase. Note that in German, only masculine singular NPs and pronouns are morphologically case-marked for nominative and accusative case (e.g., *der Professor*, *den Professor*) whereas masculine plural forms have ambiguous case (*die Professoren* for both nominative and accusative).

In the ERPs elicited by the case-marked clause-initial masculine singular pronouns in the relative clauses and those elicited by the masculine singular clause-initial noun phrases in the complement, we observed a positive wave for the accusative marked pronouns indicating object-first structures compared to the nominative marked pronouns indicating subject-first structures between 600 and 900 ms after the onset, and between 1000 and 1200 ms after the onset for the noun phrases.

The ERPs elicited by the sentence final auxiliary for case ambiguous sentences with clause-medial disambiguating elements, (11)-(14), showed a somewhat different pattern. While no difference between subject-first and object-first sentences was found in the sentence final auxiliary complement clause condition, a positivity was observed at the sentence final auxiliary in the relative clause condition even though case marking information was available in the preceding words. This result suggests that the case-marked clause-medial NP in the relative clause did not trigger a process of ultimate assignment, whereas the case-marked clause-medial NP in the complement clause did.

For the critical case-marked noun phrase in the complement clause sentences we observed a very late positivity (900-1100 ms) with a larger amplitude for the object-first complement clauses compared to the subject-first complement clauses. The ERP elicited by the case-marked clause-medial noun phrases following the ambiguous pronoun in the relative clauses showed more negativity between 300 and 400 ms in the nonpreferred object relative clause compared to the subject relative clause.

Before turning to an interpretation of the observed positivities we will briefly comment on the unexpected positivity for the sentence final auxiliary and the unexpected negativity for the case-marked clause-medial NP in relative clause sentences. The positivity at the sentence final auxiliary seems to indicate that no structural revision has taken place at the disambiguating element. This interpretation appears to be supported by the finding that no positivity was observed at the disambiguating element. Instead we found a centro-parietal negativity between 300 and 400 ms, a response usually correlated with lexical processes. Lexical processes for the case-marked element in this material could only be assumed insofar as the correct interpretation of the case-marked element, i.e., the article is dependent on accessing the gender information encoded in the lexical entry of the noun. Such lexical processes are, in fact, necessary. The article *der* is itself case ambiguous, as it could be either nominative masculine, or dative feminine, or genitive feminine. Thus the article *der* as such does not require reanalysis. For example, it could be read as a dative marker, as in (15).

(15) Das sind die Sekretäre, die *der* Professorin den Film gezeigt haben.
These are the secretaries, that the professor the film shown have.
(DAT sg, fem)

The need for reanalysis in sentences like (12) only becomes obvious when accessing the noun's gender (*Professor,* masculine, versus *Professorin,* feminine).

Recall that the article was not presented in isolation but together with the following noun. Upon encountering the NP, the parsing system has two possibilities: (a) it could follow the principle 'Attach anyway' formulated by Fodor (1996)[6] trying to look for the least costly revision, which in this case would require the addition of the feminine suffix *-in* thereby changing the gender of the noun under consideration; or (b) it could reanalyze the initial structure completely. Further research is definitely needed to clarify this issue.

6 The Late Positivity

The difference in the *amplitude* of the centro-parietal positivity between subject-first and object-first structures observed at the disambiguating elements at sentence final and clause initial position in relative clauses and in complement clauses suggest that this positivity can be taken to reflect revision processes. This view is compatible with the interpretation of Osterhout & Holcomb (1992) and Osterhout *et al.* (1994) who propose that the amplitude of the positivity reflects the 'cost of reprocessing' necessary for revision. The finding that the positivity is present both clause-finally and clause-initially suggests that revision

6 *Attach Anyway*: Having established that there is no legitimate attachment site in the current partial phrase marker (CDPM) for the current input word, attach the input word to the CPPM whenever it least severily violates the grammar, and subject to the usual preference principles that govern *Attach*.

processes become necessary not only under the condition that the reader is already 'led down the garden path' having built the simplest structure compatible with the preceding input, but also under the condition that the expectation of the simplest structure is not met independent of the preceding input. Here the question arises of whether the positivity in clause initial position can reflect processes of the actual reanalysis, given that no preceding input was available to build a complete initial structure. Alternatively, the positivity at clause initial position may reflect aspects of a mismatch between implicit structural expectations and incoming information.

The finding that the *onset latency* of the positivity varied as function of clause type with a shorter onset latency for the relative clause sentences than for the complement clause sentences, both clause initially and clause finally, suggests that this aspect of the positivity may be connected to a particular aspect of the revision process, namely, to the time necessary to detect the need for revision rather than the actual reanalysis *per se*.

The general difference in the onset latency between clause initial disambiguation and clause final disambiguation may be taken to indicate that more time is necessary to detect the need for revision in the former than in the latter case. It could be possible that this is due to the fact that the situation is less clear when the first element of a clause does not match the structural expectation, as at this point a variety of different structures are still open, at least in a language with relatively free word order such as German. The situation may be clearer in the clause final disambiguation condition since all but one element of the particular structure are already given, thus leaving only two possible structures among which the clause final element has to decide.

The finding that the *duration* of the positivity seemed to vary as a function of the type of reanalysis required leads us to consider that the duration of the positivity may also mark some (other) aspect of the revision process, namely, the actual reanalysis itself. The data from the present experiment, however, only allow a speculative interpretation of the 'duration' of the positivity as we can only rely on the significance of its presence in subsequent time windows. Thus, under the assumption that this analysis can be taken as an indicator for 'duration' we may consider the difference in duration of the positivity found at the sentence final auxiliary, and the absence of difference at clause-initial disambiguating elements to be worth discussing. Recall that the difference in duration was not independent of the position of the disambiguating element: it was only present at the clause final disambiguating elements, but not at the clause-initial disambiguating elements. Under the assumption that actual reanalysis only takes place after a reader or listener is 'led down the garden path', i.e., has built the initial structure on the basis of incoming information which then has to be revised upon encountering mismatching information (sentence final disambiguation condition), we may take the positivity's duration to reflect the actual amount of reanalysis required, with longer durations (and possibly higher amplitudes) for more difficult reanalyses than for easy reanalyses. Under this view the longer duration of the positivity observed for the complement clause sentences than for the relative clause sentences could be interpreted as representing the different types of reanalysis illustrated in Figures 1 and 2 assumed to underlie the processing of object relative clauses and object-first complement clauses, respectively.

7 Conclusion

We propose a two stage parsing system in which the first stage is compatible with the initial stage of garden-path models, which assume that the parser initially builds the simplest structure justified by the input (Frazier, 1978, 1987; Frazier & Clifton, 1996; Gorrell, 1995). In our parsing system, the second stage consists of two subprocesses taking place when initial structures have to be revised. The initial subprocess consists of diagnosing the need for reanalysis, while the subsequent subprocess represents the actual reanalysis, i.e., making the structural alterations necessary to recover from a structure that has been identified to be incorrect. Fodor & Inoue (1994) take the ease or difficulty of diagnosis to determine the difficulty of the revision process, and Gorrell (1996) takes the changes necessary to recover from a misparse to be the primary determinants of the difficulty of revision. We assume that *both* aspects play a role in determining the difficulty of revision. Moreover, on the basis of earlier ERP data concerning the onset latency of the late centro-parietal positivity observed in correlation with the processing of garden-path sentences as well as on the basis of theoretical considerations concerning the duration of different types of reanalyses required by different structures, we hypothesize that the diagnosis of need for reanalysis and the reanalysis itself may be reflected in two different aspects of the positive component, namely, its onset latency and its duration.

The data from two experiments investigating the processing of temporarily ambiguous subject-first and object-first sentences provide some support for this view. The onset latency of the positivity observed for the processing of the disambiguating element was shorter for the recovery of object relative clauses than for object-first complement clauses, independent of the position of the diagnostic element, indicating easier diagnosis for reanalysis in the former than in the latter. The duration of the positivity seemed to be shorter for relative clauses than for complement clauses, but only at sentence final position, i.e., at a point at which the structure to be revised was already completely built. At clause-initial position, the disambiguating element elicited a positivity which differed in onset latency (shorter for relative clauses than for complement clauses), but not in duration. This differentiation is taken to suggest that diagnosis and reanalysis may constitute two independent aspects in the revision process.

Max-Planck-Institute of Cognitive Neuroscience, Leipzig

References

Bader, M. & Lasser, I. 1994. German verb-final clauses and sentence processing: Evidence for immediate attachment. In C. Clifton, L. Frazier, & K. Rayner (eds.), *Perspectives on Sentence Processing*, 225-242. New York: Erlbaum.

Blumstein, S.E., Milberg, W., & Shrier, R. 1982. Semantic processing in aphasia: Evidence from an auditory lexical decision task. *Brain and Language*, 17, 301-315.

De Vincenzi, M. 1991. *Syntactic Parsing Strategies in Italian.* Dordrecht: Kluwer Academic Publishers.

Fodor, J.D. 1996. Garden path recovery: The grammatical dependency principle. Paper presented at *Architectures and Mechanisms for Language Processing (AMLaP) Conference 1996*, Torino, Italy.

Fodor, J.D. & Inoue, A. 1994. The diagnosis and cure of garden paths. *Journal of Psycholinguistic Research*, 23, 407-434.

Frazier, L. 1978. *On comprehending sentences: Syntactic parsing strategies.* Unpublished doctoral dissertation, University of Connecticut, Storrs, CT. Distributed by the Indiana University Linguistics Club, Bloomington, IN.

Frazier, L. 1987. Syntactic processing: Evidence from Dutch. *Natural Language and Linguistic Theory*, 5, 519-560.

Frazier, L. 1990. Exploring the architecture of the language processing system. In G.T. Altmann (ed.), *Cognitive Models of Speech Processing.* Cambridge, MA: MIT Press, 409-433.

Frazier, L. & Flores d'Arcais, G.B. 1989. Filler driven parsing: A study of gap filling in Dutch. *Journal of Memory and Language*, 28, 331-344.

Frazier, L. & Rayner, K. 1982. Making and correcting errors during sentence comprehension: Eye movements in the analysis of structurally ambiguous sentences. *Cognitive Psychology*, 14, 178-210.

Friederici, A.D. 1983. Aphasics' perception of words in sentential context: Some real-time processing evidence. *Neuropsychologia*, 21, 351-358.

Friederici, A.D. 1995. The time course of syntactic activation during language processing: A model based on neuropsychological and neurophysiological data. *Brain and Language*, 50, 259-281.

Friederici, A.D., Hahne, A., & Mecklinger, A. 1996. The temporal structure of syntactic parsing: Early and late effects elicited by syntactic anomalies. *Journal of Experimental Psychology: Learning, Memory and Cognition*, 22, 5, 1219-1248.

Friederici, A.D. & Mecklinger, A. 1996. Syntactic parsing as revealed by brain responses: First pass and second pass parsing processes. *Journal of Psycholinguistic Research*, 25, 157-176.

Friederici, A.D., Pfeifer, E., & Hahne, A. 1993. Event-related brain potentials during natural speech processing: Effects of semantic, morphological and syntactic violations. *Cognitive Brain Research*, 1, 183-192.

Gibson, E.A.F. 1991. *A Computational Theory of Human Linguistic Processing: Memory Limitations and Processing Breakdown.* Unpublished doctoral dissertation, Carnegie Mellon University, Pittsburgh, PA. Available as Center for Machine Translation Technical Report CMU-CMT-91-125.

Gorrell, P. 1987. *Studies in human syntactic processing: Ranked-parallel versus serial models.* Unpublished doctoral dissertation, University of Connecticut, Storrs, CT.

Gorrell, P. 1995. *Syntax and Parsing*. Cambridge, MA: University Press.

Gorrell, P. 1996. Parsing theory and phrase-order variation in German V2 clauses. *Journal of Psychologistic Research*, 25, 135-156.

Gunter, T.C., Vos, S.H., & Mulder, G. 1995. Syntactic violations and ERPs: P600 or P3b? Paper presented at *Eighth Annual CUNY Conference on Human Sentence Processing*, Tucson, AZ.

Hagoort, P., Brown, C., & Groothusen, J. 1993.The syntactic positive shift as an ERP-measure of syntactic processing. *Language and Cognitive Processes*, 8, 439-483.

Hemforth, B. 1993. *Kognitives Parsing: Repräsentation und Verarbeitung sprachlichen Wissens.* Sankt Augustin: Infix.

Hickok, G. 1993. Parallel parsing: Evidence from reactivation in garden-path sentences. *Journal of Psycholinguistic Research*, 22, 239-250.

Inoue, A. & Fodor, J.D. 1995. Information-paced parsing of Japanese. In R. Mazuka & N. Nagai (eds.), *Japanese Sentence Processing*. Hillsdale, NJ: Lawrence Erlbaum Associates, 6-63.

Kutas, M. & Hillyard, St.A. 1983. Event-related brain potentials to grammatical errors and semantic anomalies. *Memory and Cognition*, 11, 539-550.

Kutas, M. & Van Petten, C. 1988. Event-related potential studies of language. In P.K. Ackles, J.R. Jennings, & M.G.H. Coles (eds.), *Advances in psychophysiology, Vol. 3*, 139-187. Greenwich, CT: JAI Press.

MacDonald, M.C. 1994. Probabilistic constraints and syntactic ambiguity resolution. *Language and Cognitive Processes*, 9, 157-202.

MacDonald, M.C., Perlmutter, N.J., & Seidenberg, M. S. 1994. The lexical nature of syntactic ambiguity. *Psychological Review*, 101, 676-703.

Mecklinger, A., Schriefers, H., Steinhauer, K., & Friederici, A.D. 1995. Processing relative clauses varying on syntactic and semantic dimensions: An analysis with event-related potentials. *Memory and Cognition*, 23, 477-494.

Münte, T.F., Heinze, H.J., & Mangun, G.R. 1993. Dissociation of brain activity related to syntactic and semantic aspects of language. *Journal of Cognitive Neuroscience*, 5, 335-344.

Neville, H.J., Nicol, J., Barss, A., Forster, K., & Garrett, M. 1991. Syntactically based sentence processing classes: Evidence from event-related brain potentials. *Journal of Cognitive Neuroscience*, 3, 155-170.

Osterhout, L. & Holcomb, P.J. 1992. Event-related brain potentials elicited by syntactic anomaly. *Journal of Memory and Language*, 31, 785-804.

Osterhout, L. & Holcomb, P.J. 1993. Event-related potentials and syntactic anomaly: Evidence of anomaly detection during the perception of continuous speech. *Language and Cognitive Processes*, 8, 413-437.

Osterhout, L., Holcomb, P.J., & Swinney, D.A. 1994. Brain potentials elicited by garden-path sentences: Evidence of the application of verb information during parsing. *Journal of Experimental Psychology: Learning, Memory and Cognition*, 20, 768-803.

Osterhout, L. & Mobley, L.A. 1995. Event-related brain potentials elicited by failure to agree. *Journal of Memory and Language*, 34, 739-773.

Rösler, F., Friederici, A.D., Pütz, P., & Hahne, A. 1993. Event-related brain potentials while encountering semantic and syntactic constraint violations. *Journal of Cognitive Neuroscience*, 5, 345-362.

Schlesewsky, M., Fanselow, G., Kliegl, R., & Krems, J. 1996. *Preferences for grammatical functions in the processing of locally ambiguous wh-questions in German*. Manuscript, Department of Linguistics, University of Potsdam.

Schriefers, H., Friederici, A.D., & Kühn, K. 1995. The processing of local ambiguous relative clauses in German. *Journal of Memory and Language*, 34, 499-520.

Travis, L. 1991. Parameters of phrase structure and verb-second phenomena. In R. Freidin (ed.), *Principles and parameters in comparative grammar*. Cambridge, MA: MIT Press, 339-364.

Trueswell, J.C., Tanenhaus, M., & Garnsey, S. 1994. Semantic influences on parsing: Use of thematic role information in syntactic ambiguity resolution. *Journal of Meaning and Language*, 33, 285-318.

Van Petten, C. & Kutas, M. 1991. Electrophysiological evidence for the flexibility of lexical processing. In G.B. Simpson (ed.), *Understanding word and sentence*. Amsterdam: Elsevier, 129-174.

Zurif, E., Swinney, D., Prather, P. , Solomon, J., & Bushell, C. 1993. An on-line analysis of syntactic processing in Broca's and Wernicke's aphasia. *Brain and Language*, 45, 448-464.

7

Syntactic Analysis and Reanalysis in Sentence Processing*

Paul Gorrell

Abstract

In this chapter I discuss the close links between first-pass syntactic analysis and reanalysis. Throughout, the focus is on the role of structural factors in sentence comprehension. Following Gorrell (1995a), I argue that the parser incrementally applies an important principle of grammar, the principle of economy of representation. This yields a general preference for minimal structure. Further, I argue that structure building operations are constrained by Structural Determinism (SD) and Right-edge Availability (REA). A number of structural ambiguities in English and German are discussed. In addition, the proposal of Phillips (1995) that the preference for local attachment has priority over the preference for minimal structure is examined. I argue that the examples used to support this view do not, in fact, require the parser to prefer local to minimal attachments. The Diagnosis Model of Fodor & Inoue (1994) is also discussed and I argue that such a model does not obviate the need for structural constraints in reanalysis. Further, attention to the details of syntactic structure shows the important role played not only by SD and REA but also by specific properties of the phrase marker in the reanalysis process. For example, the insights of the Diagnosis Model, in conjunction with specific properties of the structure computed, leads to a detailed account of the parser's inability to correctly resolve English reduced-relative ambiguities.

* I would like to thank Josef Bayer, Angela Friederici, Colin Phillips, and two anonymous reviewers for comments on earlier versions of this chapter. The discussion in section 5 is a revised version of a talk given at the Ninth Annual CUNY Conference on Human Sentence Processing (March, 1996), where I received many valuable comments and criticisms. Note that the discussion in section 5 does not address the proposals in Fodor & Inoue (this volume).

J.D. Fodor and F. Ferreira (eds.), Reanalysis in Sentence Processing, 201–245.

1 First Pass as Prelude

Any theory of syntactic reanalysis in sentence processing is connected in numerous ways to a theory of first-pass analysis. For example, if one assumes a parallel approach to the processing of structural ambiguities, then reanalysis mechanisms will differ in fundamental ways from those required by a serial model. Also, the representational properties of the output of first-pass operations are important determinants of the properties of reanalysis. Thus, an articulated theory of reanalysis must be embedded within a parsing model which delineates both first-pass mechanisms and the assumed grammatical framework. The properties of syntactic processing I will outline below focus on the role of a particular property of grammar which, I will argue, has broad implications for parsing theory. Briefly, I will argue, following work of Frazier and colleagues (e.g., Frazier, 1978; Frazier & Fodor, 1978; Frazier & Rayner, 1982), that the parser exhibits a general preference for minimal structure (see also Frazier & Clifton, this volume). Following earlier work (Gorrell, 1995a, 1996a), and in contrast to the garden-path model, I will argue that this preference is best analyzed not as an indirect reflection of parsing operations but as a direct reflection of a property of grammar: the principle of economy of representation proposed by Chomsky (1986). The incremental application of economy of representation is called Simplicity (Gorrell, 1993, 1995).

One important property of analysis and reanalysis operations is Structural Determinism (SD) (Gorrell, 1995a). SD claims that attachments of new items which alter the dominance and precedence relations of the computed structure are more costly than attachments which preserve these primary relations.[1] I will also argue that the attachment site for a new item must meet the condition of Right-Edge Availability (REA), proposed in Gorrell (1996b). Throughout, the emphasis will be on the close connection between analysis and reanalysis operations. For example, Frazier & Fodor (1978) observed that "...trying the simplest attachment first ensures that revisions will be uniform—they will all consist of adding extra nodes to the phrase marker" (p. 321). The discussion below, which emphasizes the link between initial, minimal, structure building and SD, can be viewed as a particular instantiation of this insight.

I will concentrate on two particular types of ambiguity. The first is the subject-object ambiguity of clause initial *wh*-phrases. Establishing an initial subject

[1] The term *primary relations* is used in very different ways in Gorrell (1993, 1995) and in Frazier & Clifton (1996). See below for discussion. Also, see Gorrell (1995a, chapter 3) for a discussion of previous versions of the Determinism Hypothesis in sentence processing.

preference will be important because, as I will show below, reanalysis from a subject to an object reading is consistent with SD, but object-to-subject reanalysis is not. Therefore *wh*-ambiguities which appear to exhibit an initial object preference are of particular interest. Phillips (1995) discusses apparent object preferences in English and Dutch and argues that these follow from a modified version of Kimball's (1973) Right Association principle (RA). Phillips (1995) argues that many preferences which have been argued to follow from Minimal Attachment (MA) can be reanalyzed as RA effects. Further, he discusses examples where the parser appears to prefer an RA attachment over the minimal attachment. This approach conflicts with the general model I will propose and offers a serious challenge to the beneficial interplay the model exhibits between minimal structuring and SD. It also conflicts with a basic property of the garden-path model (Frazier 1978, 1990) that the preference for attaching minimally takes priority over the preference for attaching locally.[2] These RA examples constitute the second type of ambiguity I will discuss.

Gorrell (1995a, pp. 165-ff.) noted that SD does not address the important issue of how reanalysis proceeds in cases where primary relations are altered, yet reanalysis is not blocked. That is, SD is but one component of a complex sentence-comprehension system. The interaction of SD and other components of the system are just beginning to be explored. One framework for this investigation is the Diagnosis Model (DM) of Fodor & Inoue (1994). I will argue that the DM approach to diagnosis and recovery, although it sheds light on many new phenomena, must also incorporate structural properties such as SD and REA, since structural properties of the computed structure play an important role in reanalysis operations. In discussing the DM, I will also discuss various examples discussed by Fodor & Inoue (1994) that are argued to obviate the need for reference to structural factors in reanalysis.

What exactly do we mean when we use the term *reanalysis*? The basic intuition behind a theory of reanalysis is that, in the process of rapidly structuring input during the first-pass analysis, the human sentence processing mechanism has made an 'error' or 'misanalyzed the input' in some way which is inconsistent with subsequent lexical material. Reanalysis is, then, the correction of the first-pass error or misanalysis. There is a tendency for this way of looking at the parse sequence to underestimate the extent to which 'misanalysis' and 'reanalysis' are properties of first-pass parsing. Further, the focus on certain types of ambiguities (e.g., argument-structure ambiguities) has led to a tendency to regard the parser's response to structural ambiguity as essentially a lexical

2 Below I discuss this in relation to the approach of Frazier & Clifton (1996).

phenomenon (e.g., MacDonald *et al.*, 1994). To be sure, as the parse sequences detailed below will show, the parser's operations are 'lexically constrained' in important ways. But lexical constraints, although necessary, are not sufficient (see Frazier, 1995, for discussion).

Consider the string in (1).

(1) John ate the apple and…

Let us assume that, after processing *John ate the apple*, the postverbal NP has been attached as the direct object of the verb, as shown in (2a). The appearance of *and* forces a change in this structure, as shown in (2b).[3]

(2) a.

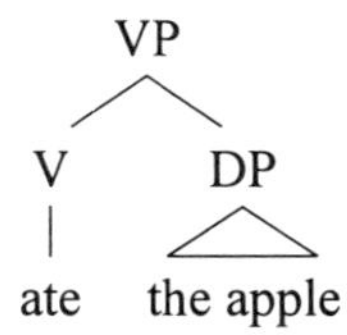

b.

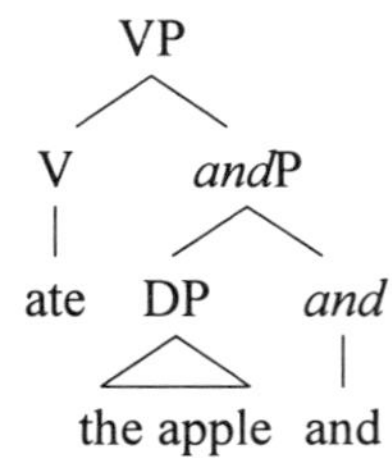

It is counter-intuitive, at best, to refer to the structuring of *ate the apple* in (2a) as an error. It is true that this structure must be revised when *and* appears. But this revision, I will argue, is a basic property of the parse sequence, i.e., the parser has added structure based on new input. This addition does require changes to some prior structural relations in the syntactic representation, but this is inevitable in the parse sequence (see the discussion below). Note that the structural analysis in (2a) is not lexically-based, i.e., the minimal structure does not result from the parser initially dispreferring the listed option of a conjoined phrase.[4]

Consider also a string such as (3) and the structures in (4).

---

[3] Assumptions concerning the structure of the conjunction do not matter here, so long as the conjoined phrases are embedded within a larger phrase.

[4] I put aside here the implausible possibility that each lexical head is listed with a conjunction option.

(3) (...) the man who...

(4)

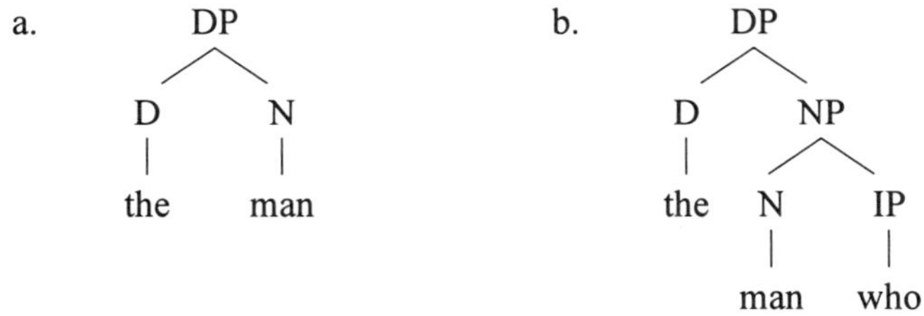

As with the previous example, the parse sequence which produces (4b) involves changing the prior structure (4a). Note that in each case the primary (dominance and precedence) relations are preserved, consistent with SD. Also, the change to the existing structure involves nodes on the right edge of the tree, consistent with REA (to be discussed below). This type of change to the existing structure is an integral part of the parse sequence. It occurs whenever a complement, modifying phrase or conjunct is added to the structure. This comes close to exhausting the attachment possibilities for a new lexical item. Abstracting away from particular node labels, we have the sequence in (5).[5]

(5)

When we turn to standard examples of 'easy' reanalysis (e.g., Pritchett, 1992; Fodor & Inoue, 1994), such as (6), we see that the parse sequence is again consistent with SD and REA. In fact it conforms to the schema in (5).

---

[5] See Sturt & Crocker (1996) for one implementation of this 'tree-lowering operation', as well as other aspects of the model proposed in Gorrell (1995a).

(6) a. John heard the noise was...

b.

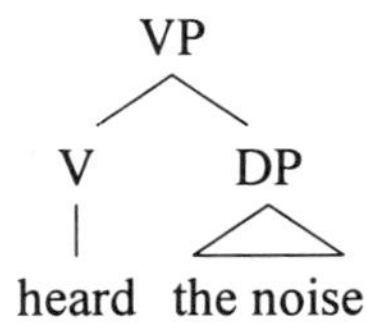

c.

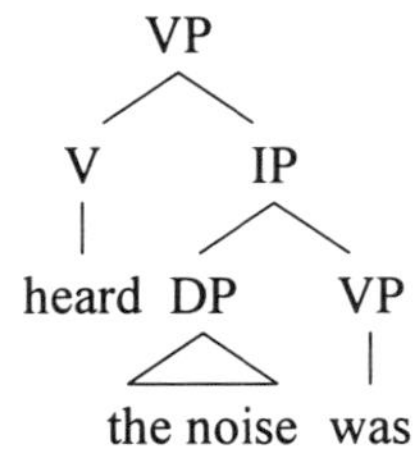

Below I will show that reanalysis is more difficult when either SD or REA (or both) must be violated to achieve a grammatical continuation of the parse sequence.[6] But first, in order to demonstrate more clearly the relation between analysis and reanalysis, it is necessary to clarify the nature of the syntactic representation which the parser is constructing.

2 Syntax

I assume that the syntactic component of the grammar includes a general economy principle, along lines suggested by Chomsky (1986 and subsequent work). One aspect of this approach, explored by Grimshaw (1993), is that phrase structure is variable, e.g., "a clause is only as big as it needs to be" (p. 5). Similar remarks apply to projection. Speas (1990, p. 46) formulates a principle of 'No Vacuous Projection'. In Gorrell (1995a) I noted that this general economy approach could be formulated as in (7).

(7) No vacuous structure.

That is, elements in a phrase-structure representation must be justified by a property of syntax. Given this, a lexical item such as *John* will be analyzed simply as an N in a syntactic structure. It need not (indeed, must not) project an additional layer of structure (cf. Higginbotham, 1985; Baltin, 1989). Further, a 'bare' verb without a complement or modification will simply be a V (the minimal structure). A V or N node in this context is both minimal (lexical) and maximal (the highest projection). Speas (1990) and others have defined a

---

[6] The focus on these factors in this chapter should not be taken as a claim that other factors are not significant. See Bader (1994) for a discussion of prosodic effects in reanalysis and Bader *et al.* (1996) for a discussion of an interesting class of case ambiguities in German. Ferreira & Henderson (1991) discuss the role of head position and ambiguity resolution.

maximal node as the highest node in an uninterrupted sequence of projections of a lexical item. This has a number of interesting implications for syntactic structure and parsing theory. For example, assuming the proposal that coordinate structures are projections of some coordinating head (Kayne, 1994; Munn, 1993), as shown in (2b), then coordination is always of maximal projections. This is because each conjoined element (e.g., N in *apples and bananas*) is dominated not by a 'coordinate NP', but by a projection of conjunction (e.g., *and*P or *and'*). In the parse sequence, attachment is always attachment of a maximal projection, with 'intermediate' nodes arising as new items are processed and branching structures required.[7]

Given this view of node projection, the structure for a tensed clause such as (8a) will be (8b). The minimal structure for a finite clause is an IP, with tense specification in I and the subject in [SPEC,IP].[8]

(8) a. John ate.

b.

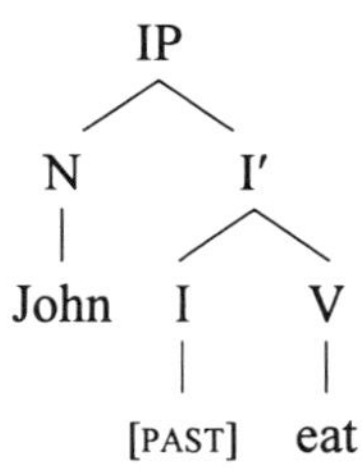

If the verb does have an object, then more structure is required, as in (9).

[7] Chomsky (1995, p. 228) proposes a constraint ('the condition of inclusiveness') which prohibits node labels from representing information not contained in the lexical items (e.g., no bar levels). I will continue to use the *XP* and *X′* notation for (visual) clarity. As Speas (1990) and Frazier (1990) note, intermediate nodes have no independent role in syntactic theory. It is heads and maximal projections which the theory makes reference to. As stated in the text, they may, in fact, be the same node.

[8] In general, I will only indicate the tense specification in I when it is relevant (see section 5 below).

(9) a. John ate apples.

b.

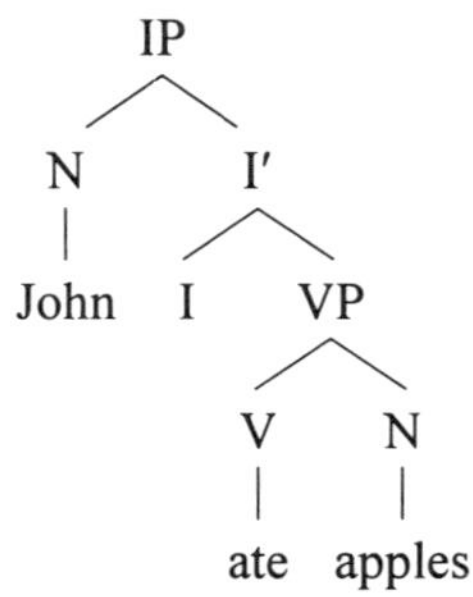

As with the verb, if the object is more complex, then more structure is required, as shown in (10).[9]

(10) a. … ate the apple.

b.

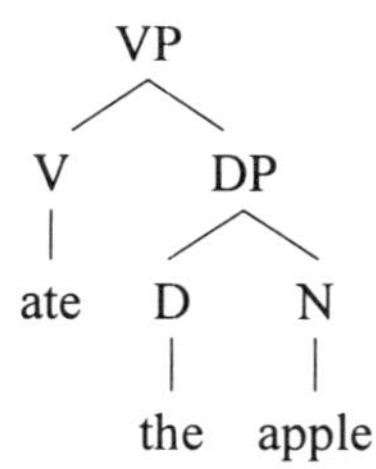

It should be clear that an incremental parse sequence will always involve adding new nodes to the structure. That is, attaching a new constituent cannot simply be an operation which affixes a phrase to the existing structure, like tacking a notice to the bulletin board. It is more accurate to refer to the *integration* of a new constituent into the phrase marker rather than attachment (Gorrell, 1989). Assuming that integration of new phrases is incremental leads to the conclusion that renalysis is incremental. No 'attachment' (however minimal) can be made without changing the existing structure. Here we see that the distinction between analysis and reanalysis becomes impossible to maintain. Furthermore, if we regard reanalysis as being triggered by an error (or, by an error signal), then it must be the case that the appearance of each new lexical item proves the existing structure to be incorrect.

---

[9] For the parsing operations discussed below, it will not matter if nominal phrases with determiners are analyzed as DP or as NP.

There is one potential caveat to this: attachment of a predicted item. A number of researchers (e.g., Frazier & Fodor, 1978; Gorrell, 1987) have proposed that the parser may precompute the structure consistent with predicted items. Consider the string (11a) and the structure (11b).

(11) a. John purchased...

b.

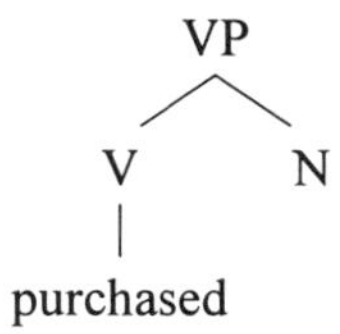

The verb *purchase* requires an object, regardless of the discourse context. It seems reasonable to assume that the parser will make use of this information and precompute the minimal structure consistent with the predicted constituent (see Wright & Garrett, 1984, and Gorrell, 1989, for a discussion of the processing of heads of predicted phrases). Given this, the appearance of a lexical item such as *apples* will require only attaching it into the existing structure. But even here there must be some form of integration if, as commonly assumed, node labels are feature bundles which contain projections (or percolations) of specific lexical information (e.g., for nouns: animacy, mass-count, number, etc.) which cannot be predicted.

Turning to the nature of clause structure, consider the embedded clauses in (12a) and (13a), and the structures given in (12b) and (13b).

(12) a. John knows Bill left.
b. John knows [$_{IP}$ Bill left

(13) a. John knows that Bill left.
b. John knows [$_{CP}$ that [$_{IP}$ Bill left

The embedded clause in (12) is an IP and the embedded clause in (13) is a CP. This follows from the 'variable' nature of clause structure, i.e., a clause is structurally as minimal as possible. In (12) there is no justification for the more complex CP structure.[10] In (13) the complementizer *that* heads a CP.[11]

[10] See Grimshaw (1991, 1993) and Gorrell (in preparation a, in preparation b) for discussion of variable phrase structure and categorial selection. One approach uses categorial identity, e.g., C and I are each [+V,–N], and D and N are each [–V,+N].

Following Grimshaw (1993), I will assume that CP and IP are verbal (extended) projections. By 'verbal' I mean that they are specified [+V,–N]. In this respect it is identical to the VP. These extended projections each have their own head.

Similar to the declarative structures in (12) and (13), *wh*-clauses will also vary in structure, as (14) and (15) illustrate.[12]

(14) a. Who likes him?
b. [$_{IP}$ who [$_{VP}$ likes him

(15) a. Who does he like?
b. [$_{CP}$ who$_1$ does [$_{IP}$ he [$_{VP}$ like t_1

In English, the variable nature of *wh*-clause structure is reflected by the presence of *do* with fronted objects and its absence with *wh*-subjects. Given the syntactic framework of Grimshaw (1993), the presence of *do* in (15), and its absence in (14), indicates that the structure for (15) contains an additional layer of verbal projection. As Grimshaw (1993) notes "[t]he one case where the requirements of an interrogative are met without any movement is when a *wh*-phrase is a subject. It is already in Specifier position, moreover it is in Specifier position of the highest phrase in the verbal extended projection" (p. 33). Assuming, as seems necessary, that the grammar of English precludes the appearance of main verbs in CP, the presence of *do* can serve as an indication of the presence of an additional projection, which, as an unselected phrase, requires a lexical head (see Grimshaw, 1993, for discussion).

As I will be discussing *wh*-ambiguities in German below, I will briefly sketch here the variation in clause structure between German *wh*-subjects (16) and *wh*-objects (17).[13]

---

[11] As Crocker (1994) observes, it is a property of functional categories such as C and I that their complement-taking properties are 'fixed'. That is, C always takes an IP complement and I always takes a VP complement. See Grimshaw (1993) for one approach to deriving this generalization. See Gorrell (1991) for an overview of the use of the complementizer phrase in generative grammar. Bader & Lasser (1994) present evidence that [SPEC,IP] position is available before the verb in the processing of German verb-final clauses (in contrast to a proposal in Pritchett, 1991).

[12] This has been proposed by (among others), Gazdar (1981), Chung & McCloskey (1983), Gazdar *et al.* (1985), Chomsky (1986), Grimshaw (1993), and Pollard & Sag (1994). See Gorrell (in press a) for the relevance of this hypothesis to the parsing of subject-object ambiguities in German declarative and *wh*-clauses. I review some aspects of the parse of German *wh*-structures below.

(16) a. Welcher Mann sah den Chef?
which man-NOM saw the boss-ACC
'Which man saw the boss?'

b. [$_{IP}$ welcher Mann [$_{I}$ sah$_1$ [$_{VP}$ den Chef t_1

(17) a. Welchen Chef sah der Mann?
which boss-ACC saw the man-NOM
'Which boss did the man see?'

b. [$_{CP}$ welchen Chef$_2$ [$_{C}$ sah$_1$ [$_{IP}$ der Mann [$_{I}$ t_1 [$_{VP}$ t_2 t_1

Unlike that of English, the grammar of German permits the raising of the verb into CP (via IP, as indicated), so *sah* is in CP in (17b). This yields a surface similarity between the *wh*-subject structure (16a) and the object structure (17a). The structures in (16b) and (17b) illustrate that the *wh*-object requires the more complex CP structure (cf. (15b)), whereas the *wh*-subject is in the [SPEC,IP] position (cf. (14b)). As I will argue in the next section, this complexity difference between *wh*-subjects and *wh*-objects is what underlies the prediction of an initial subject preference in syntactic processing. That is, 'no vacuous structure' is viewed as a central property of both the grammar and the parser.

In Gorrell (1995a, p. 119-ff.), in keeping with this minimal view of syntactic structure, I argued that utterances such as those in (18) should be analyzed as independent phrases, unattached to higher clausal structure.[14]

(18) a. While Mary was practicing the piano...
b. Before dinner...

Given this, (18a) and (18b) are simply prepositional phrases which may independently appear in an appropriate discourse context (e.g., in answer to the question *When did Bill leave?*). Note that this syntactic analysis is forced by SD, i.e., utterances such as (18) would require deletion of the nodes for the main clause. The grammatical alternative to this is to require that each PP be attached to some higher 'main' clause which is empty. I am unaware of any (currently-

---

[13] The specific syntactic assumptions are justified in Gorrell (in preparation b). But see Schwartz & Vikner (1989) for a defense of the traditional view (e.g., Thiersch, 1978) that in German verb-second clauses the preverbal constituent is in CP. See Travis (1984, 1991), who initially proposed that IP is head initial in German.

[14] I will refer to both (18a) and (18b) as PPs, taking *while* to be a preposition with a clausal complement (see Emonds, 1985, chapter 6).

applicable) arguments for this type of complex structure. Below we will see that this approach has interesting implications for the parsing of structural ambiguities within string-initial PPs such as (18a).

3 The Parser

In section 2, I discussed the proposal that the generation of structure within the grammar was constrained by a general economy principle: no vacuous structure. The computation of structure by the parser, no less than the generation of structure by the grammar, must be constrained. In Gorrell (1995a) I argued that the structure-building operations of the parser are governed by the incremental application of the principle of economy of representation. This is the principle of Simplicity, given in (19). Simplicity is a general constraint on the incremental process of structure building.

(19) No vacuous structure building.

Although in one respect Simplicity is but one way of instantiating MA (Frazier, 1978; Frazier & Fodor, 1978), there are two important differences. The first is that I am assuming, in particular, that the parser is building a phrase-structure tree. MA, on the other hand, does not presuppose a particular type of structural representation (see Gorrell, 1995a). The second difference concerns the underlying grammatical assumptions. MA is not stated as a distinct parsing principle, but follows from the assumption of a ruled-based grammar and the temporal advantages of minimal rule accessing. Frazier & Fodor (1978) argued that MA need not be stated as an independent parsing strategy; rather it follows from the parser's attempt to build all the structures consistent with ambiguous input, with the first structure computed being the one which is pursued. Under this model, the minimal attachment, because it involves the least amount of structure building, is the first to be computed.

MA and Simplicity make similar predictions across a wide range of ambiguities. But the recent *Construal* framework (CF) of Frazier & Clifton (1996) provides support for a grammar-based approach. In the garden-path model, the two basic preferences were MA and Late Closure (LC). These preferences were argued to stem from a single source: the parser's pursuit of the first available analysis of ambiguous input. Frazier (1978) states that LC "is simply part of the characterization of the operation of the first-stage parser; it does not have to be stated as a specific strategy" (p. 114). Similar remarks apply to MA.

A novel property of the CF is that a new input item may be connected to the existing structure in one of two ways. The first is *attachment*, which, in previous work, was the only type of connection within the garden-path model. We can think of attachment as *full* syntactic integration. The second type of connection is *association*. Association is a form of *partial* syntactic integration in which a new phrase is connected, not to a unique attachment site, but to a particular region of the phrase marker. In the CF this region is defined by the Current Thematic Processing Domain, which, for present purposes, is roughly the current clause. The first clause of the Construal Principle (Frazier & Clifton, 1996) states "[a]ssociate a phrase XP that cannot be analyzed as instantiating a primary relation into the current thematic processing domain" (p. 41). Primary relations in the CF are: (i) the subject and main predicate of a clause and (ii) complements and obligatory constituents of primary phrases.

Roughly put, primary relations are arguments or potential arguments. Thus the distinction between the phrases which are attached and those which are associated is defined by the grammar, and it is not an indirect result of the parser's operations. This distinction is very difficult to explain under a 'race model' view of parsing preferences (under which the parser pursues the first structure computed). For example, if parsing preferences are the indirect result of a 'race' between competing structures, how does the race get turned off just for the subset of phrases which are not supposed to be attached? To answer this question, we must first recognize that (i) none of the ambiguities which fall into the 'associate' column involve complexity differences, and (ii) all of the ambiguities which fall into the 'attach' column do. That is, MA doesn't say anything at all about where a relative clause or a secondary predicate is attached.[15] Put another way, if an ambiguity involves a complexity difference, it is subject to (minimal) attachment. This distinction is obscured within the CF, but from the grammar-based perspective proposed above, the difference between the attachment and associate ambiguities can be stated straightforwardly: the difference is whether or not the principle of economy (incrementally applied) determines a unique attachment site. Putting aside important details concerning locality principles (e.g., the effects of clause boundaries), I will assume for present purposes that, in the absence of a complexity difference, the parser prefers low attachments.

This way of looking at the distinction appears more parsimonious than the listing of primary relations required within the CF. Frazier & Clifton (1996, p.

---

15 But see Frazier & Clifton (1996, chapter 5) and Gorrell (in press b) for a discussion of Minimal Chain Principle effects in the processing of extraposed relative clauses.

45-ff.) note two distinguishing properties of non-primary relations, given in (20).[16]

(20) a. No general structural preference is observed.
b. Semantic information can contribute to the identification of the (initial) preferred determinate analysis.

The first property gives the empirical basis for the distinction we want the parsing model to capture. The second simply fails as a distinguishing feature of non-primary relations. As it stands, (20b) appears undeniable. But this is also a property of primary relations.[17] Instead of listing phrase types which are subject to structural factors (or not), the grammar-based approach captures the right distinction by having Simplicity apply wherever it can.

But Simplicity, although in general producing the locally most-minimal structure, is not a 'node counting' procedure. For example, consider the incremental parse sequence for a string such as *John ate*. When the noun is processed only an N node is created, rather than any one of an infinite number of possible alternatives (e.g., attached as subject of a clause, first member of a conjoined clause, etc.). This is clearly the minimal structure. But this structure is computed, not because it has the fewest nodes *per se*, but because additional structure is not justified by the input and would violate economy of representation (for similar proposals, but based on distinct principles, see Pritchett, 1988, and Abney, 1989). In section 4 below I will discuss

---

[16] In addition, Frazier & Clifton (1996) state that "...the presence of a nonprimary phrase is not required by—nor does it interact with—syntactic properties of individual lexical items. Put bluntly, to determine the grammatical properties of the lexical items in a sentence, one could ignore nonprimary relations" (p. 46). I take it that 'syntactic' and 'grammatical' properties in this context refer to combinatorial properties. For example, the relative clause in (i) below determines the number of the ambiguous head noun; in (ii) it determines gender. Putting aside these 'non-combinatorial' properties, it must still be the case that what is meant is something close to 'participation in primary relations'. This is because (iii) and (iv) show that the relative clause interacts with properties of the prior nouns to establish an attachment site in the phrase marker. Given this, lack of interaction with syntactic properties of lexical items fails as a distinguishing feature.

(i) the sheep that is/are in the barn
(ii) the doctor who enjoys her work
(iii) the owner of the sheep that are in the barn/that is selling his farm
(iv) the mother of the doctor who enjoys her work

[17] If this wasn't true, the 'modularity' debate in sentence processing wouldn't be so focused on ambiguities involving primary relations (e.g., main clause-reduced relative; NP versus IP complement; etc.)

ambiguities, due to Phillips (1995) and Phillips & Gibson (1996), which distinguish the effects of MA (as its role is characterized within the garden path model) and Simplicity. This approach is consistent with the approach to structure generation for PPs such as (18), discussed above.

In addition to being constrained by Simplicity, structure building by the parser is driven by the grammar. That is, node projection and syntactic integration are justified by principles of grammar. This licensing of structure, called Incremental Licensing in Gorrell (1995a), is stated in (21).

(21) The parser incrementally attempts to satisfy principles of grammar.

The similarity to Pritchett's (1992) Generalized Theta Attachment is clear. One important distinction is that, as we shall see below, Incremental Licensing does not refer to 'maximal satisfaction' of grammatical principles.[18] The formulation of Incremental Licensing in (21) is the minimal statement necessary to drive structure-building by a grammar-based parser. Similarly, Simplicity is the minimal statement required to constrain such computation. Structure building must be constrained for two reasons. The first is grammatical (the principle of economy of representation; Chomsky, 1991). The second is perceptual (the preference for minimal structure at points of ambiguity; Frazier, 1978). Simplicity unites both the grammatical and the perceptual constraints on structure building.

Building on the D-theory approach of Marcus *et al.* (1983), Gorrell (1993, 1995) proposed that changes to the existing structure are less costly if they preserve dominance and precedence relations. A brief discussion of the parse sequence for (22) will illustrate the predictions of SD with respect to ambiguity resolution by structure addition.

(22) John heard the noise was due to a design flaw.

In (22) the parser will initially attach the NP *the noise* as dominated by the VP and preceded by the verb. If the next item processed is a verb (e.g., *was*), then the embedded-clause structure is added to the existing phrase marker (see (6b) and (6c) above). In the new structure, the matrix verb still precedes the NP and the VP still dominates it (i.e., primary structural relations are unaltered). Although structure addition is not a 'cost-free' operation, the efficiency of the

---

[18] As discussed in Gorrell (1995a, 1996a) Incremental Licensing is distinct from head-driven parsing.

parse of (22) is due to the fact that the parse sequence requires only the continued application of structure building to new input. That is, the primary structural relations of the tree prior to disambiguation are unaltered in the subsequent structure.

Note that if it were the case that the appearance of *was* in (22) produced parse failure or marked difficulty, then we could readily say that (i) *noise* is such a good object for *hear* that the parser can't bear to tear them apart; (ii) the postverbal NP was initially analyzed as having accusative case and a theme theta role, but must be reanalyzed as having nominative case and a cause role; and, (iii) the postverbal NP must be taken out of one clause and put in another. Interestingly, all of these are applicable to (23), where marked difficulty is observed. Thus the comparative lack of difficulty in (22) allows us to isolate the proper factor.

(23) While Mary was mending the sock fell off her lap.

Recall from Section 2 that a PP such as *While Mary was mending the sock* may stand on its own, i.e., there is no grammatical requirement for a main clause (computation of a new clause would require specific justification (e.g., an inflected verb). As argued in Gorrell (1995a, p. 119), when the NP *the sock* appears, the only attachment site in the current structure is as object of *mend*. Of course the parser could build a new clause for which the NP could serve as subject, but Simplicity precludes this option. Incremental Licensing justifies the attachment as object within the *mend* VP. Here, in contrast to (22), as Weinberg (1992) observes, the change in structure forced by the appearance of a new verb requires that dominance relations be altered, violating SD.

Similar remarks apply to (24), where a strong garden-path effect is also evident. Here the parser will initially structure the two postverbal NPs (*the man* and *the report*) as objects of the verb *give*. In this structure they are in a precedence relation. The computation of the required relative clause (*the man (whom) the report criticized*), in which the NP headed by *report* is dominated by the NP headed by *man*, forces a retraction of the precedence relation between these nodes (because two nodes in a well-formed phrase-structure tree cannot be in both a precedence and a dominance relation; see Partee *et al.*, 1993, and Gorrell, 1995a, for discussion).

(24) John gave the man the report criticized a demotion.

An additional structural factor in reanalysis is REA, mentioned in section 1 (see Gorrell, 1996b). This is based on the proposal of Abney (1989, p. 142) that the parser, when faced with a dispreferred resolution of an ambiguity, searches the right edge of the tree for an abandoned choice point consistent with the new input. Given standard assumptions concerning well-formedness conditions on trees (e.g., no crossed branches; see Gorrell, 1995a, chapter 2), the right-edge of the parse tree is the only possible attachment site for new input.[19] For example, consider the attachment of an extraposed relative clause. Attachment of this phrase must be to the right-edge of the tree, and a connection to the head noun must be formed by trace insertion or some other device (e.g., feature percolation) for discontinuous dependencies. Consider a strong garden path such as (25).

(25) The horse raced past the barn fell.

Here the grammatical attachment of *fell* not only violates SD, as in (23), but REA fails as structure changing beyond the right edge is required. (This reanalysis is discussed in more detail in section 5.) The lack of REA is one factor which accounts for the fact that (25) is virtually impossible for the uninitiated, whereas (23) is a noticeable problem with a clear solution. This is in contrast to (22) where detecting the effect of the ambiguity requires experimental investigation (e.g., Frazier & Rayner, 1982). We can see the contribution of each factor to processing difficulty as follows (where * indicates violation of SD or REA, and ✓ indicates consistency with SD or REA):

(26)	a.	John heard the noise was due to a design flaw.	✓ SD, ✓ REA
	b.	While Mary was mending the sock fell off her lap.	* SD, ✓ REA
	c.	The horse raced past the barn fell.	* SD, * REA

Although it is clearly not the case that SD and REA are the only factors which influence sentence processing, SD and REA do appear to play a significant role in determining the parsability of sentence types such as those listed in (26). It should also be clear that the attachments in a normal parse sequence will be consistent with both SD and REA (cf. the structures discussed in sections 1 and 2).

---

19 Note that for left-branching structures, REA is still applicable. The only difference is that in a left-branching structure the new phrase will dominate projections of prior material, whereas in right-branching structures, it is a projection of some prior element which dominates the new phrase.

One additional ambiguity that needs to be discussed is the subject-object ambiguity of clause initial *wh*-phrases. Consider the strings in (27) and (28).

(27) a. I wonder who likes Bill.
b. I wonder who Bill likes.

(28) a. Welche Frau sah den Chef?
which woman-NOM/ACC saw the boss-ACC
'Which woman saw the boss?'

b. Welche Frau sah der Mann
which woman-NOM/ACC saw the man-NOM
'Which woman did the man see?'

In contrast to the German examples (16) and (17) discussed earlier, the initial feminine *wh*-phrase *Welche Frau* in (28a) and (28b) is case ambiguous, i.e., its form is consistent with either a nominative or an accusative reading. In conjunction with the possibility of a pre-verbal accusative NP (as shown in (17)), (28a) and (28b) are temporarily ambiguous, like English *who* in (27). Here the disambiguation is at the postverbal NP, as indicated.

Given the syntactic assumptions discussed in Section 2, Simplicity predicts an initial subject preference, i.e., an initial preference for the minimal structure (the *wh*-phrase in [SPEC,IP]). This is because *wh*-objects require a more-complex CP structure. This preference is compatible with SD in the following way.[20] Recall that both CP and IP are analyzed as [+V,–N]. That is, they are formally the same node type. Thus the parser is initially structuring the *wh*-phrase as specifier of a [+V,–N] phrase. If the subject reading proves correct, no additional structure building is required. On the other hand, if an object reading is forced, then an additional layer of structure must be created. But this additional structure building, although it involves some cost (see below), does not lead to marked processing difficulty. This is because the initial *wh*-phrase is specifier of a [+V,–N] phrase, whether or not this phrase has the contextually-determined role of an IP or a CP. On the other hand, an initial object preference, because it would initially involve the computation of a more-complex structure, could not be changed to a subject reading without violating SD. This is because an object-to-subject change would require deletion of computed structure. Thus it is important to examine experimental studies of *wh*-

20 See Gorrell (in press a) for detailed discussion.

ambiguities with an eye, not only to the initial preference, but also to the implications for reanalysis.

3.1 Simplicity and *Wh*-Ambiguities

Experimental evidence for a subject preference in ambiguous *wh*-structures in German is reported in a number of recent studies. For example, in a self-paced reading study, Meng (1995) tested sentences with initial case-ambiguous *wh*-phrases such as those in (29), as well as case-unambiguous structures. Disambiguation is by the number specification on the auxiliary.

(29)	a.	Welche Lehrerin	der Stadtschule	hat die Eltern	angerufen?
		which teacher	of the city school	has the parents	phoned
		'Which teacher of the city school phoned the parents?'			
	b.	Welche Lehrerin	der Stadtschule	haben die Eltern	angerufen?
		which teacher	of the city school	have the parents	phoned
		'Which teacher of the city school did the parents phone?'			

Meng reports a clear garden-path effect at the auxiliary (e.g., *haben*) when the *wh*-object reading is forced. Interestingly, in a second self-paced reading experiment, Meng found that if the disambiguation was by the post-auxiliary NP (e.g., *Welche Bewerberin hat der Chef…* 'Which applicant has the boss-NOM…'), there was no evidence of processing difficulty (as measured by reading times compared to an unambiguous structure). Meng argues that revision is more difficult when an agreement mismatch signals the error because the mismatch (assuming an initial *wh*-subject analysis) is a syntactic violation, i.e., a subject-verb agreement error. On the other hand, he argues that revision in the unambiguous NP condition is comparatively easy because no syntactic violation is produced, simply the need to change the computed structure. No matter how this difference is interpreted, the results of Meng's experiments clearly indicate a subject preference for ambiguous *wh*-questions established when the *wh*-phrase is processed. Interestingly, the difference Meng reports between what I will call *verbal* and *nominal* disambiguation may indicate why Stowe (1986) failed to find evidence for a subject preference in English embedded *wh*-structures, e.g., (30).

(30) My brother wanted to know who Ruth will bring us home to at Christmas.

Stowe reported a 'filled-gap effect' at the object position following *bring* in (30), i.e., as compared to a [–*wh*] control, reading times in a self-paced reading study were significantly longer for *us*. But such an effect was not evident in subject position (e.g., *Ruth* in (30)). Note that Stowe used *nominal* disambiguation at the subject position, as in Meng's second experiment. Thus it may be that the lack of a filled-gap effect in subject position in Stowe's experiment is due to the type of disambiguation and the use of a self-paced reading task. In English, an additional factor is the lack of inversion in selected phrases, such as those tested by Stowe. That is, in parsing a sequence such as *know who Ruth*, the parser will initially attach the *wh*-phrase into the specifier position of the verbal projection it has created. Here it is important to recall that the preference is not for a *subject* in the sense of an argument position, but for the simpler structure. Thus when *Ruth* is processed, the parser simply creates another layer of projection and attaches the NP into the specifier position of this projection.

For German structures similar to those tested by Meng, but with a simpler *wh*-phrase (e.g., *Welche Frau* instead of *Welche Lëhrerin der Stadtschule*), Schlesewsky *et al.* (in press) also found a subject preference for ambiguous *wh*-phrases. In addition, Schlesewsky *et al.* also tested 'long-distance' *wh*-structures, i.e., sentences in which the initial *wh*-phrase is associated with an argument position in an embedded clause, as shown in the examples in (31). Disambiguation was either by the number specification on the verb (31a) or by the case marking on the postverbal NP (31b) and (31c).

(31) a. Welche Frau glaubst du sahen die Männer am Freitag im Park?
which woman believe you saw-PL the men on Friday in the park
'Which woman do you believe the men saw on Friday in the park?'

b. Welche Frau glaubst du sah der Mann am Freitag im Park?
which woman believe you saw the man-NOM on Friday in the park
'Which woman do you believe the man saw on Friday in the park?'

c. Welche Frau glaubst du sah den Mann am Freitag im Park?
which woman believe you saw the man-ACC on Friday in the park
'Which woman do you believe saw the man on Friday in the park?'

The results confirm a clear subject preference for the ambiguous *wh*-phrase. Reading times were significantly longer when disambiguation forced the *wh*-

object reading.[21] In order to understand the subject preference in long-distance *wh*-structures, we need to compare the embedded-clause structures for the subject (32a) and object (32b) readings.

(32) a. Welche Frau_1 glaubst du $[_{IP}\ t_1\ \text{sah}_2\quad [_{VP}$ den Mann t_2
b. Welche Frau_1 glaubst du $[_{CP}\ t_1\ \text{sah}_2\quad [_{IP}$ der Mann $t_2\quad [_{VP}\ t_1\quad t_2$

In these embedded-clause structures, in the absence of a complementizer, the verb is in the head position of the highest projection (as we saw in (16b) and (17b) above). In (32a), the highest projection is IP. In (32b) it is CP.[22]

The parse sequence for the embedded clause with an ambiguity such as (31b) and (31c) is as follows. When the verb *sah* is processed, the parser attaches it into the head position of a verbal projection and also attaches a trace of the *wh*-phrase in specifier position. If the next phrase processed is an accusative NP, as in (31c), then this is simply attached within the VP. On the other hand, if the next phrase is a nominative NP, then the parser must compute additional structure so that the preceding trace and verb remain within the highest verbal projection (now with a CP role) and the nominative NP is attached into [SPEC,IP]. This is formally identical to the parse sequence of any (temporarily) ambiguous *wh*-structure with an object disambiguation. The generalization across the different types of *wh*-structures considered here is that *wh*-subjects are less complex than *wh*-objects, and that the parser exhibits a consistent preference for the simpler structure.[23]

Schlesewsky *et al.* (1996) report the results of three experiments which suggest a subject preference for case-ambiguous *wh*-phrases associated with verb-final *daß* ('that') clauses. They tested sentences such as those in (33), with disambiguation by the case marking of the NP following *daß*.

---

21 The disambiguation by the unambiguous NP was significant only in the subject analysis. Both subject and item analyses were significant for the verb-agreement condition. Note that a verb such as *glauben* requires a dative object (e.g., *der Frau* or *Welcher Frau*) so the form of the initial *wh*-phrase is incompatible with a matrix-object reading.

22 See Gorrell (in press a, in preparation b) for a discussion of the syntactic structures assumed here.

23 A subject preference is also evident in German relative-clause constructions with a case-ambiguous relative pronoun. See Schriefers *et al.* (1995), Mecklinger *et al.* (1995), Friederici & Mecklinger (1996) and Friederici (this volume).

(33) a. Welche Studentin glaubst du daß der Professor beobachtet?
which student believe you that the professor-NOM observed
'Which student do you believe the professor observed?'

b. Welche Studentin glaubst du daß den Professor beobachtet?
which student believe you that the professor-ACC observed
'Which student do you believe observed the professor?'

In one experiment using a self-paced reading task, reading times were significantly faster for the accusative determiner *den* in (33b), which forced a subject reading of the *wh*-phrase, than for the nominative *der* in (33a), which forced an object reading. We can see the reason for this subject preference if we examine the parse sequence in detail. Similar to (32a) above, the parser will initially compute the structure given in (34). Recall that, as mentioned in fn. 21, for all the test sentences, the case marking of the *wh*-phrase was incompatible with a matrix-object reading.

(34) Welche Studentin_1 glaubst du $[_{IP}\ t_1$

In contrast to (31), the next word processed is not a verb in a V2 clause, but the complementizer *daß*, which heads a CP. When *daß* is processed, a CP is projected and inserted into the structure, with an intermediate trace (t'_1), as shown in (35). Given the presence of the CP (forced by the lexical complementizer *daß*), this intermediate trace is required for a well-formed link between the *wh*-phrase and the trace in [SPEC,IP].

(35) Welche Studentin_1 glaubst du $[_{CP}\ t'_1$ daß $[_{IP}\ t_1$

Because the subject position ([SPEC,IP]) is filled by the trace t_1, this structure is consistent with the subsequent appearance of an accusative NP, as in (33b). The appearance of a nominative NP, as in (33a), makes reanalysis necessary, accounting for the longer reading times for the nominative determiner in Schlesewsky *et al*'s (1996) materials. Furthermore, this parse sequence follows from the general preference for minimal structure. A CP is not postulated until there is evidence for it. Also, an intermediate trace is only posited when it is required. This one basic principle predicts a general subject preference for all *wh*-ambiguities. Consistent with this principle, experimental investigations into the processing of subject-object *wh*-ambiguities in German do reveal a subject preference, regardless of the particular *wh*-structures tested. These results yield general support for the principle of Simplicity as well as SD.[24] This is because, as noted, reanalysis from subject to object *wh*-structures can be accomplished without violating SD. On the other hand, an initial object analysis would be problematic, as object to subject reanalysis violates SD.

3.2 The Active Filler Strategy

This analysis of the subject preference as a subcase of the preference for minimal structure differs from 'fill-the-first-gap' approaches such as the Active Filler Strategy (AFS) of Frazier & Flores D'Arcais (1989), given in (36).

(36) Assign an identified filler as soon as possible; i.e., rank the option of a gap above the option of a lexical noun phrase within the domain of an identified filler (p. 332).

An apparent counterexample to the proposal that AFS effects are due to a complexity difference is the gap-filling ambiguity tested by Frazier & Clifton (1989, experiment 2). Consider the sentences in (37).

(37) a. What did the very nice preschool teacher sing at Wildwood School during rest period yesterday?

b. What did the very nice preschool teacher sing at Wildwood School for during rest period yesterday?

Sentence (37a) is an *early-gap* structure because the *wh*-phrase must be interpreted as the object of *sing*. Sentence (37b) is a *late-gap* structure because the *wh*-phrase must be associated with the object of the preposition *for*. The AFS predicts a preference for early-gap structures, despite the fact that "the verbs used in these sentences were generally verbs whose preferred usage is intransitive..." (Frazier & Clifton, 1989, p. 101). Frazier & Clifton report a processing advantage for the early-gap sentences, supporting the prediction of the AFS. But there is another, independently-motivated, parsing preference which also accounts for these results: incrementally fill argument-structure slots

[24] The results in German are also consistent with the Minimal Chain Principle of de Vincenzi (1991). But, in contrast to the specific prediction that the parser will distinguish *who* and *which*-N phrases (due to a syntactic difference with respect to chain formation), Schlesewsky *et al.* (in press) found no difference in German (a subject preference for both). As they point out, these results pose a problem for revising the AFS along the lines suggested by De Vincenzi. As with the results of studies in Dutch discussed below, it may be that apparent conflicts are due to syntactic differences between the languages being investigated.

when possible (e.g., Pritchett, 1988; Abney, 1989; Frazier, 1990; Gibson, 1991; Weinberg, 1992; Gorrell, 1995a). Although the precise mechanisms underlying this preference may differ among the different theoretical approaches, there is a general consensus that, whether or not an identified filler is involved, the parser prefers to fill argument-structure slots when possible. This is clearly seen in the fact that the preference reported for the *wh*-structures tested by Frazier & Clifton (1989) is also evident in non-*wh*-structures such as (38).

(38) a. Before the teacher sang the songs he asked for quiet.
b. Before the teacher sang the songs were approved by the principal.

There are two ways of viewing the AFS. The first is that it is a construction-specific parsing strategy. The second is that it is a construction-specific *instance* of a more general principle. This second view seems more consistent with the original intent of the AFS. As Frazier & Clifton (1989) note "the gap-filling process is driven by the requirements of grammar... [T]he parser employs principled strategies for choosing between alternative grammatical structures" (p. 116). Given this, the results reported by Frazier & Clifton (1989) should not be interpreted as support for the construction-specific view of the AFS. Both *what* in (37) and *the songs* in (38) are processed as potential arguments of the verb. In each case the parser exhibits a preference to attach potential arguments into currently available argument positions.[25]

Consider a recent study by Boland *et al.* (1995), who tested *wh*-questions in which the *wh*-phrase was associated either with the object of a simple transitive verb, or with verbs (such as datives) which provide more than one potential gap site for the *wh*-filler. Boland *et al.* (1995) found a clear plausibility effect at the verb for the simple transitive verbs (i.e., implausible fillers producing 'stopped making sense' judgments at the verb), i.e., where there was a grammatical imperative to fill the direct-object gap. But such an effect was absent for the multiple-gap verbs when the first gap was implausible but the second gap was consistent with a plausible interpretation, e.g., *Which audience did the salesman show (the movie to)*. A fill-the-first-gap approach such as the AFS incorrectly predicts a consistent preference to fill the first object position in the Boland *et al.* (1995) multiple-gap condition. This prediction was disconfirmed. But, if the putative AFS-induced subject preference is a preference for the simpler structure (and not a preference to fill the first gap), then we have a straightforward explanation for the lack of an AFS effect in the Boland *et al.* (1995) results. It

[25] As Frazier (1995) points out, this preference must be a general, syntactic preference and not one determined by the lexical preference of the particular verb.

may well be that, once the subject-object complexity difference is analyzed as a separate phenomenon, the processing of gaps within verb-initial VPs is best accounted for by a lexical-expectation model similar to Fodor's (1978) original proposal. Given our syntactic assumptions, the subject-object contrast always involves a complexity difference.

3.3 Right Association and *Wh*-Ambiguities

A serious challenge to this view of analysis and reanalysis is presented by Phillips (1995), who proposes a new version of Kimball's (1973) principle of Right Association. Phillips' formulation is given in (39). I will refer to Phillips' Right Association as PRA.

(39) For any pair of overt terminal elements X Y, where X is the last terminal attached, reject attachments of Y which require unnecessary steps in the path(s) between X and Y.

For present purposes, we can informally interpret a 'step' as a branch between nodes in a structure (see Phillips, 1995, for details). PRA incorporates a locality component (proximity to the last overt terminal) and a complexity component (number of branches). To understand how PRA applies to *wh*-ambiguities, consider the ambiguity studied by Stowe (1986), as discussed above. For a string such as (40), the parser will evaluate the attachment possibilities in (41). The paths in each attachment set are listed, with the number of steps in parentheses. Note that the beginning of each path (the left-most member) is a head.

(40) I know who... *t*

(41) a. *subject reading*
wh-CP-C (2)
C-C′-IP-*t* (3)

b. *object reading*
wh-CP-C (2)
C-C′-IP (2)
I-IP-VP (2)
V-VP-*t* (2)

Phillips states that the object reading is preferred because the subject reading requires the path of longest length (3 steps), despite the fact that the object reading involves a more complex structure (more paths). The crucial difference between the subject and object readings is that, in English, an object follows a verbal head but precedes an inflectional head. For the subject reading, this means that the I head is unavailable as the beginning of a new path (i.e., it fails to intervene between the *wh*-phrase and the subject trace site), forcing the trace to be part of the longer C path, as shown in (41a). On the other hand, the *wh*-trace in the object analysis is part of the two-step V-path, because a null verbal head intervenes between the *wh*-phrase and the object trace. Because path length takes priority over number of paths, the subject reading is dispreferred. Thus, PRA can account for the lack of a filled-gap effect in subject position (Stowe 1986). That is, the lack of such an effect is taken to indicate that English exhibits an object preference for *wh*-ambiguities, in main as well as embedded clauses. Thus PRA predicts that the *wh*-object sentences (42b) and (42d) produce less processing difficulty at the auxiliary than the *wh*-subject sentences in (42a) and (42c). This prediction clearly contrasts with native-speaker intuitions.[26]

(42) a. Which actor is planning to interview the directors?
b. Which actor are the directors planning to interview?
c. Which actors are planning to interview the director?
d. Which actors is the director planning to interview?

For a language such as German, the prediction is that there is a subject preference for matrix, case-ambiguous, *wh*-phrases. This is because, in German, the object precedes the verb within VP. This means that there is no null V-head which intervenes between the *wh*-phrase and a trace in object position. Given this, a *wh*-trace in object position is part of the path headed by the inflectional head (I), as indicated in (44b). The absence of a V head intervening between the *wh*-phrase and its trace site means that there is no V path and, consequently, the I path must be longer. Given this, (unlike in English) path length no longer is a basis for rejecting the subject reading. Further, it is now the object analysis which is rejected because it involves more paths than the subject reading.

(43) Welche Frau... *t*

(44)

a. *subject reading*		b. *object reading*	
wh-CP-C	(2)	*wh*-CP-C	(2)
C-C′-IP-*t*	(3)	C-C′-IP	(2)
		I-IP-VP-*t*	(3)

[26] In conjunction with Fernanda Ferreira, experimental verification of this intuition is underway.

For German long-distance *wh*-structures, on the other hand, the prediction is that an object reading of the *wh*-phrase will be preferred. Consider an ambiguous string such as (45).

(45) Welche Studentin glaubst du daß...

(46)	a.	*subject reading*		b.	*object reading*	
		V-VP-CP-*t*	(3)		V-VP-CP	(2)
		t-CP-C	(2)		C-CP-IP	(2)
		C-C′-IP-*t*	(3)		I-IP-VP-*t*	(3)

Phillips argues that the grammar permits a well-formed direct link between a matrix *wh*-phrase and a trace in object position of the embedded clause (e.g., in examples such as (33a)). But a link to a trace in subject position requires an intermediate trace in [SPEC,CP] of the embedded clause. In part, this is due to the fact that subjects are generally regarded as islands for extraction (see Phillips, 1995, for discussion). The effect is that the subject reading, as shown in (46), requires two 3-step paths, whereas the object reading requires only one 3-step path. The crucial difference between local and long-distance *wh*-structures is that for long-distance structures it is only the subject reading which requires a 3-step V-path between the prior verbal (null) head and an intermediate trace in [SPEC,CP].[27]

It should be clear that the PRA prediction of an initial object preference for long-distance *wh*-structures is not borne out by the experimental evidence presented above for German. The experiments reported by Meng (1995), Schlesewsky *et al.* (in press) and Schlesewsky *et al.* (1996) reveal a consistent subject preference in both local and long-distance *wh*-structures. Phillips notes that a number of studies in Dutch report an object preference for long-distance *wh*-structures (e.g., Jordens, 1991; Frazier, 1993), consistent with the predictions of PRA. There are a number of issues to be sorted out with respect to the Dutch data. The first is that Kaan (1996a) reports an object preference for embedded *wh*-questions, as in (47).

[27] Recall that the (underlying) verb position is clause final, so the matrix subject is not the last head in the structure, despite surface appearances.

(47) a. Ik vroeg welke vrienden hem in het dorp aan de kust
I asked which friends him in the village at the coast
hadden opgezocht.
had visited
'I asked which friends had visited him in the village at the coast.'

b. Ik vroeg welke vrienden hij in het dorp aan de kust
I asked which friends he in the village at the coast
had opgezocht.
had visited
'I asked which friends he had visited in the village at the coast.'

Disambiguation is by the form of the masculine pronoun in the embedded clause (*hem* is accusative, *hij* is nominative). In a word-by-word continuous grammaticality judgment task (1996, experiment 2), Kaan found that response times to nominative pronouns were significantly faster than response times to accusative pronouns, indicating a preference for the subject reading for the ambiguous *wh*-phrase. Similar results are reported for a self-paced reading task (1996, experiment 3).[28] Interestingly, PRA predicts a subject preference for embedded questions, similar to local matrix *wh*-structures. This is because, in each case, there is a local *wh*-structure which must connect a *wh*-phrase in [SPEC,CP] with either the subject or object position. Given this, the path sets for (47a) and (47b) would be (44a) and (44b) respectively (repeated here as (48)).

(48) a. *subject reading*
wh-CP-C (2)
C-C′-IP-*t* (3)

b. *object reading*
wh-CP-C (2)
C-C′-IP (2)
I-IP-VP-*t* (3)

A second issue concerns the difference between German and Dutch. In (49) I have listed the experimental findings (initial subject or object preference) for these two languages, along with the predictions of PRA and Simplicity.[29]

---

28 Although the data are less clear, Kaan (1996b) reports an object preference for structures where the disambiguating pronoun is replaced by a full NP, with disambiguation by the number specification of the auxiliary verb.

29 Michael Meng (p.c.) reports two experiments which demonstrate a significant subject preference for embedded questions in German (self-paced reading and speeded-grammaticality judgement studies).

(49)

Wh-structure	German	Dutch	PRA	Simplicity
matrix *wh-*	subject	subject	subject	subject
embedded *wh-*	subject	**object**	subject	subject
long-distance *wh-*	subject	**object**	**object**	subject
relative clause	subject	subject	subject	subject

The prevalence of the subject preference in German is important because, as noted above, reanalysis from subject to object readings is consistent with SD. The differences between German and Dutch with respect to embedded and long-distance *wh*-structures are puzzling because German and Dutch appear quite similar in terms of complement clause word order. (Note that the object preference is only evident in Dutch when a complement clause is involved.) But there do appear to be differences, albeit poorly-understood.

Koster (1986) notes that, for Dutch, "[i]t is indeed the case that extraction from [embedded-clause] subject position… is slightly less good than extraction from object position…" (p. 206). But it is unclear if this is due to a property of the grammar or some aspect of the perceptual mechanism. Further, as Koopman (1983) observes, "…the data concerning subject extraction in *wh*-questions [in Dutch] do not seem to be well-established…" (p. 201). Concerning long-distance *wh*-structures, Koopman notes that subject extraction is more difficult if (i) the verb is ergative, (ii) the verb is passive, and (iii) the object is indefinite. There is an active debate whether or not there are dialectical differences regarding extraction (see Koster, 1986, for discussion), but it is clear that a number of properties of clause structure interact with subject extraction in embedded clauses that are not involved with object extraction. It should also be noted that Dutch displays Superiority effects that are absent in German (see Haider, 1993, for discussion), suggesting that the subject position in Dutch exhibits grammatical properties distinct from German (despite the superficial similarity). Again, the reason for this is not understood at all. But it does appear to be the case that subject extraction from Dutch embedded clauses must meet more stringent conditions than object extraction.[30]

[30] There are other differences of potential relevance, e.g., (i) in Dutch, but not German, embedded clauses, the auxiliary may precede the participle; (ii) Dutch expletive *er*, which may improve the acceptability of subject extraction in embedded clauses by appearing in subject position, has no counterpart in German (cf. *Wie denk je dat er verdwenen is*? 'Who do you think that has disappeared?').

Frazier (1993) attempted to account for the object preference in Dutch long-distance *wh*-structures by making crucial reference to specific properties of Dutch syntax (specifically, the direction of canonical government). In general, this appears to be the right approach because (as Frazier argues) the optimal hypothesis is that the parser does not differ, but is simply responsive to grammatical variation. Given this, the solution to the puzzle concerning differences in German and Dutch sentence processing is most likely to be found in differences between the grammars of Dutch and German. It should be noted that, given our current understanding of German syntax, Frazier's approach to the parsing of Dutch long-distance extractions would incorrectly predict an object preference for those structures in German.

Given this discussion, I will tentatively assume that there is a general (initial) subject preference for ambiguous *wh*-phrases, with the hope that future theoretical and experimental studies will shed new light on the important questions raised by the experimental work of Kaan and others. Note also that there is an outstanding issue concerning English, as mentioned above in the discussion of Stowe (1986). But the experimental results listed in (48) show a predominant subject preference, consistent with Simplicity, which allows for reanalysis of this minimal structure (if forced) to proceed in accord with SD.

4 Right Association and Locality

Phillips (1995) and Phillips & Gibson (1996) discuss a class of ambiguities which they argue demonstrate that a preference for local attachment takes precedence over the preference for the simplest structure. Consider the sentences in (50) and (51).

(50) a. Because the conference organizers liked the caterers they hired for the banquet they asked them back the following year.
b. Because the conference organizers liked the caterers they hired them for the banquet in honor of the former president.

(51) a. Whenever Mary started to think the class had finished there was still an hour remaining.
b. Whenever Mary started to think the class had finished and everybody had left.

The ambiguity in these examples is the attachment of *they* in (50) and *the class* in (51). In (50) the pronoun may be attached either as subject of a relative clause modifying the prior NP (50a), or as subject of a new clause (50b). In (51) the NP may either be attached as subject of a complement clause of *think* (51a), or as subject of a main clause. In each case the preference is for attachment to the structure projected from the prior lexical item (a locality effect). The question is whether or not this preference overrides the preference for minimal structure.

As discussed above, initial prepositional phrases such as *Because the conference organizers liked the caterers* are processed simply as PPs, not phrases attached to dominating clausal nodes. Therefore, when *they* is processed in (50), the choice is between attachment as a relative clause adjoined to the NP, or creation of a new clause to which the PP is adjoined.[31] In either case the pronoun is subject of a new clause. As the structures in (52) indicate, there is no structural difference and Simplicity fails to apply.

(52) a.

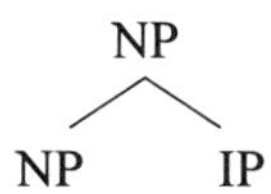

b.

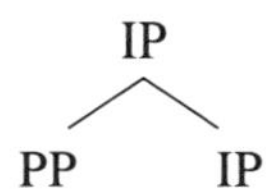

In structure (52a), the relative clause (the IP) is adjoined to the NP it modifies. In structure (52b), the *because* PP is adjoined to a 'main clause'—an IP. In each case, the pronoun is attached in [SPEC,IP]. As discussed above, when Simplicity fails to determine a unique attachment site, the parser prefers low attachments. For (50), the relative-clause analysis is the low attachment and it is preferred to the creation of a new clause.[32]

---

[31] See Sag (1996) and Gorrell (in preparation a) for syntactic justification of the analysis of object relatives lacking a relative pronoun or complementizer. In Gorrell (in preparation a) the analysis is similar to that for the complement clause lacking a complementizer in (12). One obvious difference is that, in the case of an object relative clause, the object position must be related to the head NP being modified. Note that, for relative clauses with a relative pronoun or complementizer, an object relative is more complex (a CP) than a subject relative (an IP). This is consistent with the analysis of *wh*-phrases given for (14) and (15). See Gorrell (in press a, in preparation b) for this analysis applied to German.

[32] Note that this analysis also answers the 'Locality Puzzle' posed by Phillips & Gibson (1996). That is, why does locality appear to take priority in (49) but not in (i)? The answer reduces to the general, structure-based, preference for argument over adjunct attachments within previously-computed clauses (see Gorrell, 1995a, for discussion).

(i) Joe bought the book for Susan.

Within the CF, the main-clause attachment would only be preferred if the parser had already computed the nodes for such a clause. Although this has generally been assumed within the garden-path model (e.g., the Partial Top Down Constraint of Frazier & Rayner, 1988, given in (53a)), it is not a necessary assumption. Frazier & Rayner (1988, p. 264) note that it may follow from the Maximal Chunk Constraint (MCC), given in (53b). CPPM refers to the Current Partial Phrase Marker.

(53) a. The first word of a sentence must be (minimally) attached to the topmost 'S'; each subsequent item must be attached into the CPPM.[33]

b. During processing, the human language processor forms the largest CPPMs possible given the inherent restrictions on its immediate memory and computational capacity and the grammar of the language being processed.

There are two ways of viewing the MCC. The first is that, *in contrast to multiple smaller chunks*, the parser prefers a single, maximal, structure. The second is that the parser just prefers bigger structures. This second view appears unlikely, given standard memory-load arguments for incremental structuring. The first view, which appears to be the original intent (see Frazier & Fodor, 1978) is consistent with the present proposal that a string-initial phrase is simply parsed as that phrase type (i.e., as a single structure—PP, NP, etc.) until there is evidence that it is attached to additional nodes.

This analysis of the relative-clause preference in (50) extends straightforwardly to the complement-clause preference in (51). The ambiguity is whether or not the NP following *think* is attached as a subject of a clausal complement or as subject of a new clause. As in (50), Simplicity does not apply as a new clause is created in either case (either one to which the PP is adjoined or as complement of a now-branching VP) so the preferred attachment is within the current thematic processing domain, the *think* clause. It is important to note that the only cases where a preference for local attachment appears to take priority over minimal attachment involve ambiguities where the putative minimal attachment requires creation of a new clause. As we have seen, these are in fact ambiguities where there is no unique, minimal, attachment.

---

[33] This presupposes a grammatical requirement for a clausal root node. If it were only an option, MA would preclude such an attachment.

This is important because the evidence presented by Phillips (1995) and Phillips & Gibson (1996) represents a strong challenge to the view that the preference for minimal structure represents a central property of the parser. In turn, this property is central to an understanding of the close connection between analysis and reanalysis, in particular, between Simplicity and SD. In the next section I discuss another challenge to the present proposal, the Diagnosis Model of Fodor & Inoue (1994), which claims, among other things, that structural factors play a role in reanalysis only insofar as they facilitate or hinder the correct recognition of the structural change required by new input.

5 Diagnosis and Structural Determinism

As Gorrell (1995a, 1996b) points out, the binary distinction between reanalyses consistent with and in violation of SD, does not adequately address the full range of processing phenomena which a theory of sentence comprehension must explain. That is, not all structure additions are of equal ease, and not all structure alterations are of equal difficulty. What SD predicts is that, *all else being equal*, structure addition will be more efficient than structure alteration. In section 3 above I discussed one additional factor, REA. The *Diagnosis Model* (DM) of Fodor & Inoue (1994) presents an interesting framework to investigate a broader spectrum of processing phenomena. In this section I will discuss the role of structure in both diagnosis and cure of attachment difficulties.

In contrast to the present focus on structural factors in processing, the DM focuses not on the type of revision required by new input but on how easy or hard it is for the parser to determine which revisions must be made.[34] Fodor & Inoue (1994) present persuasive arguments that an adequate theory of syntactic processing must include some form of diagnostic component, that is, some mechanism for resolving conflicts between new input and prior structure computed by the parser. The DM makes the further claim that revision type is not a factor in the observed differences in the parser's response to ambiguity resolution, but rather that, "... *any* revision can be easy as long as the parser can *spot* that this is the revision that is needed" (p. 409, emphasis in original). I will argue that structure does play a significant role, and that incorporating a diagnostic component into parsing theory does not obviate the need for distinguishing structure addition from structure alteration (see also Gorrell, 1996b).

---

[34] See Friederici (this volume) for an approach which incorporates both diagnostic and structural factors.

The process of ambiguity resolution within the DM is initiated by a principle of Attach Anyway (AA) that, despite an apparent ungrammaticality, attaches problematic new input into the computed structure, producing a conflict which, when productive, leads to a successful reanalysis. But the diagnostic parser is shortsighted. Costly moves, even if they would eventually result in successful reanalysis, are avoided. If the correct reanalysis is blocked by the avoidance of a costly move, a garden path may result. AA is given in (54).

(54) Make an attachment, the *least unacceptable* one you can find, and then follow the dictates of the grammar to adjust the rest of the CPPM to mesh with it (Fodor & Inoue, 1994, p. 414, emphasis in original).

Consider the process of reanalysis for ambiguities such as those in (55).

(55) a. She put the candy in her mouth on the table.
b. She put the candy in her mouth onto the table.

For (55a) and (55b), the parser will initially attach the first prepositional phrase as the locative argument of the verb *put*. When the second prepositional phrase is processed, structure alteration is required to reanalyze the first PP as modifying the NP. Fodor & Inoue (1994) point out that reanalysis appears to be easier in (55b) than in (55a). There are various reasons for this—e.g., *on* but not *onto* can be attached as a nominal modifier; *onto* has an unambiguous locative interpretation which facilitates its association with the verb *put*; etc. Fodor & Inoue (1994) argue that this difference between (55a) and (55b) is a problem for proposals, such as the structure-addition model, which argue that structure alteration is a comparatively-costly operation. But this is not the case. Notice that in these examples two factors are involved: cost of revision and clarity of the error signal. In (55a) and (55b), the cost of revision is held constant whereas the clarity of the error signal is greater in (55b) than in (55a). Given this, it is not surprising that the overall effect is that (55b) is easier than (55a).[35]

But, in addition to demonstrating that different types of error signals have differential effects on reanalysis, we want to ask more specifically how reanalysis is facilitated when the error signal is more informative. First, what does it mean to be more informative? For sentences such as (55), *onto* is more informative than *on* because it can only head a phrase attached as a verbal

[35] Similar remarks apply to the processing of Japanese 'double-relative' constructions discussed by Fodor & Inoue (1994).

modifier. Therefore, determination of the correct attachment site is facilitated: the attachment site must be a VP and a VP is available on the right edge of the tree. Attachment is then made to VP, as a locative argument of *put*. Now what happens? The grammar only permits one locative argument, so the prior PP *in her mouth* requires a new attachment site. The NP satisfies REA with respect to this PP (it is now the only attachment site to do so) and is a grammatical option. So the first PP is then attached to the NP. This violates SD, but it is the only grammatical possibility and the garden-path effect is less pronounced than in (55a), where the parser, seeking to maintain SD, will initially attempt to find an alternative attachment site for the second PP.

This sequence is consistent with the DM, but attends more to the role of structure in reanalysis. The unambiguous nature of *onto* allowed the parser to efficiently determine the correct attachment site from among the REA sites (VP, PP, NP within PP). Correct reanalysis requires two new attachments, each (in turn) uniquely determined. In the absence of this unambiguous preposition in (55a), the first attachment site is not uniquely determined and the parser will attempt incorrect alternatives which are consistent with SD and REA.

Consider a strong garden path such as (56a). The structure prior to the appearance of *fell* is given in (55b). The reason for including the tense indication here will be discussed below as it directly relates to the important role of the parser's prior structural analysis in the reanalysis process.

(56) a. The horse raced past the barn fell.

b.

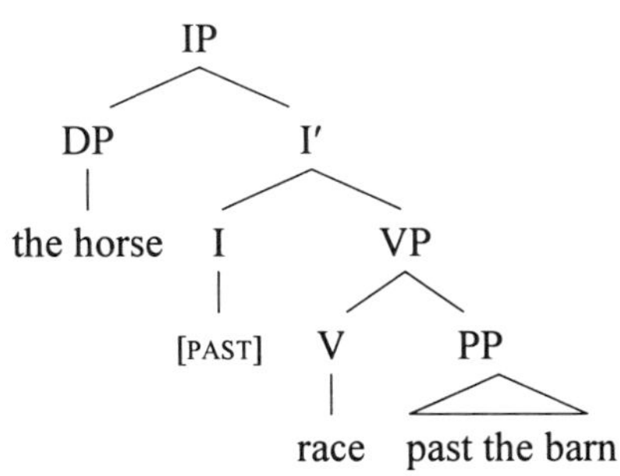

Here the parser will have initially computed the main-clause structure for *The horse raced past the barn*. When *fell* is processed, the right edge of the tree is: IP, I′, VP, PP. There is no grammatical attachment consistent with SD. Fodor & Inoue note that "...what does *not* seem to occur to the parser is that the problem is not about the attachment of *fell* but about the attachment of *raced*"

(1994, p. 415). Why not? Fodor & Inoue (1994) state that recognition of the necessary reanalysis of the *raced* VP is hindered by the fact that this VP must be detached so that the *fell* VP can take its place. That is, the correct attachment site is not REA. An important property of reanalysis that emerges from Fodor & Inoue's (1994) work is the crucial role of the initial attachment site (within DM, AA initiates the reanalysis process). In (55) we saw that *onto* unambiguously signals the correct attachment site (the VP). Importantly, this attachment site is REA. But when *fell* is processed in (56a), there is no REA site that, as Fodor & Inoue (1994) demonstrate, leads to a correct reanalysis.

Assume that *fell*, as an inflected verb, projects either to an IP (which is the normal case) or just to a VP (see below). So, the REA sites are IP and VP.[36] Consider first attachment of the IP. Where can it be attached? Intuitively, attachment of the *fell* IP requires detaching the *raced* IP. But the parser cannot detach the *raced* IP for the simple reason that it is the root node of the tree (i.e., detach it from what?). It is important to note that the *raced* IP is a complex unit (with daughters such as DP, VP, etc.). So, to detach the IP is to detach this node *along with its daughter nodes* (just as detaching the first PP in (55) detached this node along with the daughter NP *her mouth*). Of course, to detach the IP along with its daughters in (56b) is a vacuous operation. So it fails to facilitate reanalysis. What is not available to the parser is an analysis of the *raced* IP without its DP daughter. This is due to the structure of the tree: the available 'seams' are the right-edge constituents. Another possibility is that, given the presence of the *raced* IP, *fell* only projects a VP and attempts to attach it to this existing IP. This means detaching the *raced* VP.

The problem for the detached *raced* VP is that it needs an IP attachment site and there is no other IP (the DP is not a grammatical attachment site for a VP). What is important here is that the verb *race* cannot project an IP because the prior parse has 'stripped' the past-tense inflection from the verb and attached it in the head of IP position (it is this inflection which justifies the IP). At this point in the parse *race* is only a verb, not an inflected verb, as shown in (56b).

[36] In section 2, I noted that a 'bare' verb is simply a V, not a VP. But recall that the V designation of a bare verb is maximal in the relevant sense (it's the highest projection) and that distinct designations are used here only for (visual) clarity of the relations between nodes in a tree. Note also that I′ is precluded as an attachment site for grammatical reasons. If there is a projection of I, it is maximal because it is the highest projection. It is simply not grammatically possible to project to an 'intermediate' node (see fn. 7). As discussed in section 2, attachment is always attachment of a maximal projection (and AA will make the 'least unacceptable' attachment). The possibilities for *fell* then are IP or VP. Note also that the I′ reanalysis proposed for certain Japanese ambiguities in Gorrell (1994, 1995b) does not involve intermediate node projection.

That is, *raced* no longer exists as a single unit which can be reanalyzed. This is close to the analysis given by Fodor & Inoue (1994, pp. 415-416). The difference is that the role of structural factors is considered in more detail. Thus we have a specific, structure-based, account of why detaching the VP "would look to the parser like a terrible idea" (Fodor & Inoue, 1994, p. 416). As Fodor & Inoue (1994) observe, the parser apparently fails to reaccess the lexical information associated with *race* to determine that there is a non-finite alternative to the finite, past-tense, analysis. Why? For VP (re)attachment, the problem is that the VP does not contain the problematic inflectional information which signals the solution. For IP (re)attachment, the DP is unavailable as a candidate site, so the question of suitability for this site is never at issue. In other words, for reanalysis of VP, there is an available attachment site but no IP to attach to it. For the reanalysis of IP, there is no (non-vacuous) detachment which would make an attachment site available. Fodor & Inoue (1994, p. 418) note that if lexical reaccess is required for subcategorization information (as in *John heard the noise was...*), the parser appears quite efficient. From a structural point of view, this is because both the problem and solution involve the information in V. As Fodor & Inoue (1994) argue, the problem is not with lexical reaccess *per se*.[37]

Consider now the role of structure in the examples in (57).

---

[37] Ford *et al.* (1982, p. 763) attribute the difficulty of reanalysis in sentences such as (56a) to the need for a new morphosyntactic analysis of *race*. There are two steps involved. The first is lexical reaccess (to determine transitivity) and the second is recategorization as a (transitive) passive participle. The first step is not difficult, as (i) demonstrates. Sentence (ii) shows that the HNPS awkwardness in (i) is also present with an unambiguous transitive verb.

(i) John raced last night two of the fastest women in the world.
(ii) John purchased last night two of the biggest diamonds in the world.

Interestingly, recategorization of a verb, when the initial tense specification is maintained, does not appear to be difficult. Consider the German examples in (iii) and (iv).

(iii) Der Mann hat den Apfel gegessen. ('The man has eaten the apple.')
(iv) Der Mann hat den Apfel. ('The man has the apple.')

As the translations indicate, *haben* (like English *have*) may be either an auxiliary or a main verb. Neither (iii) nor (iv) is difficult. Assuming a serial, incremental, parse, one or the other must involve morphosyntactic recategorization. (Note that the postverbal NP in (iv) would complete the functional structure consistent with the main-verb reading. Furthermore, lengthening the postverbal NP does not lead to noticeable processing difficulty.) If this account is correct, then we have additional evidence in support of the I-V structural distinction as an important source of processing difficulty in (55a). See also Friederici (1995) for a discussion of analysis and reanalysis with German *werden*, which is also ambiguous between an auxiliary and main-verb reading.

(57) a. John heard the noise was due to a design flaw.
b. While Mary was mending the sock fell off her lap.

As Pritchett (1987, 1988) and others have observed, reanalysis in (57b) is more difficult than in (57a).[38] In section 3, I noted that reanalysis in (57a), but not (57b), is consistent with SD (see the discussion of (22) and (23) above). Within the DM, where structural factors are de-emphasized, how is this difference to be accounted for? In fact, it does not appear that diagnosis is a factor as, in each case, the disambiguating verb is preceded by an NP which could serve as subject. One potential candidate is the Thematic Overlay Effect (TOE) proposed in Inoue & Fodor (1995, p. 39), given in (58).[39]

(58) When a syntactic analysis is revised, it is essential that any semantic interpretation based on the initial incorrect analysis be erased.

With respect to (57b), this means that the difficulty is due to the fact that, in the initial analysis, the postverbal NP has been assigned a theme semantic role which, given reanalysis, must be removed without being replaced. Erasure takes place when a semantic role (or argument slot) vacated by reanalysis is replaced. In (57a), the clausal complement replaces the nominal complement of *hear*. But in (57b) there is no replacement for the removed nominal complement of *mend*. Given this, consider sentences in (59a) and (59b).

(59) a. John bet the man was leaving early.
b. John bet Fred (that) the man was leaving early.

Unlike verbs such as *hear*, the verb *bet* can take two internal arguments, as shown in (59b). From a structure-based approach this makes no difference, and

---

38 See Pritchett (1987) for off-line evidence, using a difficult/not difficult judgment task.

39 Another possibility, not discussed here, involves adapting a proposal due to van de Koot (1990). The proposal originally involved distinguishing the parser's decision to use, or not use, its look-ahead mechanism in (57a) and (57b), respectively. Briefly, the ambiguity in (57a) is between a nominal and clausal complement. A postverbal NP fails to disambiguate (causing the parser to make use of lookahead). On the other hand, in (57b), the ambiguity is between a transitive and intransitive reading of the verb and, here, the postverbal NP appears to disambiguate (causing the parser to fail to use lookahead). Within DM, it could be argued that, in (57b), the parser has concluded that the subcategorization ambiguity has been resolved and, therefore, omits this as a candidate for reanalysis. But one potential problem is that HNPS structures with optionally transitive verbs are predicted to produce a comparable failure to correctly determine the locus of reanalysis (cf. (i) in fn. 37).

the parse of (59a) and (57a) is essentially the same: a postverbal NP is initially attached as an object and then, via structure addition, reanalyzed as an embedded subject. But from the perspective of the TOE, the fact that *bet* takes two internal arguments makes for different predictions. That is, in (59a) the postverbal NP is initially attached as the first argument of *bet*. The appearance of the verb *was* forces reanalysis such that this NP is now the subject of the second argument position. That is, the first argument slot is vacated without being replaced. Yet there is no TOE-predicted garden-path effect. This makes it unlikely that the TOE is responsible for the processing difficulty observed in (57b). Further, for *wh*-structures such as (60a), a strong garden path is incorrectly predicted if a first-resort strategy causes the parser to initially associate the *wh*-phrase with an optional, first internal argument of *say* (as shown in (60b)). Here an argument is removed, without being replaced, when the embedded verb is processed (see Gorrell, 1995a, for a discussion of this reanalysis consistent with SD). As in (59a), the predicted processing difficulty in (60a) is absent.

(60) a. To whom did John say the letter was addressed?
b. John said to Bill the letter was too long.

The discussion of these different ambiguity types reveals that structure must play a significant role in ambiguity resolution. This is particularly clear in the analysis of the difficulty evident in (56a) presented above. It is also the only relevant factor which distinguishes reanalysis in (57a) and (57b). In particular, it appears that SD is a significant factor in reanalysis, although, as we have seen, other factors may be present which can either inhibit or facilitate reanalysis. A brief discussion of (61a), presented by Fodor & Inoue (1994) as a counter-example to SD, reveals the importance of the close connection between analysis and reanalysis which has been a focus throughout this chapter.

(61) a. Our son doesn't tell us what he's thinking about anymore.
b. John said that Bill will leave yesterday.

In contrast to (61b), where raising *yesterday* out of the embedded clause is a difficult operation, in (61a) there is an apparent lack of difficulty attaching *anymore* to the higher clause. As a negative polarity item, *anymore* must be in the scope of a negative operator which, in (61a) requires the higher attachment. Fodor & Inoue (1994, p. 431) state that the attachment of *anymore* within the embedded clause is ungrammatical, whereas attachment of *yesterday* is syntactically well-formed but incongruous.[40] The locus of this difference in the parse sequence is argued to be in the process of reanalysis. That is, in each case the ambiguous item is initially attached in the lower clause (following RA), with reanalysis in (61a) facilitated by the ungrammaticality of the attachment. No such help is available in (61b) because the DM is more responsive to syntactic illformedness than incongruity.

But, given this distinction, Incremental Licensing (section 3), in contrast to a grammar-blind application of RA, predicts that the parser will never make the lower attachment of *anymore*, as there would be no licenser (i.e., no justification) for the lower attachment. Thus, the distinction between (61a) and (61b) is due to where *anymore* and *yesterday* are initially attached. In (61b) attachment is to the lower clause, and SD correctly predicts processing difficulty in reanalysis. In (61a) the higher attachment is initially made and SD simply plays no role.[41]

6 Summary

In this chapter I have discussed the role of structural factors in sentence analysis and reanalysis. The preference for minimal structure receives wide support from both theoretical and experimental investigations. This general preference allows for close links, not only between analysis and reanalysis operations, but also between the grammar and the parser. The parser respects a central property of grammar (economy of representation) and the form of the syntactic representation computed by the parser plays a significant role in determining

---

[40] For example, consider the June 3, 1996, *Doonesbury* cartoon by Gary Trudeau. In the final panel, one character, confused as to the correct implication of the International Dateline, asks a friend embarking on a trip to 'Call me yesterday'.

[41] Fodor & Inoue (1994) treat *anymore* as two lexical items, arguing that *any* is attached before *more* is processed. This is significant because *any* is not necessarily a negative polarity item, but *any+more* is. But (at least for my dialect) it is incorrect to treat *anymore* in (61a) as two distinct items. For example, the *Oxford American Dictionary* (1980) lists *anymore* as a single item (no space between *any* and *more*). Further, it states "Do not confuse *anymore* with *any more*" and gives the following examples:

(i) I do not see him anymore.
(ii) Any more would be too many.

Of course, what is important is the psychological status of *anymore* (with respect to the lexicon and to syntactic processing), not its dictionary form. Further research is needed to choose between the distinct analyses discussed here.

sources of processing difficulty, such as violations of Structural Determinism and Right-edge Availability.

Max-Planck-Institute of Cognitive Neuroscience, Leipzig

References

Abney, S. 1989. A computational model of human parsing. *Journal of Psycholinguistic Research*, 18, 129-144.

Bader, M. 1994. *Sprachverstehen: Syntax und Prosodie beim Lesen*. Unpublished doctoral dissertation, University of Stuttgart.

Bader, M., Bayer, J., Hopf, J.-M., & Meng, M. 1996. Case assignment in processing German verb-final clauses. *MIT Occasional Papers in Linguistics, 9: Proceedings of the NELS 26 Sentence Processing Workshop*, 1-25.

Bader, M. & Lasser, I. 1994. German verb-final clauses and sentence processing: Evidence for immediate attachment. In C. Clifton, L. Frazier, & K. Rayner (eds.), *Perspectives on Sentence Processing*. New York, NY: Erlbaum, 225-242.

Baltin, M. 1989. Heads and projections. In M. Baltin & A. Kroch (eds.), *Alternative Conceptions of Phrase Structure*. Chicago, IL: University of Chicago Press, 1-16.

Boland, J., Tanenhaus, M., Garnsey, S., & Carlson, G. 1995. Verb argument structure in parsing and interpretation: Evidence from *wh*-questions. *Journal of Memory and Language*, 34, 774-806.

Chomsky, N. 1995. *The Minimalist Program*. Cambridge, MA: MIT Press.

Chomsky, N. 1991. Some notes on economy of derivation and representation. In R. Freidin (ed.), *Principles and Parameters in Comparative Grammar*. Cambridge, MA: MIT Press, 417-454.

Chomsky, N. 1986. *Knowledge of Language: Its Nature, Origin and Use*. New York, NY: Praeger.

Chung, S. & McCloskey, J. 1983. On the interpretation of certain island facts in GPSG. *Linguistic Inquiry*, 14, 704-713.

Crocker, M. 1994. On the nature of the principle-based sentence processor. In C. Clifton, L. Frazier, & K. Rayner (eds.), *Perspectives on Sentence Processing*. New York, NY: Erlbaum, 245-266.

De Vincenzi, M. 1991. *Syntactic Parsing Strategies in Italian*. Dordrecht: Kluwer Academic Publishers.

Emonds, J. 1985. *A Unified Theory of Syntactic Categories*. Dordrecht: Foris Publications.

Ferreira, F. & Henderson, J. 1991. Recovery from misanalyses of garden-path sentences. *Journal of Memory and Language*, 30, 725-745.

Fodor, J.D. 1978. Parsing strategies and constraints on transformations. *Linguistic Inquiry*, 9, 427-474.

Fodor, J.D. & Inoue, A. (this volume). Attach Anyway.

Fodor, J.D. & Inoue, A. 1994. The diagnosis and cure of garden paths. *Journal of Psycholinguistic Research*, 23, 407-434.

Ford, M., Bresnan, J., & Kaplan, R. 1982. A competence-based theory of syntactic closure. In J. Bresnan (ed.), *The Mental Representation of Grammatical Relations*. Cambridge, MA: MIT Press, 727-796.

Frazier, L. 1995. Constraint satisfaction as a theory of sentence processing. *Journal of Psycholinguistic Research*, 24, 437-468.

Frazier, L. 1993. Processing Dutch sentence structures. *Journal of Psycholinguistic Research*, 22, 85-108.

Frazier, L. 1990. Parsing modifiers: Special purpose routines in the human sentence processing mechanism? In D. A. Balota, G. B. Flores d'Arcais, & K. Rayner (eds.), *Comprehension Processes in Reading*. Hillsdale, NJ: Lawrence Erlbaum Associates, 303-330.

Frazier, L. 1978. *On Comprehending Sentences: Syntactic Parsing Strategies*. Unpublished doctoral dissertation, University of Connecticut, Storrs, CT. Distributed by the Indiana University Linguistics Club, Bloomington, IN.

Frazier, L. & Clifton, C. (this volume). Sentence reanalysis, and visibility.

Frazier, L. & Clifton, C. 1996. *Construal*. Cambridge, MA: MIT Press.

Frazier, L. & Clifton, C. 1989. Successive cyclicity in the grammar and the parser. *Language and Cognitive Processes*, 4, 93-126.

Frazier, L. & Flores d'Arcais, G. 1989. Filler-driven parsing: A study of gap filling in Dutch. *Journal of Memory and Language*, 28, 331-344.

Frazier, L. & Fodor, J.D. 1978. The sausage machine: A new two-stage parsing model. *Cognition*, 6, 291-325.

Frazier, L. & Rayner, K. 1988. Parameterizing the language processing system: Left- versus right-branching within and across languages. In J. Hawkins (ed.), *Explaining Language Universals*. Oxford, UK: Basil Blackwell, 247-279.

Frazier, L. & Rayner, K. 1982. Making and correcting errors during sentence comprehension: Eye movements in the analysis of structurally ambiguous sentences. *Cognitive Psychology*, 14, 178-210.

Friederici, A. (this volume). Diagnosis and reanalysis: Two processing steps the brain differentiates.

Friederici, A. 1995. The time course of syntactic activation during language processing: A model based on neuropsychological and neurophysiological data. *Brain and Language*, 50, 259-281.

Friederici, A. & Mecklinger, A. 1996. Syntactic parsing as revealed by brain responses: First-pass and second-pass processes. *Journal of Psycholinguistic Research*, 25, 157-176.

Gazdar, G. 1981. Unbounded dependencies and coordinate structure. *Linguistic Inquiry*, 12, 155-184.

Gazdar, G., Klein, E., Pullum, G., & Sag, I. 1985. *Generalized Phrase Structure Grammar*. Oxford, UK: Basil Blackwell.

Gibson, E.A.F. 1991. *A Computational Theory of Human Linguistic Processing: Memory Limitations and Processing Breakdown*. Unpublished doctoral dissertation, Carnegie Mellon University, Pittsburgh, PA. Available as Center for Machine Translation Technical Report CMU-CMT-91-125.

Gorrell, P. (in preparation a). Minimal structure and parsing theory. Manuscript, Max Planck Institute of Cognitive Neuroscience, Leipzig.

Gorrell, P. (in preparation b). The variable structure of German clauses. Manuscript, Max Planck Institute of Cognitive Neuroscience, Leipzig.

Gorrell, P. (in press a). The subject-before-object preference in German clauses. In B. Hemforth (ed.), *German Sentence Processing*. Dordrecht: Kluwer Academic Publishers.

Gorrell, P. (in press b). Review of *Construal*. *Journal of Linguistics*, 33, 2.

Gorrell, P. 1996a. Parsing theory and phrase-order variation in German V2 clauses. *Journal of Psycholinguistic Research*, 25, 135-156.

Gorrell, P. 1996b. Diagnosis and determinism. Paper presented at *Ninth Annual CUNY Conference on Human Sentence Processing*, New York, NY.

Gorrell, P. 1995a. *Syntax and Parsing*. Cambridge, UK: Cambridge University Press.

Gorrell. P. 1995b. Japanese trees and the garden path. In R. Mazuka & N. Nagai (eds.), *Japanese Sentence Processing*. Hillsdale, NJ: Erlbaum, 331-350.

Gorrell, P. 1994. Structural relations in the grammar and the parser. *Folia Linguistica*, XXVIII, 1-2, 101-137.

Gorrell, P 1993. Incremental structure building and the determinism hypothesis. Paper presented at *Sixth Annual CUNY Conference on Human Sentence Processing*, Amherst, MA.

Gorrell, P. 1991. COMP in formal grammar. *The Oxford International Encyclopedia of Linguistics*. Oxford, UK: Oxford University Press, 637-639.

Gorrell, P. 1989. Establishing the loci of serial and parallel effects in syntactic processing. *Journal of Psycholinguistic Research*, 18, 61-73.

Gorrell, P. 1987. *Studies of Human Syntactic Processing: Ranked-Parallel versus Serial Models*. Unpublished doctoral dissertation, University of Connecticut, Storrs, CT.

Grimshaw, J. 1991. Extended projections. Manuscript, Brandeis University, Waltham, MA.

Grimshaw, J. 1993. *Minimal Projection, Heads, and Optimality*. Technical Report #4 of the Rutgers University Center for Cognitive Science, Piscataway, NJ.

Haider, H. 1993. *Deutsche Syntax*. Tübingen: Gunter Narr Verlag.

Higginbotham, J. 1985. On semantics. *Linguistic Inquiry*, 16, 547-594.

Inoue, A. & Fodor, J.D. 1995. Information-paced parsing of Japanese. In R. Mazuka & N. Nagai (eds.), *Japanese Sentence Processing*. Hillsdale, NJ: Lawrence Erlbaum Associates, 9-63.

Jordens, P. 1991. Linguistic knowledge in second language acquisition. In L. Eubank (ed.), *Point Counterpoint: Universal Grammar in the Second Language*. Philadelphia, PA: John Benjamins, 201-219.

Kaan, E. 1996a. Parsing embedded *wh*-questions in Dutch. In R. Jonkers, E. Kaan, & A. Wiegel (eds.), *Language and Cognition 5: Yearbook 6/5 of the Research Group for Experimental and Theoretical Linguistics*. Groningen: University of Groningen, 71-85.

Kaan, E. 1996b. Gap filling in Dutch. Poster presented at *Ninth Annual CUNY Conference on Human Sentence Processing*, New York, NY.

Kayne, R. 1994. *The Antisymmetry of Syntax*. Cambridge, MA: MIT Press.

Koopman, H. 1983. *The Syntax of Verbs*. Dordrecht: Foris Publishers.

Koster, J. 1986. *Domains and Dynasties*. Dordrecht: Foris Publishers.

Kimball, J. 1973. Seven principles of surface structure parsing in natural language. *Cognition*, 2, 15-47.

MacDonald, M., Pearlmutter, N., & Seidenberg, M. 1994. The lexical nature of syntactic ambiguity resolution. *Psychological Review*, 101, 676-703.

Marcus, M., Hindle, D., & Fleck, M. 1983. D-theory: Talking about talking about trees. *Association for Computational Linguistics*, 21, 129-136.

Mecklinger, A., Schriefers, H., Steinhauer, K., & Friederici, A. 1995. Processing relative clauses varying on syntactic and semantic dimensions: An analysis with event related brain potentials. *Memory and Cognition*, 23, 477-497.

Meng, M. 1995. Processing *wh*-questions in German and Dutch: Differential effects of disambiguation and their interpretation. Poster presented at the conference on *Architectures and Mechanisms for Language Processing (AMLaP) Conference 1995*, Edinburgh.

Munn, A. 1993. *Topics in the Syntax and Semantics of Coordinate Structures*. Unpublished doctoral dissertation, University of Maryland, College Park, MD.

Oxford American Dictionary 1980. Oxford, UK: Oxford University Press.

Partee, B., ter Meulen, A., & Wall, R. E. 1993. *Mathematical Methods in Linguistics*. Dordrecht: Kluwer Academic Publishers.

Phillips, C. 1995. Right association in parsing and grammar. *MIT Working Papers in Linguistics*, 26, 37-93.

Phillips, C. & Gibson, E. 1996. The strength of the local attachment preference. Paper presented at *Ninth Annual CUNY Conference on Human Sentence Processing*, New York, NY.

Pollard, C. & Sag, I. 1994. *Head-Driven Phrase Structure Grammar*. Chicago, IL: University of Chicago Press.

Pritchett, B. 1992. *Grammatical Competence and Parsing Performance*. Chicago, IL: University of Chicago Press.

Pritchett, B. 1991. Head position and parsing ambiguity. *Journal of Psycholinguistic Research*, 20, 251-270.

Pritchett, B. 1988. Garden path phenomena and the grammatical basis of language processing. *Language*, 64, 539-576.

Pritchett, B. 1987. *Garden Path Phenomena and the Grammatical Basis of Language Processing*. Unpublished doctoral dissertation, Harvard University, Cambridge, MA.

Sag, I. 1996. English relative clause constructions. Unpublished manuscript, Stanford University, Stanford, CA (June).

Schlesewsky, M., Fanselow, G., Kliegl, R., & Krems, J. (in press). Preferences for grammatical functions in the processing of locally ambiguous *wh*-questions in German. In B. Hemforth (ed.), *German Sentence Processing*. Dordrecht: Kluwer Academic Publishers.

Schlesewsky, M., Krems, J., Kliegel, R., Fanselow, G., Brueck, U., & Mackedan, K. 1996. Syntaktisches Priming bei Subjekts- und Objekts-Fragesätzen. Paper presented at *Second Meeting of the Gesellschaft für Kognitionswissenschaft*, Hamburg, Germany.

Schriefers, H., Friederici, A., & Kühn, K. 1995. The processing of locally ambiguous relative clauses in German. *Journal of Memory and Language*, 34, 227-246.

Schwartz, B. & Vikner, S. 1989. All V-2 clauses are CPs. *Working Papers in Scandinavian Syntax*, 43, 27-50.

Speas, P. 1990. *Phrase Structure in Natural Language*. Dordrecht: Kluwer Academic Publishers.

Stowe, L. 1986. Evidence for on-line gap location. *Language and Cognitive Processes*, 1, 227-245.

Sturt, P. & Crocker, M. 1996. Monotonic syntactic processing: A cross-linguistic study of attachment and reanalysis. *Language and Cognitive Processes*, 11, 449-494.

Thiersch, C. 1978. *Topics in German Syntax*. Unpublished doctoral dissertation, MIT, Cambridge, MA.

Travis, L. 1991. Parameters of phrase structure and verb-second phenomena. In R. Freidin (ed.), *Principles and Parameters in Comparative Grammar*. Cambridge, MA: MIT Press, 339-364.

Travis, L. 1984. *Parameters and Effects of Word-Order Variation*. Unpublished doctoral dissertation, MIT, Cambridge, MA.

van de Koot, J. 1990. *An Essay on Grammar-Parser Relations*. Dordrecht: Foris Publishers.

Weinberg, A. 1992. Parameterizing the parser: A grammar-based theory of garden-paths. Paper presented at *Fifth Annual CUNY Conference on Human Sentence Processing*, New York NY.

Wright, B. & Garrett, M. 1984. Lexical decision in sentences: Effects of syntactic structure. *Memory and Cognition*, 12, 31-45.

8

Reanalysis and Limited Repair Parsing: Leaping off the Garden Path*

Richard L. Lewis

Abstract

This chapter develops a theory of reanalysis called limited repair parsing. Repair parsers deal with the problem of local ambiguity in part by modifying previously built structure when the chosen structure later proves to be inconsistent. This modification of existing structure distinguishes repair parsing from parallel or multi-path parsing, least-commitment parsing, backtracking, or reparsing strategies. Parsers with a limited capability for repair are psycholinguistically important because they can potentially explain the contrasts between difficult garden path structures (when repair fails) and unproblematic local ambiguities (when repair is successful or easy). Although the idea of repair has been implicit in some psycholinguistic work (and emerged explicitly in the diagnosis model of Fodor & Inoue, 1994, and the NL-Soar model of Lewis, 1993), there has been no clear formulation of the general class of repair parsers. This chapter makes a first step toward such a formulation, shows how repair parsing offers significant computational advantages over other alternatives for reanalysis, and proposes a particular repair mechanism, *snip*, that explains a wide range of cross-linguistic reanalysis phenomena. Snip is a proposal for a simple, automatic, on-line repair process. The chapter concludes by briefly describing how snip can be embedded in a more comprehensive sentence processing architecture that maintains the structural sensitivity of purely syntactic theories like Pritchett's (1992), yet still accounts for the flexibility of parsing as revealed by interactive studies.

---

* Many thanks to Jill Lehman and the late Allen Newell, who provided invaluable contributions to this work. Thanks also to Julie Boland and two anonymous reviewers, who provided useful comments on this chapter.

J.D. Fodor and F. Ferreira (eds.), Reanalysis in Sentence Processing, 247–285.

1 Introduction

Two central questions that a theory of human parsing must answer are: (1) How do people interpret locally ambiguous material? (2) How do people revise their interpretations of ambiguous material based on later disambiguating information? This chapter is an attempt to make progress on the second question by developing a theory of reanalysis called *limited repair* parsing (Lewis, 1992). Limited repair explains how the human sentence processor can sometimes rapidly leap off the garden path and find its way back onto the path to a successful parse. The theory has been implemented in a computational model of sentence comprehension, NL-Soar (Lehman *et al.*, 1991; Lewis, 1993a; Lewis, 1993b).

Repair parsers deal with the problem of local ambiguity by modifying previously built structure when the chosen structure proves to be inconsistent with the disambiguating material. The explicit modification of existing structure distinguishes repair parsing from parallel or multi-path parsing, minimal commitment parsing, and backtracking/reparsing strategies. Although the idea of repair has been implicit in some psycholinguistic work (and has recently emerged quite explicitly in the diagnosis model of Fodor & Inoue, 1995), there has been no clear formulation of the general class of repair parsers. This chapter makes a first step toward such a formulation, shows how repair parsing may offer significant computational advantages over other alternatives for reanalysis, and proposes a particular repair mechanism which explains a wide range of cross-linguistic reanalysis phenomena.

Why is understanding reanalysis just as important as understanding ambiguity resolution? Frazier & Rayner (1982) put it most strongly: "... it is emphasized that an understanding of the parser's revision procedures is essential to an explanation of why certain linguistic structures cannot be successfully parsed by humans" (p. 178). Indeed, one important source of data that can be used to reveal the nature of reanalysis processes concerns the contrast between ambiguous structures that can give rise to noticeable garden path effects, such as the subject/object ambiguity in (1) (Frazier & Rayner, 1982), and those ambiguous structures that cause little or no perceptible difficulty, such as the subject/object ambiguity in (2) (Juliano & Tanenhaus, 1994; Mitchell, 1987; Pritchett, 1988):

(1) Although Mary forgot her husband didn't seem very upset yesterday.

(2) a. Mary forgot her husband at the airport yesterday.
b. Mary forgot her husband needed a ride yesterday.

The structure in (1) can give rise to an impression of ungrammaticality, indicating a failure of reanalysis. The structure in (2) may produce longer reading times in the disambiguating region (e.g., an extra 50 ms on *needed* compared to unambiguous structures with overt complementizers; Ferreira & Henderson, 1990), but does not usually cause noticeable difficulty, regardless of which interpretation is required. A theory of reanalysis is required to explain the contrasts. Why does reanalysis fail in structures such as (1), and succeed in structures such as (2)? Apparently, reanalysis processes are not all-powerful, but are constrained in some way. The particular model proposed below limits repair by a locality assumption that increases computational efficiency and leads to interesting predictions about difficult and easy reanalyses. Furthermore, it provides a concrete hypothesis about exactly what is going on in that extra 50 ms or so in the disambiguating regions of the easier sentences.

The remainder of the chapter is organized as follows. Section 2 describes how reanalysis can be understood as a functional requirement on human parsing, independently of how that function is realized. This will permit us to see how four rather different classes of reanalysis are all responsive to the same functional requirement. In section 3, each of the four major parsing models will be described in terms of the spaces they search and the strategies they use for searching them. This leads us to an interesting theoretical result: repair parsing is an effective parsing method because it *reformulates* the parsing search space so that it better supports efficient depth-first search. Section 4 describes a specific kind of repair mechanism, limited cue-based repair, and shows how it accounts for a wide range of cross-linguistic reanalysis phenomena. Section 5 sketches how the repair mechanism is embedded in a more comprehensive model of sentence processing.

2 Reanalysis as a Functional Requirement

Reanalysis is a function that must be performed by any system for parsing natural language. The following gives a functional definition of reanalysis:

(3) Reanalysis is the function of revising the interpretation of previously perceived linguistic material based on information that follows later.

Local ambiguity is the phenomenon that gives rise to the requirement for reanalysis: the intended interpretation of linguistic input is often determined by information that comes later in the sentence. For example, consider the familiar subject/object ambiguity in (4):

(4) I know the little boy hiding under the table...

The comprehender might adopt one of the following options for the initial interpretation:

(5) a. Interpret the string as meaning *I know who the boy is.*

b. Interpret the string as meaning I know something (to be made explicit immediately) about the boy.

c. Interpret the string as meaning either *I know who the boy is*, or *I know something about the boy.*

d. Delay interpretation.

If the input now continues:

(6) ...will bump his head

the comprehender must revise the initial interpretation if it happened to select some option other than (5b). It is irrelevant what kind of ambiguity resolution process is used, no process can always make the correct decision. Nothing in this analysis hinges on the difficulty or ease of making the revision. The only point is a functional one: in some cases the revision must be made if the material is to be understood. (Parallel models and minimal commitment models may seem to provide counterexamples to the requirement for reanalysis, but we shall see in the next section that this is not the case.)

One might argue that the pure delay strategy (5d) is in fact a way of avoiding reanalysis, since there is no interpretation to be revised. However, such a strategy cannot be systematically sustained if the comprehender is constrained to emit some interpretation incrementally (within a finite time bound). The problem is that local ambiguities in natural language can stretch on indefinitely. For example, in long distance filler-gap ambiguities such as (7) below there is never a point at which one can be sure that it is safe to commit to a decision about the location of the gap.

(7) I saw the landlord that Amparo believes Ted knows Janet...

3 Four Theories of Reanalysis

The functional definition in (3) abstracts away from the process that is used to realize reanalysis. In this section we consider the computational properties of four major classes of possible reanalysis processes: reanalysis by backtracking, reanalysis by selection from parallel alternatives, reanalysis by refining commitments, and reanalysis by repair.

3.1 Reanalysis by Backtracking (Reparsing)

Frazier & Rayner's (1982) classification of reanalysis processes in reading provides a good starting point for understanding the space of possible processes. They distinguished between forward, backward, and selective reanalysis. *Forward* reanalysis occurs when the reader returns to the beginning of the sentence and recomprehends the sentence, presumably looking for choice points at which to make alternative decisions. In *backward* reanalysis, the reader works backward through the sentence, trying out different alternatives. In *selective* reanalysis, the reader attempts to focus only on the portion of the sentence that caused the problem. Frazier & Rayner looked for evidence for these different reanalysis types from explicit eye movements in reading. Most of the behavior was consistent with selective reanalysis, although subjects sometimes did start at the beginning and reread. The data did not support backward reanalysis at all.

All three kinds of reanalysis can be classified as *backtracking* schemes (Winograd, 1983), because they involve the comprehension system returning to previous states in the parse and pursuing alternative analyses by reparsing or recomprehending the ambiguous material. Reanalysis by backtracking to prior states is possible if the parser has a memory of previous choice points and states. If the pursued interpretation is incompatible with disambiguating material, the parser can revisit earlier choice points and try alternative paths.

Which state the parser returns to is determined by the particular control strategy used. *Chronological backtracking* systematically revisits previous choice points in reverse order. For example, a push-down stack can be used in ATN parsing to implement chronological backtracking. Unfortunately, the result is exponential search (Winograd, 1983). *Dependency-directed backtracking* uses information about the error itself in an attempt to return directly to the choice point that was responsible for the misanalysis. The ranked flagged serial model of Inoue & Fodor (1995) is an example of a selective backtracking model.

These various control strategies for backtracking yield the forward, backward, and selective reanalysis distinction of Frazier & Rayner (1982).

Figure 1 shows how different kinds of backtracking can be viewed as variations on depth-first search in a space of legal parsing operations. Each node in the search space represents a partial, well-formed parse tree. Each operator or transition in the space represents a parsing operation (for example, the application of a phrase-structure rule) that extends the parse tree and pushes the system into a new state in the space. Some of the state transitions correspond to consuming input. Local ambiguity corresponds to choice points in the parsing space: multiple legal parsing operations are applicable at a given point. The goal state is a well-formed interpretation of the input. If the parser takes a wrong turn at an ambiguity, a dead-end is reached on a garden path and the parser must backtrack by revisiting prior states and pursuing alternative paths.

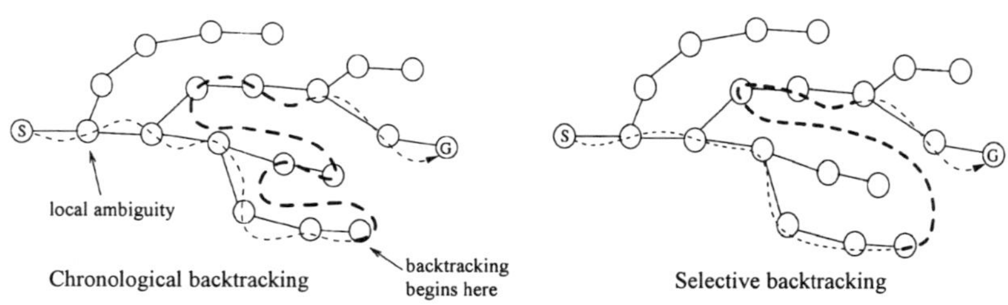

FIGURE 1: Two kinds of reanalysis by depth-first backtracking. The dashed lines indicate the path the parser takes in the search space; the heavy dashed lines indicate the reanalysis. *S* indicates the starting state, *G* indicates the goal state (a well-formed syntactic representation of the input).

There must be sufficient memory of previous states and choice points to support the control strategy used. Exhaustive chronological backtracking (Figure 1, left), requires a complete memory of parser states at all the previous choice points. Selective backtracking (Figure 1, right) can achieve some savings by only storing a limited number of prior parser states. This was the method used by the finite-state parser of Blank (1989). Blank's parser is an example of a *limited-memory selective backtracking* system. The parser was sometimes garden-pathed because the necessary parse states were not always available to backtrack to. Blank fixed, in advance, a small set of *boundary registers* that saved states at specific kinds of phrasal boundaries. Blank noted that the type and number of such registers is unconstrained—he simply chose a set that seemed reasonable and predicted certain kinds of strong garden path effects.

We have implicitly assumed so far that backtracking in reading results in overt regressions and reparsing.[1] However, as Frazier & Rayner (1982) point out, and as subsequent eye-tracking studies have demonstrated, reanalysis need not involve regressive eye movements. Often reanalysis is detected by longer times spent on the disambiguating region as the eye fixations continue forward through the sentence. In fact, all backtracking reanalysis strategies can be realized covertly, without explicit eye movements and reparsing. The cost for doing so is additional short-term memory storage. Overt backtracking reparses the actual input, while covert backtracking reparses a memory of the input. This distinction was never an issue for natural language parsing systems in artificial intelligence or computational linguistics, but it is clearly an important one for psycholinguistics.

Thus, the backtracking strategy that places the least demands on memory is forward reanalysis by overt recomprehension from the beginning of the sentence. This strategy requires no memory for input or prior parsing states—it needs just enough memory for the parser to remember not to continue going down the same path.[2] The drawback of this method is time, but it is a reliable strategy when all else fails.

As a theory of *covert*, rapid reanalysis—i.e., as a theory of what is happening in the longer fixations of disambiguating material when the eye continues to move forward, or as speech continues to flow in—standard backtracking suffers from two drawbacks. First, it may require an implausible amount of wasted reparsing. For example, reanalyzing the object NP to subject position in (8) below would require reparsing the entire NP over again (Winograd, 1983):

(8) Mary knew the bright red Honda parked next to hers belonged to the landlord.

Variations on standard backtracking avoid this wasted reparsing by keeping track of, and reusing, well-formed subphrases in the parse (e.g., Abney, 1989; Holbrook *et al.*, 1992; Konieczny, 1996). The second drawback is unavoidable in principle: in addition to the current parse state, the parser must keep track of

---

1 Backtracking can occur in speech processing as well, when the listener repeats something to herself that she did not understand, or recomprehends as the speaker repeats himself. A kind of covert backtracking occurs when the listener covertly rehearses and recomprehends something, or reinterprets material in the short-term phonological trace without rehearsal (Gathercole & Baddeley, 1993).

2 O(N) bits for N choice points for exhaustive search of the space.

prior states and input, and have extra mechanisms available for reinstantiating and managing the prior states (e.g., the stack used in chronological backtracking).

3.2 Reanalysis by Selection from Parallel Alternatives

While backtracking searches depth-first, Figure 2 shows how parallel parsing is a breadth-first search through the parse space. Parallel parsing may seem to present an obvious counterexample to the claim that analysis is a functional requirement, because it does not appear to engage in any revision processes. This objection confuses the kind of parsing process with the function that it realizes. It is true that parallel models do not need to make changes to their structural representations when the disambiguating information arrives, because the required structure can be selected and carried forward, and the incorrect structure dropped from further consideration. Nevertheless, the process of ruling out the incorrect structure (e.g., explicit pruning operations (Gibson, 1991), or redistribution of activation (Just & Carpenter, 1992)) is precisely what carries out the reanalysis function. This also holds of models in the constraint-based lexical framework (MacDonald *et al.*, 1994; Trueswell *et al.*, 1994) that adopt a kind of weighted-parallel scheme.

All-paths parsing (Figure 2, left) carries forward all possible interpretations in parallel. This places unrealistic memory demands on the human parser, and quickly runs afoul of empirical data on garden path effects (it predicts there should never be noticeable garden paths). Computationally, breadth-first search is more memory-intensive than depth-first search, and should be avoided unless depth-first search runs the risk of getting lost in deep or infinite paths (Winston, 1992).

Thus, the critical theoretical and empirical issue is how to limit the parallelism (Figure 2, right) so that the parser can still handle easy local ambiguities. Gibson (1991), following Gorrell (1987), proposed a limited parallel model motivated by short-term memory limitations. Gibson's theory took the form of a syntactic metric which measured memory load. The metric was used to make precise predictions about which alternatives will be pursued and which will be abandoned, turning the breadth-first search into a limited beam search (see e.g., Winston, 1992).

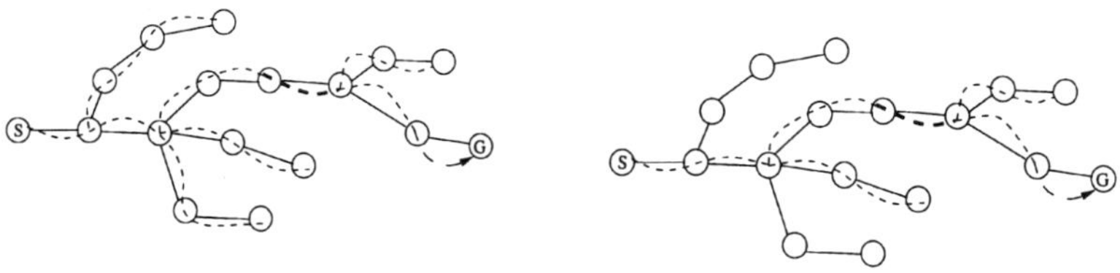

All-paths parallel parsing   Limited path parallel parsing

FIGURE 2: Reanalysis by selection from parallel alternatives. The dashed lines indicate the path the parser pursues in the search space; the heavy dashed lines indicate the reanalysis that takes place when some paths are dropped from consideration. *S* indicates the starting state, *G* indicates the goal state (a well-formed syntactic representation of the input).

The impressive empirical coverage of Gibson's metric would seem to provide additional support for the plausibility of a memory-limited parallel model. However, the way the metric is actually applied points away from such an account. Gibson's model works in the following way: it computes multiple parse trees in parallel, and assigns a memory cost to each partial tree based on the metric (the metric counts the number of unsatisfied syntactic relations of various types). Certain structures are then pruned based on their memory metrics. However, the pruning rule does not eliminate structures when they jointly or individually exceed some posited memory bound. Instead, the rule computes the *difference* in memory load between two structures, and if the difference is greater than some constant *P*, it prunes the higher cost structure. Multiple high-cost structures may be maintained in parallel as long as they do not differ too much in cost. Furthermore, this way of using the metric, and the pruning constant *P*, has no relation to the use of the metric to predict processing overload effects on center-embedded structures (Gibson, 1991). There, the metric is used more straightforwardly as a measure of memory load: structures are predicted to be unprocessable (and pruned) if they exceed some posited bound *K* (different from *P*).

One interpretation of the Gibson metric, therefore, is that it actually reflects the operation of a depth-first single-path parser, which has some limited capacity to repair or transform one structure into another.[3] Under this view, the metric implicitly serves as a metric of structural closeness or similarity. If the two structures are not too different, the repair process of transforming one to the other is easy, but if they are structurally too far apart, the process is difficult.

[3] Gibson (1991) acknowledges such an interpretation, but does not pursue it.

Another interpretation of the metric is that it reflects a parallel system that is not maintaining completely independent structures, but using some structure sharing technique to conserve space. The more two structures share substructure, the closer their metrics will be, and the less memory they will require. Hence, it is less likely that one of them will be pruned.

Structure sharing addresses, in part, a difficult problem that any parallel parser must solve. When a parallel parser reaches an ambiguous point with two or more possible paths, it must create new copies of the original structure in order to pursue all the attachments. This kind of powerful copy-on-demand mechanism is an implausible candidate for a subcomponent of the human sentence processor.[4]

The alternative is that the parser engage in some kind of structure sharing or sophisticated lazy evaluation (delaying copying until absolutely necessary; Godden, 1990; Lytinen & Tomuro, 1996). The choice of mechanism depends in part on the nature of the grammatical representation. Simple context free grammars admit straightforward structure sharing, but sharing can be more complicated with other kinds of grammars (Winograd, 1983). For example, unification grammars do not readily admit sharing at all, but demand either copying of structure, or lazy (delayed) copying. A dependency grammar representation that shares structure requires careful bookkeeping of which link goes with which interpretation (Lombardo, this volume).

Finally, note that none of these arguments against parallel, breadth-first parsing are arguments against parallel *generation* of syntactic alternatives at ambiguous points (Altmann & Steedman, 1988). These are orthogonal issues. The arguments are against *maintaining and pursuing* distinct interpretations in parallel. The distinction can be seen clearly in the Soar-based comprehension model of Lewis (1993a). This architecture separates the parallel generation and selection of potential parsing operators from their serial application. At each ambiguous point, multiple operators are generated that correspond to the intention to produce different syntactic structures. Of these multiple possibilities, one operator is selected,[5] and the execution of that operator produces the single selected structure.

---

[4] This is the process used in Gibson's computational implementation of the theory, though he made no psychological claims about this aspect of the model.

[5] Possibly on the basis of semantic or contextual factors (Lewis, 1993a; Lewis, 1996a).

3.3 Reanalysis by Monotonic Refinement of Commitments

Like parallel parsers, minimal commitment parsers seem to be obvious counterexamples to the functional requirement for reanalysis. Minimal commitment parsers only make monotonic additions to the representations of the parse tree they are incrementally building (Gorrell, 1993; Weinberg, 1993). But note that although the representation itself evolves monotonically over time, *what* the representation represents (the parse tree) is revised non-monotonically. In other words, minimal commitment parsers do revise their structural interpretations in the face of disambiguating information. In our earlier example, a minimal commitment parser would change its interpretation from (5a) to (5b). The fact that the same process (adding dominance and precedence relations) is used for both initial interpretation and reanalysis does not mean that there are not two distinct functions being accomplished. It simply means this particular approach has achieved some economy of mechanism (though we will question this achievement below). Both parallel models and minimal commitment models can therefore be seen as theories that are designed specifically to respond to the requirement for on-line reanalysis.

The way minimal commitment parsers effect reanalysis has several desirable properties that distinguish them from backtracking and parallel parsers:

1. There is no need to keep track of prior states or choices points, as in backtracking.

2. There is no need to reparse ambiguous input as in standard backtracking.

3. There is no need for arbitrary copy mechanisms or structure sharing strategies, as in parallel parsing.

4. The memory requirements are less than in parallel parsing.

Minimal commitment models therefore seem to handle the problem of reanalysis with considerable computational simplicity and economy. Yet all of the advantages listed above have little to do with monotonicity or under-specification. They instead derive from a restructuring of the parse space so that the search can always continue forward, effecting successful reanalysis (most of the time) without explicit backtracking. The next section shows how repair parsers can be formulated that have all these desirable properties of minimal commitment parsers, while abandoning monotonicity and under-specification.

Why abandon monotonicity and underspecification? Minimal commitment representations lead to some paradoxes when considering their role in a functionally complete system engaging in semantic interpretation (Lewis, 1993a). The most plausible assumption is that the syntactic representations are immediately and incrementally interpreted (Weinberg, 1993). This presumably requires determining which syntactic relations actually hold. Because the dominance assertions do not explicitly specify which relations hold, additional computation must be performed to make the *immediate* dominance relations explicit. These computations are purely syntactic in nature, since they process purely syntactic representations. Whether this process is considered part of the parser itself, or assigned to the semantic interpreter (an odd partitioning of function), monotonicity is violated since the immediate dominance relations change nonmonotonically throughout the parse. In short, it is not clear how to reconcile minimal commitment parsers with immediacy of interpretation, without abandoning monotonicity. Since, as argued above, the desired computational features do not depend on monotonicity, this is not such a bad move.

3.4 Reanalysis by Limited Repair

Limited repair is a way of reformulating the parsing problem space so that it efficiently supports depth-first search without backtracking. The starting point is to note that we can cast the parsing process as a search for a well-formed syntactic representation (e.g., Fong & Berwick, 1990), rather than a search through legal applications of grammatical rules. The parsing search space can therefore be formulated in several ways. In addition to legal attachment operators, we are free to include any kind of structure building operators, including non-standard attachment operations that may momentarily violate some well-formedness constraint. We can also include operators that undo or destructively modify existing structures, such as operators that detach phrases and operators that move phrases.

These new modification operators are at the heart of repair parsing. The basic idea is to augment the standard parsing space used in depth-first backtracking parsing with repair operators that enable the system to continue moving through the space when it reaches a dead-end (or, more accurately, what once was a dead-end). Figure 3 shows what the structure of a new repair space might look like. In short, the parser can sometimes leap off the garden path, rather than explicitly backtracking to prior decision points. In making the repair to the correct state, it is possible that the parser may visit states that have no counterpart in the space explored by a standard backtracking parser. The repair process may also revisit a prior state, but only through a process of reconstruction (or de-construction), not by retrieving it from some short-term store.

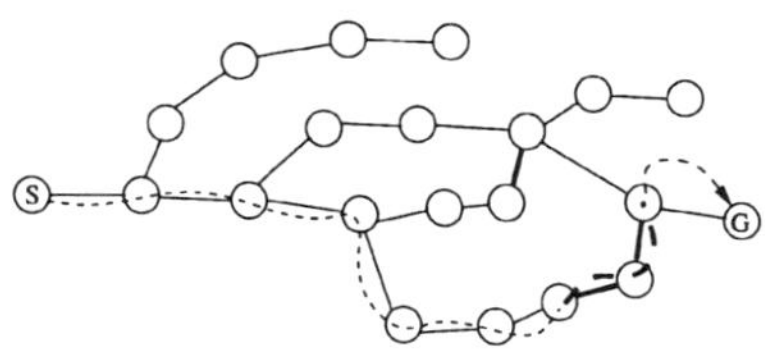

FIGURE 3: Reanalysis by repair of the existing interpretation. The dashed lines indicate the path the parser pursues; the heavy dashed lines indicate the reanalysis that takes place during repair. The heavy state transitions denote new repair operators that augment the original space. *S* indicates the starting state, *G* indicates the goal state (a well-formed syntactic representation of the input).

In no way does this problem space reformulation change the *task* of parsing. The grammatical constraints on the parser output are not relaxed in any way. The only thing that changes is the structure of the space in which the parser searches for a well-formed representation.

What kind of repair operators should be added to the space? It might be possible to augment the parsing space with some highly general repair operators that can be applied to any state (perhaps a kind of move-α for repair). This would ensure that the full search space is reachable from any given state, yielding reanalysis as powerful as general backtracking. However, that could also yield a combinatoric search that is as at least as bad as chronological backtracking, and possibly worse.

The generation and application of the repair (modification) operators must therefore be constrained in some way. Figure 3 depicts a constrained version of repair. Two features of limited repair spaces are apparent in this little example. First, the additional repair operators are only available from a small subset of the total set of states. Second, there are no guarantees of completeness: it is still possible to go irreparably down the garden path. For example, if the parser takes the wrong branch at the first choice point in Figure 3, there is no way to repair from the garden path back to the correct path.

Even before specifying the details fully, we can see that limited repair would have several desirable computational and psycholinguistic properties as a theory of covert reanalysis:

- It uses memory-efficient depth-first search, rather than breadth-first search.
- It avoids the additional memory overhead of backtracking.
- It avoids the need for copy mechanisms or structure sharing techniques.
- It incrementally produces interpretable, fully specified syntactic structures.
- It potentially distinguishes between difficult-to-repair and easily repaired structures.

It is worth noting that reformulating problem spaces to make problem solving easier for some task is an old and important idea in artificial intelligence (Newell & Simon, 1972). In fact, *repair* in particular has been used in some domains to great effect (Minton *et al.*, 1992). A dramatic demonstration was recently made using the n-queens problem, a classic search puzzle that requires finding a way to position n-queens on an $n \times n$ chessboard so that no queen can attack any other queen. The standard algorithms, which performed backtracking search in a space of (locally) legal queen placements, were able to solve n-queens problems with n up to about 100 (Nadel, 1990). The problem space was then reformulated as a repair space, which started with a board full of queens in illegal positions, and used a repair operator ('swap') for making minor modifications to queen positions. The result was a system that could solve the n-queens problem in polynomial time (Sosic & Gu, 1990). The authors were able to solve problems with $n = 500{,}000$ on 25MHz workstations.

3.5 Summary of the Four Major Theoretical Classes

We can summarize the four kinds of reanalysis models and their computational properties as follows:

- *Depth-first backtracking* parsers accomplish reanalysis by revisiting prior choice points or states in the parse, and pursuing alternative paths by reparsing the ambiguous material. Different control strategies (e.g., chronological backtracking, dependency-directed backtracking) yield the forward, backward, and selective reanalysis distinction of Frazier & Rayner

(1982). The different strategies place different demands on memory, with forward reanalysis making the least demands. Reanalysis by backtracking can be overt (corresponding to regressive eye fixations in reading) or covert (corresponding to a reparsing of an internal memory of the input). The primary disadvantage of backtracking, particularly as a theory of covert reanalysis, is the memory overhead required to maintain prior states and input (relative to minimal commitment and repair parsers) and the additional mechanism needed to manage this memory.

- *Parallel* and *limited parallel* parsers accomplish reanalysis by pursuing multiple structural interpretations in parallel, and disposing of those interpretations that are not consistent with later input. Parallel parsers effect a breadth-first search in the space of partial interpretations. The primary disadvantage of any breadth-first search is the increased space requirement (relative to depth-first alternatives). Standard techniques for reducing the memory requirements and the need for structure copying (structure sharing or lazy evaluation) require complicated mechanisms for grammars more complex than context-free grammars. Finally, the most detailed attempt yet to work out a memory-limited parallel account of difficult and easy local ambiguities (Gibson, 1991) yielded a theory that is at least as consistent with single-path repair parsing as parallel parsing—perhaps more so.

- *Minimal commitment* parsers accomplish reanalysis by making monotonic additions to underspecified parse tree representations. They require less memory than either backtracking or parallel models, and require no structure sharing or structure copying. Furthermore, no additional mechanism is required to effect the reanalysis. The primary disadvantage relative to all the other models is that additional computation is necessary to make explicit the syntactic relations necessary for immediate, incremental semantic interpretation. These relations change nonmonotonically, therefore some other component of the system must be effecting what is essentially a destructive syntactic revision.

- *Limited repair* parsers accomplish reanalysis by destructively modifying the current parse tree. They augment the standard parsing space used in depth-first backtracking parsing with repair operators that enable the system to continue moving forward when it reaches a dead-end. In short, limited repair parsers reformulate the search space to support *single-state depth-first search*. The primary advantage over backtracking and parallel parsers is reduced memory load—only a single state must be maintained at any time. There is no need for structure sharing or structure copying mechanisms, and unlike minimal commitment parsers, repair parsers produce fully specified, interpretable syntactic structures. The disadvantage, relative to all the other models, is that explicit modification operators must be added to the search space.

Table 1 lists some of the explicit reanalysis theories proposed, classified into variations on the four major classes discussed above.[6] Although repair parsers are clearly a viable class on purely theoretic grounds, they have been little explored relative to the other models. Nevertheless, repair parsing was used in one of the earliest and most successful natural language processing efforts in artificial intelligence: the PROGRAMMAR parser of Winograd's SHRDLU system (Winograd, 1972, 1983). Winograd's system used a set of specific rules mapping problem situations onto structure modifying actions. Lombardo's (this volume) parser is one modern theory pursuing a similar approach.

One important theory of reanalysis that defies this classification is Pritchett's (1988, 1992) model. Pritchett's *On-line Locality Constraint* (OLLC) provides an abstract syntactic characterization of easy reanalysis. The OLLC is computed over the preferred and correct structures. If the preferred interpretation is structurally too distant (in some precisely defined sense) from the correct structure, Pritchett's theory predicts a strong garden path effect. This model is interpreted naturally in terms of a depth-first parser with some rapid repair or revision process. Like the Gibson (1991) metric, the OLLC can be construed as a characterization of when the correct interpretation is out of reach of on-line repair. Pritchett in fact used this kind of language himself in describing the theory, but made no explicit commitment to single-path or parallel parsing.

The theoretical analysis presented in this section is insufficient to rule out backtracking, parallel parsing, or minimal commitment parsing as candidates for theories of reanalysis, but it raises a set of computational concerns that may be addressed by limited repair parsers. The putative theoretical advantage of repair parsers depends in large part on finding simple candidate repair operations. The empirical success of repair parsers depends in large part on providing good accounts of the reanalysis phenomena foreshadowed in section 1 above. The next section presents a repair parser intended to meet these theoretical and empirical goals.

---

6 Hybrid approaches are also possible. For example, limited repair and backtracking show up together in the models of Lewis (1993a) and Konieczny (1996).

TABLE 1: Some theories of reanalysis

Backtracking
- Overt backtracking
  - Forward (Frazier & Rayner, 1982; Lewis, 1993a)
  - Backward (Frazier & Rayner, 1982)
  - Selective (Carpenter & Daneman, 1981; Frazier & Rayner, 1982; Ferreira & Henderson, 1991; Inoue & Fodor, 1995)
- Covert backtracking
  - Forward
  - Backward (Kaplan, 1972; Wanner & Maratsos, 1978)
  - Backward, reuse of well-formed subphrases (Holbrook *et al.*, 1992)
  - Selective, limited memory (Blank, 1989)
  - Selective, reuse of well-formed subphrases (Abney, 1989; Konieczny, 1996)

Parallel Parsing
- All-paths parsing
- Ranked limited path parsing (Kurtzman, 1985; Gorrell, 1987)
- Multi-path parsing with limited memory (King & Just, 1991; Gibson, 1991; Just & Carpenter, 1992)

Minimal Commitment Parsing
- Lookahead/delay (Marcus, 1980)
- Under-specified representations (Weinberg, 1993; Gorrell, 1993)
- Under-specified representations, language-specific control knowledge (Sturt & Crocker, 1995)

Repair Parsing
- Limited mechanism (Konieczny, 1996; Lehman *et al.*, 1991; Lewis, 1993a; Stevenson, 1994)
- Limited control knowledge (Fodor & Inoue, 1995; Lombardo, this volume; Winograd, 1972)

4 Limited Cue-Driven Repair

The particular repair mechanism described in this section was developed in the context of a detailed computational model of human sentence comprehension, NL-Soar (Lewis, 1993a). NL-Soar is based on the Soar cognitive architecture (Newell, 1990; Laird *et al.*, 1987). We will only mention here briefly three points about Soar and NL-Soar that are relevant to understanding the repair theory. First, Soar is a problem space architecture: all tasks, including language comprehension, are formulated as a series of applications of cognitive operators to states in a short-term working memory. The operators move through some problem space until a desired or goal state is found. Second, Soar adopts the *single-state assumption*: only one state per problem space is accessible in working memory at any given time. There is no architectural support for maintaining prior states in service of backtracking (Newell, 1990). Third, Soar is a theory of both deliberate and automatic behavior, so it is suitable not only for modeling long stretches (tens of seconds to minutes) of problem solving, but immediate cognitive behavior in the hundreds of milliseconds range (Newell, 1990). Embedding the comprehension model in Soar has deep implications for many aspects of sentence processing, including ambiguity resolution, but this chapter focuses only on the repair mechanism itself.

4.1 The Snip Operator

NL-Soar posits a set of rapid cognitive operators for parsing and interpretation. The most primitive parsing operations are *link* operators, which perform syntactic attachments (Figure 4), incrementally building up a parse tree.[7] Since Soar maintains only a single state, reanalysis must be achieved by either deliberate recomprehension (rereading) of the input or repair of the existing state.

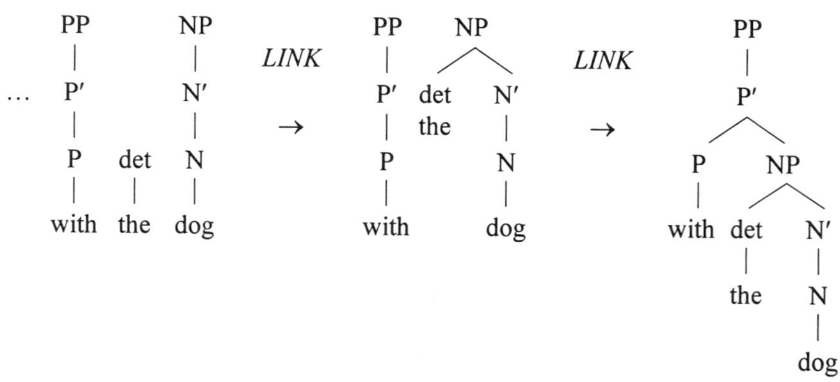

FIGURE 4: Building syntactic structure in NL-Soar. At the left is the partial structure after projecting *with* to a PP and projecting *dog* to an NP (via a series of link operators not shown). Next, a link operator attaches the determiner *the* to the NP, forming [$_{NP}$ the dog]. Finally, a link operator attaches [$_{NP}$ the dog] as the complement of the PP.

[7] The tree is built in a head-driven, bottom-up fashion, though that is not a commitment that is crucial to the repair theory.

The minimal amount of new mechanism required to effect on-line repair is an operator that breaks an existing relation in the parse tree. We call this operator *snip* (Lewis, 1992). In fact, snip does not complete the repair; it just destroys a bit of structure and then lets the other link operators take over to finish the job.

As an example of how snip works, consider what happens with the subject/object ambiguity in (9) below:

(9) Thad knows Shaq is tall.

Shaq is initially attached in the complement position of *knows*. When *is* arrives, it is projected to the sentential complement node CP.[8] Next, a link is proposed to attach the CP in the complement position of *knows*. This proposal is made because *knows* can take sentential complements as well as nominals.

Figure 5 shows what happens next. The result is a momentary superposition of two separate interpretations, with two nodes competing for the same structural position ([COMP,V′] of *knows*). This inconsistency triggers a local snip operator, which breaks the link between [$_{V'}$ knows] and [$_{NP}$ Shaq]. Next, [$_{NP}$ Shaq] is attached in subject position ([SPEC,IP]), and the repair is complete.

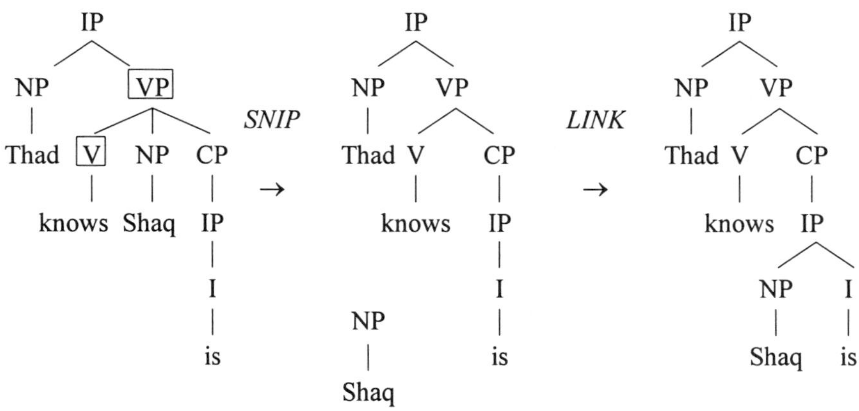

FIGURE 5: An example of simple cue-driven, destructive repair with the snip operator. The incoming CP competes for the same complement position as *Shaq*, triggering a snip to detach *Shaq*. Next, *Shaq* is attached as the subject of the incoming clause. The boxed nodes identify the locality of the inconsistency, which delimits the generation of snip operators.

---

8 CPs are projected in the absence of overt complementizers, following Pritchett (1992).

The initial attachment of the sentential complement was attempted despite the fact that another constituent was already occupying the complement position. This is the only way in which the attachment operators are nonstandard: they relax the constraint on uniqueness of complements and specifiers. Fodor & Inoue (1995) adopted a similar strategy, which they dubbed 'attach anyway'. The critical thing to note is that the constraints on the final output have *not* been relaxed. Only the set of processes and intermediate states that finally lead to the well-formed representation have changed.

4.2 Constraining the Generation of Snip

It was argued above that repair operators must be constrained in some way, else they risk opening the system up to combinatoric search as costly as arbitrary backtracking. The generation of snip is highly constrained in the following way. Snip is proposed only for structural relations that are *local* to a detected inconsistency (where *local* is defined precisely as within the maximal projection containing the inconsistency). The boxed nodes in Figure 5 identify the locality of the inconsistency. These nodes delimit the scope of consideration for generating snip operators.

The mechanism relies on simple, local structural cues to detect that something has gone wrong with the parse. This way of triggering snip serves as a way of focusing the repair directly on the problem. A free generation of snip for every link in the utterance model is possible, of course, but would radically increase the search space even for moderately-sized syntactic structures.

As an example of how the theory predicts a difficult garden path, consider the following subject/object ambiguity (Frazier & Rayner, 1982):

(10) Since Jay always jogs a mile seems like a short distance to him.

Here, *a mile* is taken initially as the complement of *jogs*, just as in (9) *Shaq* is initially attached as the complement of *knows*. Because *jogs* does not take sentential complements, the initial phrase *Since Jay jogs* is adjoined to the incoming *seems*. In fact, this is its correct final position. However, $[_{IP}$ seems$]$ is still missing its subject. But in this case a snip operator is not generated for the complement relation between $[_{V'}$ jogs$]$ and $[_{NP}$ a mile$]$, because the relation is not local to the detected inconsistency (the missing obligatory subject). This situation is shown in Figure 6, with the boxed nodes again representing the locality of the inconsistency. As a result, $[_{NP}$ a mile] is not reanalyzed as the subject of $[_{IP}$ seems], and the necessary repair fails.

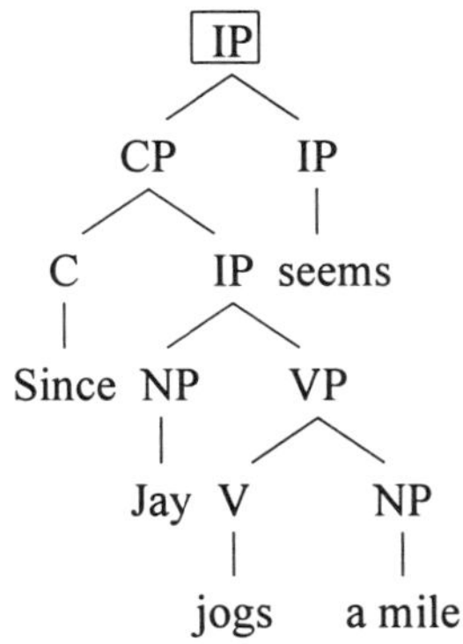

FIGURE 6: Failure to repair a subject/object ambiguity.

In addition to being a repair theory, this theory of reanalysis has a number of important features:

- The theory is formulated *independently of what guides the initial choice* at the ambiguity point. Thus, the theory classifies structure types as *potential* garden paths, not definite garden paths. The repair theory determines whether or not a given inconsistent structure can be repaired. Whether a local ambiguity gives rise to a strong garden path effect in any particular context is a function *both* of the ambiguity resolution process itself, and of the efficacy of the repair.

- The theory is a *cue-driven* theory of repair, because it depends on a few simple local cues to trigger the repair process.

- The theory is a *functional* theory, in that it posits mechanisms to efficiently carry out the functions of comprehension. NL-Soar is not a linguistic metric that distinguishes easy and difficult ambiguities. It is an implemented computational theory that classifies certain sentences as potential strong garden paths because it may fail to parse those sentences.

- The theory posits that *on-line repair is not costly*; in fact, the prediction is that these small local repairs are a frequently occurring part of normal sentence comprehension. Furthermore, the realization of repair in the Soar architecture yields the prediction that this repair may take as little as 50-100 ms more (the cost of the additional snip and reattachment processes).

- The theory posits a *minimal amount of additional new mechanisms and control* to carry out the repair. The only new operator is snip; repairs are carried out by snip and a sequence of the existing parsing operators. The only significant new piece of control knowledge is a rule that says roughly: *don't relink what you just snipped.*

4.3 Some Cross-Linguistic Predictions

This section explores predictions that the snip-based repair mechanism makes across a wide range of structural ambiguities, including some that derive from lexical categorial ambiguities. The structures presented here are a subset of the roughly 70 structures analyzed in Lewis (1993a) and Lewis & Lehman (1994).

4.3.1 Object/Subject Ambiguities

We have already seen how the theory handles two cases involving object/subject ambiguities ((9) and (10) above). The unproblematic ambiguity in (9) arises in Mandarin as well (Pritchett, 1992):

(11) a.

Wo	wang	le	Zhangsan.
I	forget	PERF	Zhangsan

'I forgot Zhangsan.'

b.

Wo	wang	le	Zhangsan	yao	qu.
I	forget	PERF	Zhangsan	will	go

'I forgot Zhangsan would go.'

NL-Soar repairs the Mandarin structure just as it does the English counterpart—the incoming clause attaches as the complement of [$_{V'}$ forgot], triggering the local snip of [$_{NP}$ Zhangsan]. NL-Soar also correctly predicts the following difficult subject/object garden paths in Mandarin (Gorrell, 1991) and Hebrew (Pritchett, 1992):

(12)

Zhangsan	yi	du	shu	jiu	diao	le.
Zhangsan	as-soon-as	read	book	then	fall	PERF

'As soon as Zhangsan read the book fell.'

(13) Axrey she-shatiti maim hitgalu be-b'er.
After COMP-drank-1st water were-found in the well
'After I drank water was found in the well.'

The explanation is the same as in the English example (9): the local snip is not generated to remove the object NP from complement position.

4.3.2 Object/Object Ambiguities

Pritchett (1991) presents a Japanese object/object ambiguity that leads to a strong garden path effect.

(14) Frank-ni Tom-ga Guy-o syookai suru to John-wa iwaseta.
Frank-DAT Tom-NOM Guy-ACC introduce COMP John-TOP said CAUSE
'John made Frank say Tom introduced Guy.'

The initial sequence through *to* (the complementizer) is taken as a complete complementized clause:

(15) $[_{CP}$ $[_{IP}$ Frank-ni Tom-ga Guy-o syookai suru] to]
'Tom introduced Guy to Frank.'

Next, $[_{NP}$ John] is encountered and left unattached, waiting for the final verb. The final verb, *iwaseta*, is a causative verb requiring three arguments, including an obligatory *ni*-marked causee. Only two arguments are available: $[_{NP}$ John] and the initial CP. $[_{NP}$ Frank-ni] must be reanalysed as an argument of $[_{V'}$ iwaseta]. However, the required snip within the CP is not local to the VP which is missing the argument, so the repair fails, resulting in a garden path effect. The same effect shows up in Korean as well (Pritchett, 1992).

4.3.3 Complement/Adjunct Ambiguities

Incoming phrases can often be interpreted as either complements or adjuncts. Consider the unproblematic sentences in (16):

(16) a. Is the block on the table?
b. Is the block on the table red?

The prepositional phrase *on the table* may be interpreted as a modifier of *block* or the complement of *is*. Assume that the complement attachment is pursued first. When *red* arrives, it is projected to an AP and attached in complement position, which triggers the snip operator to detach [$_{PP}$ in the box] in the same manner that we have seen above. Once detached, [$_{PP}$ on the table] is simply adjoined to [$_{N'}$ block]. A similar explanation predicts the acceptability of complement clause/subject-relative ambiguities (Gibson, 1991):

(17) a. John told the man that Mary kissed Bill.
b. John told the man that kissed Mary that Bill saw Phil.

However, other complement/adjunct ambiguities do cause difficulty. Crain & Steedman (1985) found that complement clause/object-relative ambiguities produce strong garden path effects:

(18) The psychologist told the wife that he was having trouble with to leave.

Prepositional phrase argument/adjunct ambiguities may also produce noticeable garden path effects (in contrast to (16) above) (Gibson, 1991):

(19) I sent the letters to Ron to Teresa.

Unfortunately, NL-Soar cannot account for these effects, because the repair succeeds in both cases, as in (16). It might be possible to find some independent source of difficulty, but as currently formulated, the theory is making an incorrect prediction.

Crain & Steedman (1985) found that a garden path arises when a clause is interpreted as a relative clause but the complement reading is required. This is the opposite of the standard complement/adjunct garden path above in (18), in which the ambiguous clause is initially taken as a complement, but the relative reading is required (Crain & Steedman induced the relative reading through a contextual manipulation, not reproduced here):

(20) The psychologist told the wife that he was having trouble with her husband.

NL-Soar can account for this effect: even if [$_{NP}$ her husband] is attached as the complement of [$_{P'}$ with], the critical snip operator required to detach the clause from [$_{N'}$ wife] will not be generated.

4.3.4 Main Verb/Relative Ambiguities

We now explore variations on the classic relative clause garden path. Consider the canonical example (Bever, 1970):

(21) The horse raced past the barn fell.

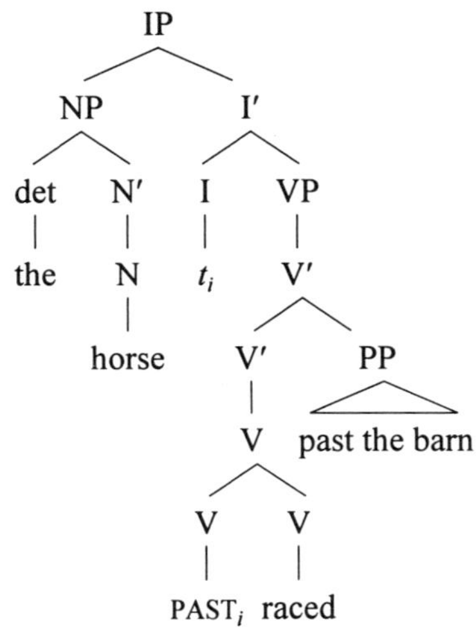

FIGURE 7: The main verb reading of *The horse raced past the barn*. The inflectional features that head the IP phrase adjoin to the verb, leaving a trace in the head of IP.

Figure 7 shows the complete structure for the main verb interpretation of (21). The inflectional features that head the IP phrase adjoin to the verb, leaving a trace in head of IP. (This joining of inflectional features to the verb is assumed in some form by many syntactic theories; e.g., McCawley, 1988, calls it *Tense-hopping*, and assumes an adjunction structure like the one presented here.)[9] On the other hand, passive forms like *driven* and *raced* are untensed. In the reduced relative reading of *the horse raced past the barn*, which uses the passive interpretation of *raced*, the inflection is not present.

Consider the repair required to successfully parse (21). The structure in Figure 7 must be repaired into the reduced relative structure. This involves removing [$_{NP}$ the horse] from [SPEC,IP] position, and snipping the adjoined inflectional

---

9 This particular adjunction analysis is not critical for the empirical predictions; what is important is that the tense information is local to the verb.

features. When *fell* arrives and is projected to VP, the only place it may attach is in complement position of I′. This produces an inconsistency local to the IP, as shown in Figure 8. However, this fails to trigger all the required snips; in particular, the crucial inflection adjunction is left undisturbed, so the passive reading cannot be recovered.

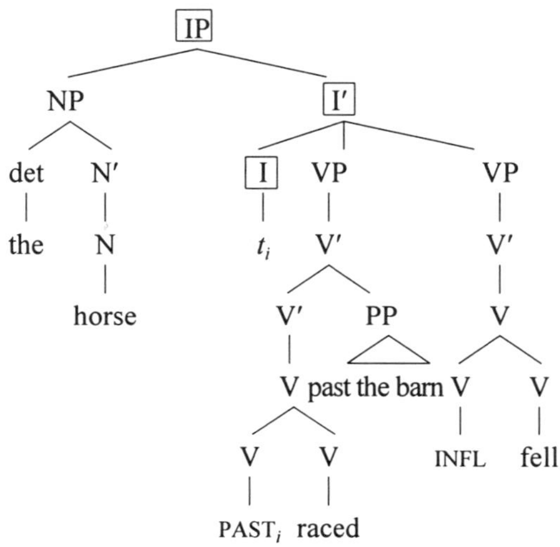

FIGURE 8: The main verb/reduced relative garden path effect. When *fell* arrives and is projected to VP, the only place it may attach is in the complement position of I′. This produces an inconsistency local to IP (denoted by the boxed nodes). However, this fails to trigger all the required snips; in particular, the crucial inflection adjunction is left undisturbed, so the required passive reading cannot be recovered.

The intervening modifier [$_{PP}$ past the barn] is irrelevant to this explanation. Thus, the theory correctly predicts the existence of very short reduced relative garden paths (Kurtzman, 1985; Abney, 1989):

(22) The boat floated sank.

Such examples are one demonstration of the independence of garden path effects from length effects (Pritchett, 1992; Lewis, 1993a). The explanation also extends to ditransitive verbs (23) (Rayner *et al.*, 1983) and embedded relatives (24) (Gibson, 1991):

(23) My friend sent the flowers smiled broadly.

(24) The dog that was fed next to the cat walked to the park chewed the bone.

Surprisingly, not all main verb/relative clause ambiguities produce garden path effects. Mazuka *et al.* (1989) present an interesting unproblematic Japanese construction involving a main verb/relative ambiguity:

(25) a.

Roozin-ga	kodomo-o	yonda.
old man-NOM	child-ACC	called

(The old man called the child.)

b.

Roozin-ga	kodomo-o	yonda	zyosee	to	hanasi-o	sita.
old man-NOM	child-ACC	called	woman	with	talk-ACC	did

(The old man talked with the woman who called the child.)

In (25a), the NP NP V sequence *roozin-ga kodomo-o yonda* is interpreted as the main clause *The old man called the child.* In (26b), the relative clause reading is required, disambiguated by the appearance of [$_{NP}$ zyosee]. Unlike the familiar English main verb/reduced relative ambiguity, NL-Soar can repair the structure in (25b). Figure 9 shows how. The main clause interpretation is pursued initially, with [$_{NP}$ roozin] in subject [SPEC,IP] position and [$_{NP}$ kodomo-o] in complement position of [$_{VP}$ yonda]. Next, [$_{NP}$ zyosee] arrives and the CP adjoins to [$_{N'}$ zyosee] as a modifying clause (unlike the English version, the relative clause is active, not passive, and therefore the clause remains tensed). The appropriate traces are generated in [SPEC,CP] and [SPEC,IP] position, in the same manner as English relative clauses. The [SPEC,IP] trace creates a local inconsistency at the IP node, triggering a snip of [$_{NP}$ roozin]. [$_{NP}$ roozin] is now available to attach as the subject of the incoming [$_{IP}$ to hanasi-o sita], and the repair succeeds.

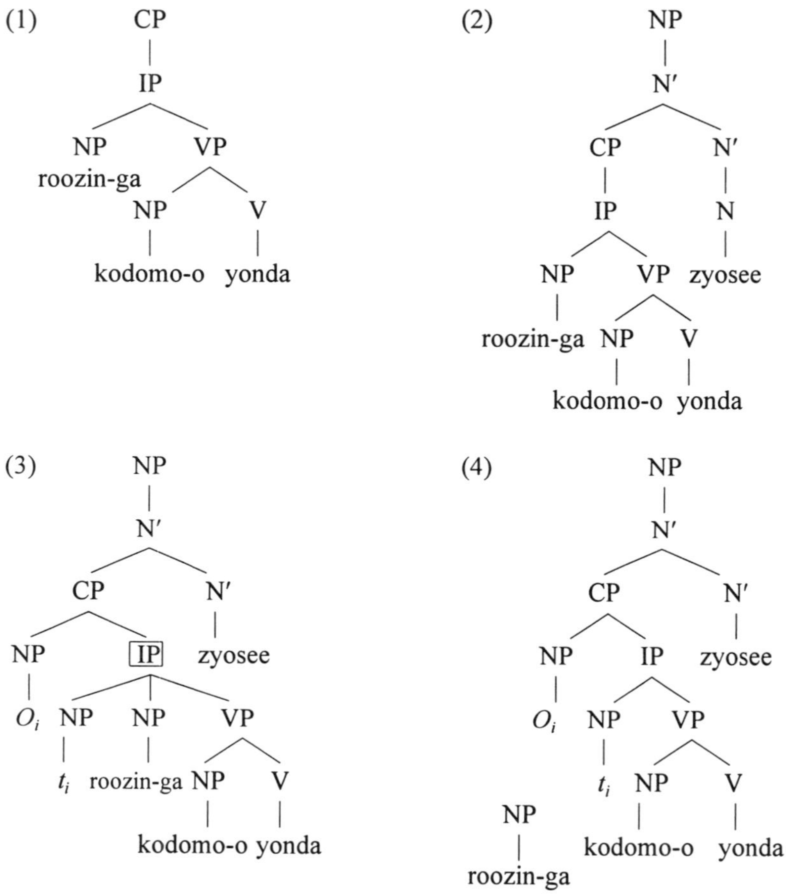

FIGURE 9: Repairing an unproblematic Japanese main verb/relative clause ambiguity. The initial CP is attached as a relative modifier of the incoming NP, leading to the creation of a trace in [SPEC,IP]. This triggers the snip of the misanalyzed NP, making it available to serve as subject of the main clause.

4.3.5 Lexical Categorial Ambiguities

Lexical ambiguity often gives rise to structural ambiguity. Consider the basic noun/adjective ambiguity in (26):

(26) a. The square is red.
b. The square table is red.

When *square* arrives, both categories are retrieved in parallel from the lexicon, and NP and AP nodes are projected. Next, the determiner *the* is attached in [SPEC,NP] position, forming [$_{NP}$ the square]. Then *table* arrives and is projected to NP. Next, the adjective phrase [$_{AP}$ square] is adjoined to [$_{N'}$ table]. Each syntactic link is well-formed, but two mutually incompatible bits of structure have been produced, since the single token *square* cannot simultaneously be an adjective and a noun.

A snip operator is immediately triggered by the inconsistency of syntactic structure attached to competing senses of the same lexical token. A locally generated snip breaks the [SPEC,NP] link between the determiner and [$_{NP}$ square]. Next, a link operator attaches the determiner in specifier position of [$_{NP}$ table], forming [$_{NP}$ the square table]. This completes the repair. In this way, the snip operator extends naturally to handle repairs involving lexical ambiguity.

We have now seen all three kinds of structural cues that trigger the snip operator:

1. multiple phrases competing for the same structural position;

2. missing obligatory phrases (e.g., missing subjects); and

3. attachments to competing categorial interpretations of the same lexical item.

NL-Soar also handles multiple lexical ambiguities. For example, noun/verb ambiguities may be preceded by adjective/noun ambiguities without causing difficulty (Milne, 1982; Pritchett, 1992):

(27) a. The square blocks the triangle.
b. The square blocks are red.

NL-Soar effects the repairs in (27) in the same manner as (26); see Lewis (1993a) for details. Yet some noun/verb ambiguities do cause difficulty. If the unproblematic ambiguity in (27) is followed by a reduced relative, the result is a strong garden path (Milne, 1982; Pritchett, 1992):

(28) The building blocks the sun faded are red.

Suppose that *blocks* is initially taken as the main verb, and *sun* as the complement. When *faded* arrives, it can be attached as a reduced relative modifying *sun*. Once *are* is projected to an IP, no additional attachments are possible. Furthermore, there are no local inconsistencies to generate a snip, so the repair is never initiated.

4.3.6 Filler-Gap Ambiguities

Filler-gap sentences provide another interesting test of the repair mechanism, because the location of the gap is often not known with certainty. Consider (29):

(29) a. John found the ball$_i$ that the boy hit *t*$_i$.
 b. John found the ball$_i$ that the boy hit the window with *t*$_i$.

In (29a), the trace or gap appears in the complement position of the verb (*the boy hit the ball*), while in (29b), the sentence continues so that the trace appears as the object of a preposition (*the boy hit the window with the ball*). Neither sentence causes difficulty. Figure 10 shows how the repair of the object trace is triggered. First, [$_{NP}$ the window] arrives and attaches as the complement of [$_{V'}$ hit]. This creates the familiar local inconsistency: two nodes (the trace, and the NP) occupying the same structural position. A snip is generated to remove the trace. When [$_{PP}$ with] adjoins to [$_{V'}$ hit], a new trace is generated as the object of the preposition.

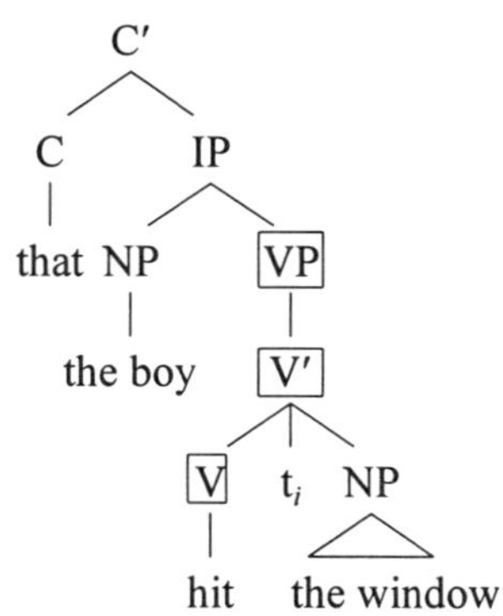

FIGURE 10: Triggering the repair of a filler-gap ambiguity.

A striking aspect of these filler-gap ambiguities, noted in the introduction, is that they may be propagated over long distances:

(30) a. Who do you believe?
b. Who do you believe Jim suspects Bob knows Pat hates?

An object trace is posited after each verb in (30b). As an NP arrives to fill the object slot, the trace is snipped, and a new one generated at the next verb. Thus, (30b) involves at least three separate repair operations. These repair operations provide an explanation for the filled-gap effect—the increased duration of eye fixations on the overt NPs that occupy the misanalyzed gaps (e.g., Stowe, 1986).

4.3.7 Other Examples

The snip-based repair mechanism is quite simple and limited, but surprisingly effective. The sentences below give some additional examples of local ambiguities that are easily repaired by snip:

(31) a. Without her we failed. (Pritchett, 1988)
b. Without her contributions we failed.

(32) a. The cop gave her earrings. (Gibson, 1991)
b. The cop gave her earrings to the dog.

(33) a. The defendant examined the evidence. (Pritchett, 1988)
b. The defendant examined by the lawyer shocked the jury.

(34) a. I like green. (Pritchett, 1988)
b. I like green dragons.

(35) a. I know that. (Gibson, 1991)
b. I know that boy.
c. I know that dogs should play.

(36) a. I saw her duck fly away. (Pritchett, 1992)
b. I saw her duck into an alleyway.

(37) a. I went to the store.
b. I went to the store and the barber.

Other examples of impossible-to-repair structures include:

(38) Without her contributions failed to come in. (Frazier, 1978)

(39) Sue gave the man who was racing the car. (Pritchett, 1992)

(40) The cotton clothing is made of grows in Mississippi. (Marcus, 1980)

(41) Before she knew that she went to the store.

(42) That coffee tastes terrible surprised John. (Gibson, 1991)

The structures in (39) and (41) are particularly interesting because they illustrate how *overt* cues are required to trigger the repair operation (Fodor & Inoue, 1995); if the parser assigns the full string a partial structure that is well-formed, there are no local inconsistencies to get the repair started, and the parser simply halts. The contrasts between the easy and difficult *that*-ambiguities are also interesting, because they clearly demonstrate the importance of local structural context in guiding the parser to the right categorial sense of ambiguous words. Switching syntactic categories *per se* is not necessarily difficult.

5 Toward a Complete Theory of Garden Path Effects

The on-line repair model presented here is actually just part of NL-Soar's account of garden path effects. The other pieces of the puzzle are NL-Soar's theory of ambiguity resolution, and its model of limited syntactic short-term memory. The following is a just a brief sketch of the theory; for further details, see Lewis (1993a, 1996b). The main point of this section is to provide a glimpse of how the simple repair mechanism described here can be embedded in a complete architecture for comprehension, and how the resulting theory can provide explanations for a wider variety of reanalysis-related phenomena.

The major components of NL-Soar are a short-term memory for syntactic structure subject to similarity-based interference (Lewis, 1996b), an open control structure for ambiguity resolution, and the limited repair mechanism outlined in this chapter. The structure of the working memory is theoretically motivated by computational concerns, and empirically motivated by difficulty with center-embedded structures. NL-Soar's ambiguity resolution is open to potentially any knowledge source (semantic and contextual) because Soar's control structure permits any long-term knowledge to be brought to bear at each decision point.[10] The combination of the snip-based repair mechanism and the

[10] However, for a semantic or contextual parsing strategy to be brought to bear on-line, it must be in a highly compiled form so that it can be retrieved in real-time at the point of the ambiguity. There are no guarantees that any given semantic or contextual strategy will be available in this

open control structure means that NL-Soar can account for both the structural regularities captured by the syntactic metrics of garden path difficulty (e.g, Pritchett, 1992; Gibson, 1991), and the flexible, context-sensitive ambiguity resolution of interactive theories (e.g, Altmann & Steedman, 1988).

The open control of parsing also means that once NL-Soar's on-line repair process has failed, it can engage in a *deliberate* recovery process by carefully rereading the problematic sentence. 'Carefully' is given a precise computational definition in Soar: in effect, it means that Soar is forcing itself to reconsider (albeit more slowly) decisions that it previously made automatically (Laird, 1988). This has three implications. First, NL-Soar predicts that, given time, people can recover from difficult garden paths. Second, because of Soar's continuous learning, the model actually acquires new ambiguity resolution strategies as a result of this more careful recomprehension. In future similar contexts, the system may not necessarily be led down the garden path. Third, this deliberate recovery process may provides a locus for developing an account of the length-based differences in reanalysis of difficult garden path structures demonstrated by Ferreira & Henderson (1991).

The limited short-term memory affects both ambiguity resolution and repair. Although NL-Soar was described here as if it kept complete parse trees in working memory, in fact that is not the case. Constraints on working memory mean that there is a severe limit on the number of possible attachment sites that can be kept open at any given time; in short, some structural ambiguities are not even detected. Working memory constraints also affect the repair processes. If there is too much structure intervening between the ambiguity and the disambiguating material, the structural relations that must be repaired may no longer be in working memory. This explains how Warner & Glass (1987) were able to turn otherwise easy subject/object ambiguities (of the *I forgot Pam needed...* variety) into severe garden path structures:

(43) The girls believe the man who believes the very strong ugly boys struck the dog killed the cats.

---

form at just the right time. As a result, the system may yield modular behavior (ignoring semantic and contextual constraints) either because some other ambiguity resolution strategy is more highly automatized and causes the system to charge down the wrong path blindly, or because there is not enough time to deliberate about the decision.

6 Conclusion

This chapter developed a theory of reanalysis based on limited repair. The theory has both computational and empirical motivation, as evidenced by the computational comparison to other theories of reanalysis, and by the account of a wide range of cross-linguistic reanalysis effects. To summarize the major points:

1. Reanalysis is a functional requirement for any natural language parser: all parsers must sometimes revise the interpretation of locally ambiguous material based on later information.

2. The four major kinds of parsing models that handle reanalysis are backtracking, parallel parsing, minimal commitment parsing, and repair parsing. As theories of covert reanalysis, the first three suffer from several computational or theoretical drawbacks which repair parsers do not share. These include increased memory demands and requirements for additional mechanisms to perform structure copying or sharing. Although backtracking does not seem suitable as a theory of covert, on-line reanalysis, selective backtracking provides a suitable theory of deliberate and overt recomprehension.

3. Repair parsers are an effective parsing technique because they reformulate the parsing search space to support efficient depth-first parsing without backtracking. Repair parsers use operations that modify or repair existing syntactic structure. These operations permit the parser to 'leap off' the garden path in certain cases back onto the path to a successful parse.

4. Repair operations must be limited in some way, otherwise repair will give way to combinatoric search as costly as general backtracking.

5. Limited cue-based repair, based on a new destructive parsing operation (snip), provides one promising mechanism for repair. This theory suggests that the repair itself is not difficult. On the contrary, limited repair is an on-line process that is frequently invoked to handle reanalysis. Difficulty arises when the appropriate local cues are not present to trigger the repair. Those structures that do not provide the right cues seem to map fairly well onto the class of structures that cause noticeable garden path effects, cross-linguistically.

6. Limited repair mechanisms can be embedded in complete architectures for comprehension, yielding more comprehensive theories of reanalysis effects which explain how short-term memory, experience, and context affect both on-line and deliberate reanalysis.

It is encouraging to see several different theoretical approaches—in particular, Stevenson's (1994) competition model, Fodor & Inoue's (1995) diagnosis model, Lombardo's dependency parser (this volume), and NL-Soar—all converge on limited repair as a fundamental component of human sentence processing. If the general analysis of repair parsing provided in this chapter is correct, this should not be surprising, because we have the beginnings of a computational basis for understanding why repair is a simple and effective way of handling local ambiguity.

The Ohio State University

References

Abney, S.P. 1989. A computational model of human parsing. *Journal of Psycholinguistic Research*, 18, 1, 129-144.

Altmann, G. & Steedman, M. 1988. Interaction with context during human sentence processing. *Cognition*, 30, 191-238.

Bever, T.G. 1970. The cognitive basis for linguistic structures. In J.R. Hayes (ed.), *Cognition and the Development of Language*. New York, NY: Wiley, 279-362.

Blank, G.D. 1989. A finite and real-time processor for natural language. *Communications of the ACM*, 32, 10, 1174-1189.

Carpenter, P.A. & Daneman, M. 1981. Lexical retrieval and error recovery in reading: A model based on eye fixations. *Journal of Verbal Learning and Verbal Behavior*, 20, 137-160.

Crain, S. & Steedman, M. 1985. On not being led up the garden path: The use of context by the psychological syntax processor. In D.R. Dowty, L. Karttunen, & A.M. Zwicky (eds.), *Natural Language Parsing*. Cambridge, U.K.: Cambridge University Press, 320-358.

Ferreira, F. & Henderson, J.M. 1990. Use of verb information in syntactic parsing: Evidence from eye movements and word-by-word self-paced reading. *Journal of Experimental Psychology: Learning, Memory, and Cognition*, 16, 555-568.

Ferreira, F. & Henderson, J.M. 1991. Recovery from misanalyses of garden-path sentences. *Journal of Memory and Language*, 30, 725-745.

Fodor, J.D. & Inoue, A. 1994. The diagnosis and cure of garden paths. *Journal of Psycholinguistic Research*, 23, 407-434.

Fong, S. & Berwick, R. 1990. The computational implementation of principle-based parsers. In M. Tomita (ed.), *Proceedings of the First International Workshop on Parsing Technologies*. Pittsburgh, PA: Carnegie Mellon University, 75-84.

Frazier, L. 1978. *On Comprehending Sentences: Syntactic Parsing Strategies*. Unpublished doctoral dissertation, University of Connecticut, Storrs, CT. Distributed by the Indiana University Linguistics Club, Bloomington, IN.

Frazier, L. & Rayner, K. 1982. Making and correcting errors during sentence comprehension: Eye movements in the analysis of structurally ambiguous sentences, *Cognitive Psychology* 14, 178-210.

Gathercole, S.E. & Baddeley, A.D. 1993. *Working Memory and Language*. Hove, UK: Lawrence Erlbaum Associates.

Gibson, E.A.F. 1991. *A Computational Theory of Human Linguistic Processing: Memory Limitations and Processing Breakdown*. Unpublished doctoral dissertation, Carnegie Mellon University, Pittsburgh, PA. Available as Center for Machine Translation Technical Report CMU-CMT-91-125.

Godden, K. 1990. Lazy unification. *Association for Computational Linguistics*, 28, 180-187.

Gorrell, P 1993. Incremental structure building and the determinism hypothesis. Paper presented at *Sixth Annual CUNY Conference on Human Sentence Processing*, Amherst, MA.

Gorrell, P. 1991. Subcategorization and sentence processing. In R.C. Berwick, S.P. Abney, & C. Tenny (eds.), *Principle Based Parsing: Computation and Psycholinguistics*. Dordrecht: Kluwer Academic Publishers, 279-300.

Gorrell, P. 1987. *Studies of Human Syntactic Processing: Ranked-Parallel versus Serial Models*. Unpublished doctoral dissertation, University of Connecticut, Storrs, CT.

Holbrook, J.K., Eiselt, K.P., & Mahesh, K. 1992. A unified process model of syntactic and semantic error recovery in serntence understanding. In *Proceedings of the 14th Annual Conference of the Cognitive Science Society*, 195-200.

Inoue, A. & Fodor, J.D. 1995. Information-paced parsing of Japanese. In R. Mazuka & N. Nagai (eds.), *Japanese Sentence Processing*. Hillsdale, NJ: Lawrence Erlbaum Associates, 9-63.

Juliano, C. & Tanenhaus, M.K. 1994. A constraint-based lexicalist account of the subject/object attachment preference. *Journal of Psycholinguistic Research*, 23, 6, 459-471.

Just, M.A. & Carpenter, P.A. 1992. A capacity theory of comprehension: Individual differences in working memory. *Psychological Review*, 99, 1, 122-149.

Kaplan, R. 1972. Augmented transition networks as psychological models of sentence comprehension. *Artificial Intelligence*, 3, 77-100.

King, J. & Just, M.A. 1991. Individual differences in syntactic processing: The role of working memory. *Journal of Memory and Language*, 30, 580-602.

Konieczny, L. 1996. *Human Sentence Processing: A Semantics-Oriented Parsing Approach*. Unpublished doctoral dissertation, University of Freiburg.

Kurtzman, H.S. 1985. *Studies in Syntactic Ambiguity Resolution*. Unpublished doctoral dissertation, MIT, Cambridge, MA.

Laird, J.E. 1988. Recovery from incorrect knowledge in Soar. In *Proceedings of the Seventh National Conference on Artificial Intelligence*, The American Association for Artificial Intelligence, 618-623.

Laird, J.E., Newell, A., & Rosenbloom, P.S. 1987. Soar: An architecture for general intelligence. *Artificial Intelligence*, 33, 1-64.

Lehman, J.F., Lewis, R.L., & Newell, A. 1991. Integrating knowledge sources in language comprehension. In *Proceedings of the 13th Annual Conference of the Cognitive Science Society*, 461-466. Also in P.S. Rosenbloom, J.E. Laird, & A. Newell (eds.), *The Soar Papers: Research on Integrated Intelligence*. Cambridge, MA: MIT Press, 1993, 1309-1314.

Lewis, R.L. 1992. Recent developments in the NL-Soar garden path theory. Technical Report CMU-CS-92-141, School of Computer Science, Carnegie Mellon University, Pittsburgh, PA.

Lewis, R.L. 1993a. *An Architecturally-Based Theory of Human Sentence Comprehension*. Unpublished doctoral dissertation, Carnegie Mellon University, Pittsburgh, PA. Available as Technical Report CMU-CS-93-226 from reports@cs.cmu.edu.

Lewis, R.L. 1993b. An architecturally-based theory of sentence comprehension. In *Proceedings of the 15th Annual Conference of the Cognitive Science Society*, 108-113.

Lewis, R.L. 1996a. Architecture matters: What Soar has to say about modularity. In D. Steier & T. Mitchell (eds.), *Mind Matters: Contributions to Cognitive and Computer Science in Honor of Allen Newell*. Hillsdale, NJ: Lawrence Erlbaum, 75-84.

Lewis, R.L. 1996b. Interference in short-term memory: The magical number two (or three) in sentence processing. *Journal of Psycholinguistic Research*, 25, 1, 93-115.

Lewis, R.L. & Lehman, J.F. 1994. A theory of the computational architecture of sentence comprehension. Unpublished manuscript, Cognitive Science Laboratory, Princeton University, Princeton, NJ.

Lombardo, V. (this volume). A computational model of recovery.

Lytinen, S.L. & Tomuro, N. 1996. Left-corner unification-based natural language processing. In *Proceedings of the 13th National Conference on Artificial Intelligence*. The American Association for Artificial Intelligence, 1037-1043.

MacDonald, M.C., Pearlmutter, N.J., & Seidenberg, M.S. 1994. The lexical nature of syntactic ambiguity resolution. *Psychological Review*, 101, 676-703.

Marcus, M.P. 1980. *A Theory of Syntactic Recognition for Natural Language*. Cambridge, MA: MIT Press.

Mazuka, R., Itoh, K., Kiritani, S., Niwa, S., Ikejiru, K., & Naitoh, K. 1989. Processing of Japanese garden path, center-embedded, and multiply left-embedded sentences. *Annual Bulletin of the Research Institute of Logopedics and Phoniatrics, Vol. 23*. University of Tokyo, 187-212.

McCawley, J.D. 1988. *The Syntactic Phenomena of English, Vol. 1*. Chicago, IL: University of Chicago Press.

Milne, R.W. 1982. Predicting garden path sentences. *Cognitive Science*, 6, 349-373.

Minton, S., Johnston, M.D., Philips, A.B., & Laird, P. 1992. Minimizing conflicts: A heuristic repair method for constraint satisfaction and scheduling problems. *Artificial Intelligence*, 58, 161-205.

Mitchell, D. 1987. Lexical guidance in human parsing: Locus and processing characteristics. In M. Coltheart (ed.), *The Psychology of Reading, Attention and Performance, Vol. 12*. Hillsdale, NJ: Lawrence Erlbaum, 601-681.

Nadel, B.A. 1990. Representation selection for constraint satisfaction: A case study using *n*-queens. *IEEE Expert*, 16-23.

Newell, A. 1990. *Unified Theories of Cognition*. Cambridge, MA: Harvard University Press.

Pritchett, B.L. 1988. Garden path phenomena and the grammatical basis of language processing. *Language*, 64, 539-576.

Pritchett, B.L. 1991. Head position and parsing ambiguity. *Journal of Psycholinguistic Research*, 20, 251-270.

Pritchett, B.L. 1992. *Grammatical Competence and Parsing Performance*. Chicago, IL: University of Chicago Press.

Rayner, K., Carlson, M., & Frazier, L. 1983. The interaction of syntax and semantics during sentence processing: Eye movements in the analysis of semantically biased sentences. *Journal of Verbal Learning and Verbal Behavior*, 22, 358-374.

Sosic, R. & Gu, J. 1990. A polynomial time algorithm for the *n*-queens problem. *SIGART Bulletin*, 1, 3, 7-11.

Stevenson, S. 1994. Competition and recency in a hybrid network model of syntactic disambiguation. *Journal of Psycholinguistic Research*, 23, 4, 295-322.

Stowe, L. 1986. Evidence for on-line gap location. *Language and Cognitive Processes*, 1, 277-245.

Sturt, P. & Crocker, M. 1995. Monotonic parsing and reanalysis. Paper presented at *Eighth Annual CUNY Sentence Processing Conference*, Tucson, AZ.

Trueswell, J.C., Tanenhaus, M.K., & Garnsey, S.M. 1994. Semantic influences in parsing: Use of thematic role information in syntactic ambiguity resolution. *Journal of Memory and Language*, 33, 285-318.

Wanner, E. & Maratsos, M. 1978. An ATN approach to comprehension. In M. Halle, J. Bresnan, & G.A. Miller (eds.), *Linguistic Theory and Psychological Reality*. Cambridge, MA: MIT Press, 119-161.

Warner, J. & Glass, A.L. 1987. Context and distance-to-disambiguation effects in ambiguity resolution: Evidence from grammaticality judgments of garden path sentences. *Journal of Memory and Language*, 26, 714-738.

Weinberg, A. 1993. Parameters in the theory of sentence processing: Minimal commitment theory goes east. *Journal of Psycholinguistic Research*, 22, 3, 339-364.

Winograd, T. 1972. Understanding natural language. *Cognitive Psychology*, 3, 1-191.

Winograd, T. 1983. *Language as a Cognitive Process, Vol. 1: Syntax*. Reading, MA: Addison Wesley.

Winston, P.H. 1992. *Artificial Intelligence, Third Edition*. Reading, MA: Addison Wesley.

9

A Computational Model of Recovery

Vincenzo Lombardo

Abstract

This paper introduces a computational model of recovery in sentence processing. The model consists of a general computational framework which defines a space of possible models and a set of heuristics which constrain the framework to a specific model. The basic idea is to *diagnose* the error source that has caused the failure and to *repair* the structure in order to solve the inconsistencies. The diagnosis of the error is accomplished through a heuristic search procedure (which makes selected accesses to the syntactic structure and returns the last safe position) operating together with a constraint on possible structural repairs. The repair component reprocesses input items only when it is not possible to reuse the structures built during the first pass analysis. This chapter describes the architecture of the general framework and the component modules, and sketches some heuristics that explain well-known cases of reanalysis in the literature.

1 Introduction

This work arises from the hypothetical claim that a convergence between the psycholinguistic models of the human parser and the efficient solutions to automatic parsing is possible. When we use realistic (i.e., wide coverage) grammars, the number of interpretations of a sentence grows dramatically, and the engineering approaches try to compact all the possible structures into a reduced memory space (for example, charts, Kay, 1980, and forests, Tomita, 1987, or to rank the various alternatives according to some criteria (Hobbs & Bear, 1990). In both cases, the semantic interpreter has to process an enormous number of structures, because, on the one hand, the compact form is exploded into individual parses, and, on the other hand, ranking does not cut off paths.

J.D. Fodor and F. Ferreira (eds.), Reanalysis in Sentence Processing, 287–325.

To reduce the number of useless structures and the waste of computation time, some of the existing systems have included psycholinguistic preferences formulated to explain the data on initial attachment. Preferences in specific configurations lead to the selection of some path (Shieber, 1983), but often they are too general to cope with the variety of structures computed with realistic grammars (Huyck & Lytinen, 1993). Moreover, path selection introduces the problem of what to do when the initial preference turns out to be erroneous. Single path parsers use chronological backtracking: when they face a breakdown, they go back to the last choice point and try another path. This strategy has two main drawbacks: first, at each choice point the parser saves a lot of information on the state of the computation, information which is restored in case that choice point is revised; second, the revision process is blind, because chronological backtracking always pursues the same search through the choice points, no matter what type of error occurred or what the structures built are like. Perhaps the only exception to this common approach is the boundary backtracking of Blank (1989), according to which the state of the computation is saved only at the boundaries of specific phrase types (e.g., NP) in a limited number of registers. When parsing fails, the backtracking handler retrieves the contents of a register and the computation restarts from that state. Since registers are bound in number, some will be overwritten, and some choice points will be lost. Boundary backtracking assigns a status to the choice points (the ones that are not stored in a register are not accessible), and provides a first rough distinction between easy and hard recoveries through a computational model. However, it suffers from the problems of how to fix the number of registers, what registers to overwrite, and how to navigate the register space, because a chronological traversal would systematically assign a higher preference to recent choice points (see, in contrast, SRH approaches below or comments in Sturt & Crocker, 1996).

The approach pursued in this paper is to devise a general mechanism of recovery which incorporates the accounts advanced in the psycholinguistics literature. The recent research in psycholinguistics on the topic of recovery has mainly focused on the distinction between computationally easy revisions and hardly recoverable garden-paths. In some models the difference is grounded in pure processing constraints. Parallel models (Gibson, 1991; Just & Carpenter, 1992) explain recoverability with the fact that the alternative structure to switch to is still available when the disambiguating material appears; otherwise, if the required alternative, for any reason, has been abandoned, garden path effects occur. In these models, a reanalysis process does not exist explicitly: the explanation of the garden path phenomena is based on the content of working memory.

An alternative approach is to derive a processing model from grammatical theory: the On-Line Locality Constraint (OLLC) (Pritchett, 1992) states that the characterization of garden-path effects must be a function of the distance between the structure of the preferred interpretation and the structure of the globally correct interpretation. In particular, OLLC claims that a constituent can be moved from a position A (if it exists) to a position B (if it exists) in the structure, only if A is in the *locality domain* of B; otherwise recovery is impossible. Locality domain is defined in terms of *government* and *dominance* relations between structural nodes. The OLLC constraint, stated in the GB framework, is then a purely structural hypothesis, which provides a good coverage of the experimental data.

Recently, two computational models have incorporated a constraint of locality, as a precondition for repairs of the syntactic structure, NL-Soar and monotonicity. NL-Soar (Lewis, 1993, this volume), the processing model based on SOAR general architecture (Newell, 1990), has one operator of structure extension, *link*, and one operator of structure deletion, *snip*. NL-Soar is a single path model: when an inconsistency occurs, the snip operator breaks a link (created by link), and the link operator rebuilds a different structure. Snip works on a limited portion of the structure, within the domain given by the maximal projection from the position where the inconsistency was detected. The applicability of snip is very constrained. There are three cases of possible triggering: when the same input token is attached to alternative syntactic structures; when two nodes occupy the same structural position; when the current projection misses an obligatory substructure. With respect to standard parsing algorithms, NL-Soar does not need to save the state of computation in order to repair the structure. However, even if described as a single path model (and in most cases it is), the treatment of lexical ambiguity is parallel in practice: the maximal projections of all the lexical entries for an input token remain active in the working memory to enable a possible activation of the snip operator.

Sturt & Crocker's (1996) approach introduces the notion of informational monotonicity in syntactic reanalysis. Following an idea originated in D-theory (Marcus *et al.*, 1983), Sturt & Crocker (1996) separate the relations of dominance and immediate dominance. At each processing stage the syntactic structure contains a mixture of dominance and immediate dominance relations. The overall assumption is that syntactic representation is formed by a monotonic set of relations (see also Weinberg, 1993; Gorrell, 1995). In other words, no retractions are possible (cf. the snip operator of NL-Soar). Sturt & Crocker (1996) introduce a formal operator, Tree Lowering, that accomplishes reanalysis while preserving coherence of syntactic relations. Tree Lowering is similar to a tree adjunction operation, but it is applied only to those nodes that are accessible after a constrained search strategy. A node is accessible if it dominates the last word attached and all the nodes in its subtree are saturated. Search strategies are devised to cope with ambiguity in reattachment on cross-linguistic examples. They are based on purely structural accounts (attach high versus attach low), and reveal processing differences between English and Japanese. The constraints on the notion of accessibility, which depends on the dominance relation and the coverage of the thematic domain, prevent some easy recoveries that modify constituents outside of the current subtree.

An alternative computational model is the hybrid symbolic and connectionist network of CAPERS (Stevenson, 1993; Stevenson, 1994), which provides a uniform competition-based explanation for both initial attachment preferences and garden path phenomena. When multiple possible grammatical attachments exist for a phrase, CAPERS executes the attachments in parallel, and then forces a competition that, in a number of cycles, leads the network to a stable state with only one active structure. The same competition game is responsible for recovery: if a new attachment causes an inconsistency, the network is forced to look for a new stable state, where all the structures are kept together through a new distribution of activations. If this new state is not reachable, a garden path effect occurs. CAPERS accounts for a large range of phenomena, especially if compared with the simplicity of its mechanism. Because of its net configuration, attachment of phrases that cause inconsistency, and thus restructuring, is only limited to the phrases along the right edge of the tree. Recoveries that involve previously structured phrases are not accounted for by the model.

As an alternative to the above, there exists a further view of the models based on processing constraints. When a breakdown occurs, the parser goes through a chain of inferences to detect the source of the error. The error may have occurred much earlier in the sentence, but the effects of the wrong choice are visible at the time of breakdown. Once it has spotted the error, the parser repairs the structure to accommodate the phrase that caused the inconsistency and forwards again the analysis. The first attempt to formulate a model of recovery in these terms goes back to the Selective Reanalysis Hypothesis (SRH) (Frazier & Rayner, 1982). The SRH suggests the existence of a human capability to "quickly identify the source of an erroneous analysis of temporarily ambiguous material, often permitting to revise just that part of its initial analysis which resulted in conflict with subsequent disambiguating material" (p. 199). Frazier & Rayner carried out an eye regression experiment and showed that subjects, most of the time, returned from disambiguating regions to the ambiguous region where the error had occurred. Recovery was not always possible; sometimes the signals provided by the disambiguating region were not sufficient to spot the error.

In this line of research, Fodor & Inoue (1994) have proposed a diagnosis model where the parser, switched into an emergency mode due to the occurrence of a breakdown, *attaches* (*anyway*) the new, incompatible constituent, then executes a chain of inferences to identify the error source, and finally repairs the structure. The fundamental revision principle is Attach Anyway, whose function is to accommodate the input phrase (which caused the breakdown) in the least unacceptable position, and then try to adjust the structure to produce well-formedness. The authors provide cross-linguistic examples and show how the theory predicts the difficulty of reanalysis in English and Japanese. Their explanation involves the difference of effectiveness of symptoms, according to how easily they take to the error source with a longer or shorter chain of inferences. At the current stage of development, the diagnosis model does not provide sufficient details to develop a computational model. In particular, Fodor & Inoue do not define how to formally relax the grammatical constraints in order to implement effectively the Attach Anyway principle (see, however, Fodor & Inoue, this volume, for some recent theoretical advances in this line of work).

The latter class of approaches (SRH approaches) seems to be more suitable for dealing with unrestricted input in a computational environment, as the variety of occurring phenomena goes beyond experimental practice in psycholinguistics. The range of possible breakdowns is unpredictable when a system uses a realistic grammar with hundreds of rules. The overgeneration of ambiguous points is mainly due to the inefficacy of semantic and pragmatic constraints, which are not very sophisticated in today's systems. Hence, the parser needs some general help to navigate the search space in reanalysis, and other models seem less suitable to scale to hundreds of choice points. Another reason for adopting an SRH model is that the line between easy and hard recoveries does not seem so sharp, and an SRH characterization, which involves chains of inferences of different lengths, could auspiciously provide a graceful degradation of performance.

The work described in this chapter is a general computational framework based on the SRH approach: it evaluates the symptoms of a breakdown, relates them to an error source, and finally repairs the structure. The architecture consists of three modules that accomplish these tasks: the symptom evaluation module, the diagnostic module, and the repair module. These modules are equipped with heuristics that implement some rationale derived from syntactic knowledge. The symptom evaluation module employs heuristics to relate the information available at the breakdown with a recognizable symptom code. The diagnosis module employs heuristics to relate the symptom code to an error source, to be found in the syntactic structure previously built. Finally, the repair module employs heuristics to reparse the input selectively, by trying to exploit at its best the structures built during the first pass analysis. A specific set of heuristics defines a model which classifies the cases of failure as recoverable or irrecoverable, depending on heuristics coverage.

The whole framework can be considered as an intelligent backtracking procedure, because it actually returns to a choice point to reparse the input (backtracking), but the search strategy is heuristics-based and reparsing does not reprocess input items (intelligent). Moreover, it does not save the state of computation at the choice points. The long term goal is the application of this approach to free text parsing. Thus far we have devised a limited set of heuristics to test the model on data taken from the pycholinguistic literature.

The organization of this chapter is as follows. The four following sections introduce the overall framework of parsing and recovery: a description of the grammatical formalism (2), the basic parser operations (3), ambiguity resolution (4), the recovery mechanism (5). We also introduce some heuristics and we go through examples to see how the model works. Finally we provide some discussion and conclusions.

2 The Grammar

This section outlines the theory of dependency grammar, which underlies the model. Dependency grammar is not a common framework in the psycholinguistic tradition, though a major exception is the work of Pickering and Barry (Pickering, 1994; Pickering & Barry, 1991). Here we sketch some basic tenets of the theory; the specific dependency formalism we use in the model is described in the Appendix (p. 318).

Dependency grammar describes the structure of a sentence in terms of binary *head-modifier* (also called *dependency*) *relations* on the words of a sentence. A dependency relation is an asymmetric relation between a word called *head* (*governor*, *parent*), and a word called *modifier* (*dependent*, *daughter*). A word in the sentence can play the role of the head in several dependency relations, i.e., it can have several modifiers, but each word can play the role of the modifier exactly once. One special word does not play the role of the modifier in any relation, and it is named the *root*. The set of the dependency relations that can be defined in a sentence form a tree, called the *dependency tree* (see Figure 1a). Note that the notion of constituency, the main theme of phrase structure grammars, is not a primitive in dependency theory; furthermore, the theory does not distinguish between various types of dependents with different structural configurations. For example, in phrase structure grammars, elements that are subcategorized for are attached differently from adjuncts, and specifiers are also attached differently from complements; in contrast, dependency trees that are structurally identical (they have the same nodes and edges) can be distinct because grammatical relations, that label the structural links, are different. Each one-level head-dependent configuration in the dependency tree satisfies the constraints associated with the head word in the lexicon; additionally, generic grammar places constraints on the syntactic categories.

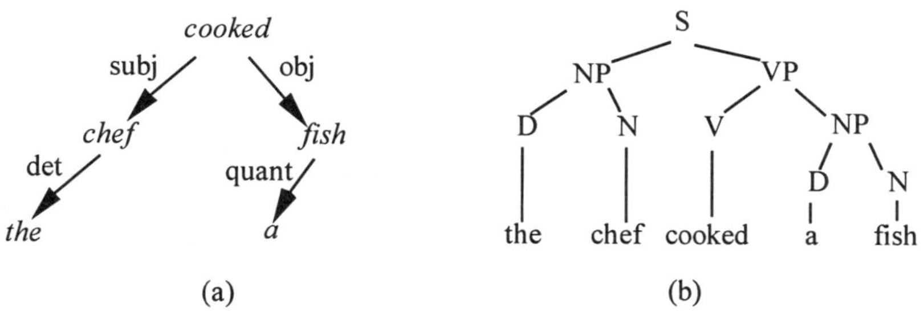

FIGURE 1: A dependency tree (a) and a phrase structure tree (b) for the sentence *The chef cooked a fish*. The leftward or rightward orientation of the arrows in the dependency tree represents the order constraints. The modifiers that precede the head stand on its left, the modifiers that follow the head stand on its right.

Phrase structure grammar assumes the notion of constituency as primitive, and describes the structure of a sentence via a *phrase structure tree*, a recursive decomposition of the whole word sequence into smaller sequences, called *phrases* or *constituents*, down to one-word units (Figure 1b). The elements of the phrase structure tree are both word and phrasal symbols. Word symbols are the leaves of the tree; phrasal symbols are the internal nodes (including the root, which is a distinct phrasal symbol spanning the whole sentence).

Dependency syntax has a long tradition in the European linguistics (Hudson, 1990; Mel'cuk, 1988; Sgall *et al.*, 1986), and some of the original insights of dependencies have found a role in the constituency formalisms, in particular, the concept of head of a phrase and the use of grammatical relations. The identification of the head within a phrase has been a major point of all recent frameworks in linguistics; in fact, most current linguistic theories include the X-bar schema (Jackendoff, 1977), which defines phrases as projections of (pre)terminal symbols, i.e., word categories. Grammatical relations are the primitive entities of relational grammar (Perlmutter, 1983), a particular form of a dependency-based theory (Mel'cuk, 1988). Dependency grammars use names that traditionally identify the grammatical relations (e.g., *subject*, *object*, *xcomplement*, etc.), to label dependency relations when the head is a verb.

Dependency syntax, like other lexicalized frameworks, does not produce spurious grammars,[1] and this facility is of practical interest, especially in writing grammars for experimental psycholinguistics settings and for parsing naturally occurring texts. Dependency trees are closely mapped to thematic domains, and this concept has shown to be relevant in many psycholinguistic theories (Pritchett, 1992; Sturt & Crocker, 1996). Finally, most of the predictions on sentence processing are grounded on constructs that rarely go beyond the basic elements of dependency grammar, or an equivalent context-free grammar (see, however, Pritchett, 1992, for an exception).

There are several dependency formalisms in the literature. In the appendix, we illustrate the Hierarchical Dependency Grammar (HDG), a dependency-based formalism where syntactic categories are arranged in a taxonomy, the formal definition of a dependency tree. The taxonomy is a tree the root of which is called a *top level* category (e.g., Verb) and whose other nodes (including the leaves) are *subcategories* (Transitive Verbs, Null-subject Verbs, etc.). The hierarchy is based on restrictions on features values. The interested reader will find further details regarding the HDG formalism in the Appendix.

3 Elementary Parsing Operations

The parsing algorithm applies the grammatical constraints by implementing a top-down strategy by which the syntactic structure is initialized at the root node, i.e., the node of a root category. At each step, on a given node, the parser predicts the existence of a category *C* dependent on the basis of the linear order constraints (HP and LP constraints—see the Appendix). These top-down

---

[1] For instance, there are no heavily ambiguous, infinitely ambiguous, or cyclic dependency grammars (such as $S \rightarrow SS$; $S \rightarrow a$; $S \rightarrow e$).

predictions are filtered through the use of left-corner information. A category *C* dependent is actually instantiated only when the current input word is of a category which can be the left corner of *C*. For example, let us assume that a noun can have just one optional dependent, a determiner, on its left. The parser instantiates a noun dependent only when the input word is a determiner or a noun itself (the latter possibility depends on the optionality of the determiner). This filtered top-down strategy accounts for two aspects of the human processor, the facility of committing to syntactic expectations, and the fact that this facility is controlled by the input data. Actually, this parser can be considered as a descendent variant of left-corner parsing,[2] which has the best performance in terms of space requirements and local ambiguities (Abney & Johnson, 1991).

The syntactic structure is always connected, which allows for implementing incremental processing at a fine-grained level of interleaving (Lombardo, 1995b). Note that the top-down strategy can overcome some shortcomings of the standard head-driven approaches (Abney, 1989; Pritchett, 1992) in dealing with some psycholinguistic phenomena. Head-final language processing (Bader & Lasser, 1994; Frazier, 1987) and referent identification in a spatial context (Eberhard *et al.*, 1995) require a commitment to a syntactic structure before parsing the head.

In dependency grammar, predicting a category *C* node corresponds to postulating the existence of a category *C* word in the sentence. The parser introduces a template (or *empty*) node labelled C_x in the structure (x is a numerical index), and then associates C_x with an actual input word. However, when the top-down parser guesses the node, it does not know which input word will 'fill' that node and what the specific features of its subcategory will be. Each guess applies only the general loose constraints provided by top level categories (*C* is a top level category). These constraints will be specialized when the actual input word, of a lower subcategory, fills the node. Two primary parsing actions, named *crlink* and *fill* (see below), implement the top-down process just described. They consist of two parts: the syntactic part, which builds the dependency tree, and the semantic part, which builds the semantic representation. This chapter does not consider the issues of semantic interpretation, but we assume that interpretation is tightly coupled with the syntactic analysis and proceeds incrementally. Let us consider each parsing action in turn.

---

[2] Using a top-down parser has some computational advantages when compiling a grammar (Lesmo & Lombardo, 1995).

Crlink(N, Cat, R) creates an empty node of the *top level* category *Cat*, and links it to (makes it depend on) the node *N* through an arc labelled with the relation *R* (see Figure 2a). *Crlink(N, Cat, R)* is invoked when the next dependent of *N* in the linear order is linked through the relation *R*, which restricts the feature category to *Cat* and the category of the input word *w* as belonging to the left corner of *Cat*.

Fill(N, w) associates (inserts) the input word *w* (of subcategory *Subcat*) with the empty node *N* (of category *Cat*) when *Subcat* is a subcategory of *Cat* (see Figure 2b).

A full node that governs all the modifiers licensed by the dependency relations defined by its subcategory is called *complete*. Note that the *crlink* top-down action creates and links a new node. Since each new node is immediately linked to an existing node, the syntactic structure is always connected.[3]

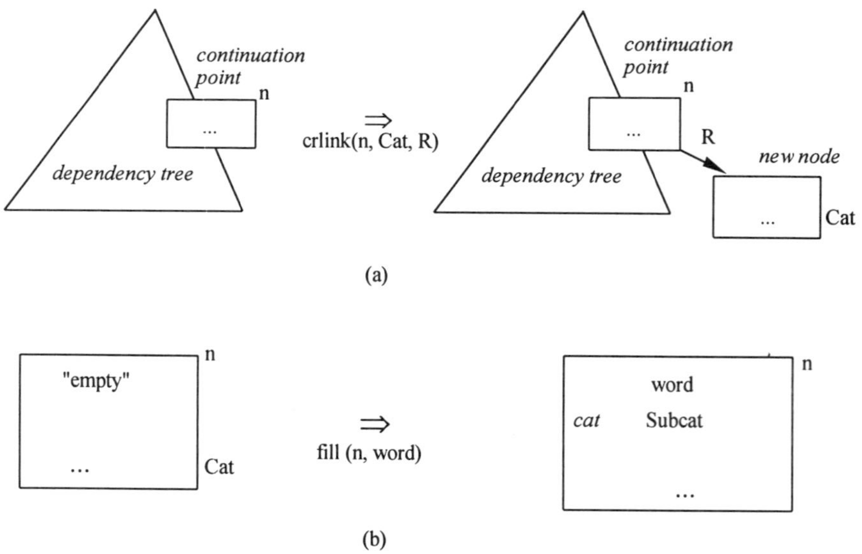

FIGURE 2: A graphical representation of *crlink* and *fill*.

[3] The problem of left recursion (how many *crlinks* to perform to insert the current input word), typical of top-down algorithms, is overcome with a constructive version of the check redundancy rule (Earley, 1970). In case of left recursive structures we instantiate the minimal unit of recursion and the new units only when necessary (Lesmo & Lombardo, 1995).

Before entering the problem of ambiguity resoultion let us describe the behavior of the parser on a simple sentence free of ambiguity, *John devoured a cake*. We consider only a reduced set of syntactic features as lexical information (see the Appendix). From an initial node V_1 of category Verb (the root category), the parser instantiates a nominal dependent N_1 with the *subj* relation. The operation *crlink*(V_1, *Noun, subj*) is licensed because *John*, a proper-noun, is in the left corner of the category Noun. Then N_1 is filled with the current input word *John*. Note that the agreement feature Number of the subject forces a value *sing* on the same feature of the main verb.

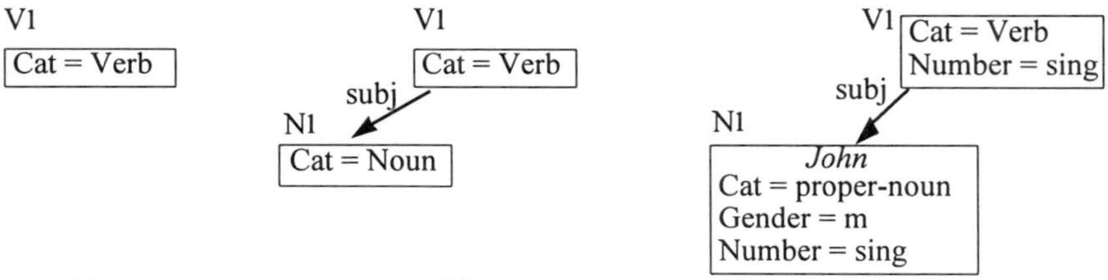

(a) (b) (c)

Then the verb *devoured*, of category *Vt* (obligatorily transitive), fills the node V_1. The subcategorization frame of the category *Vt* requires an obligatory object dependent, represented graphically by the dangling arc labelled 'obj' and the question mark. Note that no arc has been actually built (no *crlink* occurred); it is only a graphical representation of this expectation, which is soon satisfied by the next input word, the indefinite determiner *a*, in the left corner of the category noun. A new nominal node N_2 is created and linked by the operation *crlink*(V_1, *Noun, obj*).

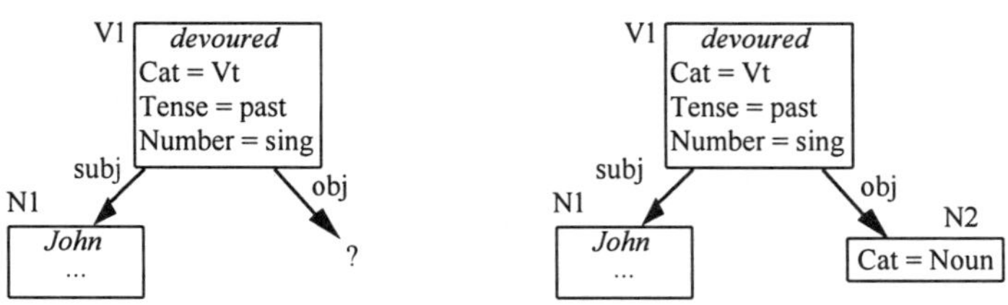

(d) (e)

The creation and filling of the determiner node D_1 (note that *a* is of the subcategory *I-Det*—indefinite determiner) follow soon after, and finally, *cake* fills the node N_2.

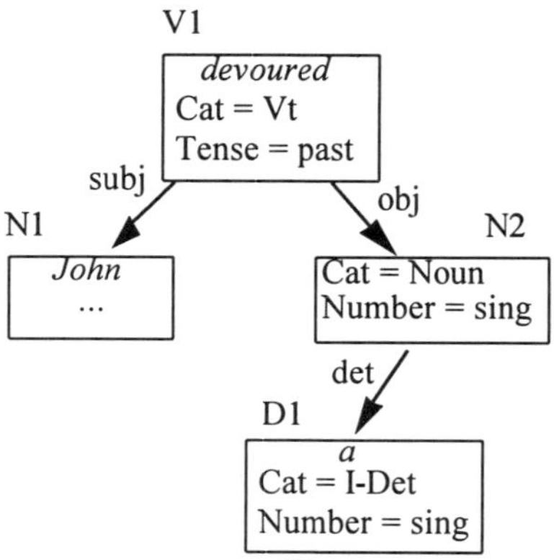

(f)

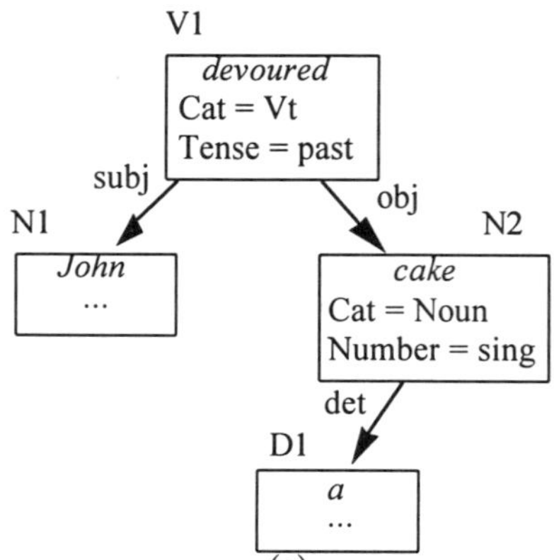

(g)

Since all the subcategorization requirements on each node are satisfied, the dependency tree is well-formed and the sentence is accepted.

The parsing operations introduced so far, *crlink* and *fill*, represent the dependency instantiation of the generic top-down parsing basic operations, *predict* and *scan* (Lombardo & Lesmo, 1996), that can be applied to any formalism when parsing follows a top-down strategy. The computational framework described in this paper can be easily extended to a non-dependency formalism, since the few dependency-based peculiarities of the operations introduced here are easily translated into a phrase structure form.

4 Ambiguity Resolution

Ambiguity resolution has been extensively studied in psycholinguistics, and many preferences devised to account for the experimental data on initial attachment have been implemented in automatic systems. Different types of preferences operate on different parameters of the parsing algorithm: the accessibility of the syntactic structure, the range of possible categories for an ambiguous input word, the set of executable operations at the same instant. The most effective characterization on the algorithmic structure is whether the parser is restricted to a single path or it can pursue multiple paths. In the first case, the parser can keep active only one path at a time and then is forced to commit to a single operation before it constructs structure. In the second case, when the parser encounters an ambiguous point in the input, it builds alternative syntactic structures for a portion of the input sentence starting at that point (called a *window* of limited parallelism). At the end of the parallel phase, when the window is exhausted, the parser can discard the least plausible structures by assigning some heuristically-based measure and then making a selection by using an appropriate threshold. Again, we can have a single selection, or a multiple selection.

'Limited' windows are present, to a certain extent, in a number of psycholinguistic models. In the Sausage Machine (Frazier & Fodor, 1978) and in Marcus' (1980) parser limited windows of about six words and three constituents, respectively, served as phrase assemblers. However, they were not windows of 'parallelism', because the windowed phase was single path, decided by preferences (Frazier & Fodor, 1978) and rule priority (Marcus, 1980). Limited parallelism models (Gibson, 1991; Just & Carpenter, 1992) assume the capacity of the working memory as the size of the window.

```
 0. initialize the root node
 1. take the word w in the next input position
 2. consult the grammar for each category of w and each
    attachment point on the structure
 3. IF at least one operation is allowed for continuation THEN
 4.    IF more than one operation and not already in a
       WINDOW of limited parallelism THEN
 5.        initialize WINDOW
 6.    execute all the operations
 7.    keep trace of the multiple paths
 8.    decrement WINDOW
 9.    IF WINDOW exhausted THEN
10.        selection of active paths and freezing of discarded
           paths
11. ELSE call recovery
12. GOTO 1
13. IF all the nodes in the dependency tree are complete
    THEN accept
14. ELSE call recovery
```

FIGURE 3: The parsing algorithm.

The algorithm in Figure 3 is a neutral parsing schema that handles ambiguity and invokes a recovery procedure in case of failure. The neutrality is in terms of the size of the window of limited parallelism, which can go from zero (single path models) to infinity (all path models). Many psycholinguistic models can be simulated within this schema (see below). It allows us to state what partial syntactic structures are stored in the working memory, when the recovery procedure comes into play.

The algorithm begins by initializing the dependency tree (with an empty root node—line 0). The loop 1-12 scans the input words. At each step there can be several nodes in the structure partially built that are suitable for continuation (attachment ambiguity). The parser accesses the lexicon to retrieve information on the current input word. The word can belong to several syntactic categories (lexical ambiguity). The parser consults the grammar for each combination of attachment node and input category (line 2). Each node in the final tree will have a configuration that satisfies the constraints of the feature structure of the node (see Figure A2 in the Appendix). During the processing, the partial node configuration can evolve in several ways, even for a single input category, this being a third source of ambiguity (continuation ambiguity). The parser produces a number of executable operations, that can be one of the two kinds *crlink* or *fill*.

Single path models of ambiguity resolution work at this level: some restrict the set of accessible attachment nodes (Late Closure or Recency models; Gibson *et al.*, 1996; Kimball, 1973); others restrict the set of input categories considered by the parser, according to the frequency of use (MacDonald *et al.*, 1994) or the activation in context (Spivey-Knowlton *et al.*, 1993); and yet others restrict the set of executable operations, including those which preferably attach the Final Argument (dependent) of a node (Ford *et al.*, 1982) and those which satisfy thematic role requirements (Trueswell *et al.*, 1994). Multiple path models wait for the execution of the operations to solve the ambiguity: limited parallelism models pursue multiple paths in parallel until the exhaustion of the working memory forces a decision (Gibson, 1991; Just & Carpenter, 1992); competition-based models pursue multiple paths in parallel until a winner is selected because of its simpler structure (Minimal Attachment; Frazier & Fodor, 1978), because it is the quickest to be computed (McRoy & Hirst, 1990), or because it is the most activated (Stevenson, 1993; Stevenson, 1994); generic constraint-based models prefer the analysis that maximizes the satisfaction of constraints—and in doing this, they also incorporate many of the preferences seen above (Spivey-Knowlton & Sedivy, 1995).

If the parser does not find any operation to continue (line 3), something has gone wrong in the analysis, and this immediately triggers a recovery phase (line 11). In the case of multiple operations (line 4), the parser enters a phase of limited parallelism. This means that for a limited amount of some dimension, the parser pursues multiple paths in parallel. The 'limited parallelism' mode is signalled by the flag WINDOW (line 5), which is set to the maximum value and is appropriately decreased during the execution (line 8). WINDOW can be counted in time slots, number of input words (the 'magic' number seven) or constituents (working memory cells). During the parallel phase, the parser keeps a trace of the alternative analysis paths (line 7), but provides a single representation for those portions of the structure that are shared by several paths (see the example below).

Lines 3-10 provide a framework for the application of the initial attachment preferences, according to the various theories illustrated above, given that the window of limited parallelism can range from zero (single-path models) to any value (multiple-path models). The framework described in this paper does not take a position on the preferences adopted for resolving initial attachments. The instantiation of a model in this framework would have to make some decisions as to which measure of plausibility should be implemented when evaluating the alternative syntactic structures. The measure could rely on syntactic, semantic or pragmatic issues. We assume an incremental parser that works in parallel with the semantic interpreter at the word level of interaction (Lombardo, 1995b).

The parallel phase can end for two reasons. A premature end occurs when only one path remains active because of grammatical constraints. In this case we simulate a wait-and-see strategy, and the window is large enough for the parser to reach the point of disambiguation. Otherwise, the parallel phase ends because the window is exhausted (line 9). Path selection depends on some specific measure of plausibility and can produce one or more *active* paths, while freezing (i.e., making *inactive*) the other paths. The inactive paths will be possibly reactivated only in reanalysis. Freezing a path means that the structures built for that analysis are not accessible in the following analysis, but remain dangling. They are transparent to the subsequent operations of the parser, and so they do not affect the computational load.

At the end of the sentence (line 13), all the nodes in the tree must be complete, in the sense they must satisfy the constraints of subcategorization provided by the respective words; otherwise recovery is invoked.

Let us now outline an example of parsing a sentence without entering recovery. We will see how the parser faces the ambiguous parts of the input with either a single path model or a multiple path model. The goal is to show what structures are created in each case. The recovery model described in section 5 works on the structures; it is therefore useful to know what differences it finds in both cases. In the following examples, to simulate parser behavior, we assume the application of various preferences and the selection of only *one* active path at the end of the parallel phase. These assumptions make the exposition of the examples easily understandable, but are not intended as a limitation of the generality of the computational framework. The example sentence is *John sent the book on the table to Anne* (Figure 4). When the parser arrives at the word *on*, there are two attachment points (*sent* and *book*), one syntactic category in the input (*P*), and two possible operations (*crlink(N2, P, p-adjunct)* and *crlink(V1, P, p-adjunct)*).

In a single path model the parser selects the operation and instantiates a unique structure. In Figure 4a we assume the parser has implemented a Late Closure strategy, by preferring the lower attachment. In a multiple path model the parser enters a phase of limited parallelism. In the example, the window is initialized to three input words (*on the table*). The parser executes the two operations, but in order to avoid the duplication of structures, it creates a unique prepositional node and links it twice, once with *N2* and once with *V1* (Figure 4b). These two arcs are mutually exclusive, and cannot belong to the same parse tree. The parser identifies two paths and names them <1.1> and <1.2>. These numerical labels have the form 'i.j', which identifies the jth alternative for the ith point of non determinism. Elements labeled 'i.j' cannot cooccur with elements labelled i.k, where $k \neq j$. The parts of the structure that do not depend on a particular choice are left unlabeled and are assumed as belonging to the structure whatever path is followed. A *path* is precisely defined as an exhaustive set of indices that can co-occur, where exhaustive means that the set contains at least one representative of each ambiguity encountered, and, because of co-occurrence, it contains exactly one representative. The structure that corresponds to one path is one possible *parse*. The path to follow results from an evaluation, in terms of syntactic preference and semantic consistency, of the various partial structures built in the parallel phase. One parse, called the *active parse* and corresponding to a specific path, is selected for continuation. The remaining partial structures are not deleted, even if not reachable in the currently active path, and are possibly reconsidered in the recovery phase. At the end of the window of limited parallelism, the selection process takes into account the semantic interpretation of the two links and prefers again the lower attachment. The active path is {1.1} and {1.2} is frozen. Its structures are pending but, because of their labeling, they are not accessible to the parser (except during recovery).

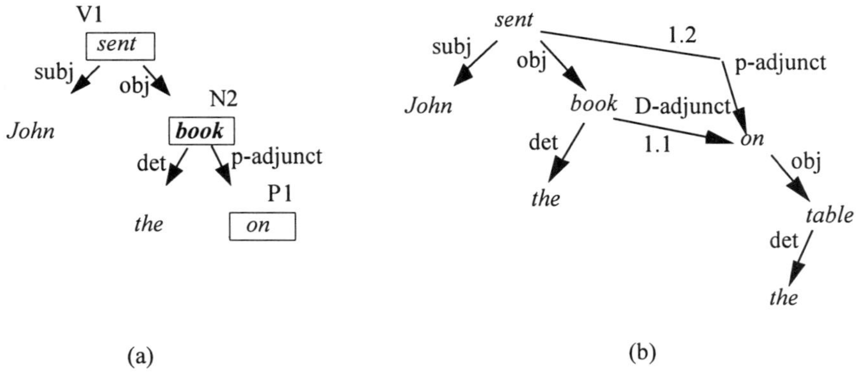

FIGURE 4: Single path (a) and multiple path (b) resolutions of ambiguity.

When the parser arrives at the word *to* (Figure 5), for both models there are three attachment points (*sent*, *book* and *table*), one syntactic category in the input (*P*), and three possible operations (*crlink(V1, P, i-obj)*, *crlink(N2, P, p-adjunct)*, and *crlink(N3, P, p-adjunct)*). In both cases, the parser prefers the attachment to *sent* because of subcategorization constraints (Final Argument preference), which corresponds to the path {1.1, 2.3} in the multiple path model (Figure 5b).

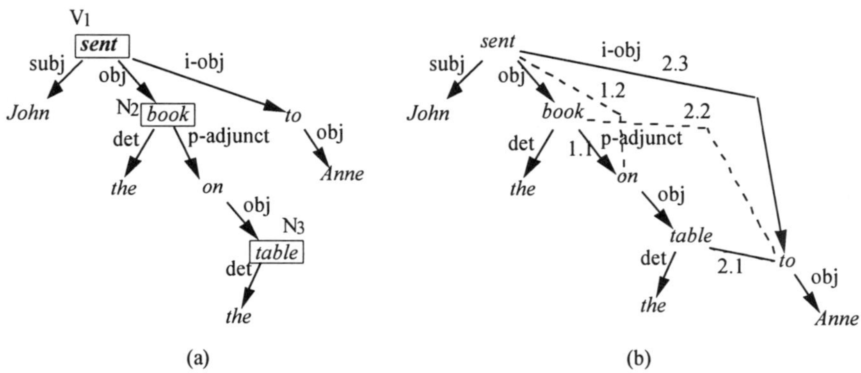

FIGURE 5: The final syntactic structures for single path (a) and multiple path (b) models.

We have illustrated how the structures are computed in the two approaches. While in the single path model alternative parses are never instantiated when the preferred parse succeeds, in the multiple path model alternative parses are partially instantiated anyway. Now we propose a mechanism of recovery that can operate using whatever strategy the parser pursues in the first-pass analysis. However, the structures instantiated in the two cases will result in different behaviors.

5 Recovery

The recovery mechanism implements a selective reanalysis, according to the SRH sketched in Frazier & Rayner (1982). In terms of a computer system, this can be translated as follows: rather than re-trying each choice point traversed in the first pass, the parser should carry on a selective search. What this hypothesis claims is that all the information available at the breakdown point should contribute to identifying the source of the error. Using Fodor & Inoue's (1994) terminology, this information is the *symptom* from which to search for the error source. Symptoms include expectations that remain unsatisfied in the currently active parse and features carried by the input material that caused the breakdown. The diagnosis (from the symptoms to the source of the error) is based on heuristic knowledge. This knowledge guides a selective search through the structures belonging to the currently active path. The effectiveness of symptoms is evaluated in the diagnosis phase: if the heuristic knowledge owned by the recovery mechanism is able to relate the symptom to the correct error source, then reanalysis will be much easier. Once the error source has been identified, the same diagnostic material contributes in the selection of a new promising path, among those previously discarded. Finally, the active parse structure is repaired complying with the path change. Repairing is an *ecological* form of reparsing. The word or the attachment where the source of the error is located corresponds to the position where a different path had been interrupted during the first pass (*error position*). From the error position, the parser forwards the analysis again, trying to add the partial structures that span the portion of the sentence between the error position and the breakdown point, and that are still valid after the path change. However, sometimes these structures are not compatible with the new active path, and some input needs to be reprocessed, i.e., assigned a different structure with respect to the first pass. This occurs especially when the parser implements a null window of limited parallelism, in which case, since it pursues a straight single path, some categories of an input word cannot be considered for continuation, because there is no way of attaching them to the reachable nodes in the tree. Take, for example, the Italian sentence:

(1) Una vecchia porta che cigola può tradire un ladro.

$$\text{An}_f \begin{Bmatrix} \text{old}_{N,f}\text{(woman) carries}_V \\ \text{old}_{A,f} \quad \text{door}_{N,f} \end{Bmatrix} \text{which creaks can reveal a theft.}$$

The sentence in (1) presents a double ambiguity noun-adjective/verb-noun (*f* indicates feminine morphology) which, if initially solved in favor of the first alternative (noun/verb), causes a breakdown at the relative pronoun. The error source is *vecchia*, which was parsed as a noun rather than an adjective, forcing the verbal reading of *porta*. When the parser diagnoses this error and goes back to *vecchia*, now turning to its adjectival reading, the structures for the noun *porta* do not exist yet and this word needs to be partially reprocessed.

In this section we describe the computational framework of recovery, and some heuristics that can simulate actual models. We deal with recovery as the process which makes a frozen path active. Models which pursue multiple paths in parallel (Gibson, 1991; Just & Carpenter, 1992) do not perform an actual recovery, but only switch to some other active path. These models would be easily accounted for by making frozen paths inaccessible. The recovery mechanism has the following schema:

1. Evaluate a symptom α.
2. Given α, diagnose an error source β.
3. Freeze the active path A.
4. Select a new path B and make B the active path.
5. Repair the structure according to B.

In this section we describe the recovery mechanism in terms of the modules that compose it: the *symptom evaluation* module (section 5.1), which takes as input the information available at the breakdown point and produces as output a *symptom code*; the *diagnostic* module (section 5.2), which takes as input the symptom code and produces as output the *error source* and an *error correction*, i.e., the syntactic structure (node or edge) badly processed (the point where the error occurred) and a constraint on subsequent processing; and the *repair* module (section 5.3) which *freezes* (i.e., makes inactive) the currently active path A, *selects* a new path B to become active, and finally *repairs* the structure according to path B, possibly reprocessing some parts of the input.

5.1 The Symptom Evaluation Module

The symptom evaluation module (SYMPEVAL) takes as input all the information available at the breakdown point and produces as output one or more symptom codes that belong to a predefined set of codes. Input information can refer to the result of the application of a parser operation that failed, e.g., feature checking; to the impossibility of accommodating the next input word within the active partial structure; or to the absence of some structural element obligatorily required by the grammar. The set of predefined symptom codes can be organized in a taxonomy (Figure 6). There are four major symptom classes: FEATURE MISMATCH, indicating a mismatch of feature values between expectations and actual data; SEMANTIC FAILURE, indicating a failure in the current semantic interpretation process; EXTRA, indicating linguistic material in excess with respect to the expectations; and MISSING, indicating that an expected element is 'missing'. The symptom is more informative if it is possible to specify the symptom further, that is, to identify a subclass of the top level classes. For example, if we have the general symptom FEATURE MISMATCH, and we know that the feature involved is GENDER, we can produce a symptom code GENDER MISMATCH; with the general symptoms EXTRA and MISSING, we can specify the syntactic category of the word or the phrase in excess (e.g., EXTRA-VERB) or expected (e.g., MISSING-VERB), or the dependency relation deducible from the surface form of a word (e.g., *she*—EXTRA-SUBJ) or predicted by the currently active subcategorization frame (e.g., MISSING-OBJ). SYMPEVAL tries to come up with a symptom as refined as possible, in order to be more informative for the diagnostic module, and whenever possible, more than one symptom code. The lowest levels of the taxonomy (not shown in Figure 6) contain very specific types that account for further syntactic features, like finiteness of verbs, etc.

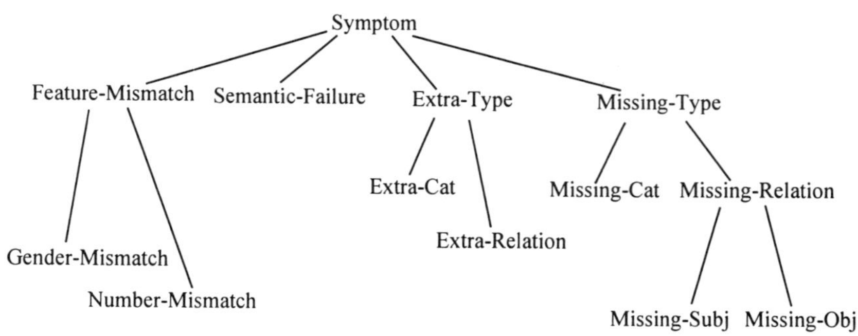

FIGURE 6: Taxonomy of symptom types: very specific symptoms have been omitted.

According to the architecture sketched above, an incremental processor guided by the syntax interprets partial syntactic structures which are totally connected. The emergence of symptoms during processing occurs at different times. The symptoms EXTRA and MISSING take place first, then FEATURE MISMATCH, and finally SEMANTIC FAILURE.

The set of symptom codes in the system is refined manually, and depends on the coverage of the grammar as well as on the possibility of relating experimental findings. As the grammar coverage increases, the symptoms allowed also increase. For example, the addition of new syntactic categories, relations, and/or features is immediately reflected in the taxonomy of symptoms. From a cognitive point of view, those elements should be introduced as soon as processing breakdown actually detected can be related to a symptom. The set (and the taxonomy) of symptom codes is one dimension of variability of the computational framework. The possibility of evaluating some symptom is the beginning of the recovery process, and the absence of a symptom code prevents some recoveries.

Below are some examples of more or less recoverable garden paths that, if interpreted in an unbiased context, originate the symptom codes in brackets. The breakdown point is indicated by a word in italics or by the symbol ◊ (end of sentence); the ambiguity point, where the wrong choice was made, is underlined.

(2) The horse <u>raced</u> past the barn *fell*. (Bever, 1970) (EXTRA-VERB)

(3) I gave <u>her</u> food for the dog ◊. (MISSING-RECIPIENT)

(4) Tom <u>heard</u> the gossip *was* true. (EXTRA-VERB)

(5) The <u>prime</u> number few ◊. (Milne, 1982) (MISSING-MAIN-VERB)

(6) <u>That</u> information is important *is* doubtful. (Tomita, 1987) (EXTRA-FINITE-VERB)

(7) L'avvocato diffida del padre della ragazza <u>che</u> si è *tradito* al processo. (De Vincenzi & Job, 1993) (GENDER MISMATCH)

'The lawyer suspects the father of the girl who betrayed himself at the trial.'

(8) The minister warned the president <u>of</u> the danger ◊. (SEMANTIC FAILURE)

The errors in sentences (2), (3), and (4) are immediately understandable. In (2) the initial lexical choice for *raced* is finite main verb; in (3) the adjectival reading of *her* is preferred; in (4) the subcategorization of *heard* containing a direct object is preferred. The choice in (5) of *prime number* as adjective-noun results in a missing main verb at the end of the sentence; in (6), *that* is disambiguated as a determiner, rather than a complementizer, and the second *is* causes on first encounter is taken to be an extra finite verb symptom. The Italian example in (7) illustrates a feature mismatch when the relative clause is attached to *ragazza* ('girl')—the past participle form has a masculine suffix and a gender mismatch occurs. Finally, the semantic failure occurs in (8) when the attachment *president-of-danger* is interpreted. Notice also that if the semantic interpreter accepts this attachment, SYMPEVAL could originate a MISSING-TOPIC error, due to the subcategorization frame of *warn*.

SYMPEVAL consists of a set of rules that take into account the situation at the moment of the breakdown in terms of the lexical features of the input word and of the attachment points in the syntactic structure to produce a symptom code. In the case of FEATURE MISMATCH and SEMANTIC FAILURE, the module just reports the results of the processes that failed, i.e., the feature unification process and the semantic interpreter respectively. EXTRA and MISSING symptoms result from an application of if-then rules that are local to the module. Generic symptoms are produced by two very intuitive rules:

RULE 1 IF *the input phrase is of category* Cat
THEN *return* EXTRA-Cat

RULE 2 Let *N* be a node
IF N *expects next a dependent with the relation* R
THEN *return* MISSING-R

When the missing relation can be one of two different relations *R1* and *R2*, and there is not enough information to discriminate between the two cases, SYMPEVAL returns the generic symptom MISSING-RELATION. But when both *R1* and *R2* require a phrase of the same category *Cat*, SYMPEVAL produces the more informative symptom MISSING-CAT. For example, the verb *load* has an ambiguous subcategorization frame between an *on-locative* grammatical relation (*I loaded the truck on the ship*), and a *with-object* grammatical relation (*I loaded the truck with beans*), but both are realized by a dependent of category *P* (preposition). In case one of the prepositions is missing, SYMPEVAL can always return MISSING-P, even if it does not know the subcategorization preferred.

5.2 The Diagnostic Module

The diagnostic module (DM) takes as input the symptom code and searches for the error source in the active syntactic structure. Each symptom has a number of heuristic search procedures associated with it that are used to individuate a candidate for revision. The candidate (i.e., the error source) is an element of the active structure that resulted in a misanalysis in the first pass. The element can be a node of the dependency tree (when the error source is a word that has been badly disambiguated), or an edge (when a whole subtree—a constituent—has been badly attached). Furthermore, the DM produces as output a constraint on the possible revisions. The repair module takes this constraint into account when adjusting the structure. At the current stage of development, the DM determines most of the behavior of the whole system, since the relation between a symptom and the error source is not always obvious. Of course, the set of symptom codes and the SYMPEVAL module also contribute to the behavior. But the class of possible symptom codes relies mostly on the grammatical theory used (a human or computational system would contain just a subset of them), and the rules of SYMPEVAL have a straightforward application. Hence, the recoverability of an error mostly depends on how clever DM is to relate the symptom code to an error source and to force some constraint on the ambiguous portion of the input. Once an error source and some further constraints are provided, the repair module restarts the parsing process as if it were in the first pass, but in an *ecological mode*. The ecological mode involves the recycling of all the substructures that were previously built and that are still valid after the path change.

The procedure that creates an edge is the one associated with the symptom FEATURE MISMATCH, possibly refined on some feature *F*. It searches for the head node *Nh* that governs the unification of the feature *F* on the node *N* that caused the mismatch, and returns the arc *Ah* directly descending from *Nh* that links the subtree that contains *N* (see Figure 7). Also, DM returns the node *Nr* at the low end of the right edge traversable from *Nh*. In this way, all the attachment points on the right edge are accessible to the repair module, which will try an arc different from *Ah*. A similar diagnosis is returned in the case of SEMANTIC FAILURE, since the attachment (arc) that failed is already reported by the semantic interpreter. Figure 7 also provides an example where SRH is an effective strategy. Attachment revision can intervene either on the *rel-clause* relation or on the *p-adjunct(of)* relation, but error diagnosis on the symptom GENDER-MISMATCH produces the *rel-clause* arc as output.

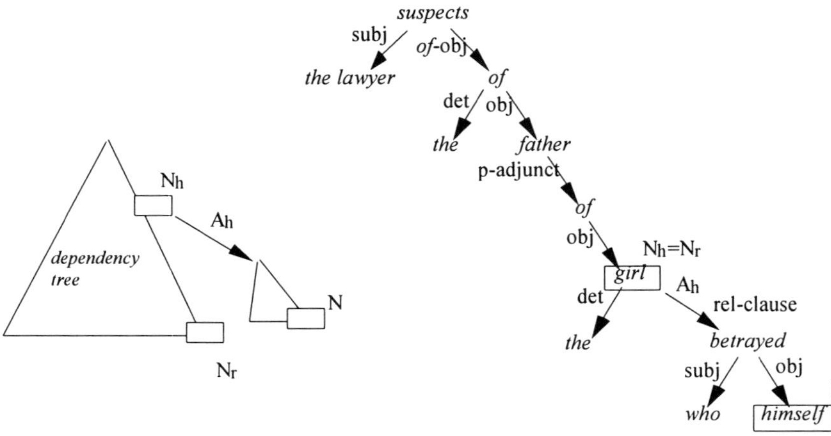

FIGURE 7: A diagnosis of an error source with the symptom GENDER-MISMATCH.

The procedure that creates a node is the one associated with the symptom MISSING-VERB. If we assume that *knew* belongs to two categories (*Vt* and *Vcomp*), thus presenting an ambiguity for its subcategorization frame (<subj, obj> and <subj, complement>), then the sentence *Tom knew the gossip* could hypothetically be parsed under the second frame (*Vcomp* category for *knew*); this results in a breakdown and SYMPEVAL outputs the symptom MISSING-VERB (Figure 8).

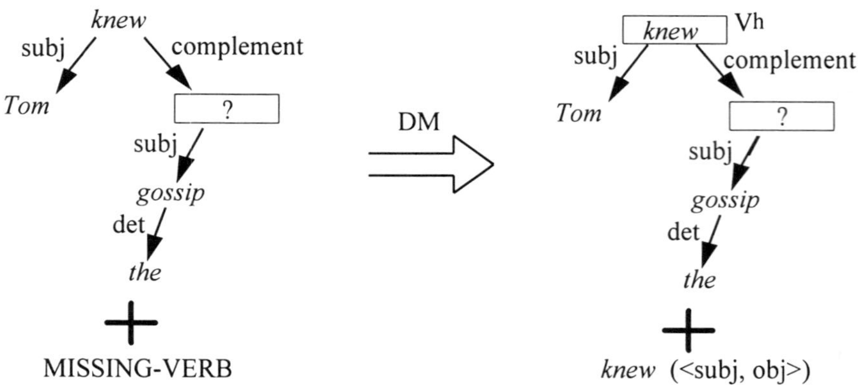

FIGURE 8: A diagnosis of an error source with the symptom MISSING-VERB.

The procedure associated with this symptom searches the structure following the arc upwards, and creates the verbal head node *Vh* since the latter has an alternative subcategorization frame which does not contain the relation 'complement', together with the new subcategorization frame (see Figure 8). The output of the diagnostic module for the example in Figure 8 is <*Vh*, <subj, obj>>.

In general, the diagnosis process that takes place with structural symptoms like EXTRA and MISSING is more complex. The search procedures associated with these cases incorporate some underlying rationale to relate the symptom with the error, but sometimes in a very subtle way (Fodor & Inoue, 1994, describe a long chain of inferences to be performed). The following three procedures, for example, are associated with the symptom EXTRA-TENSED-VERB:

S1 *Search for the local verbal head node* N *(that contains the word* w*)*
IF w *has an alternative subcategorization that introduces a tensed verb expectation*
THEN *create* N *and the new active subcategorization of* w

S2 *Search for the local verbal head node* N *(that contains the word* w*)*
IF w *has an alternative untensed interpretation*
THEN *create the node that contains the word that precedes* w *and restricts the input category of* w *to the untensed entry*

S3 *Search for the local verbal head* h
IF h *is a tensed verb*
and h *can have a sentential subject*
THEN
Search for a word w *that precedes* h *and has an alternative reading as a complementizer*
Create the node that contains the word that precedes w *and restricts the input category of* w *to complementizer*

These three procedures are invoked in this order, which corresponds to their increasing complexity. All of the three searches center on the current verbal head; if the parser can accommodate this word in an alternative way, its structural position will be released and the new verb could take over. S1 guesses that the current verbal head has an alternative subcategorization which introduces an expectation for a tensed verb, like a sentential complement dependency relation. S1 creates the verbal head node and the new subcategorization frame (*Tom heard the gossip was true*). S2 guesses that the current verbal head *w* has an alternative lexical entry which is untensed, and returns to the position immediately preceding the verb by also restricting *w* to the untensed entry (*The bird found in the room was dead*—Figure 9). Finally, S3 looks for a word *w* that precedes the current verbal head and has an alternative lexical entry as a Complementizer. If DM finds such a suitable word w, it creates the node that contains the word that precedes *w* and restricts the category of *w* to complementizer (*That information is important is doubtful*).

We can see that structural errors are more difficult to recover from than feature mismatching and semantic failures and that this is consistent with the higher inherent difficulty detected in experimental practice. But we should also consider that theories of semantic interpretation both in psychological and computational linguistics are at a lesser degree of development, hence, the space for possible ambiguities and recoveries is reduced with respect to the high sophistication of syntactic theories, and navigation in a reduced space is usually easier and less time consuming.

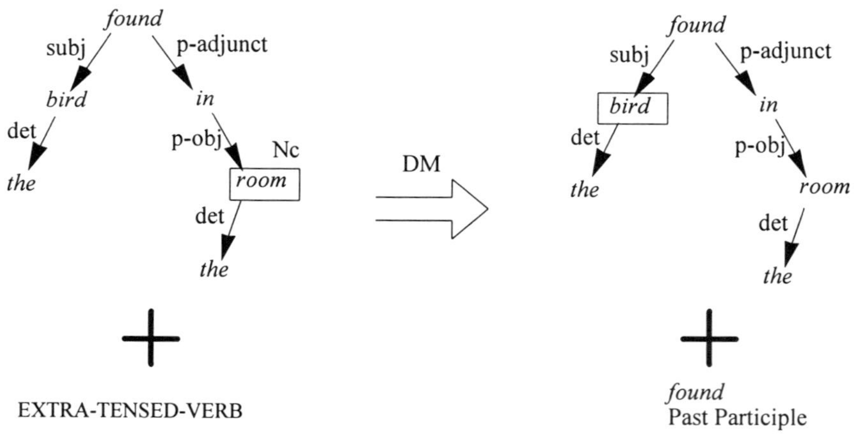

FIGURE 9: A diagnosis of an error source with the symptom EXTRA-VERB.

5.3 The Repair Module

The repair module (RM) accomplishes the actual task of building the new active structure after the old active path has been abandoned. It is in this task that RM recycles all the pieces that can belong to paths that were previously active or discarded but that are still valid in the new path. RM takes as input all elements of the syntactic structure and the constraints produced by DM. (Recall that when the element is a node *N* with a word *w*, DM either returns a new subcategorization frame for *w* or a restriction on the syntactic category of the word that follows *w*; when the element is an arc *A*, DM also returns the node at the low end of the right edge of the tree rooted by *A*.) RM works as the parser did in the first pass analysis, but does not reprocess the input items that were parsed in a structural position which is consistent with the repair (as such, RM operates in an *ecological mode*).

The node *N*, the output of DM (in either case), represents the point from which to start the repair process. RM works left to right: it reprocesses the input portion from *N*'s position to the position where the breakdown occurred. RM uses the same parser operations, *crlink* and *fill*, as in the first pass analysis, but RM checks if the structural elements to be created are already present in the structure. In the case of a single path first pass, these elements are in the old parse (the one that failed); in the case of a multiple path first pass, thay can be in both the active parse (that failed) or in one of the inactive parses. When some structural elements are reusable, RM relinks a whole subtree, and the analysis can continue from the input position that follows the portion spanned by that subtree. We now turn to the difference of behavior with the operations *crlink* and *fill* between the so-called *normal mode* and *ecological mode*, by assuming that we are on a node *N* and the word to reprocess is *w*.

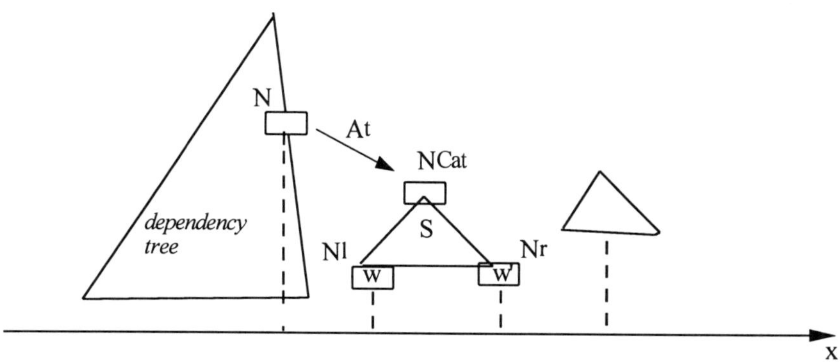

FIGURE 10: Execution of a *crlink* in ecological mode.

In *normal mode*, the operation *crlink(N, Cat, R)* instantiates a node of category *Cat* and links it to the node *N* with an arc labelled with the relation *R*. In *ecological mode* (Figure 10), RM checks whether *w* is in a node, say *Nl*. If *Nl* is the left corner of some subtree *S* rooted in a node of category N_{Cat}, then the parser is in a situation already accounted for in the first pass and N_{Cat} can be reused instead of creating a new node. To find N_{Cat}, RM climbs the structure on the leftmost edge, while checking whether it encounters a node of category *Cat*. The climb is over when the node reached is no more a leftmost daughter of the next higher node. At this point there are two possibilities: (i) If RM has found a node of category *Cat* during its climb, this node becomes N_{Cat}; the old link to N_{Cat} is deleted; a new arc *At* is generated to link *N* with N_{Cat}; now, to identify the right edge of the whole substructure *S* which can be included in the parse, RM descends from the N_{Cat} on the rightmost edge and takes the lowest node *Nr* which contains the word *w'*; *Nr* becomes the new current node, the input position is updated to the position following *w'* and the repair continues. (ii) Otherwise, when RM does *not* find a suitable node to link, it is compelled to create a new one, which becomes the new current node, and the repair continues.

In *normal mode*, the operation *fill(N, w)* fills the node *N*, previously created by a crlink operation, with the word *w*. In *ecological mode*, there are three possibilities: (i) *N* has been created anew by a crlink in RM and we have to fill it as usual; (ii) *N* has only been linked by the RM and is full, in which case fill is never invoked because the processor jumped over the whole subtree all the way to its rightmost word; (iii) *N* has only been linked but is empty, in which case the processor jumped to a word preceding the word that will fill *N*, and fill can executed as usual. After filling, repair continues from *N*.

The goal of this strategy for RM is to save computation time by reusing the structures that are compatible with the new active path. RM is invoked on the portion of the input sentence that begins with the word produced by DM as output and the word that caused the breakdown; then the normal mode analysis restarts. Note that the task of RM is computationally lighter when it works after a multiple path parsing model. Most of the structures that it needs are built in some phase of limited parallelism and are now ready for a simple reactivation.

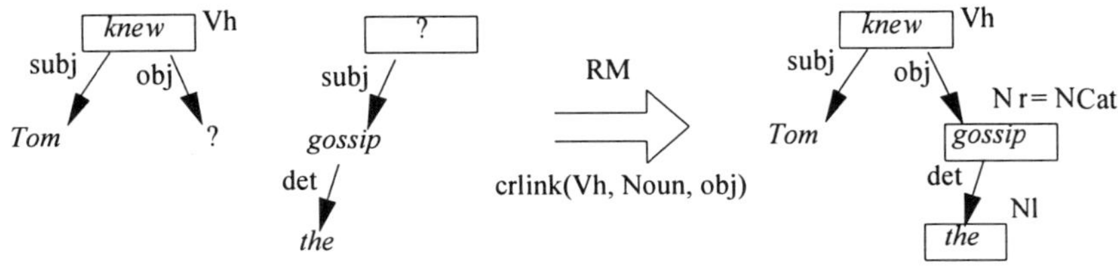

FIGURE 11: Repairing from the diagnosis in Figure 8.

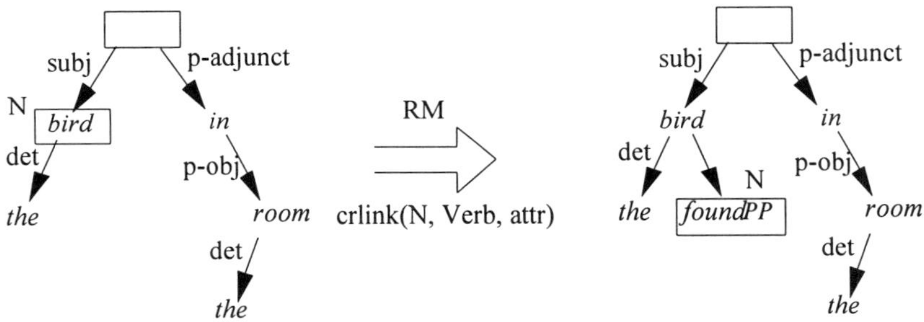

FIGURE 12: Repairing from the diagnosis in Figure 9.

Let us close this section with two examples which follow from the examples seen in the description of DM above. In the first one (Figure 11, see Figure 8), from the attachment node *Vh* and with the word *the* (Determiner) as the next input word, we have an operation *crlink(Vh, Noun, obj)*. Climbing the leftmost edge from *the*, we find a node of category noun, filled with *gossip*. This node is linked via a new arc. With N_{Cat} as the new current node we can continue the analysis in normal mode.

In the second example (Figure 12), RM begins its repairs from the node *N* (*bird*), and the next word *found* is constrained to a past participle reading (PP). The operation to be executed is *crlink(N, Verb, attr)*. Since a node containing the next input word is not present in the structure, we create a new node and link it to *N*.

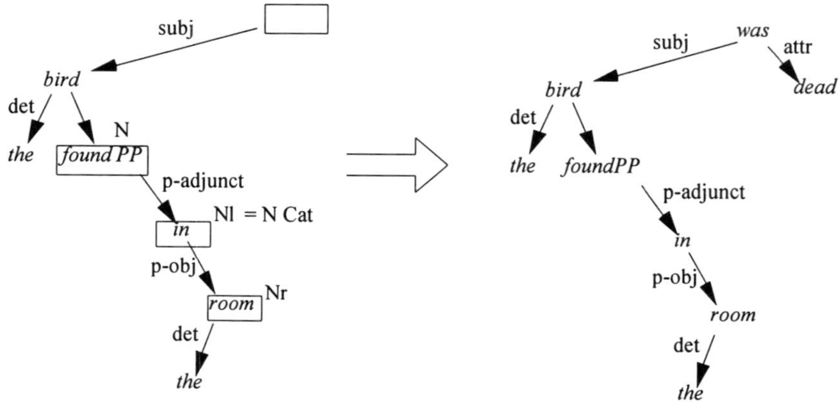

FIGURE 13: Continuing repair from Figure 12 and finishing it.

At the next step (Figure 13), we can save some computation time by attaching the subtree rooted by *in* to *N*. Now the repair phase has concluded and the parser can restart the first-pass analysis and will eventually reach successfully the end of the sentence.

6 Discussion and Conclusions

This chapter has presented a general computational framework for recovery which can be parameterized to a range of models by introducing a well defined set of heuristics. The framework implements an SRH approach in terms of a three module architecture: a symptom evaluation module, a diagnostic module, and a repair module. We are aware that some heuristics used as examples in the paper correspond to the solutions of irrecoverable garden paths. The goal is to provide an idea of the possibilities offered by the framework in terms of parameterization.

The mechanism presented is able to recover from breakdowns by pursuing an intelligent backtracking strategy. We insist on these two terms, *backtracking* and *intelligent*, for several reasons. First, even if the parser does not save any phase of the computation, in fact it 'backtracks' to a safe point in the structure to start the repair phase; moreover, as in standard backtracking, the repair consists in reparsing, since the system does not use any predefined restructuring operator or any other knowledge other than some constraints on syntactic knowledge. Second, we refer to the term intelligent with regard to the search for the return point, which is accomplished selectively through the elements in the existing structure (given the detected symptom), and repair maximally exploits the work already done during the first pass.

The model is an independent model for the first pass analysis, in that it works with both single path and multiple path parsers. A previous version of this model was limited to recovery with multiple path parsers (Lombardo, 1995a). The characteristic of independence makes the model applicable to several analysis schemas. Moreover, with a flexible definition of the heuristics in the symptom evaluation and the diagnostic modules, we can apply the mechanism to any of several grammar formalisms.

In the introduction we stated that an SRH mechanism can deal with parsing unrestricted texts better than other computational models. Let us now support this claim with two comments on the model described in this paper, even if we believe that proof can only come from a thorough experimental work on the implementation. First, our recovery model has a flexible search strategy for discovering the error source. The heuristics in the diagnostic module are small chunks of knowledge that are invoked in relation with specific symptoms. This assures the extendibility of the system to deal with further error sources. The practice with computational systems is to trace executions and expanding coverage when necessary. In the case of a recovery mechanism we will force some failure and trace the behavior of the system. We will introduce new heuristics when we detect that some failures are particularly relevant. The fact that a heuristic rule covers a reduced number of configurations helps us in devising more rules without affecting the functioning of the whole system. Other computational models rarely address the problem of what strategies are used to search through the structure to selectively find where the repair applies. The type of breakdown occurred never contributes to the search of the error source. The necessity of defining some strategies in reanalysis has been observed by Sturt & Crocker (1996), who recognize that their bottom-up (i.e., recency-based) search is only an approximation of more sophisticated procedures.

Second, the repair module is a grammar-based repairing-as-reparsing procedure. This has two advantages: (i) the module can account for structural corrections that go beyond the right edge of the tree; (ii) it is not necessary to verify the correctness of modifications, which is required in the case of ad hoc procedures. Other computational models do not address this problem, mostly because they limit the recovery to the right edge or the rightmost substructure of the tree (e.g., Stevenson, 1994). When we move from sentences in the psycholinguistic literature to sentences in unrestricted texts, the length generally increases, as do the chances to commit to erroneous choices. Thus, the distance between the error source and the breakdown point can go beyond the limits proposed in most models for revision.

The behavior of the repair module is also a major difference between our model and Fodor & Inoue's (1994) model, which involves specific chains of operations depending on the error identified. Hence, the measure of the difficulty of recovery changes for the two models. In Fodor & Inoue's model, recovery is a chain of inferences dominated by the Attach Anyway principle. These inferences lead the parser from the diagnosis of the error to the repair of the structure, and the difficulty is relative to the length of this chain. In our model, difficulty is measured in terms of the execution of the search procedure(s); then repair contributes to difficulty depending on the elements that have to be built anew.

The current implementation of the system recovers from any error because the parser is able to 'remember' the failed paths it has pursued with a bookkeeping technique based on the arc labels i.j described in section 4 (see also Lombardo, 1995a). In order for the model to be psycholinguistically interesting, we must introduce some criteria for distinguishing between easily recoverable processing errors and irrecoverable garden paths. Some criteria are under study and include the accessibility of structural elements in terms of the completeness of their substructure (assigned thematic roles) (Ferreira & Henderson, 1991), the locality constraints on path change expressed in terms of a thematic domain (Pritchett, 1992), and the rank of the relationship between symptoms and errors (Fodor & Inoue, 1994).

Future improvements on this model include empirical testing of the system with unrestricted texts. We are confident that this computational methodology will shed new light on the recovery phenomenon.

Universitá di Torino

References

Abney, S.P. 1989. A computational model of human parsing. *Journal of Psycholinguistic Research*, 18, 129-144.

Abney, S.P. & Johnson, M. 1991. Memory requirements and local ambiguities of parsing strategies. *Journal of Psycholinguistic Research*, 20, 3, 233-250.

Bader, M. & Lasser, I. 1994. German verb-final clauses and sentence processing: evidence for the immediate attachment. In C. Clifton, L. Frazier, & K. Rayner (eds.), *Perspectives on Sentence Processing*. Hillsdale, NJ: Lawrence Erlbaum Associates, 225-242.

Bever, T. 1970. The cognitive bias for linguistic structures. In J. Hayes (ed.), *Cognition and the Development of Language*. New York: John Wiley and Sons, 279-352.

Blank, G.D. 1989. A finite and real-time processor for natural language. *Communications of the Association for Computing Machinery*, 32, 10, 1174-1189.

De Vincenzi, M. & Job, R. 1993. Some observations on the universality of the Late-Closure strategy. *Journal of Psycholinguistic Research*, 22, 2, 189-206.

Earley, J. 1970. An efficient context-free parsing algorithm. *Communications of the Association for Computing Machinery*, 13, 94-102.

Eberhard, K., Spivey-Knowlton, M., Sedivy, J., & Tanenhaus, M. 1995. Eye movements as a window into real-time spoken language comprehension in natural contexts. *Journal of Psycholinguistic Research*, 24, 409-436.

Ferreira, F. & Henderson, J. 1991. Recovery from misanalyses of garden-path sentences. *Journal of Memory and Language*, 30, 725-745.

Fodor, J.D. & Inoue, A. 1994. The diagnosis and cure of garden paths. *Journal of Psycholinguistic Research*, 23, 5, 407-434.

Ford, M., Bresnan, J., & Kaplan, R. 1982. A competence-based theory of syntactic closure. In J. Bresnan (ed.), *The Mental Representation of Grammatical Relations*. Cambridge, MA: MIT Press, 727-796.

Frazier, L. 1987. Syntactic processing: Evidence from Dutch. *Natural Language and Linguistic Theory*, 5, 519-559.

Frazier, L. & Fodor, J.D. 1978. The sausage machine: A new two-stage parsing model. *Cognition*, 6, 291-325.

Frazier, L. & Rayner, K. 1982. Making and correcting errors during sentence comprehension: Eye movements in the analysis of structurally ambiguous sentences. *Cognitive Psychology*, 14, 178-210.

Gibson, E.A.F. 1991. *A Computational Theory of Human Linguistic Processing: Memory Limitations and Processing Breakdown*. Unpublished doctoral dissertation, Carnegie Mellon University, Pittsburgh, PA. Available as Center for Machine Translation Technical Report CMU-CMT-91-125.

Gibson, E.A.F., Pearlmutter, N., Canseco-González, E., & Hickok, G. 1996. Recency preference in the human sentence processing mechanism. *Cognition*, 59, 23-59.

Gorrell, P. 1995. *Syntax and Parsing*. Cambridge: Cambridge University Press.

Hobbs, J.R. & Bear, J. 1990. Two principles of parsing preferences. In *Proceedings of the Thirteenth International Conference on Computational Linguistics (COLING 90)*, Helsinki, 162-167.

Hudson, R. 1990. *English Word Grammar*. Oxford, UK: Basil Blackwell.

Huyck, C.R. & Lytinen, S.L. 1993. Efficient heuristic natural language parsing. *Proceedings of the National Conference on Artificial Intelligente (AAAI 93)*, 386-391.

Jackendoff, R. 1977. *X-bar Syntax: A Study of Phrase Structure*. Cambridge, MA: MIT Press.

Just, M.A. & Carpenter, P.A. 1992. A capacity theory of comprehension: Individual differences in working memory. *Psychological Review*, 99, 1, 122-149.

Kay, M. 1980. *Algorithm Schemata and Data Structures in Syntactic Processing*. Technical Report No. CSL-80-12. Xerox Park, Palo Alto, CA.

Kimball, J.P. 1973. Seven principles of surface structure parsing in natural language. *Cognition*, 2, 15-47.

Lesmo, L. & Lombardo, V. 1995. *Efficient Dependency Parsing*. Technical Report No. 13-95. Dipartimento di Informatica, Università di Torino.

Lewis, R.L. 1993. *An Architecturally-based Theory of Human Sentence Comprehension*. Unpublished doctoral dissertation, Carnegie Mellon University, Pittsburgh, PA. Available as Technical Report CMU-CS-93-226.

Lombardo, V. 1995a. Parsing and recovery. In *Proceedings of the 17th Annual Meeting of the Cognitive Science Society*, 648-653.

Lombardo, V. 1995b. Splitting the use of syntax and lexicon in incremental processing. Paper presented at *Architectures and Mechanisms for Language Processing (AMLaP) Conference 1995*, Edinburgh.

Lombardo, V. & Lesmo, L. 1996. An Earley-type recognizer for dependency grammar. In *Proceedings of the 16th International Conference on Computational Linguistics (COLING 96)*, 723-728.

MacDonald, M., Pearlmutter, N., & Seidenberg, M. 1994. Lexical nature of syntactic ambiguity resolution. *Psychological Review*, 101, 4, 676-703.

Marcus, M. 1980. *A Theory of Syntactic Recognition for Natural Language*. Cambridge, MA: MIT Press.

Marcus, M., Hindle, D., & Fleck, M. 1983. D-Theory: Talking about talking about trees. *Association for Computational Linguistics*, 21, 129-136.

McRoy, S. W. & Hirst, G. 1990. Race-based parsing and syntactic disambiguation. *Cognitive Science*, 14, 313-353.

Mel'cuk, I. 1988. *Dependency Syntax: Theory and Practice*. Albany, NY: State University of New York Press.

Milne, R. 1982. Predicting garden path sentences. *Cognitive Science*, 6, 349-373.

Newell, A. 1990. *Unified Theories of Cognition*. Cambridge, MA: Harvard University Press.

Perlmutter, D. 1983. *Studies in Relational Grammar 1*. Chicago, IL: University of Chicago Press.

Pickering, M. J. 1994. Processing local and unbounded dependencies: A Unified Account. *Journal of Psycholinguistic Research*, 23, 4, 323-352.

Pickering, M.J. & Barry, G. 1991. Sentence processing without empty categories. *Language and Cognitive Processes*, 6, 229-259.

Pritchett, B. 1992. *Grammatical Competence and Parsing Performance*. Chicago, IL: University of Chicago Press.

Sgall, P., Haijcova, E., & Panevova, J. 1986. *The Meaning of Sentence in its Semantic and Pragmatic Aspects*. Dordrecht: Dordrecht Reidel Publishing Company.

Shieber, S.M. 1983. Sentence disambiguation by a shift-reduce parsing technique. *Association for Computational Linguistics*, 21, 113-118

Spivey-Knowlton, M. & Sedivy, J. C. 1995. Resolving attachment ambiguity with multiple constraints. *Cognition*, 55, 3, 227-267.

Spivey-Knowlton, M., Trueswell, J., & Tanenhaus, M. 1993. Contexts effects in syntactic ambiguity resolution: Discourse and semantic influences in parsing reduced relative clauses. *Canadian Journal of Experimental Psycology*, 47, 2, 276-309.

Stevenson, S. 1993. A competition-based explanation of syntactic attachment preferences and garden path phenomena. *Association for Computational Linguistics*, 31, 266-273.

Stevenson, S. 1994. A unified model of preference and recovery mechanisms in human parsing. In *Proceedings of the 16th Annual Meeting of the Cognitive Science Society*, 824-829.

Sturt, P. & Crocker, M. 1995. Incrementality and monotonicity in syntactic processing. In D. Milward & P. Sturt (ed.), *Incremental Interpretation. Edinburgh Working Papers in Cognitive Science, Vol. 11*. Edinburgh: Centre for Cognitive Science, 23-66.

Sturt, P. & Crocker, M. 1996. Monotonic syntactic processing: a cross-linguistic study of attachment and reanalysis. *Language and Cognitive Processes*, 11, 15, 449-494.

Tomita, M. 1987. An efficient augmented-context-free parsing algorithm. *Computational Linguistics*, 13, 31-46.

Trueswell, J., Tanenhaus, M., & Garnsey, S.M. 1994. Semantic influences on parsing: Use of thematic role information in syntactic ambiguity resolution. *Journal of Memory and Language*, 33, 285-318.

Weinberg, A. 1993. Parameters in the theory of sentence processing: Minimal commitment theory goes east. *Journal of Psycholinguistic Research*, 22, 3, 339-364.

Appendix: Hierarchical Dependency Grammar

In this appendix, we introduce the formalisms of Hierarchical Dependency Grammar (HDG), which has some similarities with the word grammar approach described in Hudson (1990). Using such formalisms is motivated given the advantages of using a lexicalized formalism in linguistics or psycholinguistics together with the possibility of defining categorical constraints as an abstraction over lexical constraints (Lombardo, 1995b).

Syntactic categories are the top level nodes of subcategory taxonomies (see Figure A1). For example, the category verb (*V*) is the top level of a taxonomy of subcategorization frames, and the category noun (*N*) is the top level of a taxonomy of nominal (sub)categories, like common nouns, pronouns, or proper nouns. The classification is grounded on the assignment of values to basic features: the more restricted a value is, the lower the subcategory. A node in the taxonomy is a feature structure; features and values are inherited. The complete set of features and values for a subcategory is determined by unification of the feature structures that subsume the subcategory together with the constraints of the subcategory itself. Among other features, there are some complex features that define the dependency relations. In Figure A1 there is a simple taxonomy of verbs: *V* is the syntactic category, the top level of the hierarchy; *Vimp* (impersonal—null subject—verbs), *Vi-t* (transitive/intransitive verbs), *Vt* (transitive verbs) and *Vcomp* (verbs with a complement) are the subcategories.

The feature structures of the taxonomy contain both syntactic and semantic information; in this chapter we have restricted ourselves to the syntactic information. The top level feature structure contains two complex features, the dependency relations *subj* and *p-adjunct*. The embedded feature structure for the dependency relation *subj* has four features: *Cat* (with the value of a syntactic category) is the top level category of the *subj* dependent; HP (Head Precedence—with value *before* or *after*) is the linear precedence of the dependent with respect to the head; LP (Linear Position—with the value of any integer greater than zero) is the linear position of the dependent with respect to the other dependents with the same HP; finally, *Iter* is an interval with the minimum and maximum number of times that this dependency relation can be instantiated for a node of this subcategory. When *Iter* is 0..1, the relation can be optionally instantiated; when *Iter* is 0..0, the relation cannot be instantiated; when Iter is 1..1, the relation must be instantiated once and only once; when Iter is 0..#, the relation can be instantiated an indefinite number of times (including none). The position in the taxonomy depends on the actual values of the following features: the inclusion of the intervals (*Iter*), the hierarchy of dependency relations, and semantic concepts (the latter two are outside the scope of this paper).

The subcategories in the taxonomy of Figure A1 represent four classes of verbs: (i) impersonal verbs *Vimp* are subjectless verbs (e.g., the Italian *piove*, 'it rains, it is raining') (note that they do not constrain the number of p-adjuncts; *In inverno piove su ogni regione d'Italia*, 'In winter it rains in every region in Italy'); (ii) intransitive/transitive verbs *Vi-t* are verbs with an optional object (e.g., *eat* in *John ate an apple* or *John ate*); (iii) absolute transitive verbs *Vt* are verbs with a mandatory object (e.g., *devour, destroy, instruct*); (iv) optionally transitive verbs with a sentential complement *Vt-comp* (e.g., *tell* in *John told his wife that Sara was sick*, or *John told that Sara was sick*) (note that the object precedes the sentential complement when both are present (LP constraint));

(v) verbs with a sentential complement and no object V_{comp} (e.g., *hear* in *Tom heard the gossip was true*) (note that most of the verbs in *Vcomp* are ambiguous between *Vcomp* and *Vt* (cf. *Tom heard the gossip*)).

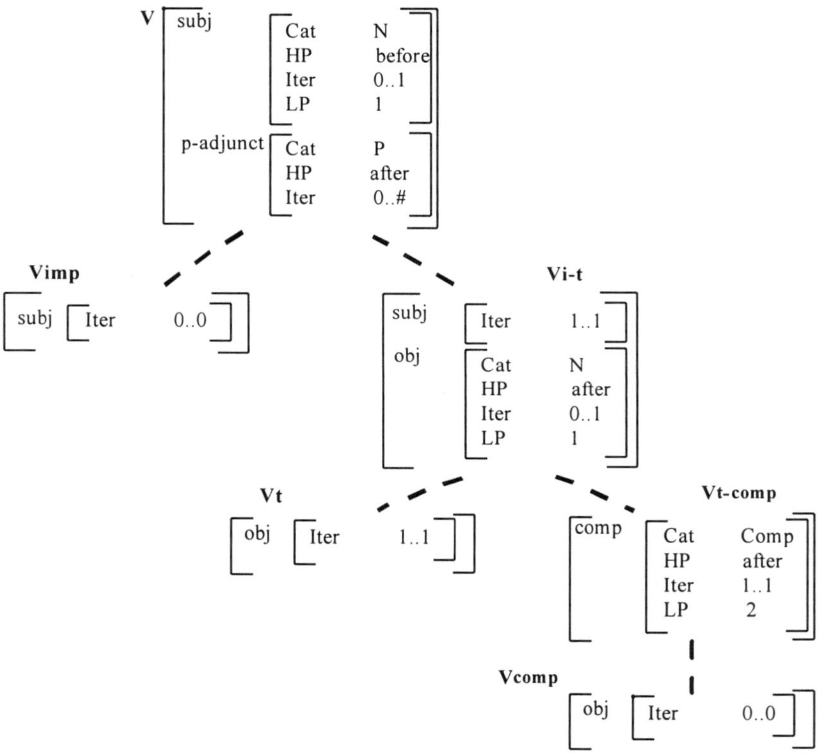

FIGURE A1: A fragment of the verb taxonomy of an HDG.

Top level categories present loose constraints that are common to all the subcategories. All the other nodes represent subcategories that are sets of lexical entries. An HDG is a set of taxonomies, a set of root categories, i.e., those categories that can be the root of a dependency tree, and a lexicon, which associates the words with the subcategories of the taxonomies.

An HDG states the constraints that a dependency tree of a sentence must satisfy in order to be well-formed. In particular, if *s* is a sentence, a dependency tree of *s* is a tree such that:

1. the nodes are triples <C, w, p>, where *C* is one of the syntactic categories, *w* is a word of the sentence of category *C*, and *p* is the input position of *w* in *s*;

2. a node N has left dependents and right dependents with a certain configuration (see Figure A2) if and only if the configuration of relations satisfy the constraints of the grammar, in terms of precedences (features HP and LP) and number of iterations for a relation (*Iter*);

3. it satisfies the *condition of projectivity* with respect to the order in s, that is, if a word a_i depends directly on a_j, and a_k intervenes between them (i<k<j or j<k<i), then either a_k depends on a_i or a_k depends on a_j (see Figure A3). Intuitively, the condition of projectivity states that a dependent is never separated from its governor by anything other than another dependent, together with its subtree, or by a dependent of its own;

4. the root is a word a_s, such that the category of a_s is a root category.

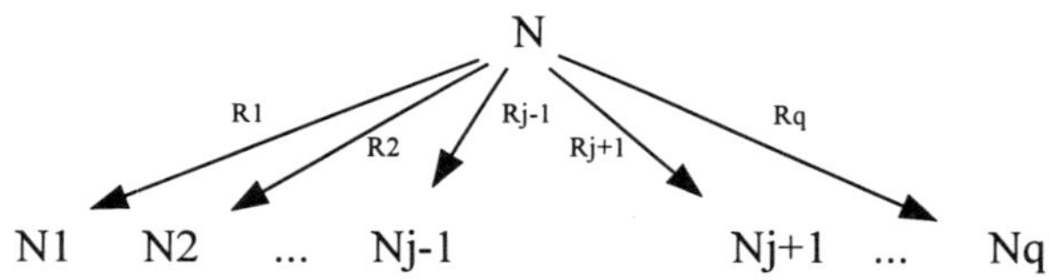

FIGURE A2: A node and its dependents.

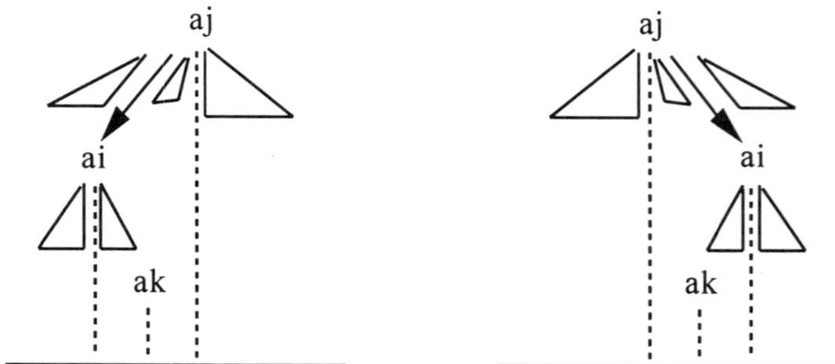

FIGURE A3: The condition of projectivity.

The dependency tree in Figure 1a (p. 293) satisfies the constraints posed by the simple taxonomy in Figure A1, if we assume an HDG with a verb as the root category, a lexicon where *chef* and *fish* are nouns, *the* and *a* are determiners, and *cooked* is of category *Vi-t* or *Vt* (cf. Figure A1 above), and three taxonomies of verbs, nouns and determiners.

The HDG formalism allows wide coverage grammars in a concise form, especially in free word order languages where linear order is only a matter of preference and the number of productions to account for all the legal permutations of words would be enormous.

10

Parsing as Incremental Restructuring

Suzanne Stevenson

Abstract

A prevalent trend in modeling human sentence processing has been to account for both initial attachment preferences and reanalysis behaviors with minimal extensions to a presumed set of initial parsing operations. Here, an entirely different formulation of the initial attachment and revision processes is suggested. Rather than assuming that all parsing is (as much as possible) initial attachment, the opposite approach is advocated: that all parsing—even initial attachment—is restructuring. The realization of parsing as restructuring arises from a set of independently motivated computational assumptions within the competitive attachment architecture, a hybrid connectionist model of the human sentence processor. Central to the model is a unique parallel attachment operation that simultaneously attaches the current input phrase, while reattaching previously structured phrases. Within this model, reanalysis is not a separate process or module, but rather a side effect of the primary means of forming syntactic structures. The ease of performing possible reanalyses is therefore determined by the same conditions, such as recency and lexical preferences, that affect initial attachments. Furthermore, independently motivated constraints on the network structure determine the allowable syntactic configurations that may undergo restructuring within the competitive attachment operation. The model thus also provides a computational explanation of garden-path sentences, in which automatic reanalysis is impossible.

1 Introduction

Models of the human sentence processing mechanism (HSPM) have traditionally focused on explaining initial preferences in response to a structural ambiguity. More recently, the emphasis has shifted to a detailed determination of the behavior of the HSPM when faced with an input that does not conform with its initial interpretation. The HSPM varies in its response to inputs that force it to revise its preferred analysis, exhibiting a range of slight to moderate

J.D. Fodor and F. Ferreira (eds.), Reanalysis in Sentence Processing, 327–363.

difficulty within recoverable misanalyses, to severe garden paths. Building on theories that specify the initially preferred structures, much current research investigates the conditions under which those structures may be successfully revised or discarded, and an alternative analysis brought into focus. This shift in attention has given rise to a number of diverse models of the reanalysis phase of sentence processing. Although they vary in precise details, it is instructive to divide these models into a few general classes based on the number and type of parsing mechanisms they rely on.

The first, and most common, general approach to accounting for reanalysis behavior proposes an explicit set of revision operations distinct from the initial parsing mechanism of the HSPM (e.g., Abney, 1989; Frazier & Clifton, 1996; Lewis, 1993; Lombardo, 1995; Pritchett, 1992; Sturt & Crocker, 1996). The separation of the two processes enables a clear formulation of what conditions allow the reanalysis routines to be successfully applied, and what costs those revisions incur. The disadvantage of this approach is that there are two distinct types of parsing mechanisms: operations which establish the initial attachments of an input phrase within the parse tree, and operations which restructure the current tree when necessary.[1]

A second class of reanalysis models avoids the problem of dual structuring mechanisms by prohibiting revision operations within the HSPM. The goal is to enhance the initial analysis process of the parser so that separate restructuring operations are unnecessary. One approach adds routines to rank and prune the multiple initial analyses of an ambiguous input (e.g., Gibson, 1991; Gorrell, 1987; Inoue & Fodor, 1995). An entirely different proposal details the diagnostic abilities (and limitations) of the HSPM in response to an error (Fodor & Inoue, 1994). Both types of approaches succeed in limiting the parser to a single structure building mechanism. However, they achieve this by proposing a second type of process—a filtering or diagnostic procedure—again adding to the repertoire of parsing mechanisms in order for the models to account for reanalysis behavior.

The final class of models—the recent constraint-based proposals—avoids multiple mechanisms of any type, by assuming that all alternative analyses are

[1] In this class of model, the distinguishing aspect of the two mechanisms may be different restrictions on attachment operations rather than different attachment operations in themselves. For example, in Frazier & Clifton (1996), separate structure building primitives may not be necessary, but the operation of those primitives in the initial attachment and reanalysis processes is constrained by necessarily different principles: Minimal Attachment for the former, and Minimal Revisions for the latter.

differentially activated during the parse of the input (e.g., MacDonald, 1994; MacDonald *et al.*, 1994; Spivey-Knowlton & Sedivy, 1995; Trueswell, 1996; Trueswell *et al.*, 1994). There is no special revision process, since reanalysis is simply a matter of increasing the activation of an already existing alternative. Neither is there an extra 'filter' to explicitly weed out excess alternatives or to constrain which less-preferred alternatives may be subsequently adopted—the ease of recovering from a misanalysis is determined by the level of activation of the alternative that must be adopted. A severe garden path occurs when the activation level of the necessary structure falls too low (Trueswell, 1996). Although this class of models achieves uniformity of mechanism, in other aspects it is highly unrestricted. Of particular relevance here, there is as yet no precise procedure proposed that can predict whether a misanalysis will cause a severe garden path effect or not.

We can see from this overview that effective models of reanalysis behavior have thus far involved the positing of additional types of parsing mechanisms. Furthermore, although attention has shifted from initial attachment preferences to reanalysis behavior, the primacy of initial parsing *mechanisms* has prevailed. Researchers have universally attempted to keep initial structuring routines intact within models of reanalysis. In fact, a prevalent trend has been to eschew a distinct revision component and to account for all parsing behavior with minimal extensions to a presumed set of initial parsing operations.

This chapter suggests an entirely different formulation of the initial attachment and revision processes. Rather than assuming that all parsing is (as much as possible) initial attachment, the opposite approach is advocated: that all parsing—even initial attachment—is *restructuring*.[2] The realization of parsing as restructuring arises from a set of independently motivated computational assumptions within the competitive attachment architecture, a hybrid connectionist model of the HSPM (Stevenson, 1993a; 1994a; 1994b). At a high level, the restructuring process in the model can be viewed as a consequence of a truly incremental approach to interpretation. Since unfilled potential attachment sites in the network make (at least weak) default assumptions, even initial attachment requires the revision of earlier structural commitments. As a

[2] A careful reading of Fodor & Inoue (1994) reveals much in common with the approach to be described here. Although they conclude the description of their diagnosis model with an argument for why it can be considered to use only initial parsing mechanisms, the initial attachment operation they propose (Attach Anyway) is highly non-standard. In fact, it incorporates the ability to build ungrammatical structures, provoke the breaking of attachments, and trigger its iterative application under the guide of the diagnosis mechanism. This proposal seems to be a short step away from the type of single automatic restructuring mechanism proposed here.

result, incorporating each new input phrase into the current parse tree is a process of reanalysis.

This novel formulation of the parsing process has three key consequences for modeling the HSPM, each of which will be briefly previewed here. First, the model yields a truly unified mechanism for both initial attachments and unproblematic reanalyses: there is a single massively parallel attachment operation that attaches the current input phrase and *concurrently* revises earlier attachments. Because this restructuring operation is the only parsing operation, there is no dichotomy in normal parsing between the initial attachment and the revision processes. By definition, exactly the same factors that affect the initial attachment for a phrase—for example, recency and lexical preferences—also affect the possible restructuring of an analysis. Furthermore, this property entails that there is no need for a separate error-detection or inferencing stage to reanalysis (as in, e.g., Frazier & Clifton, 1996; Frazier & Rayner, 1982; and Fodor & Inoue, 1994), since reanalysis is the single automatic operation of the parser.

Second, the domain of the restructuring operation is determined by independent processing principles. The nodes of the connectionist network correspond to parse tree nodes. General constraints imposed by the distributed competition mechanism restrict the allowable configurations of the nodes in the network, so that only a limited range of attachments is accessible to the current input phrase. Any structure that can be formed from the set of accessible attachments is predicted to correspond to a possible reanalysis. A revision that falls outside of this domain of restructuring—one in which the needed attachments involve inaccessible nodes—incurs a conscious garden path. The independently required network restrictions eliminate the need for explicit principles within the model that determine whether a reanalysis induces a severe garden path or not (e.g., cf. the Thematic Overlay Effect, Inoue & Fodor, 1995; structural determinism, Gorrell, 1995; the On-Line Locality Constraint, Pritchett, 1992).

Finally, because of the parallel distributed control of the parser, the restructuring operation applies concurrently at multiple potential attachment sites, so that all possible attachments and re-attachments are attempted simultaneously. The model thus avoids the disadvantage of an explicit serial ordering of attempted attachment or revision operations, as in Abney (1989) or Sturt & Crocker (1996). For example, Sturt & Crocker (1996) must determine some *a priori* threshold for maintaining an analysis, leading to situations in which the parser may give up a mediocre analysis without guarantee of finding a better one, or conversely may maintain a mediocre analysis that it could have improved on.

The concurrency of the competitive attachment model also has an advantage over race-based models (e.g., Frazier & Fodor, 1978; Gorrell, 1987; McRoy & Hirst, 1990), since different analyses explicitly compete with each other and therefore can affect each other's activation (for evidence of competition in ambiguity resolution, see MacDonald, 1994). Furthermore, because there is a single concurrent restructuring mechanism with these two properties—the lack of a hard-coded ordering of attempted attachments, and the interacting competition of all accessible attachments—there is also no ordering of initial attachment *before* reanalysis. Thus, attachments that necessitate reanalysis are not inherently dispreferred; we will examine data that bears on this issue, favoring the competitive attachment approach.

Following a description of the relevant aspects of the computational model, each of the above consequences of the architecture will be discussed.

2 Competition and Restructuring

The competitive attachment parser is an implemented hybrid connectionist model that integrates simple symbolic processing with numeric spreading activation. The model builds syntactic analyses by activating network processing nodes that directly represent a parse tree structure; that is, the nodes of the network correspond one-to-one to nodes and links in a parse tree. Because many configurations of the nodes may represent grammatical substructures, competition for activation is a crucial mechanism for determining the attachments that comprise the preferred analysis at any point in processing. This section will describe the basic functioning of the parser and the constraints on the competition mechanism that lead to the unique restructuring operation.

2.1 The Parsing Network

Syntactic structures are created in the network by dynamically activating two types of processing nodes in response to the input. The first type represents the nodes of a single $\overline{X}$ projection. These phrasal nodes are allocated from a pool of $\overline{X}$ templates, which represent syntactic phrases as a set of processing nodes (X, X′, XP) that are connected in the network. The phrasal nodes have symbolic features (e.g., category or subcategorization frames) that are initialized based on the features of the head of the phrase, which are retrieved from the lexicon. Figure 1 shows a sample $\overline{X}$ template and its instantiation. Additionally, the phrasal nodes are given an initial maximal activation of 1.0, which decays over time. (All processing nodes necessarily incorporate an aspect of decay into their activation function; see Stevenson, 1994a. This leads to general recency effects in the parser, which will be discussed in Section 3.)

FIGURE 1: An $\overline{X}$ template and its instantiation as a verb phrase.

The second type of processing node encodes the potential attachment relations between nodes in different $\overline{X}$ phrases. The grammaticality of attachments is determined by licensing conditions (cf. Abney, 1989; Gorrell, 1995; Pritchett, 1992; Weinberg, 1995; among others), which are primarily satisfied within a sisterhood relation. Therefore, attachment nodes are established between two phrasal nodes that are potential sisters in the parse tree. For example, the attachment of an NP as the complement of a verb is represented by an attachment node connected to the NP node and to the V node, as shown in Figure 2.

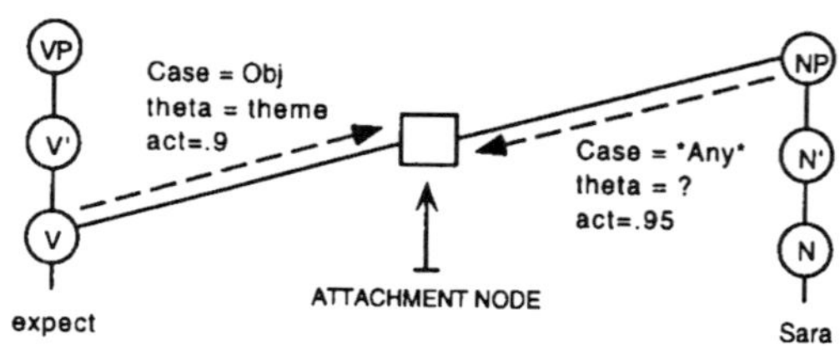

FIGURE 2: An example attachment of an NP as a complement to a verb.

Figure 3 more generally illustrates the basic $\overline{X}$ relations (with ordering among nodes as in English), and their representation using phrasal and attachment nodes in the network. In this and all figures, the level of activation of an attachment node is indicated by how dark it is—i.e., white is inactive and black fully activated. Each type of $\overline{X}$ node serves as an attachment site for a phrase (an XP node) to attach to. The X node of a phrase is the attachment site for a single complement to its right. The X′ node is the attachment site for a specifier to its left, and may also be the attachment site for a complement to its right, if the head of the phrase takes two internal arguments. The XP node is the attachment site for modifiers (adjuncts) to the right. Each XP node in turn (except for the root of the partial parse tree) must activate an attachment to an X, X′, or XP node, by which its phrase is licensed as a complement, specifier, or modifier. Thus, in Figure 3, WP is licensed as a modifier of XP, YP is licensed as a specifier of X′, and ZP is licensed as a complement of X.

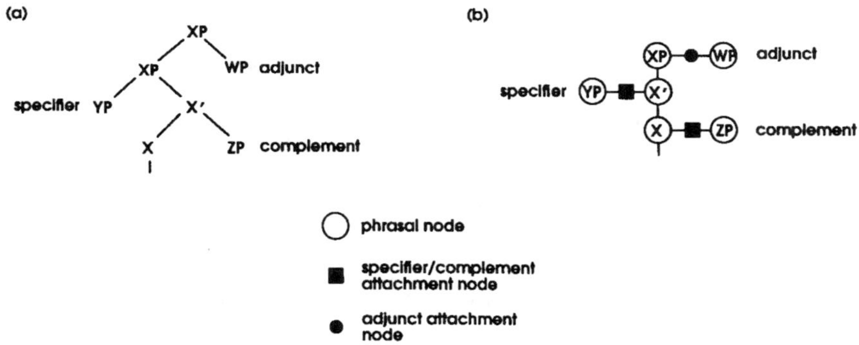

FIGURE 3: The structure of an example $\overline{X}$ phrase (a) and its representation in the competitive attachment network (b).

When an input token is processed, the parser retrieves its lexical entry from the lexicon, activates an $\overline{X}$ template, and instantiates it with the features from the lexical entry. Next, the parser allocates attachment nodes to represent the potential attachments between the current phrase and previously structured phrasal nodes, as shown in Figure 4. Once the new phrasal nodes are connected to the existing partial parse tree, the network enters its feature passing and spreading activation phase. Grammatical features from the phrasal nodes determine whether an attachment is valid or not; numeric activation levels represent the level of preference for a given attachment alternative. An invalid attachment node—one which receives incompatible features—cannot represent a grammatical attachment in the parse tree, and so becomes inactivated. A valid attachment node determines its level of activation by processing the numeric activation that it receives from each of its two phrasal nodes. This process is an iterative one in which activation is propagated among the nodes in the network, and the activation level of each attachment node gradually becomes fixed. The resulting activation level indicates the strength of preference for establishing an attachment in the current parse tree between the two associated phrasal nodes. The network has settled on a set of attachment decisions when the activation level of each attachment node is either above a certain threshold (the attachment node is 'on'), or below a certain threshold (the attachment node is 'off'). Figure 5 shows the network structure for a complete sentence, and the corresponding parse tree that it represents.

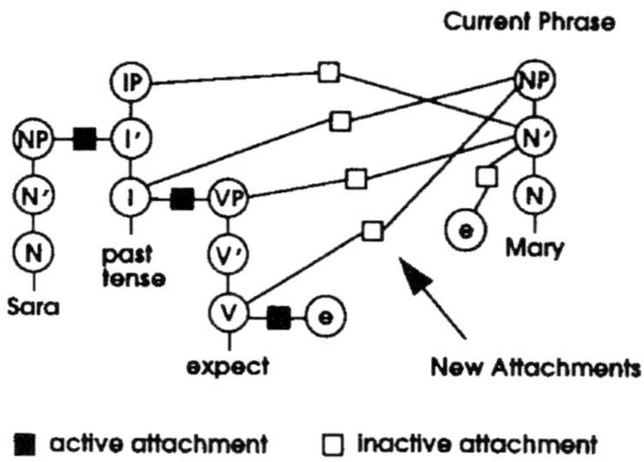

FIGURE 4: The parser allocates new attachment nodes between the current phrase and the existing partial parse tree.

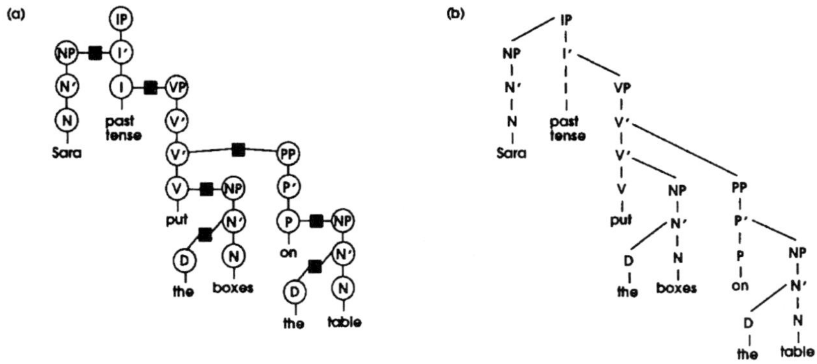

FIGURE 5: An example network structure for a complete sentence (a) and the corresponding parse tree representation (b).

2.2 The Competition Mechanism

The model differs crucially from most other approaches in that there is no central control mechanism that can oversee structure building and directly compare alternative analyses for an ambiguous input (as is required, e.g., to apply heuristics such as Minimal Attachment, as in Frazier, 1978; or to calculate differences in processing loads, as in Gibson, 1991). Here the task of determining the preferred structure must be distributed among the processing nodes of the network. The goal is for activation in the network to be focused onto a consistent set of parse tree attachments, so that the preferred analysis is highly activated and the alternatives are inactive.

One option for focusing activation in the network would be to put inhibitory links between all pairs of mutually exclusive attachment nodes, bringing about direct competition between them. This approach has the disadvantage of complicating the network structure and making its mapping to a parse tree representation less simple and direct. Furthermore, it matches neither our intuitions nor the experimental evidence (MacDonald, 1994; Trueswell, 1996; Trueswell *et al.*, 1993) which indicates that it is properties of the *phrasal nodes* (e.g., subcategorization frames and lexical preferences) that determine the strength, and therefore competitiveness, of an attachment. Instead of viewing competition as direct inhibition between attachments, we more naturally view it as a phrasal node making choices about which attachment is best for it. The competitive attachment model embodies this view by putting the attachment decision process under the direct control of the phrasal nodes. This is accomplished by having each phrasal node use a competitive output function to allocate activation differentially among its attachment nodes. That is, since multiple attachments for a phrasal node may be valid, each phrasal node must determine which of those choices to activate. A phrasal node divides its output activation among its potential attachments, proportional to their current activation level. Attachment nodes with higher activation levels will receive more of the phrasal node's output activation, and attachment nodes with lower activation levels will receive less of the output activation. This competition for a limited resource—the output activation of the phrasal node—brings about indirect inhibition among the attachment nodes, so that only a subset of the nodes is able to become fully activated.

Note that the determination of the final activation level of an attachment node is an iterative process, and one that depends on the input from both its phrasal nodes. In order for an attachment node to become fully active, it must receive the entire output from each of its two phrasal nodes. Specifically, for an attachment node to have a consistent interpretation, the two phrasal nodes connected to it must 'agree' either to turn the attachment node on, by each sending all of its output to the attachment node, or to turn the attachment node off, by neither one sending any of its output to the attachment node. Thus a phrasal node may favor one attachment initially, but later send more activation to a different attachment, because of the propagation of the competitive processing through the network.

This propagation of competitive effects is due to the distributed nature of the attachment competition. Although the competitive attachment process is mediated by individual phrasal nodes, the competition for activation occurs simultaneously at all attachment nodes that are established in the network. This leads to one of the basic results of the model, that both initial attachments (involving newly established attachment nodes that connect to the current phrase) and revision of earlier attachments (involving previously established attachment nodes within the partial parse tree structure represented by the network) are decided on in a single concurrent process. As described thus far, this competitive attachment process is fairly unconstrained. However, the competition mechanism has limitations that arise from its inherent computational weaknesses. The following subsections describe these weaknesses and the restrictions that must be imposed on the network architecture in order for it to be able to correctly parse a grammatical input. These restrictions are responsible for the status of the single attachment mechanism in the parser as a restructuring operation that applies within a limited configurational domain.

2.3 Imprecision of the Competition Mechanism

In order for a particular network configuration to represent a valid partial parse tree, each phrasal node must activate a number of attachment nodes in accordance with its grammatical properties. As discussed above, because every phrase must be licensed in the parse tree, each (non-root) XP node must activate exactly one attachment node to a phrasal node (an X, X′, or XP) that licenses it (see Figure 3). Each specifier and complement site may license at most one attachment node, while adjunct (modifier) sites permit multiple attachments.[3] For simplicity of exposition, we can ignore modifiers here and assume that every phrasal node licenses zero or one sister. Unfortunately, the competitive output function, which determines the amount of activation to output to attachment nodes, is not a very precise mechanism, and cannot be successfully parameterized to activate a variable number of attachments. Specifically, the competitive output function can be tuned to effectively activate exactly one attachment—as needed for an obligatorily transitive verb. But it cannot be adjusted to allow the activation of zero or one attachment node—as needed for an optionally transitive verb, or an obligatorily transitive verb whose complement has not been reached in the input. Since the competitive output function can bring about activation of *one* attachment node, but not *zero or one*, in order for it to allow attachment at all, the function must be parameterized to activate exactly one attachment node *at all times*.

This is potentially problematic, since phrases are activated incrementally as a sentence is processed—that is, a phrasal node may be activated in the parsing network earlier than the phrasal node it will attach to in the final tree. For example, in English, a V node will be activated before the XP node that represents its complement. To accommodate this, the parser allocates a dummy phrasal node, called an *empty node*, which serves as a default node that a phrasal node can activate an attachment to. The attachment to an empty node provides

[3] Complement sites license at most one attachment because multiple arguments each have their own attachment site to mediate the assignment of the individual theta roles. By contrast, since the number of adjuncts is not determinable in advance, an adjunct site must allow for an arbitrary number of attachments (Stevenson, 1995). That is, in Figure 3, the XP node may have multiple WP nodes attached to it, represented by each such modifier phrase activating an attachment node between it and the modified XP node. Adjunct sites therefore use a different competitive output function that allows arbitrary numbers of attachment nodes to be activated.

an attachment node to activate even when no overt phrase is available to attach to. For present purposes, we can think of the activation of the attachment to an empty node as an explicit representation in the network of the lack of an attachment to an overt phrase. This can occur for two reasons: (i) an attachment to that site is not required (e.g., for an (optionally) intransitive verb), or (ii) an attachment is required, but a suitable XP to attach there has not been projected (e.g., for an obligatorily transitive verb, which is activated before its complement is reached in the input).[4]

To maintain uniformity of numeric processing across all phrasal nodes, every phrasal node uses the same competitive output function, which activates exactly one attachment node at all times. Thus, each phrasal node must posit an attachment to an empty node when it is allocated. Figure 6 shows the empty nodes that are automatically activated with each $\overline{X}$ template; each attachment site connects to an attachment node that in turn connects to an empty node. (Empty nodes are labeled *e* in the figures, and are omitted in remaining figures where they are irrelevant.)

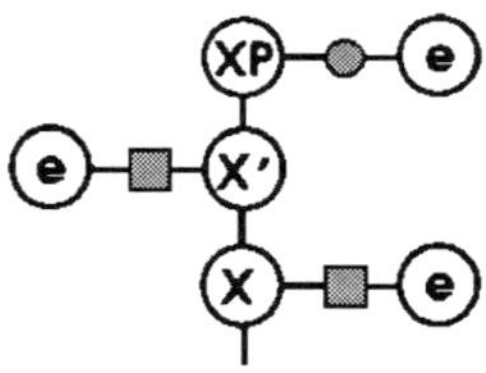

FIGURE 6: Empty nodes are activated in conjunction with every phrase, at each attachment site.

Empty nodes have the same computational properties as an XP node of an overt phrase, and therefore do not extend the parsing mechanisms used in the model. However, because an empty node is just a dummy placeholder for a phrase, it has no overt evidence from the input and thus has only minimal activation. Using the same competitive output function as a non-empty phrasal node, an empty node sends its entire output activation to the single attachment node that it connects to. Because of the weak activation of the empty node, the attachment node also can become only weakly activated. If an empty node occurs in a structural location that does not require attachment of a phrase (e.g., as the

---

4 Empty nodes are also used in the parser to represent null elements—i.e., empty categories or traces. See Stevenson (1993b, 1994a) for the effects of the active binding mechanism on filler-gap preferences and reanalysis.

complement to an intransitive verb), a grammatical network structure may include the attachment to the empty node. However, often an attachment to an empty node is a temporary 'default' attachment that is replaced in the attachment competition by an attachment to an overt phrase projected from the input. This occurs, for example, in the case of a verb which takes either an optional or obligatory complement, before the complement phrase is activated by the input. If an overt phrase competes with an empty node for attachment to the same site, the attachment to the more highly activated overt phrase will win the competition over the attachment to the weakly activated empty node. Note that if the attachment to the empty node turns off, the empty node is deactivated as well, since it has lost its connection to the rest of the parse tree.

The requirement that the competitive output function have a 'default' attachment to activate is thus the underlying reason that even initial attachment in the parser involves reanalysis. An attachment to an empty node acts as a default attachment hypothesis for an attachment site, which must be overridden in order to attach an overt phrase at that site. The initial attachment of a phrase to an attachment site has to compete with the default attachment to an empty node at that site, and therefore involves a revision of structure. The attachment of the overt phrase takes more or less time, depending on the strength of the attachment of the empty node to that site. Although all empty nodes have the same weak activation level, the activation level of the attachment to an empty node depends also on the properties of its other phrasal node, such as whether the attachment is optional or obligatory.

It should be emphasized that the use of empty nodes is independently motivated by the requirements of the competitive output function. Furthermore, they are the minimal mechanism necessary to support the aspect of processing that necessitates them—i.e., the requirement to always activate an attachment node. The use of these 'default' attachments is therefore independently justified and not just established to effect some particular psycholinguistic behavior.

2.4 Locality of Competition

While the necessity of default attachments means that all attachment entails restructuring, another computational limitation of the competition mechanism leads to a precise specification of the domain of the restructuring operation. The second limitation is the inherent locality of the competition mechanism. A model with inhibitory links could establish direct competition between any pair of attachment nodes. By contrast, in the competitive attachment model, competition can only be brought about as a consequence of a single phrasal node choosing among its possible attachment nodes. Since only attachments that connect to a single phrasal node can compete with each other, the competition mechanism is unable to rule out the simultaneous activation of more distantly connected attachment nodes that are incompatible in a valid syntactic structure (e.g., those that would correspond to 'crossing links' in the parse tree represented by the network). In order to prevent invalid parse trees, the incremental allocation of the network of potential attachments must conform to the Right Edge Restriction: new attachment nodes can only represent an attachment between the current phrase and the right edge of the developing parse tree (cf. similar restrictions in Abney, 1989, and Sturt & Crocker, 1996).

Maintaining the required network structure to support this restriction entails the use of a parsing stack. The stack is a single phrasal node that can activate multiple attachments; a phrase puts itself on the stack by activating an attachment node that is connected to the stack. Therefore, as with empty nodes, the use of a stack entails no extension to the basic processing mechanisms of the parser. The required Right Edge Restriction is enforced by allocating new attachment nodes only between the current input phrase and the right edge of the partial parse tree on top of the stack, as shown in Figure 7. Enforcing this constraint on the network connectivity—at each step in attaching a new input phrase—prevents invalid parse trees that the competition mechanism could not otherwise rule out.

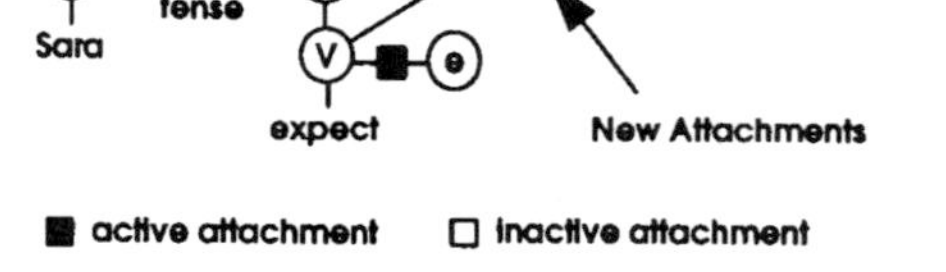

FIGURE 7: The stack node is used to enforce the Right Edge Restriction, by limiting new attachments to connect to the right edge of the partial parse tree on the top of the stack.

Moreover, with the use of empty nodes and the stack, the competitive relationships in the network now completely define a highly constrained set of choices of attachment nodes that can be simultaneously activated in a stable state of the parser. The logical attachment possibilities, an example of which is shown in Figure 8, follow directly from the propagation of local attachment competitions through the restricted network structure. Each phrasal node must activate a single attachment node, and the constrained connectivity of the network now ensures that this local restriction on all of the individual attachment competitions propagates through the network in a globally consistent manner. The logical attachment possibilities necessarily restrict the domain of the restructuring operation of the parser: only attachments that occur within this constrained set of possibilities can participate in the newly formed partial parse tree structure at each step of the incremental analysis of a sentence. Consistency of the parse tree structure cannot be guaranteed if arbitrary restructuring in the network were allowed.

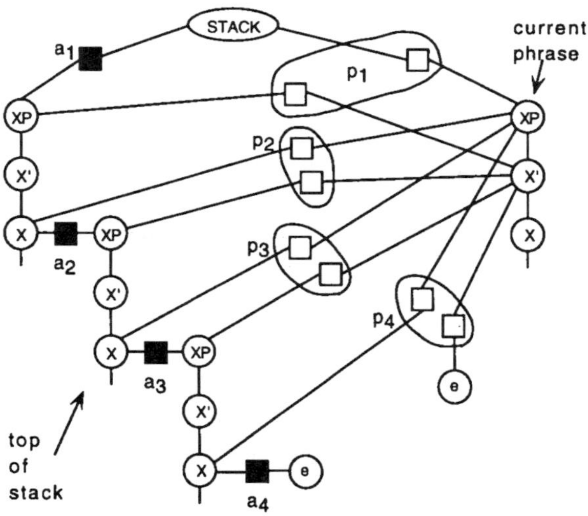

FIGURE 8: One example of competitive relationships in the parallel restructuring operation. Attachments a_1–a_4 were previously activated. To attach the current phrase to the tree on the stack, the following must occur: exactly one of the prior attachments, a_i, must become inactive, and the corresponding pair of attachments, p_i, must become active. This relationship holds for a tree of arbitrary depth on the stack.

Restrictions on the competitive mechanism therefore define a circumscribed set of attachment possibilities that concurrently determine both initial and revised attachments in the parser. The result is a unique parallel restructuring operation that is the sole structural analysis mechanism in the parser. Thus, the competitive attachment model, in contrast to other approaches, uses a single, restricted mechanism to account for preference and reanalysis behavior. The remainder of this chapter will discuss the performance of the model on some key examples from the psycholinguistic literature.

3 Modeling Reanalysis

The preceding section discussed the computational basis of the following properties of the competitive attachment parser, which were first presented in the introduction to this chapter:

1. The model uses a single, unified restructuring mechanism for initial attachment and reanalysis.
2. Computational limitations impose independently motivated constraints on the restructuring mechanism that yield a precisely defined domain of application.
3. All initial and revised attachments compete concurrently, with no externally imposed ordering on attachment possibilities.

This section will discuss illustrative behaviors of the model related to each of these properties.

3.1 Unified Mechanism for Attachment and Reanalysis

The competitive attachment model has a conceptual advantage over other approaches in proposing a single, restrictive parsing mechanism for initial attachment and reanalysis. A single mechanism approach also makes a strong claim concerning the factors that affect initial preferences as well as the ease and choice of revision. Since there is a single attachment process, exactly the same factors necessarily affect the time course and preferences exhibited in both initial attachment and reanalysis behavior. If we observe a certain factor at work in one case, we would expect it to play a role in the other. If we fail to find similar factors affecting the two processes, this is evidence against the model. Here we will examine two different factors that have been shown to affect human initial preference and reanalysis behavior—recency and lexical preferences—and demonstrate how they shape the behavior of the model in analogous ways. It will be seen that the available evidence supports the single mechanism approach of the competitive attachment model.

3.1.1 Recency

The ease of making attachments to more recently established syntactic structure has long been incorporated into theories of initial attachment preferences in a variety of formulations—e.g., Right Association (Kimball, 1973); Late Closure (Frazier, 1978); Recency Preference (Gibson, 1991); or decay of activation (Stevenson, 1990; 1994a). The effect of recency in the competitive attachment parser follows from the necessary element of decay in the activation function for a phrasal node. (See Stevenson, 1994a, for a detailed motivation of the decay mechanism and for additional discussion surrounding the following examples.) We will first see how decay influences initial attachment preferences in the parser. For example, in the following sentence, the particle up has two attachment possibilities, to the verb *called* and to the verb *smashed* (example from Church, 1980):

(1) I called the guy who smashed my brand new car up.

Although sentence (1) is ambiguous, it is very difficult to interpret it as meaning *I called up the guy who smashed my brand new car*, which requires the attachment of the particle to the more distant site (*called*). In the competitive attachment model, the phrasal nodes in the VP of *called* have decayed significantly, due to the length of the postverbal NP. The more recent attachment site (*smashed*) has more activation to output to the attachment node connecting to the particle *up*, and the attachment within the subordinate verb phrase therefore wins the attachment competition.

Accounting for recency effects in terms of decay is very different from accounting for them in terms of a disambiguation principle that only applies in cases of ambiguity (e.g., Frazier, 1978; Gibson, 1991). In the competitive attachment model, the same decay mechanism explains recency effects even in cases where the input is not ambiguous (Stevenson, 1994a). This conforms to the observed facts, but was previously unexplained by the models of locality effects mentioned earlier. (Though see Hawkins, 1994, for a very different type of approach that does capture absolute locality effects, and also Frazier & Clifton, 1996, for a more recent proposal within the Garden Path approach in terms of visibility.) For example, the attachment of *a rotten driver* is unambiguous in both of the following two sentences (unlike the particle *up*, which has an ambiguous attachment in sentence (1) above):

(2) I called the guy a rotten driver.

(3) I called the guy who smashed my brand new car a rotten driver.

The contrast in acceptability between sentences (2) and (3), with the second much more difficult than the first, indicates that increased distance between the current phrase and its only possible attachment site can cause processing difficulty. This effect receives a straightforward account in the competitive attachment model. The earlier an attachment site has been allocated, the more its activation has decayed, and the longer it takes for an attachment node to that site to accrue sufficient activation to participate in a stable configuration of the network.

Next we can explore the role of recency in determining the preferred reanalysis when the parser has more than one option for revising an initial preference. Since the single attachment mechanism of the parser also performs any revision of structure, the decay of phrasal node activation also affects the choice of reanalysis to make. Consider the following example from Stevenson (1994b), in which an ambiguous initial substring of a sentence has a main verb (*believes*) and a subordinate verb (*suspect*) that each have an NP/S subcategorization ambiguity—i.e., both verbs can take either an NP or a clausal complement:

(4) Sara believes the report that women suspect Laika to have...

The evidence for an IP (the word *to*) triggers reanalysis in the parser. There are two choices for that revision, indicated by the following two possible continuations:

(5) Sara believes the report that women suspect [Laika to have committed the crime].

(6) Sara believes the report that [women suspect Laika] to have been published.

In both of these sentences, the initial attachment of a postverbal NP as object of the verb must be broken and replaced by the attachment of a clausal complement. In sentence (5), the attachment of *Laika* is replaced by the attachment of *Laika to have committed the crime* as complement of the lower verb *suspect*. In sentence (6), the attachment of *the report* is replaced by the attachment of *the report to have been published* as complement of the higher verb *believe*. Although I know of no experimental evidence that bears on this issue, my intuitions are that sentence (5), in which the reanalysis involves the lower, more recent verb, is strongly preferred (cf. similar assumptions made by Sturt & Crocker, 1996). The competitive attachment parser explains this preference of choosing the reanalysis that involves more recent, and therefore less decayed, nodes. Note that this occurs for exactly the same reason that the model prefers to make *initial* attachments to more recent material. In both initial and revised attachments, the decay mechanism has the side effect of making attachments to more recently allocated phrasal nodes more competitive.

In cases where there is a single reanalysis possibility—i.e., a single alternative analysis for the parser to adopt when its initial preference is proven wrong—recency effects also obtain. For example, Frazier & Rayner (1982) compared pairs of sentences with an NP/S ambiguity analogous to the following, in which the second differs only from the first in having a lengthier ambiguous region (the postverbal NP):

(7) Mary knows the answer was correct.

(8) Mary knows the answer to the difficult physics problem was correct.

Even though in both cases the parser has only a single option for successfully revising its initial preference, Frazier & Rayner (1982) found increased reading times in the disambiguating region for sentences with a longer postverbal NP (sentence (8)). In the competitive attachment model, decay again affects the revision involving an earlier attachment site. The observed increase in reading time corresponds to an increase in the time it takes for the network to settle on a consistent set of attachment decisions at the point of processing the word *was* (from 24 iterations of network processing after a short NP to 31 iterations after a long NP).

Ferreira & Henderson (1991) investigated the source of length effects in ambiguity resolution, and found that it is not the complexity of the ambiguous phrase per se, but rather the distance between the head of the ambiguous phrase and the disambiguating word that affects processing difficulty.[5] This is

[5] Ferreira & Henderson (1991) used a different ambiguity in their experiments, but I will continue with the NP/S ambiguity for consistency of presentation. Of course, this makes the assumption that effects of length in attaching ambiguous NPs are consistent across different types of constructions. In any case, this is the prediction made by the competitive attachment parser.

precisely the case in the competitive attachment model. For example, in the contrast between sentences (7) and (8), the number of words occurring after the head of the NP, rather than the precise structure of the intervening material, determines the degree to which the nodes involved in the necessary reanalysis have decayed (in this case, the V node of the main verb and the NP node for the ambiguous NP).

Ferreira & Henderson (1991) also found that material prior to the head of the ambiguous NP did not affect processing in the disambiguating region. This follows in the competitive attachment model as a consequence of the interaction between the decay mechanism and the Right Edge Restriction. Because only nodes along the right edge of the developing parse tree are accessible for later attachment, nodes within the parse tree (not on this frontier) are irrelevant to new attachment competitions—intuitively, these phrases are 'closed' (cf. Church, 1980; Ford *et al.*, 1982; Frazier, 1978; Gibson, 1991). Nodes on the right frontier of the tree, however, participate in current attachment competitions, counteracting the effect of decay by increasing their activation level.[6] Thus, the activation level of phrases depends not just on when they are allocated, but also on where they are attached in the tree. The interaction of these two effects results in phrasal nodes being more to less activated from the bottom to the top of the accessible (right-edge) frontier of the parse tree. Since prenominal modifiers do not affect the configuration of accessible attachments along the right frontier of the tree, they do not contribute to a recency effect in a sentence such as the following:

(9) Mary knows the very difficult physics problem was confusing.

In this example, the activation level of the nodes corresponding to the main verb and the postverbal NP would be the same as in example (7) above, and both sentences are easily processed.

3.1.2 Lexical Preferences

Beginning with Ford *et al.* (1982), researchers have also noted the important influence of individual lexical preferences on attachment decisions. Also in this area, the competitive attachment parser, because of its single attachment mechanism, provides a unified account of the effects of lexical preferences in

---

6 The activation level of a phrase necessarily depends in part on the activation level of the attachments it participates in—i.e., the spread of activation in the network is actually two-way between phrasal nodes and attachment nodes. See Stevenson (1994b) for details.

both initial attachment and in reanalysis. Lexical strength is represented by the weights on the links between a phrasal node and its potential attachments, and these weights reflect the frequency of a phrasal node licensing a certain category of XP attachment. This means that, as with recency, lexical preferences always affect activation levels, not just in an overt choice between ambiguous attachments.

Continuing the example of a verb with an NP/S subcategorization ambiguity, we can observe the operation of the model in first attaching the postverbal NP, and then in revising that attachment given evidence of a clausal complement. Figure 9 illustrates the attachment choices when processing the postverbal NP in *Mary expected Sara to come.*

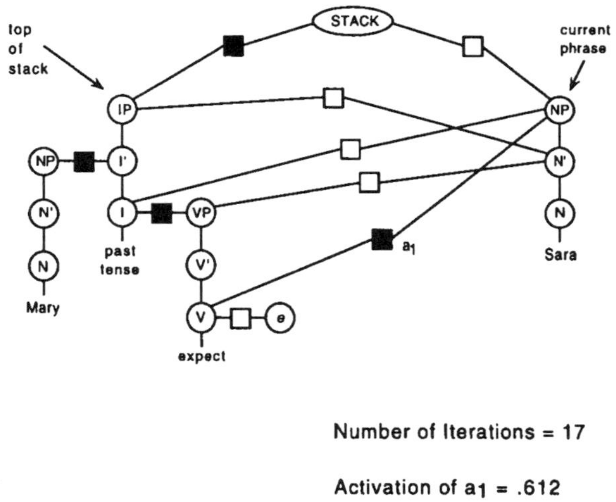

FIGURE 9: The attachment competition at the point of processing the NP following a verb with an NP/S subcategorization ambiguity.

In the competitive attachment model, the initial attachment of the NP is not ambiguous, at least not in the sense of choosing between an attachment as the object of the verb or as the subject of the clausal complement of the verb. The NP node activated by *Sara* can attach as the complement of the verb, or can push itself onto the stack. Attachment as the subject of a clausal complement of *expected* is not an option, since there is no evidence in the input of a subordinate clause (Stevenson, 1994b). The V node in turn has a choice between activating an attachment to the NP, or to an empty node (the 'default' attachment, as described in section 2). Recall that the attachment from the V to the empty node has only weak activation because the empty node has no overt evidence, and so the V node favors sending more activation to the attachment to the NP. The attachment node between the V node and the NP node will always become the most highly activated attachment in this situation, as long as the verb can take an NP complement.

Experimental evidence reveals that a strong preference for a sentential complement (i.e., an S-biased verb) can slow reading times at the postverbal NP in an NP/S ambiguity (Garnsey *et al.*, 1996; Trueswell *et al.*, 1993).[7] Given no option of attaching the NP as a subordinate subject, how does the model account for this fact? If the attachment of the NP to the verb is not competing with an attachment of the NP to a subordinate clause, then why does the S-bias affect the activation of the initial NP-to-V attachment? Recall that the NP must compete with an attachment to an empty node. As the verb divides its output proportionally between the attachment to the empty node and the attachment to the NP, the relative weight on the link to the NP attachment affects the proportion of activation that is sent to it and to the empty node. For an S-bias verb, the weight will be less than for an equi-biased verb. Thus, a verb with a strong S-bias will send less activation to an attachment to an NP node, even when there is no attachment to a sentential complement (IP or CP node) competing with it. Decreasing the preference for an NP complement therefore increases the time it takes for the NP to make an attachment to the V node (from 17 to 20 iterations of network processing).

Again we would expect, given the single mechanism approach of the model, that the same lexical preference effects are evident in the revision of this initial attachment configuration. Garnsey *et al.* (1996) report additional results relevant to this situation. They found that reading times at the point of disambiguation were longer for NP-bias verbs than for S-bias verbs. Here again the competitive attachment model accounts for the data. Given an NP-bias verb, the new potential attachment of the subordinate clause has to compete with a

---

[7] The data concerning processing of the NP/S ambiguity given differential subcategorization biases is quite complex, and space precludes a detailed analysis here—see Garnsey *et al.* (1996) for a thorough investigation of the effects and a comprehensive discussion of related studies. Although several effects reported in the literature were not replicated in their larger study (e.g., the *that*-bias effect found in Trueswell *et al.*, 1993), the increase in reading times on the postverbal NP following a strongly S-biased verb was a fairly robust finding.

strong NP attachment; Figure 10 illustrates the network at this step in processing. Note that there is only one choice of reanalysis to perform; however, the strength of the lexical preference for the initial attachment (of the NP to the verb) and the strength of preference for the new attachment (of the IP to the verb) interact to influence the time course of reanalysis. The attachments appropriate to the revision will become activated, but it takes longer to do so for an NP-biased verb compared to an equi-biased verb (30 versus 24 iterations of the network). By contrast, given an S-bias verb, the time to successfully make the revision is shorter (22 iterations), and is in fact getting close to the same amount of time as to initially attach the NP in this case.

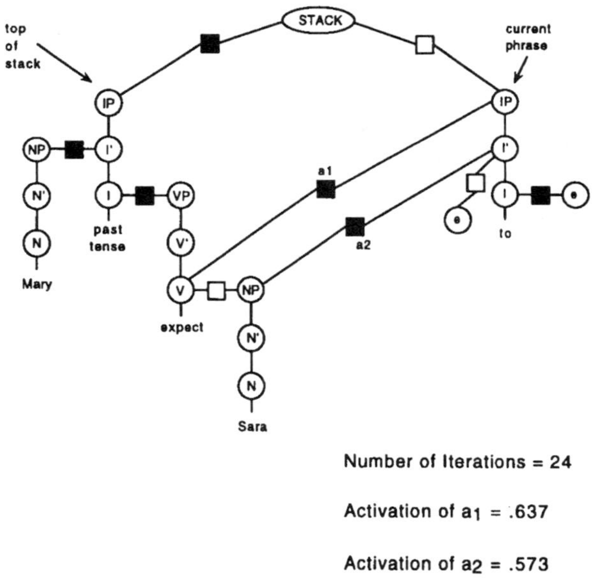

FIGURE 10: The attachment competition at the point of processing the IP following a verb with an NP/S subcategorization ambiguity.

Both in the initial attachment of the NP and in the necessary reanalysis, the model has been shown to exhibit the absolute effects of lexical preferences, analogous to the absolute effects of recency demonstrated above. The model also easily accounts for the effects of lexical preferences in choosing between two possible initial attachments, since the difference in proportion of output activation sent to each depends directly on the lexical preference information. In fact, recency and lexical preferences typically interact in these cases to yield a range of behavior; see Stevenson (1994b) for additional examples.

3.2 Restricted Domain of Restructuring

The discussion until now has assumed that necessary reanalyses are possible within the competitive attachment model. This is clearly not the case in general, given the rather severe restrictions on allowable attachment configurations detailed in section 2. Here we turn to a description of the types of reanalyses that are possible within the automatic attachment (restructuring) operation of the parser, as well as those that are not amenable to analysis without recourse to special recovery procedures. The model can perform reanalyses that conform to a restricted attachment configuration, one whose properties hold across different constructions that instantiate the general structural form. Within those possible reanalyses, the parser experiences a range of mild to moderate difficulty (exhibited in increased number of iterations to determine a consistent attachment configuration), depending on factors such as recency and lexical preference, described above. On the other hand, the model is stymied, mimicking severe garden path effects, when required reanalyses do not conform to the constraints on the restructuring mechanism. We will examine each of these situations in turn.

3.2.1 Easy Reanalyses

The possible reanalyses are precisely defined in the competitive attachment model as those involving competing attachments along the right edge of the partial parse tree on the top of the stack. Only revisions of this nature can be processed within the normal attachment operation of the parser. This type of reanalysis has been illustrated on the following sentence; see Figure 10:

(10) Mary expected Sara to come.

Note that the Garden Path theory of Frazier and her colleagues (Frazier, 1978; Frazier & Rayner, 1982; Frazier & Clifton, 1996) claims that this sentence causes a garden path effect, but one from which it is easy to recover. By contrast, there is no such garden path effect in the competitive attachment model. A reanalysis of the initially preferred attachment of the NP to the verb is required, but this is accomplished within the normal attachment operation of the parser. The network is able to revise its initial preference because the competitions of the new attachment nodes draw sufficient activation away from the attachment node between the V and the NP. In effect, the new attachments between the V and the IP, and the NP and the I′, conspire to break the old attachment between the V and the NP. The number of iterations required for this network configuration to settle is 24, which is longer than the 17 iterations required for the simpler initial NP attachment to the verb, but not indicative of great processing difficulty. A reanalysis of this type, which involves attachments to a recent portion of the right edge of the parse tree, are not only possible but are fairly easy for the parser. However, there is a cost to pay for a reanalysis of this type, in that it generally involves a stronger competition among the attachment nodes than in the original attachment of the NP (which only competes with an empty node). Unlike the Garden Path model, no recovery strategies are necessary for an easy reanalysis of this type, but neither is the reanalysis cost-free, as in a ranked parallel model (Gibson, 1991; Gorrell, 1987).

The general constraints on reanalysis hold across all constructions, so that reanalysis is possible as long as the relevant attachments conform to the general structural configuration, regardless of category. For example, the following sentence is also easy for the competitive attachment parser:

(11) The daughter of the king's son's butler admires herself.

The sentence requires two analogous reanalyses, each of which involves only right edge attachments; Figure 11 illustrates the first of these reanalyses, where the interpretation changes from referring to 'the daughter of the king' to 'the daughter of his son'. Note that the structural configuration is exactly as in the NP/S ambiguity example shown in Figure 10, and that both follow the logical attachment possibilities illustrated in Figure 8 (p. 341).

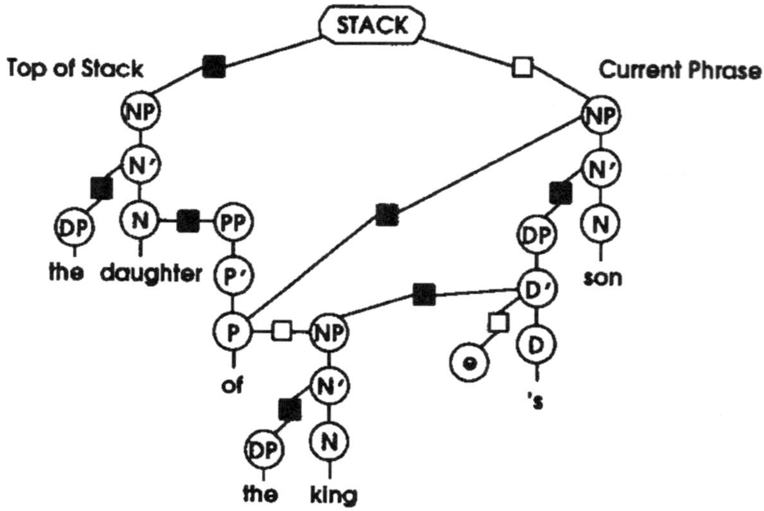

FIGURE 11: Allowable reanalysis of a genitive NP.

Recall that the restriction of making attachments only to the right edge of the tree on the top of the stack is independently motivated by properties of the competitive activation mechanism of the parser. Thus, the ability to make the necessary revisions in this type of structure follows from fundamental properties of the competitive attachment architecture. Interestingly, the structural configurations in which the competitive relations allow reanalysis are very similar to those captured by explicit restructuring strategies in other approaches. For example, the revisions within the model roughly conform to the restrictions imposed by the right-edge continuation heuristic of Abney (1989), the 'Steal' operation of Fodor & Inoue (1994) (borrowed from Abney, 1987), the 'On-Line Locality Constraint' of Pritchett (1992), and the accessibility constraint on tree-lowering proposed by Sturt & Crocker (1996); the competitive attachment restructuring operation is also similar to the 'snip' operation in Lewis (1993), but is more tightly constrained. In contrast to these other approaches, the restrictions on reanalysis in the competitive attachment model are an emergent property of the general attachment mechanism of the parser, enabling the model to avoid explicit heuristics defining allowable reanalyses.

3.2.2 Reanalyses of Intermediate Difficulty

Reanalyses that conform to the restrictions of the restructuring operation may be more difficult than examples (10) and (11) due to other performance factors. The competitive behavior of the model provides an account of the range of difficulty of possible reanalyses, incorporating precisely the same factors as affect initial preferences (for example, recency and lexical strength). Examples of this were discussed above in Section 3.1. It is worth emphasizing here that all of the reanalysis examples presented earlier are revisions that are possible within the automatic attachment operation of the parser. Recency and lexical preferences cannot make a reanalysis that involves inaccessible attachment nodes possible. What they can do is to affect the amount of time it takes for the network to settle on the appropriate set of attachments, and to influence the choice it makes among multiple possible reanalyses.

3.2.3 Garden Paths

Although the types of structural reanalysis discussed above do not cause a garden path effect in the parser, it is not the case that any arbitrary restructuring is possible in the network. Garden pathing does occur for required revisions which do not conform to the possible attachment configurations that form consistent attachment sets on the right edge of the developing parse tree. For example, consider the following sentences, which are illustrated in Figures 12-14:

(12) I convinced her children *were* noisy.

(13) Jamie gave the child the dog *bit* a bandaid.

(14) When Kiva left the room *got* quiet.

In each of these sentences, the competitive attachment model initially activates the attachments corresponding to the preferred interpretation of the ambiguous phrase. However, at the point of disambiguation (shown in italics in the examples), the parser cannot activate the set of attachments corresponding to the correct analysis of the sentence. In each case, the set of competing attachment nodes between the current (disambiguating) phrase and the partial parse tree does not include the attachments necessary for the reanalysis.

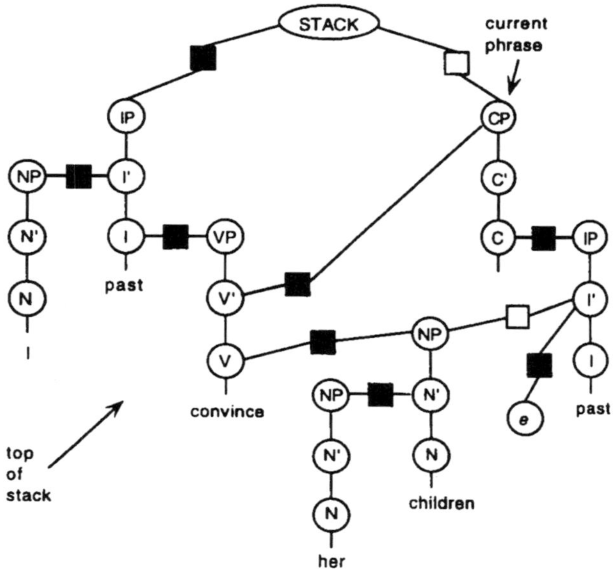

FIGURE 12: The network at the point of processing *were* in the garden path sentence *I convinced her children were noisy.*

For example, consider Figure 12, which shows the parser when processing *were* in the sentence *I convinced her children were noisy.* (The CP and IP in the current phrase in the figure are projected based on the tense features of the verb *were.*) Note that a reanalysis has already occurred previously in the input. The word *her* had initially been attached as the first complement of *convince*, and has been reanalyzed as the specifier of *children*; this revision is structurally identical to those shown earlier in Figures 10 and 11. At the point of processing *were* in Figure 12, a correct analysis of the sentence now requires that *children* attach as the subject of the current IP, and *her* re-attach as the first complement of the verb. Although the first of these attachments is possible (represented by the attachment node between the NP for *children* and the current I'), the second attachment is no longer available—the attachment node between the NP node for *her* and the V node for *convince* having been deleted when *her* was reanalyzed. Because *her* is now attached as the specifier of *children*, it is not on the right edge of the parse tree, and thus is not available for restructuring. Since the attachment between *her* and *children* cannot be broken, the network cannot represent the correct structure for the sentence, and the parser is garden pathed.

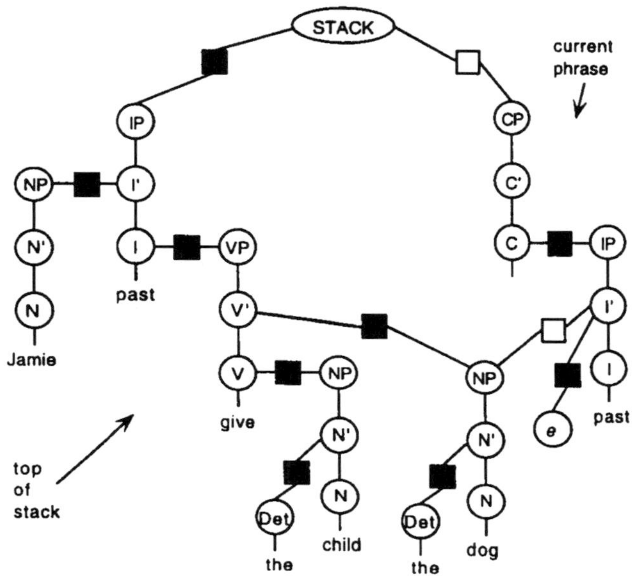

FIGURE 13: The network at the point of processing *bit* in the garden path sentence *Jamie gave the child the dog bit a bandaid.*

Figure 13 illustrates a similar case in processing *Jamie gave the child the dog bit a bandaid*, at the word *bit*. Here again, in order to arrive at a valid analysis of the input, the network needs access to nodes that are not on the right edge of the partial parse tree. The current CP node needs to attach as a modifier of the NP node of *child*, but the appropriate attachment node cannot be established, and again the parser is garden pathed.

The processing of *When Kiva left the room got quiet* differs in an interesting respect. Figure 14 shows the network at the point of processing the word *got*. The postverbal NP needs to break its attachment to the verb and reattach as the specifier of the current IP. The network could do this by de-activating attachment node a_1 and activating attachment node a_2. However, a_2 is not able to win the competition with a_1 for the output activation from the NP. The difference from the case in Figure 10 (p. 349), where reanalysis is possible, is that there, the attachment node between the verb and the NP was competing with two new attachments, which were together able to draw activation from the NP-to-V attachment. In the network shown in Figure 14, there is no attachment node for the V node to redirect its output to, and so it continues to activate the

NP attachment. The attachment of the NP to the I′ is not strong enough by itself to win the competition with the attachment of the NP to the V. The current I′ thus activates the default empty node attachment, leading to a clause with an empty (and unbound) subject. Since the network settles on an irrecoverably ungrammatical analysis, the model correctly predicts a garden path.

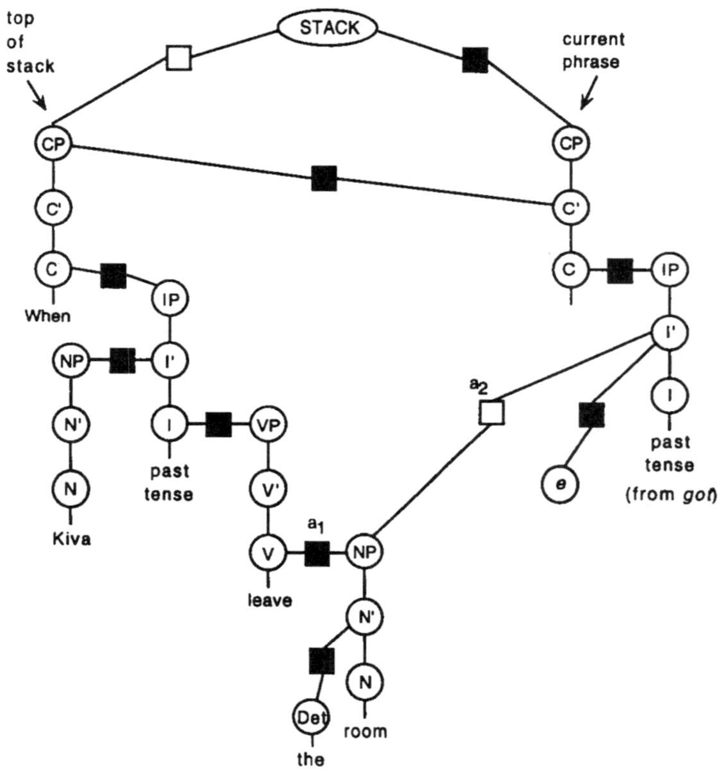

FIGURE 14: The network at the point of processing *got* in the garden path sentence *When Kiva left the room got quiet.*

However, this garden path situation differs in an important respect from those in Figures 12 and 13. Figure 14 shows that what is preventing a correct analysis of sentence (14) is that the V node in the subordinate clause needs to be able to activate an attachment to an empty node. Except for missing an empty node to signal the lack of an attachment for the subordinate verb, the attachments necessary for a correct revision are in the current competing group of attachments on the right edge of the existing parse tree. Because the source of the error can be localized within a single phrasal node that needs to be able to re-activate an attachment to an empty node, a simple recovery strategy could be added to the parser to allow a phrasal node to resurrect an attachment node to a defunct empty node. This would make this sentence a recoverable misanalysis for the model, but one which requires the addition of an explicit recovery procedure outside of its normal restructuring operation—we could think of this as a moderate garden path. However, no such simple strategy would help with the examples in Figures 12 and 13. In these examples, the attachments needed to form a correct analysis involve access to phrasal nodes not along the right edge of the partial parse tree. Each of these cases would require a more open-ended search procedure to locate the appropriate attachments (for *her* in Figure 12 and for the CP of the current phrase in Figure 13). Thus, the difference in attachment configurations within the competitive attachment model in these cases matches the intuition that sentences (12) and (13) lead to a more severe garden path effect than sentence (14).

3.3. Concurrent Processing of Attachments

The final property of the restructuring operation that results from the constraints on the competitive mechanism is that all attachments and revisions are attempted simultaneously in the parser. One effect of this is that even in possible reanalyses, there is an explicit competition between the initial and revised attachments that leads to a measurable slow down in the operation of the parser, as we saw above. This conforms with the on-line experimental data that have revealed the effects of revising a misanalysis even when there is no conscious awareness of either the ambiguity or the error in initial interpretation (as, for example, in the NP/S ambiguity). Note that ranked parallel models (e.g., Gorrell, 1987; Gibson, 1991) have not been able to provide a consistent account of this type of data. Furthermore, even if such an account were proposed, it cannot explain the uniformity of effects of factors such as recency and lexical preferences on the time-course of both initial attachment and reanalysis. Other activation-based models (e.g., MacDonald *et al.*, 1994) can account for this reanalysis time in terms of activation switching from one structural alternative to another, but cannot also account for the stringent restrictions on reanalysis for which severe garden paths are evidence.

A second, less obvious result of the concurrency of attachment competitions in the parser is that both initial attachments and reanalyses directly compete with each other. We have looked at cases above where multiple initial attachments for a phrase are competing, and at other cases where multiple possible revisions are competing. But because the model makes no distinction between initial and revised attachments, an initial attachment for a phrase will also compete with revisions of earlier material that involve that phrase. The result is that there is no explicit ordering of initial attachment before reanalysis. This differs from serial models, which only resort to restructuring when the initial attachment of a phrase is not consistent with the current analysis. Thus the model accounts for the extra time it takes to perform a reanalysis, without building in a bias for trying simple initial attachments first.

To explore the effect of not favoring initial attachment over revision, consider the following initial sentence fragment:[8]

(15) The man who believes the countess killed...

There is a temporary ambiguity at the verb *killed*, which can be the main verb, or the embedded verb in a sentential complement of *believes*, as shown in the following completions:

(16) The man who believes the countess killed herself will testify today.

(17) The man who believes the countess killed himself after the testimony.

Serial models (e.g., Frazier & Clifton, 1996; Sturt & Crocker, 1996) would interpret *killed* as the main verb, as in sentence (17), since that requires no reanalysis, while the interpretation as the embedded verb entails breaking the attachment of *the countess* to *believes*. Example (16) is thus predicted to be a garden path. My intuitions are the opposite—namely, that sentence (16) is easier than sentence (17). In the competitive attachment model, both analyses compete with each other. The sentential phrase projected in response to *killed* tries to push itself onto the stack, and attach *the man* as its subject, representing the main verb interpretation. It simultaneously tries to activate an attachment as the complement of believes, and attach *the countess* as its subject. Both of these

[8] This example is adapted from Sturt & Crocker (1996), who embed the initial NP as the complement of a verb with an NP/S ambiguity, yielding a temporary ambiguity with two possible reanalyses, as in example (4). Here I look at the NP as the subject of a sentence, to compare an initial attachment and revision, rather than two revisions.

attachment configurations are valid in the parser.[9] In the absence of any biasing effects, the verb *killed* is most likely to attach as the complement of a recent verb, and thus sentence (16) is preferred. However, since both analyses are available and compete with each other, biasing context could bring about the alternative (main verb) interpretation.

4 Discussion

Although a review of all related models of reanalysis is not possible here, some proposals have particularly strong parallels to the competitive attachment approach. For example, Sturt & Crocker (1996) develop a computational formalization of the monotonic parsing proposal in Gorrell (1995), which leads to a more restrictive range of possible parsing operations. They propose a tree-lowering operation which performs structural revisions that are very similar to the restructurings allowed in the competitive attachment parser. One advantage of the competitive attachment approach is that it derives restrictions on possible reanalyses from fundamental limitations of the competition mechanism. Another advantage that has been discussed earlier is that the concurrent restructuring operation eliminates the need for specifying explicit ordering heuristics and precise thresholds, as necessary in the serial search approach taken by Sturt & Crocker (1996).

The competitive attachment model also has some important similarities to the proposal in Frazier & Clifton (1996), which postulates two independent and interacting principles, Minimal Revisions and visibility, that determine the possibilities for reanalysis and how easy or difficult a particular reanalysis is. Visibility accounts for the kinds of recency effects that are captured here through the decay mechanism of the parser, and Minimal Revisions has similar consequences to the right edge restriction on the restructuring operation. In both theories, the interaction of these two properties accounts for a number of psycholinguistic behaviors. As with the comparison to Sturt & Crocker's (1996) proposal, an advantage here is the independent justification of the parser's properties in terms of the computational architecture. Another advantage is that the framework proposed by Frazier & Clifton (1996) requires two principles whose intent is to choose the minimal (re)structuring of an

---

9 Attaching *the man* as the subject of the main verb *killed* (roughly) corresponds to activating the pair of attachment nodes labeled p_1 in Figure 8 (p. 341). Attaching *the countess* as the subject of the embedded verb *killed* roughly corresponds to activating the pair of attachment nodes labeled p_3 in Figure 8. The actual structure of the current sentence is more complex than in that abstract example, but the network configurations are similar in the relevant respects.

input—Minimal Attachment, which operates solely in determining initial attachment preferences, and Minimal Revisions, which applies only to reanalysis. By contrast, in the competitive attachment model, factors that affect attachment decisions apply equally to both initial attachment and revision.

In spite of the fact that the competitive attachment model avoids error detection and analysis procedures, a very similar approach to the spirit of this work can be found in the diagnosis model of Fodor & Inoue (1994). Although they concentrate on the inferencing requirements of their parsing model, the Attach (Anyway) operation is responsible for much of the interesting work in this account. In fact, an admittedly biased view is that Attach (Anyway) can be seen as a higher-level, serialized description of the simultaneous attachment and restructuring operation of the competitive attachment model. Attach (Anyway) incorporates pressure to make attachments that is mirrored in the competitive attachment parser in the requirement that every attachment site has to activate an attachment node. As in Attach (Anyway), here the new phrase tries its best to activate a good attachment, possibly triggering the reattachment of an earlier phrase. But this is all an *automatic* operation, not a deliberate process of making an ungrammatical attachment and then trying to fix it, as in Fodor & Inoue's approach. The competitive attachment model also accounts for the overt versus covert symptom distinction noted by Fodor & Inoue. Here, an overt phrase that, in order to attach, forces an earlier phrase to reattach, does so within the normal attachment operation of the parser. On the other hand, arriving at the end of the sentence with some grammatical constraints unsatisfied does not lead to reanalysis within the normal restructuring operation.[10] A point of contrast with the Fodor & Inoue proposal is that necessary restrictions on the allowable network configurations in the competitive attachment parser currently are the sole determinant of whether a misanalysis is revisable or not. However, if it becomes necessary to augment the model with simple recovery strategies, such as the empty node postulation scheme suggested in section 3.2.3, then the two models may converge even more.

[10] Stevenson (1993b) discusses this in the context of filler-gap ambiguities, where a late obligatory gap may force the filler to abandon an earlier (optional) gap. This leads to an easier reanalysis than with a missed early gap, in which the end of the sentence signals that the filler has failed to bind a gap, but does not automatically trigger activation of an earlier possible gap.

5 Conclusions

Taken strictly, incremental interpretation during parsing means that incorporating each input word into the current tree requires revision of some (at least default) hypotheses. This insight leads to the exploration of the proposal that *all* attachment involves reanalysis. Such a view leads to a single uniform mechanism for both initial attachments and revisions. Other approaches have tried to give a unified account of the parsing process by minimally extending the initial parsing operations. The competitive attachment model instead embodies an approach of parsing as incremental restructuring, which allows it to capture a broad range of human behaviors with a single, parallel attachment operation.

Rutgers University

References

Abney, S. 1989. A computational model of human parsing. *Journal of Psycholinguistic Research*, 18, 1, 129-144.

Church, K. 1980. *On Memory Limitations in Natural Language Processing*. Master's thesis, MIT, Cambridge, MA.

Ferreira, F. & Henderson, J.M. 1991. Recovery from misanalyses of garden-path sentences. *Journal of Memory and Language*, 30, 725-745.

Fodor, J.D. & Inoue, A. 1994. The diagnosis and cure of garden paths. *Journal of Psycholinguistic Research*, 23, 5, 407-434.

Ford, M., Bresnan, J., & Kaplan, R. 1982. A competence-based theory of syntactic closure. In J. Bresnan (ed.), *The Mental Representation of Grammatical Relations*. Cambridge, MA: MIT Press, 727-796.

Frazier, L. 1978. *On Comprehending Sentences: Syntactic Parsing Strategies*. Ph.D. thesis, University of Connecticut, Storrs, CT. Distributed by the Indiana University Linguistics Club, Bloomington, IN.

Frazier, L. & Clifton, C. 1996. *Construal*. Cambridge, MA: MIT Press.

Frazier, L. & Fodor, J.D. 1978. The sausage machine: A new two-stage parsing model. *Cognition*, 6, 291-325.

Frazier, L. & Rayner, K. 1982. Making and correcting errors during sentence comprehension: Eye movements in the analysis of structurally ambiguous sentences. *Cognitive Psychology*, 14, 178-210.

Garnsey, S.M., Pearlmutter, N.J., Myers, E., & Lotocky, M.A. 1996. The relative contributions of verb bias and plausibility to the comprehension of temporarily ambiguous sentences. Submitted for publication.

Gibson, E.A.F. 1991. *A Computational Theory of Human Linguistic Processing: Memory Limitations and Processing Breakdown*. Unpublished doctoral dissertation, Carnegie-Mellon University, Pittsburgh, PA. Available as Center for Machine Translation Technical Report CMU-CMT-91-125.

Gorrell, P. 1987. *Studies of Human Syntactic Processing: Ranked-Parallel versus Serial Models*. Unpublished doctoral dissertation, University of Connecticut, Storrs, CT.

Gorrell, P. 1995. *Syntax and Parsing*. Cambridge, UK: Cambridge University Press.

Hawkins, J.A. 1994. *A Performance Theory of Order and Constituency*. Cambridge, UK: Cambridge University Press.

Inoue, A. & Fodor, J.D. 1995. Information-paced parsing of Japanese. In R. Mazuka & N. Nagai (eds.), *Japanese Sentence Processing*. Hillsdale, NJ: Lawrence Erlbaum Associates, 9-63.

Kimball, J. 1973. Seven principles of surface structure parsing in natural language. *Cognition*, 2, 15-47.

Lewis, R. 1993. *An Architecturally-based Theory of Human Sentence Comprehension*. Unpublished doctoral dissertation, Carnegie Mellon University, Pittsburgh, PA. Available as Technical Report CMU-CS-93-226.

Lombardo, V. 1995. Parsing and recovery. In *Proceedings of the 17th Annual Conference of the Cognitive Science Society*, 648-653.

MacDonald, M., Pearlmutter, N., & Seidenberg, M. 1994. Lexical nature of syntactic ambiguity resolution. *Psychological Review*, 101, 4, 676-703.

MacDonald, M.C. 1994. Probabilistic constraints and syntactic ambiguity resolution. *Language and Cognitive Processes*, 2, 157-201.

McRoy, S.W. & Hirst, G. 1990. Race-based parsing and syntactic disambiguation. *Cognitive Science*, 14, 313-353.

Pritchett, B. 1992. *Grammatical Competence and Parsing Performance*. Chicago, IL: University of Chicago Press.

Spivey-Knowlton, M. & Sedivy, J.C. 1995. Resolving attachment ambiguity with multiple constraints. *Cognition*, 55, 3, 227-267.

Stevenson, S. 1990. A parallel constraint satisfaction and spreading activation model for resolving syntactic ambiguity. In *Proceedings of the 12th Annual Conference of the Cognitive Science Society*, 396-403.

Stevenson, S. 1993a. A competition-based explanation of syntactic attachment preferences and garden path phenomena. *Association for Computational Linguistics*, 31, 266-273.

Stevenson, S. 1993b. Establishing long-distance dependencies in a hybrid network model of human parsing. In *Proceedings of the 15th Annual Conference of the Cognitive Science Society*, 982-987.

Stevenson, S. 1994a. Competition and recency in a hybrid network model of syntactic disambiguation. *Journal of Psycholinguistic Research*, 23, 4, 295-322.

Stevenson, S. 1994b. *A Competitive Attachment Model for Resolving Syntactic Ambiguities in Natural Language Parsing*. Unpublished doctoral dissertation, University of Maryland, College Park, MD. Available as Technical Report TR-18 from Rutgers Center for Cognitive Science, Rutgers University.

Stevenson, S. 1995. Arguments and adjuncts: A computational explanation of asymmetries in attachment preferences. In *Proceedings of the 17th Annual Conference of the Cognitive Science Society*, 748-753.

Sturt, P. & Crocker, M. 1996. Monotonic syntactic processing: A cross-linguistic study of attachment and reanalysis. *Language and Cognitive Processes*, 11, 5, 449-494.

Trueswell, J.C. 1996. The role of lexical frequency in syntactic ambiguity resolution. *Journal of Memory and Language*, 35, 566-585.

Trueswell, J.C., Tanenhaus, M.K., & Garnsey, S.M. 1994. Semantic influences on parsing: Use of thematic role information in syntactic ambiguity resolution. *Journal of Memory and Language*, 33, 285-318.

Trueswell, J.C., Tanenhaus, M.K., & Kello, C. 1993. Semantic influences on parsing: Use of thematic role information in syntactic ambiguity resolution. *Journal of Experimental Psychology: Learning, Memory, and Cognition*, 19, 3, 528-553.

Weinberg, A. 1995. Licensing constraints and the theory of language processing. In R. Mazuka & N. Nagai (eds.), *Japanese Sentence Processing*. Hillsdale, NJ: Lawrence Erlbaum Associates, 235-255.

11

Generalized Monotonicity for Reanalysis Models*

Patrick Sturt & Matthew W. Crocker

Abstract

A common assumption in psycholinguistic theory is that reanalysis is constrained by a preference to preserve certain aspects of the representation built in response to previous input. In this chapter, we discuss this notion of representation-preservation in the wider context of models of reanalysis as a whole, and point out that in order to define a representation-preserving constraint on reanalysis, we must specify not only which aspects of representation should be preserved, but what is meant by the notion of preservation. We propose that the appropriate notion of preservation is that which is assumed in monotonic models of parsing, where structural relations between linguistic elements are updated totally non-destructively from state to state. Previous monotonic theories of parsing have limited themselves to consideration of phrase structure representations. In contrast, we propose a general framework within which one may formulate models which apply the same notion of preservation to other representation types. The framework is discussed with reference to a model which preserves thematic structure.

* Much of the material in this chapter was presented at seminars given at the University of Freiburg, Germany, and the University of Torino, Italy, during July and September 1996. We would like to thank the seminar participants for their instructive comments, especially Barbara Hemforth, Lars Konieczny, Leonardo Lesmo, Vincenzo Lombardo, and Gerhard Strube. We would also like to thank Suzanne Stevenson and an anonymous reviewer for their comments and suggestions which have greatly improved the quality of this chapter. Any remaining errors are our own. The research reported here was supported by the award of ESRC studentship No. R00429334338 to the first author.

J.D. Fodor and F. Ferreira (eds.), Reanalysis in Sentence Processing, 365–400.

1 Introduction

One of the goals of reanalysis models is to predict differential costs associated with different types of revision. In attempting to achieve this goal, a number of models have been proposed which we call representation-preserving (Pritchett, 1988; Weinberg, 1993; Gorrell, 1995; Sturt & Crocker, 1996). These models constrain revision by appealing to a preference encoded in the processor to preserve certain features of the representation built up to the point when reanalysis occurs. Representation-preserving models contrast with theories which constrain reanalysis directly in terms of limitations on working memory, inferential ability, and other computational resources.

Our goal in this chapter is not to argue that representation-preserving models are better than alternative accounts—in fact, we have no doubt that representation, resource boundedness, and many other factors will turn out to be relevant to reanalysis. Instead, we have settled on two less ambitious goals. Firstly, we aim to situate the notion of representation-preservation within the context of reanalysis models in general. Secondly, we aim to provide a general framework within which precisely formulated representation-preserving models can be built and evaluated. Specifically, we will propose a general framework for building monotonic models, a particular subclass of representation-preserving models. The idea of monotonicity provides us with a notion of 'preservation' which can be applied to different types of representation.

2 What Is Reanalysis?

2.1 A Definition of 'Reanalysis'

Loosely speaking, 'reanalysis' may be taken to mean 'discarding one reading of an ambiguity in favor of another. However, exactly what counts as 'reanalysis' varies considerably from model to model. For example, in Gibson's (1991) restricted parallel system, 'reanalysis' refers only to recovery from 'parsing breakdown' situations, which are predicted to occur exactly in those cases where a previously discarded parse has to be re-introduced. The re-ordering of alternatives still under parallel consideration, which presumably must occur at some level, is not regarded as reanalysis. Similarly, in 'constraint satisfaction' models (e.g., MacDonald *et al.*, 1994), which are characterized by the parallel competitive activation of multiple alternatives, minor changes in relative activation levels are not usually classed as 'reanalysis', but some researchers working in this tradition (Trueswell *et al.*, 1993) do not deny the existence of 'true garden path' effects, which are indeed associated with 'reanalysis'. Presumably, reanalysis in a constraint satisfaction model corresponds to the re-activation of an alternative whose activation has dropped below some threshold to a level close to zero.

By contrast, within a serial framework, the Garden Path model (Frazier, 1978; Frazier & Rayner, 1982) assumes that normal processing is accompanied by any number of minor reanalyses, as initial attachments based on restricted grammatical knowledge are discarded by higher level processing modules. However, even within the Garden Path tradition, it is not always clear which varieties of structural change count as reanalysis. For example, in models influenced by the Garden Path tradition a distinction is often made between the attachment of postmodifiers of verbs, which are incorporated into the representation via sister adjunction, and the attachment of postmodifiers of nouns, which are incorporated via Chomsky adjunction (see Clifton *et al.*, 1991, for an example of this distinction). Adams (1995) uses this distinction to argue that the attachment of NP modifiers is, in some sense, more destructive than the attachment of VP modifiers, and therefore we should presumably see attachment of NP modifiers as involving some form of reanalysis, and attachment of VP modifiers as not.

Given this wealth of subtly different nuances associated with the term, we propose to clarify what *we* mean by 'reanalysis', before discussing the notion any further. We believe that it is useful to view the processing of a string as a series of states, where each word induces a transition from one state to the next. For the sake of simplicity of definition, we assume a processing model in which a single preferred analysis is always unambiguously available at each state.[1] Now, we assume that whatever syntactic representation is used in the model, it will include information about grammatical dependencies, which could be modelled using licensing relations, coindexation, structure sharing, unification, argument cancellation or any number of alternative means, depending on the variety of grammar that the processing model uses.[2] We will use the

[1] Our definition does not necessarily exclude parallel models; it merely insists that, in the case of a parallel model, of the alternative analyses available, one has a higher *value* (which could be determined by activation, processing load units, structural preferences, or other means) than all the others.

[2] We see dependencies as separate from the structural conditions that license them; for example, we would include "X is a modifier of Y", or "X is a complement of Y" as a dependency relation, but not "X is a daughter of Y", or "X is a sister of Y".

abbreviation Dep^S to stand for the following proposition: "*Dep* is the set of dependencies holding in the preferred analysis at state *S*". We will abbreviate the notion of 'a transition from state *S* to state *T*' as $S \Rightarrow T$. Now, we define reanalysis as follows:[3]

$$\text{A transition } S \Rightarrow T \text{ involves reanalysis iff } Dep^S \not\subseteq Dep^T.$$

From the definition, it can be seen that by 'reanalysis' we mean 'breaking at least one dependency'. From this it follows that, for example, attaching a postmodifier is not a case of reanalysis, since it involves adding rather than breaking a dependency. On the other hand, in a ranked parallel system, changing the relative preference order of analyses in such a way that the preferred analysis at *S* is no longer the preferred analysis at *T* will count as reanalysis, if there are any dependencies at *S* which do not hold at *T*.

2.2 The Nature of Reanalysis

Until recently, the phenomenon of reanalysis has been of concern to experimental psycholinguistics chiefly for the light it can shed on preferences for initial attachment. For example, in the following sentence, the detection of processing disruption at the word *was*, in an on-line task, may be taken as evidence that the processor has decided to attach *the cake* as a direct object of *saw*, rather than as the subject of an embedded clause, on the assumption that the disruption is the result of reanalysis.

(1) The wedding guests saw the cake was still being decorated.

However, reanalysis has rarely been treated as anything more than a diagnostic test for mis-attachment. Experimental research on ambiguity resolution has shown us *when* reanalysis occurs, but there have so far been very few experimental studies examining the question of *how* reanalysis occurs, or what preferences exist in reanalysis (but for examples of experimental studies which examine reanalysis for its own sake see Frazier & Rayner, 1982; Rayner *et al.*, 1983; Warner & Glass, 1987; Ferreira & Henderson, 1991; Sturt, in preparation).

---

[3] Note that the definition makes the simplifying assumption that it will always be possible to identify one particular transition where the preference for one alternative is replaced by the preference for another.

In the remainder of this section, we give a general discussion of the abstract problem of reanalysis, as compared with initial attachment. The aim of this discussion is simply to point out that reanalysis is an inherently more complex process than initial attachment, and that this complexity has consequences both for the human language processing system that has to perform the task, and for the models which psycholinguists need to build in order to understand the phenomenon. To understand the complexity of reanalysis as compared to initial attachment let us restrict our attention to a maximally incremental processing system, where each word is incorporated into single totally connected syntactic representation before the processor moves on to consider the next word (see Sturt & Crocker, 1996, and Lombardo, this volume, for examples of processing systems which has this property). Consider the problem of incorporating a new word into the representation, as informally illustrated in Figure 1.

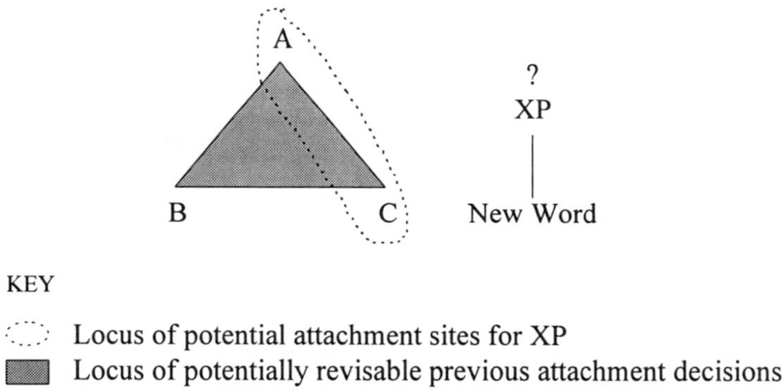

FIGURE 1: Incorporating a new word into the tree.

Assuming that the processor attaches in accordance with the theory of trees, then the locus of initial attachment possibilities for the projection of the new word corresponds with the right frontier of the tree built so far—that is, depending on the processing system used, the constituent XP could be attached as a daughter of any of the nodes on the path from C to A, or alternatively, the root A could be attached as the left daughter of XP (see Stevenson, 1994a, 1994b and Sturt & Crocker, 1996, for particularly clear examples of 'right-frontier based' attachment). However, no other attachments are possible if the processor wants to obey the theory of trees, retain a connected structure, and preserve all dependencies.

Now consider the possibilities for reanalysis. It may be the case that XP cannot find a felicitous attachment site on the right frontier. If this is true, then, according to most models, the processor will attempt to revise a previous decision. Recall example (1), repeated below:

(1) The wedding guests saw the cake was still being decorated.

Assume that *the cake* is initially attached as the direct object of *saw*, and that the processor attempts to reanalyze this decision at *was*. Assume also that the processor is serial to the extent that it does not have the sentential complement reading available.[4] Then, the reanalysis must involve at least the following operations:

1. *the cake* must be 'detached' from its current position as the direct object of *saw* (we will call this position the *detachment site*).

2. *the cake* must be re-attached as the subject of *was* (we will call this position the *target site*).

3. The (projection of the) new word must be attached into a position in the representation (we will call this position the *attachment site* of the new word).

Items 2 and 3 are each tasks comparable in complexity to standard initial attachment. Thus, in general, reanalysis must involve at least as much search as initial attachment. Note also that, while in this particular case the detachment site is on the right frontier of the tree at the point when reanalysis occurs (and incidentally, this is part of the reason why both Sturt & Crocker, 1996, and Stevenson, 1994a, predict example (1) to be unproblematic for the human language processor), in the general case, the *a priori* locus of candidate detachment sites corresponds to the entire tree, as illustrated in Figure 1, and not just the right frontier. This means that, generally speaking, reanalysis is likely to involve considerably more search than initial attachment.

Of course, all this is a statement of the obvious. However, we think it is a good idea to reflect seriously on the nature of reanalysis, particularly as, from reading the literature on psycholinguistic experiments, we could be forgiven for assuming that reanalysis is a much simpler phenomenon than it really is. Most experiments that are written to test hypotheses about ambiguity resolution are

---

[4] In a parallel system, such as that of Gibson (1991), the processor simply has to discard the structure corresponding to the direct object reading from its working set, and attach *was* into the structure corresponding to the sentential complement reading.

carefully controlled to contain only the one ambiguity under investigation. This means that, if evidence for reanalysis is found, the researcher can be relatively sure that this reanalysis involves revision of the single choice point involved. However, the sentences which readers have to process in real life are unlikely to conform to this ideal. In fact, at any given point where reanalysis is necessary, there may be any number of candidate choice points—corresponding to suitable detachment sites throughout the tree representation—which could be revised in any number of ways. Given this, one of the major aims of a theory of reanalysis must be to make predictions about how the processor deals with reanalysis ambiguity. That is to say, when the processor is faced with a choice of more than one possibility for reanalysis, we want to know what, if anything, influences the choice of detachment site and target site; (see Sturt & Crocker, 1996, and Sturt, in preparation, for a discussion of reanalysis ambiguity).

As far as theoretical models of reanalysis are concerned, we believe that the complexity of reanalysis motivates models that are computationally implementable. In models of initial attachment, where the task is to predict how the current word incorporates itself into the right edge of the current partial phrase marker, it is often very easy to ascertain the predictions of models. One of the reasons why the principles of Minimal Attachment and Late Closure (Frazier, 1978) have been so influential (and so acrimoniously debated) is that, in any given situation, it is usually clear what predictions these principles make. By contrast, when we are attempting to model the more complex process of reanalysis, we are much more likely to miss loopholes, where the model either over-predicts or under-predicts, unless we have a foolproof way of testing the consequences of a model. Furthermore, given the complex nature of the reanalysis problem, we would expect to find that the human language processing system, which has to perform this daunting task, imposes constraints on the search involved in reanalysis. Given that the number of analyses for a string grows exponentially in the length of the input, it is unlikely that the processor considers every alternative when the current analysis is discarded. This leads us to consider a further aim of reanalysis models—to define the exact nature of the constraints which the human language processor imposes on reanalysis search. It is this aim that has occupied most of the attention of researchers working on reanalysis, and in the next section we will give a brief review of how these constraints have been defined.

3 Accounting for Constraints on Reanalysis

As we stated above, recent models of reanalysis have concentrated on the aim of accounting for differential costs associated with different reanalyses by postulating various constraints on the possibilities for revision. In this section we will take a very brief look at some of these proposals, and identify two dimensions within which such constraints may vary; firstly, models vary in the extent to which they constrain the *diagnosis* versus the *cure* of garden paths (terms we have borrowed from Fodor & Inoue, 1994). Secondly, models vary in the nature of the computational limitations which are assumed to be the ultimate motivation for the constraints. Specifically, while some models attribute their constraints directly to limits in the computational resources available to the processor (such as bounded working memory, for example), others express the computational limitations less directly, by appealing to a preference encoded in the processor to preserve certain core aspects of representation. We will call the former class resource bounded and the latter class representation-preserving models. It is with the problem of defining representation-preserving models that the remaining sections (4-7) will concerned.

3.1 Diagnosis versus Cure

As we mentioned above, there is still not a great deal of experimental evidence available on the nature of reanalysis, and many researchers have relied on intuitive distinctions, between degrees of difficulty associated with different types of reanalysis. An example of such a distinction is that between 'conscious' garden paths (which, typically are claimed to cause noticeable processing difficulty) and 'unconscious' garden paths (which intuitively cause only a minor disruption to processing). Contrast (1), repeated below, which would on most accounts be classed as an unconscious, or easy garden path, with (2), which on many would be classed a conscious, or difficult garden path (c.f. Pritchett, 1988, 1992; Gorrell, 1995).

(1) The wedding guests saw the cake was still being decorated.

(2) While the wedding guests ate the cake was still being decorated.

Using the intuitive distinctions such as these as a clue, researchers have attempted to define constraints on reanalysis which exclude garden paths from which recovery is difficult, but include easy garden paths. Recall from the previous section that reanalysis typically involves finding a detachment site, finding a target site to re-attach the detached constituent, and finding a new attachment site for (the projection of) the new word. The constraints in the following models can be defined in terms of one or more of these notions:

> *Pritchett (1988)*: The target site must be in the same *theta-domain* as the detachment site.[5]
>
> *Pritchett (1992)*: The detachment site must govern or dominate the target site.
>
> *Gorrell (1995)*: The detachment site must dominate the target site. (N.B., this is a consequence of the indelibility of dominance and precedence relations, rather than a stipulation.)
>
> *Lewis (1993)*: The detachment site must be local to the new attachment site of the incoming word (where the notion of local corresponds to 'within the same maximal projection').
>
> *Fodor & Inoue (this volume)*: The detachment site must be accessible to the new attachment site of the incoming word through a chain of grammatical dependencies.
>
> *Sturt & Crocker (1996)*: The detachment site must be on the right frontier of the tree description built so far. The detachment site, reattachment site and new attachment site must be local to each other, as defined by the *tree-lowering* parsing operation. (The result is a system which obeys Gorrell's constraints.)
>
> *Stevenson (1994a, 1994b)*: Similar constraints to Sturt & Crocker (1996), but derived from the architecture of a hybrid Competitive Activation model.

In addition to the above, a *recency preference* has been proposed for the detachment site. This is captured, for example, in Stevenson (1994a, 1994b),

---

[5] α is in the γ θ-domain of β iff α receives the γ θ-role from β or α is dominated by a constituent that receives the γ θ-role from α (Pritchett, 1988, p. 555).

via decay of activation, and in Sturt & Crocker (1996) via an explicit search strategy.[6]

It can be seen from the above that the models differ with respect to the relative importance attached to the *detachment site* and the *target site*. For example, Lewis (1993) and Fodor & Inoue (this volume) impose no constraints on the *target site*, other than the constraints that apply to initial attachment, but impose strong constraints on the *detachment site* with respect to the position where the projection of the new word is attached. In terms of search, this implies that the search for the attachment error that is the ultimate cause of the need for reanalysis is more tightly constrained than the search for an alternative attachment. On the other hand, Pritchett (1988, 1992) imposes no constraints on the position of the detachment site itself, but does impose constraints on the position of the *target site* relative to the detachment site. Pritchett's model implies that the search for an alternative attachment is more tightly constrained than the search for the error. We can call models of the former kind, which constrain the search for the error more heavily than the search for alternative attachments, 'diagnosis-constrained models', and models of the latter kind, which constrain the search for alternative attachments more heavily than the search for the error, 'cure-constrained models'. Of course, many models contrain elements of both diagnosis and cure; for example, Sturt & Crocker (1996) impose a right-frontier accessibility constraint on the search for a *detachment site*, and to this extent is *diagnosis*-constrained. On the other hand, the model also strongly constrains the space of possible *target positions*, and to this extent it is also *cure*-constrained. This shows that diagnosis-constrained models and cure-constrained models are not mutually exclusive. Rather, diagnosis and cure should be seen as two aspects of search which, in any particular processing model, may independently be constrained to a greater or lesser extent. To the extent that a model can be seen to constrain diagnosis at the expense of cure, that model can be called diagnosis-constrained, and vice versa.

3.2 Resource-Boundedness versus Representation-Preservation

It is likely that the ultimate motivation for the constraints on reanalysis is computational. Given the combinatorial explosion of ambiguity in natural language, and the *a priori* complexity of search involved in reanalysis which we

---

6 Ferreira & Henderson (1991) show evidence that this recency preference should be sensitive to the point at which the *head* of the detachment site is read.

discussed in the previous section, it is unlikely that all alternatives to an initially chosen analysis are equally available to the processor. However, models vary with respect to how these limitations manifest themselves in processing behavior. Specifically, while some models express the computational limitations directly in terms of, for example, bounds on working memory, or constraints on inferential ability, others propose that the processor acts in such a way as to preserve, to as great an extent as possible, the representation that it has built up to the point where reanalysis occurs. We will call models of the first type *resource-bounded* models, and models of the second type *representation-preserving* models.

Gibson (1991) is a clear example of a *resource-bounded* model, since in this model, the bounds on computational resources play a direct role in the constraints imposed on reanalysis. In Gibson's model, the processor maintains multiple analyses in parallel, but, to avoid memory overload, prunes away analyses which exceed a certain processing cost relative to the preferred analysis. The necessity for re-introducing a pruned structure is predicted to correspond to the conscious garden path effect in human processing. In this system, the constraint on reanalysis is clearly motivated by working memory limitations. Conserving working memory also plays a key part in the more serial model of Lewis (1993), where attachment sites waiting to be filled are pruned from the parser's memory under certain conditions.

By contrast, *representation-preserving* models attribute to the processor an unwillingness to destroy representation, or propose that there is a difficulty involved in doing so. The ultimate motivation for this may very well be limitation in computational resources; after all, representations presumably require computational resources to build and modify. However, the link between bounds on computational resources and constraints on processing is much less direct in these models than in the resource bounded models. Instead, the claim is that there is something about destroying structure which is intrinsically dispreferred. The model described in Fodor & Inoue (this volume) contrasts strongly with a representation-preserving model, since it claims that there is no difficulty involved in destroying structure *per se*, just so long as the limited inferential capabilities of the processor allow it to determine *which* structure needs to be destroyed.

An example of a principle which is clearly motivated by representation-preservation is Frazier & Clifton's (this volume) *Minimal Revisions* Principle (c.f. Frazier, 1990a):

> *Minimal Revisions*: Don't make an unnecessary revision. When revision is necessary, make the minimal revision consistent with the error signal, maintaining as much of the already assigned structure and interpretation as possible.

Of course, there are various ways in which a representation-preserving principle like this could be interpreted, depending on precisely what is meant by 'minimal revision', and 'maintaining as much of the already assigned structure and interpretation as possible'. The question is, what general metric would be appropriate to quantify destructiveness to representations? One possibility, which would be consistent with our dependency-based definition of reanalysis, is to count the number of dependencies which have to be broken by the revision in question. This metric was behind the explanation we suggested for differences, described in Sturt & Crocker (1996), between reanalysis preferences in head-initial versus head-final languages, and is also consistent with the data which Frazier & Clifton discuss in their chapter of this volume.

However, the simple *number* of dependencies which are broken is unlikely to provide a *complete* answer to the question—in many cases, both 'hard' and 'easy' garden paths involve breaking only one dependency. In the reputedly 'easy' garden path in (1) repeated below, one dependency (between *saw* and *the cake* is broken, and the same is true of the 'hard' garden path in (2), where the broken dependency is between *ate* and *the cake*.

(1) The wedding guests saw the cake was still being decorated.

(2) While the wedding guests ate the cake was still being decorated.

Furthermore, there is evidence that the preferred interpretation of certain relative clause attachment ambiguities in Italian (De Vincenzi & Job, 1995) and Japanese (Kamide & Mitchell, 1997) may be derived via the breaking of one dependency even in the absence of any syntactic or semantic error signal (see Sturt & Crocker, to appear, for discussion).

This leads us to another side to this question, which is the consideration that there might be certain *aspects* of representation that are, in some sense, more sacred to the processor than others, and which the processor is therefore more reluctant to destroy. This has been the basic assumption behind many of the reanalysis models that have been recently proposed. Thus, Pritchett's (1988) *Theta Reanalysis Constraint* encodes a preference to preserve certain aspects of *thematic* structure, as defined by his 'thematic domains'. Meanwhile, Gorrell

(1995) and Weinberg (1993, 1995), encode a preference to preserve (description based) *constituent* structure representations. On the other hand, Bader (1996) argues that *multiple* representation types (a mixture of syntactic, lexical-morphological and prosodic representations) should be preserved.

As with the diagnosis/cure distinction, resource-boundedness and representation-preservation are not mutually exclusive characteristics. That is, a processor may be resource bounded in some way, say, due to limitations on working memory, but may use representation-preservation as a heuristic for keeping the computational cost of reanalysis within these bounds. Similarly, a processor may be primarily motivated to preserve representations, but be further limited by rather modest inference capabilities.

4 The Monotonicity Framework

As we mentioned in the previous section, the assumption of a representation-preserving processor leaves open two questions:

1. How should we formalize the notion of preservation?

2. Which aspects of representation should be preserved?

As an answer to the first question, we will argue that the most natural notion of 'preservation' is provided by the *monotonicity* paradigm, by which we mean the family of parsing models descended from Description theory (henceforth D-theory, Marcus *et al.*, 1983). However, D-theory has hitherto been applied to purely *constituent structure* representations. Therefore, we propose to generalize the paradigm in a way such that it can be applied to other representation types. This yields a framework within which models can be built to test proposed answers to the second question (see Sturt & Crocker, to appear, for a model which uses the generalized monotonicity framework to define monotonicity at a *thematic* level of representation).

What, precisely, do we mean by 'representation-preservation'? We can regard a representation as a set of (possibly binary) linguistic or structural relations. Now, recalling that a parse is viewed as a series of transitions from one state to the next, the notion of 'preservation' implies that, once a relation has been added to the representation, it is not removed. Monotonic models (Gorrell, 1995; Weinberg, 1993; Sturt & Crocker, 1996) use a form of representation called a *description* which can be 'preserved' in this manner, while tolerating certain classes of *reanalysis*. Recalling our definition of reanalysis, this means that, while at the level of linguistic *dependencies*, a relation holding at some state *S* may fail to hold at the next state *T*, at the level of the *description*, all relations holding at state *S* also hold at state *T*.

4.1 The Essence of Monotonicity

We can think of the dynamics of processing in monotonic models on three levels, as illustrated in Figure 2. On the first level, the *description*, is a set of statements describing certain aspects of the syntactic representation. Following Marcus *et al.* (1983), the description standardly consists of a set of *dominance* relations; for example, at State 1, the description consists of the statement "*a* dominates *b*". As we shall see, the fact that the dominance relation is *transitive* (i.e., if *X* dominates *Y* and *Y* dominates *Z*, then *X* dominates *Z*) gives D-theory its flexibility and power. At any state, the description can be interpreted as an infinite set of 'possible trees', which we have depicted in the middle level of the diagram, corresponding to all the trees which are consistent with the dominance statements, along with the axioms of the theory of trees. At any point in processing, a minimal 'default' tree can be generated from the description. In the simplest case, the 'default' tree at some state *S* is simply the result of assuming all dominance relations in the description at *S* encode *immediate* dominance, and assuming all nodes not mentioned in the description do not exist, that is, assuming the description is a 'closed world'. If we take state 1 in Figure 2, for example, the 'possible trees' comprise the infinite set of trees corresponding to the statement "*a* dominates *b*", including trees in which other nodes exist on the domination path between *a* and *b*. However, at this state, the default tree contains only the unique member of the set of possible trees for which there is evidence, namely, the tree in which *a* dominates *b*, and no other nodes exist; in other words, where *a directly* dominates *b*.

The constraint of monotonicity says that the description must be preserved—that is, once a dominance relation has been added, it cannot be deleted. This means that the description can be seen as a *monotonically increasing* set, where the description at each state will be a subset of all descriptions at subsequent states. Conversely, the 'possible trees' comprise a *monotonically decreasing* set, in that adding new relations to the description removes 'possible trees', but never adds them. Consider the effect of adding the new relation *dom(a,c)* at state 2. This has the effect of removing from the set of possible trees all structures in which *c* does not exist, for example, or all trees in which *c* dominates *a*. However, all the trees which are compatible with the description at state 2 are also compatible at state 1.

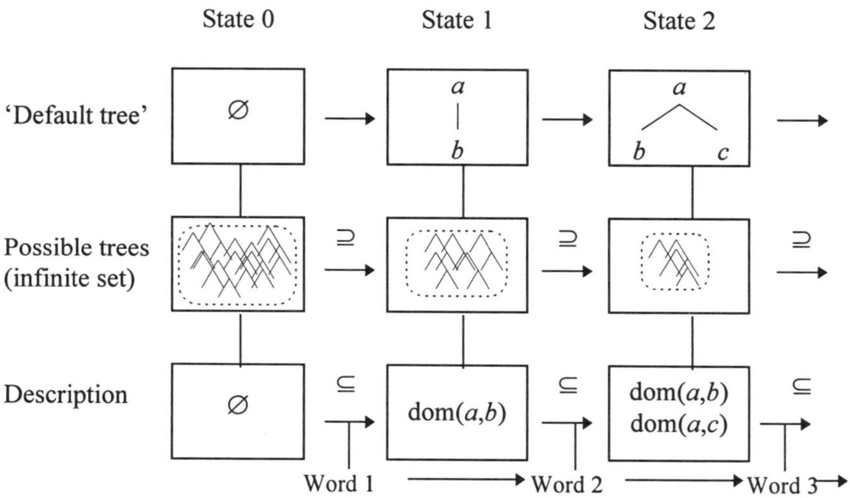

FIGURE 2: The essence of monotonicity.

In this sense, the monotonicity framework shares common features with the classical *cohort* model of word recognition (Marslen-Wilson, 1987). The 'cohort' in Marslen-Wilson's system is simply the set, at a given state of word recognition, of all word candidates consistent with the string of phonemes processed up to that point. As subsequent phonemes are recognized, word candidates which become inconsistent with the input are removed. If it subsequently becomes necessary to reintroduce a candidate that has been eliminated at a previous state, then a processing cost is predicted. Thus, the cohort is a monotonically decreasing set, and is equivalent to the level of 'possible trees' in the monotonicity framework. Of course, one of the major differences between syntax and word recognition is that, unlike the set of word candidates in a cohort, the set of continuations of a *syntactic* prefix is infinite, and thus impossible to enumerate.[7] The *description* in a monotonic processing model may therefore be viewed as an underspecified representation which, at

[7] This distinction does not hold in languages which exhibit cyclical agglutinative morphology, where the number of word candidates for a prefix is potentially infinite.

any state *S*, encodes the infinite locus set of possible changes which the representation may undergo as new material is processed subsequent to state *S*.

4.2 Infinite Local Ambiguity

Infinite local ambiguity may arise in circumstances such as the following. Imagine the following string of words has been processed:

(3) I saw the man...

Now, let us say that the minimal 'default' interpretation contains the following information:

(4) (State S:) I [$_{VP}$ saw [$_{NP_x}$ the man]]

Because of the transitivity of the dominance relation, the set of 'possible trees' will include trees in which various numbers of nodes intervene on the domination path between VP and NP_x. However, the minimal default tree will include only the single tree indicated above, in which VP *immediately* dominates NP_x. Now imagine that the input proceeds so that at state *T*, the default tree includes the following information:

(5) (State T:) I [$_{VP}$ saw [$_{NP_y}$ [$_{NP_x}$ the man]'s wife]]

By the time of state *T*, the default tree at state *S* has been removed from the set of possible trees, and, since the dependency between the verb *saw* and NP_x has also been removed, we class this change as a *reanalysis*. However, the new minimal interpretation at state *T* has existed in the set of possible trees at all previous states, including that of state *S*. In fact, the input could continue indefinitely in the same manner, and the set of possible trees would at each stage be monotonically *narrowed down*, with the description simultaneously monotonically increasing.

(6) I saw the man's wife's friend's sister's…

The type of local ambiguity exemplified in (3)-(6) is more pervasive than might be thought. We can expect to find similar examples in all cases where right branching and left-branching structures meet—a situation which, as pointed out by Inoue & Fodor (1995), is extremely pervasive in head-final languages such as Japanese.

It should be clear at this point that the D-theory formalism is extremely powerful, in that it allows a compact encoding of an infinite number of possible trees. This property makes the monotonicity paradigm an interesting alternative to parallelism. In contrast to, for example, ranked parallel models (e.g., Gibson, 1991), in which alternative analyses are explicitly built, and structures pruned when they exhibit a particular relative or absolute processing cost, in the monotonic framework, multiple analyses are simply implicit in the description, and the 'pruning' is simply the by-product of adding new relations to the description.

4.3 Problems with Monotonicity

Despite the conceptual attraction of the monotonicity framework, we have argued (Sturt & Crocker, to appear), that existing models that have been proposed within the framework have been too inflexible to provide an account of the available data. One of the examples which we gave in that paper concerns the attachment of modifiers. Consider the following well-known sentence from Cuetos & Mitchell (1988).

(7) The journalist interviewed the daughter of the colonel who had had the accident.

There are two possible interpretations for sentences such as (7), corresponding to the attachment of the relative clause as a modifier of *daughter* on the one hand (high attachment) and as a modifier of *colonel* on the other (low attachment). Notice that, if the relative clause is initially attached in the low site, and subsequently reanalyzed to the high site, then, at the level of constituent structure, this reanalysis will break a dominance relation. This is because, in the low site, it will be dominated by the NP headed by *colonel*, while reanalysis to the high site will remove the relative clause to a position where it is no longer dominated by this NP. Thus, standard, constituent structure based D-theory models make a clear prediction that reanalysis of this type should cause conscious processing difficulty.

However, recent experimental evidence from Italian (De Vincenzi & Job, 1993, 1995) and Japanese (Kamide & Mitchell, 1997), suggests that, in sentences similar to (7) in these languages, although the initial, on-line preference is for for the *low* site, the final, off-line preference is for the *high* site. Specifically, questionnaire studies in both Italian (De Vincenzi & Job, 1993) and Japanese (Kamide & Mitchell, 1997) show a high attachment preference for globally ambiguous sentences similar to (7). However, self-paced reading studies in both languages (De Vincenzi & Job, 1993, 1995; Kamide & Mitchell, 1997) show evidence for an initial on-line commitment to the low attachment site.

This suggests that the revision from low attachment to high attachment, far from causing conscious processing difficulty, as predicted by standard monotonic models, may actually be the preferred course of action for the processor.[8]

5 A General Definition of Monotonicity

Despite this problem and others which we mention in Sturt & Crocker (to appear), we argue that the monotonicity framework should not be rejected as a paradigm for studying reanalysis. The reason for this is that previous monotonic models represent only a small subset of possible monotonic models. Specifically, the representation which they preserve using monotonicity is a description which mentions all nodes in the phrase structure tree at each state. Because of this, we can see these models as defining monotonicity over constituent structure representations. However, there is nothing to prevent us from defining similar constraints over other representation types. If we can provide a general definition of monotonicity capable of being applied to different types of representation, then we can use this framework to examine specific versions of the representation-preserving hypothesis. That is, we can keep the notion of preservation constant (using the general definition of monotonicity) while varying the type of representation to which it applies.

5.1 Monotonicity at the Constituent Structure Level

In what follows, we will give a brief review of the constraints imposed in one monotonic model (Gorrell, 1995). This model predicts processing cost associated with any reanalysis which deletes either precedence or dominance relations. Since the dominance and precedence relations constrained by this definition of monotonicity are between all nodes, this can be seen as a definition of monotonicity at the constituent structure level of representation. In the following, we again use the abbreviation '$S \Rightarrow T$' to stand for the transition from state S to state T.

---

[8] Due to certain characteristics of left-branching languages a monotonic account of the Japanese results is possible within the type of framework we have been discussing here. However, we do not go into the details of this, due to lack of space. The (right-branching) Italian results remain problematic for the type of models we have discussed here.

Thus, Gorrell's constraint can be defined as follows:[9]

> *Dominance Constraint*: For each transition $S \Rightarrow T$, if X dominates Y at state S, then X dominates Y at state T.
>
> *Precedence Constraint*: For each transition $S \Rightarrow T$, if X precedes Y at state S, then X precedes Y at state T.[10]

We will take these two constraints in turn, to see how they predict some intuitive distinctions. The Dominance Constraint predicts the intuitive difference between the 'easier' sentence in (1) and the 'harder' one in (2), repeated below:

(1) The wedding guests saw the cake was still being decorated.

(2) While the wedding guests ate the cake was still being decorated.

Assuming that *the cake* is initially attached as the direct object of the immediately preceding verb, then the reanalysis required to convert this NP to the subject of the complement clause in (1) involves only the *addition* of (at least) one node dominating the NP (i.e., at least the maximal sentential node dominating the complement clause). However, in the case of (2), the NP has to be 'moved' to a position from where it is no longer dominated by any of the nodes in the preposed clause, thus there exist dominance relations which hold at the state before reanalysis occurs but fail to hold at following states.

As an example of a violation of Gorrell's version of the Precedence Constraint, consider the following well-known garden path, which is 'hard' in the null (unbiasing) context:[11]

---

9 Although this constraint is equivalent to Gorrell's, it is not stated in identical terms.

10 To avoid cluttering these definitions, we avoid explicit mention of the universal quantifiers over the variables X and Y. We continue to make this omission in subsequent definitions, where we believe there is no danger of misinterpretation.

11 Clifton (to appear) describes an eye-tracking experiment which investigated garden path sentences of this type. Though the experiment was intended to investigate a separate issue, Chuck Clifton informs us (p.c.) that, in addition to garden path effects found in the eye-movement data, response accuracy to comprehension questions was extremely low for the dispreferred relative clause continuation, in comparison with the preferred complement clause continuation (34% versus 85% correct). This indicates that reanalysis is extremely hard and often impossible in this type of garden path.

(8) The doctor persuaded the woman that he was having trouble with to leave.

Assuming that the *that*-clause is initially attached as an argument of *persuaded*, (and, on standard analyses, is therefore preceded by *the woman*), the reanalysis necessary to reinterpret the that-clause as a relative clause will result in the that-clause being *dominated* by *the woman.* Hence the reanalysis requires the deletion of the precedence relation between *the woman* and the *that*-clause, and is therefore predicted to be difficult—that is, at least one precedence relation holds at the state before reanalysis occurs, but fails to hold after it.

5.2 Generalizing Monotonicity in Terms of Properties

In what follows, we will present two methods of generalizing monotonicity. The inspiration for both of these methods comes from Barker & Pullum (1990), who introduce two similar methods of generalizing *command relations*, based on *properties* on the one hand, and *relations* on the other. In this section, we describe a definition of monotonicity which is generalized in terms of *properties* of nodes. The central idea is that representation types can be defined by picking out, from a phrase structure tree, subsets of nodes which share a certain property, which we will call the *Generator Property* (borrowing some terminology from Barker & Pullum, 1990).

We will illustrate this with reference to the tree for (7), given in Figure 3. The most fine-grained representation is the phrase-structure tree (marked 'PS tree' in the diagram). It is the most fine-grained representation because it specifies all the nodes. However, we can also pick out less-fully specified representations by picking out only *subsets* of nodes which share a particular generator property. In the diagram, we have drawn a circle around all the nodes which we call *thematic assigner* nodes—that is, nodes which share the property of being the (extended) maximal projection of a theta-assigning head. (We make the assumption—along with Frazier & Clifton, 1996; De Vincenzi & Job, 1995; and Gilboy *et al.*, 1995—that the noun *daughter* assigns a thematic role to NP3, *the colonel*. Hence NP2, the maximal projection of *daughter* is a thematic assigner node.) The nodes which have been enclosed in squares correspond to the set of what we call *thematic receiver* nodes. These are nodes which have received a thematic role from some theta-assigning head. Let us say that the set of *thematic nodes* consists of the union of the thematic assigner and thematic receiver nodes. Then we can envisage three different levels of specification, according to which generator property we consider: the phrase-structure tree consisting of all the nodes, the thematic tree consisting of all and only the thematic nodes, and the thematic assignment tree consisting of all and only the thematic assigner nodes. Notice that the trees become 'flatter' as the membership of the relevant set of nodes becomes smaller.[12] It is possible to define monotonicity specifically, in terms of any one of these three levels, or in general, in terms of any arbitrary generator property.

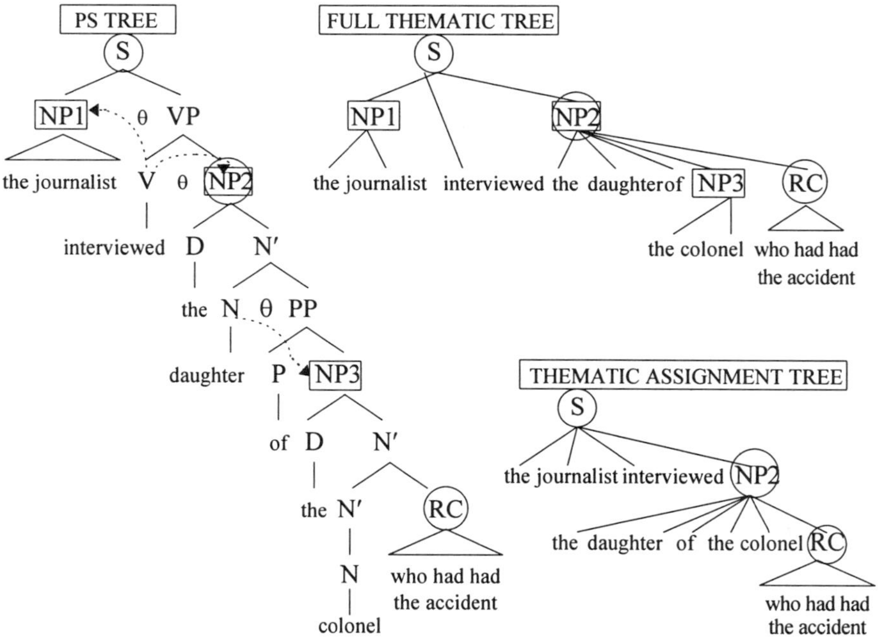

FIGURE 3: A representation showing thematic *assigner* nodes (enclosed in circles) and thematic *receiver* nodes (enclosed in squares) for a modifier attachment ambiguity.

What, then, is the role played by the structural relations of dominance and precedence, and how does this role relate to the notion of generator properties?

The statement "*A* dominates *B*" can be interpreted as a statement that domain *A* contains element *B*. On the other hand, a precedence relation between *C* and *D*

---

[12] Of course, given a phrase structure tree labelled with the necessary thematic feature information, the 'thematic trees' are purely derivative constructs and do not need to be built separately by a parser. We depict them in the diagram (including terminal symbols for clarity) purely for expository convenience.

can be interpreted as a statement that *C* and *D* are independent domains (i.e., neither one contains the other), since, by the theory of trees, a precedence relation between two nodes implies that the two nodes are not related by dominance.[13] The requirement that structural relations be updated monotonically can therefore be seen as a dynamic constraint on the construction of domains; that is, the constraint that both the membership (dominance) and the independence (precedence) of domains should be preserved.

When we move on to consider monotonic models defined in terms of some arbitrary generator property *P,* we simply use *P* to define the relevant notion of domain; the domains whose membership and independence we wish to preserve consist of subtrees rooted in nodes of which *P* holds (we will call such nodes *P*-nodes). Thus, in a system defined by the generator property *P,* the *membership* of a domain is the set of nodes dominated by some *P*-node, while the *independence* of two domains is captured by a precedence relation between two *P*-nodes. So, for example, if we were to take the generator property to be that of *thematic nodes* (i.e., the union of thematic assigner and thematic receiver nodes), then, in Figure 3, NP1 and NP2 would be independent domains (since NP1 and NP2 are each thematic nodes, and a precedence relation holds between them), while NP3 would be a member of the domain of NP2, because NP2 dominates NP3.

We now move on to a general definition in which any arbitrary generator property can be used to define a domain. In the following definitions, the *P*-Dominator Monotonicity Constraint ensures that although each node can become a member of a new domain (where domains are defined in terms of the generator property *P*), no node can cease to be a member of an existing domain. On the other hand, the *P*-Precedence Partner Monotonicity Constraint ensures that once a pair of independent domains has been established, (i.e., two nodes, each with property *P* are in a precedence relation), that independence must be preserved.

> *P-Dominators*: The *P-dominators* for *Y* at state *S* (abbreviated as $D(Y, P)^S$) is the set of all nodes *X*, such that property *P* holds of *X* at state *S*, and *X* properly dominates *Y* at state *S*

[13] The exclusivity condition of the theory of trees forbids two nodes from being simultaneously in a dominance and a precedence relation. See Wall (1972) for an introduction to the theory of trees.

(where *X properly dominates Y* iff X dominates Y and $X \neq Y$).[14]

P-Dominator Monotonicity Constraint: For each transition $S \Rightarrow T$, and for each node X, $D(X, P)^S \subseteq D(X, P)^T$.

P-Precedence Partners: The set of *Precedence Partners* at state S (written $PRP(P)^S$) is the set of all ordered pairs of nodes X and Y, such that property P holds of both X and Y at state S, and X precedes Y at state S.

P-Precedence Partner Monotonicity Constraint: For each transition $S \Rightarrow T$, $PRP(P)^S \subseteq PRP(P)^T$

This generalized definition allows one to recreate Gorrell's (1995) constraints by simply setting the generator property P to the trivial property of being a node. This will have the effect of preserving dominance and precedence relations between all nodes. However, it also allows any number of alternative definitions to be made. For example, we can set the generator property to be the property of being a thematic assigner node. Recalling Figure 3, imagine that, as in De Vincenzi & Job's (1995) Italian experiments, we have evidence for an initial on-line commitment to the low attachment of the relative clause (the reading in which the relative clause modifies *colonel*, as illustrated in the Figure), followed by a final preference for the high attachment site (where the relative clause modifies *daughter*), and that this reanalysis is therefore of the 'easy' kind. Let us say that this reanalysis occurs in the transition $S \Rightarrow T$. Then, in Gorrell's (1995) system, the relative clause will lose at least one dominator (e.g., NP3), and the reanalysis will be incorrectly predicted to be 'difficult'. However, if we alter the generator property so that it picks out, say, only the set of thematic assigner nodes, then the reanalysis will be correctly predicted to be unproblematic, since both dominators for the relative clause (i.e., both S and NP2) remain dominators for RC in both attachment positions.

5.3 Generalizing Monotonicity in Terms of Relations

The second, more powerful way in which we can generalize monotonicity is in terms of *relations*. In the previous section, where monotonicity was defined in

[14] The use of the predicate 'Properly Dominates' rather than 'Dominates' allows a close convergence with the generalized command theory of Barker & Pullum (1990).

terms of *properties*, the *P*-dominators for a node *N* were defined exclusively in terms of the generator property *P*, along with the predicate 'properly dominates'. By contrast, when we define monotonicity in terms of *relations*, the membership of the set of dominators of *N* may depend partly on features of *N* itself. This allows us to make different types of nodes sensitive to different types of domains.

Before providing a concrete example, we will give the definitions. In what follows, we use the the abbreviation $R(X, Y)^S$ to stand for "the relation *R* holds between *X* and *Y* at state *S*". We will refer to *R* as the *Generator Relation.*

> *R-Dominators*: The *R*-dominators for *Y* at state *S* (abbreviated as $D(Y, R)^S$) is the set of all nodes *X* such that $R(X, Y)^S$, and *X* properly dominates *Y* at state *S*.
>
> *R-Dominator Monotonicity Constraint*: For each transition $S \Rightarrow T$, and for each node *X*, $D(X, R)^S \subseteq D(X, R)^T$.
>
> *R-Precedence Partners*: The set of *R-Precedence Partners* at state *S* (written $PRP(R)^S$) is the set of all ordered pairs of nodes *X* and *Y*, such that $R(X, Y)^S$ and $R(Y, X)^S$, and *X* precedes *Y* at state *S*.[15]
>
> *R-Precedence Partner Monotonicity Constraint*: For each transition $S \Rightarrow T$, $PRP(R)^S \subseteq PRP(R)^T$.

An example of a monotonicity constraint defined in terms of a relation is 'Thematic Monotonicity' (Sturt & Crocker, to appear). This constraint is defined in terms of a generator relation which we call 'visibility'. The visibility relation captures the idea, proposed in recent years, that the attachment of modifiers is, in some sense, less constrained than the attachment of obligatory constituents (see Frazier, 1990b; Frazier & Clifton, 1996). The visibility relation yields a model which behaves as though it were based on two generator properties simultaneously, by making modifiers and nonmodifiers sensitive to different kinds of domains. Specifically, the model behaves as though the

---

[15] Note that, for the sake of generality, we have defined *R*-Precedence Partners 'symmetrically', assuming no difference in priority between the left and right members of a pair of nodes in a precedence relation. An anti-symmetric definition would also be possible, where only one of *R(X, Y)* or *R(Y, X)* would have to hold. This would require independent justification of the directionality of the relation.

reanalysis of modifiers is constrained by the generator property of *thematic assignerhood*, while the reanalysis of non-modifiers is constrained by the generator property of being a *thematic node*. Thus, all and only the *thematic assigners* are visible to modifiers, while (depending on certain conditions, which we will discuss below) both thematic assigners and thematic receivers are visible to *non*-modifiers.

The definition of the visibility relation, taken from Sturt & Crocker (to appear) is as follows:

Visibility:

1. *A* is visible to a modifier *M* iff *A* is a thematic assigner node.[16]
2. *A* is visible to a non-modifier *N* iff

   either there is no modifier that dominates *N* but not *A*, and *A* is a thematic node (i.e. a receiver or assigner),
   or there is a modifier that dominates *N* but not *A*, and *A* is a thematic assigner node (see below).

The 'either-or' statement in part 2 of the definition requires some explanation. The actual processing system which employs the thematic monotonicity constraint propagates configurational information relevant to visibility in a strictly local fashion, with the consequence that modifiers act as what can informally be thought of as 'visibility filters' to their descendants.[17] Recall Figure 3, for example. Because the relative clause, (labelled RC) is a modifier, only thematic assigner nodes are visible to the RC, and, moreover, none of the nodes *inside* the RC can 'see' anything other than thematic assigner nodes 'beyond' the RC, even though, if they are non-modifiers, they can 'see' all thematic nodes 'up to' the most immediately dominating modifier. Thus, NP3, because it is not a thematic assigner node, is not visible to the RC or to any nodes dominated by the RC. On the other hand, both S and NP2 are thematic assigner nodes, and so *are* visible to the RC and to nodes within the RC.

---

[16] This and the remainder of the definitions in this section are intended to be relativized to *states*. Strictly speaking, this particular clause of the definition of visibility should read "*A* is *visible* to a modifier *M* at State *S* iff *A* is a thematic assigner node at state *S*". We omit mentioning states to avoid cluttering the definitions.

[17] We lack the space to discuss the details of implementation here, but sese Sturt (in preparation) for further details, including a discussion of the inheritance mechanism used.

However, *all* thematic nodes, that is both assigners and receivers, are visible to non-modifiers, unless they are 'filtered out' by a modifier in this way. Thus, for example, NP1 is visible to NP3, and vice versa, but neither NP1 nor NP3 are visible to any nodes inside the RC.

Using the visibility relation as a generator relation in the above definitions we can see that the *R*-dominators for the relative clause (which is a modifier) consist of NP2 and S, the two thematic assigner nodes properly dominating the RC. Meanwhile, the *R*-dominators for a non-modifier, such as the head noun immediately dominating *colonel*, for example, consist of NP3, NP2, and S, the three thematic nodes properly dominating this node. Thus, the *Thematic Monotonicity Constraint*, which defines monotonicity using visibility as a generator relation has the effect of 'anchoring' each node into representations, which are more or less specified according to the features of the node in question. This allows us to apply to modifiers a constraint which is similar to *Construal* (Frazier & Clifton, 1996), while non-modifiers are subject to a constraint which is similar to Pritchett's (1988) *Theta Reanalysis Constraint*. We need the extra power of relations to do this; it would be impossible to reproduce the same behavior in a system which only used properties as generators.

We will now illustrate the visibility relation with reference to two concrete examples. The first example demonstrates how we handle the effect of preposition type which has been found in the processing of sentences similar to that illustrated in Figure 3. Consider Figure 4, which shows the translation of an Italian attachment ambiguity from De Vincenzi & Job (1995). The relative clause is a modifier, so, assuming the notion of thematic structure which we discussed in section 5.2, its dominators are the two circled nodes: the NP, which is the maximal projection of *father*, and the Matrix S node, which is the (extended) maximal projection of the verb *suspects*. Even if the relative clause is initially attached in the low site, its attachment can later be revised to the high site (modifying *father*) without violating the monotonicity constraint.

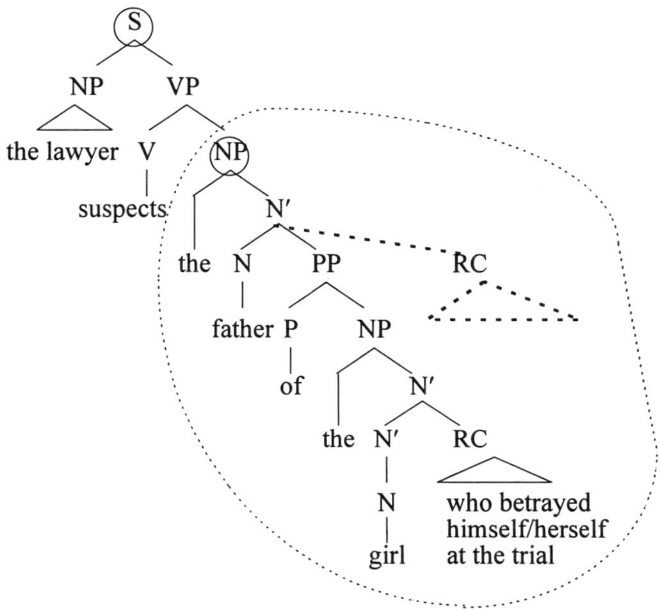

FIGURE 4: A relative clause attachment ambiguity. The dotted line encloses the locus of possible re-attachment sites for the relative clause once it has been attached in the low site. The high site is available here. (After De Vincenzi & Job, 1995.)

Now let us consider the situation in which the preposition inside the complex NP assigns a thematic role in its own right, as shown in Figure 5. In this case, the PP is a thematic assigning node, and therefore acts as a thematic dominator for the relative clause. This means that, once the relative clause has been attached in the low site, it cannot be re-attached to the high site without violating the Monotonicity Constraint. This pattern is consistent with De Vincenzi & Job's finding that, although an initial low attachment was found for the relative clause, for conditions including both non-thematic and thematic prepositions (illustrated by Figures 4 and 5 respectively), a final, off-line preference was found only for the condition including the *thematic* preposition (illustrated by Figure 5).

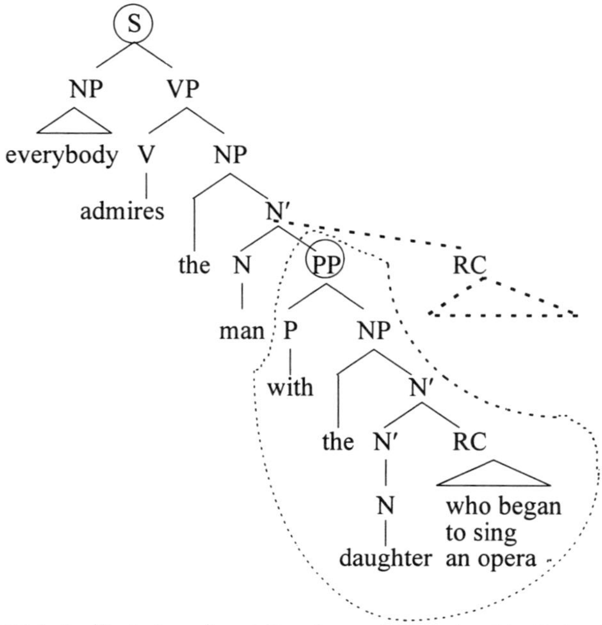

FIGURE 5: An illustration of a relative clause attachment ambiguity involving a preposition which assigns a thematic role. The locus of possible attachment sites for the relative clause now excludes the high site. (After De Vincenzi & Job, 1995.)

The second example applies to the reanalysis of a *non*-modifier. Consider again sentence (8), repeated below, which we cited as an illustration of Gorrell's (1995) Precedence Ponstraint, which, we recall, is known to cause considerable 'difficulty' in a null context:

(8) The doctor persuaded the woman that he was having trouble with to leave.

Assuming that the *that*-clause is originally attached as an argument of *persuaded*, and assigned a thematic role, then the clausal node will be a thematic receiver. The NP dominating *the woman* will also be a thematic receiver. Given also that neither the NP nor the clausal node are modifiers, they will be visible to each other. Hence, taking visibility as a generator relation, the NP and the clausal node will be *R*-Precedence Partners on the initially preferred attachment. However, reanalyzing the *that*-clause as a relative modifying the NP will result in a configuration in which the NP *dominates* the clause, and therefore, the precedence partnership will cease to hold, against *R*-Precedence Partner Monotonicity.

6 Reflections on the Monotonicity Framework

At this point we would like to step back and consider the nature of the monotonicity framework from a wider perspective. As we have pointed out, our purpose in this paper has not been to motivate any one particular instantiation of monotonicity, but rather to point out how the general concepts of D-theory can be applied to a wider range of models than has previously been considered. In this section we will consider some of the more general properties that are implied by the framework.

6.1 Consequences of Defining Monotonicity in Terms of Arbitrary Properties and Relations

We have seen in the preceding sections that monotonicity defined at the level of *constituent structure* (as in Gorrell, 1995) is equivalent to defining monotonicity with respect to the property that holds of all nodes, and thus has the effect of preserving all dominance and precedence relations in a tree. However, we have also seen that it is possible to define monotonicity with respect to properties that do not necessarily hold of all nodes. For monotonic models defined in terms of *properties*, it is true to say that there is an inverse correlation between the restrictiveness of the generator property and the restrictiveness of the resulting processor. That is to say, generator properties which are more general, in the sense that they hold of more nodes, will impose more restrictions on the possibilities for reanalysis, while generator properties which are more restrictive, in the sense that they hold of fewer nodes, will impose less strong constraints on the possibilities for reanalysis.[18] This means that monotonicity defined at the level of *constituent structure* yields the monotonic model which has the most restricted possibility for reanalysis, simply because the generator property necessarily holds of all nodes. Conversely, a generator property which necessarily holds of no nodes (i.e., the empty set) will impose no constraints on reanalysis at all. Generator properties which are intermediate between these two extremes will 'pick out' more or less underspecified representations, and subsequently allow more or less freedom for reanalysis. One of the consequences of defining a model in terms of a generator property *P*, for example, is that it will be impossible to 'raise' a constituent past the nearest dominating node of which *P* holds. In Gorrell's system, this means no nodes can be raised at all. In a system in which the generator property *P* is *thematic*

[18] This is related to the fact that, as proved by Barker & Pullum (1990), intersection over command relations corresponds to union over their generating properties.

assignerhood, no node can be raised past the nearest dominating thematic assigner. In a system in which the generator property is clause-hood, no constituent can be raised past the nearest clausal node, and so on.

In this paper, we have given some statically defined definitions but said very little about the *dynamics* of processing. In particular, we have not considered the question of when properties are 'assigned' to nodes. In a constituent-based model of monotonicity, where the generator property is simply *nodehood*, this question does not arise, as a node trivially cannot exist unless it has the generator property. However, in systems with smaller generator properties, there exists the possibility that a node may be attached into a phrase structure tree at some state, but acquire the generator property at a subsequent state. This allows monotonic models to capture some notion of 'delayed commitment', since a node may be in a position in which it could *potentially* have the generator property, but the processor may not necessarily *commit* itself to assigning the property to this node immediately. In Sturt & Crocker (to appear), for example, we assumed a processor which *attached* nodes immediately, but in which the *confirmation* of nodes holding the relevant properties was *head-driven* (in this case, the relevant properties were thematic assigner-hood and thematic receiver-hood, properties which are used in the definition of the 'visibility' relation on which the model is based).

6.2 Consequences of a Binary Monotonic/Non-monotonic Distinction

In this chapter, we have implicitly presented monotonicity as though it were a necessary condition for parse success—we have made the implicit assumption that a revision which violates monotonicity (in whichever monotonic model is proposed) is not possible for the parser. However, it is clear that people *do* manage to make sense of a number of 'conscious' garden paths, and, moreover, it is well known that the effort required to (re)process these structures can be lessened by manipulating factors such as subcategorization frequency and semantics. There are various ways of viewing the conscious/unconscious garden path distinction. The stronger view, due to Pritchett (1992), is that reanalysis of hard garden paths is possible, but that, unlike reanalysis of easy garden paths, it is not performed within the language module. A monotonic model does not necessarily commit itself to this position. The framework is equally consistent with a view that sees monotonicity not as a necessary condition for parsability but rather as a condition that the processor attempts to meet if it can. On this view, the processor is capable, if necessary, of destroying parts of its favored representation (as defined by the monotonicity model under consideration), but *prefers*, all other things being equal, to reanalyze in such a way that this representation is preserved.

Whichever view one takes, we believe a useful way to evaluate reanalysis models is to test what must be, after all, their most central prediction: the *preference* for one reanalysis over another, when more than one possibility is available. For example, a monotonic model would make clear predictions about the pair of sentences in (9):

(9) a. Once the students had understood the homework was easy they quickly finished it.
b. Once the students had understood the homework was easy and they quickly finished it.

In (9), the verb *understood* can either be intransitive, or subcategorize for either a clause or an NP. We would assume that in both (9a) and (9b), the NP *the homework* is initially attached as the direct object of *understood.* However, on the appearance of *was*, there are two possibilities for reanalysis: either *the homework* can be reanalyzed as the subject of a complement clause (a monotonic revision) or *the homework* can otherwise be reanalyzed as the subject of the main clause (which would violate monotonicity under most models). The former reanalysis is supported by the continuation in (9a) and the latter by the continuation in (9b). According to our intuitions, (9a) is indeed easier. Though we recognize the necessity for carefully controlling such materials (for example, in (9), we would need to consider the relative subcategorization frequencies for *understand*), we believe this general tactic is a useful one for reanalysis research.

One phenomenon for which monotonic models appear to be ill-suited is that of *graded* difficulty. That is, even *within* the class of either monotonic or non-monotonic revisions, there may be discernible *levels* of difficulty. For example, consider the following sentences, from Fodor & Inoue (1994):

(10) a. She put the candy in her mouth on the table. HARDER
b. She put the candy in her mouth onto the table. EASIER

Experiments investigating structures similar to this (Adams, 1995) suggest that *both* of the sentences in (10) cause processing disruption, and in fact, both are predicted to require non-monotonic revision in both constituency-based models (Gorrell, 1995; Sturt & Crocker, 1996) and the model based on the thematic notion of visibility described in Sturt & Crocker (to appear). However, as Fodor & Inoue (1994) point out, there is an intuition that (10a) is harder to resolve than (10b). How can we account for this in a model which treats both examples on a par? Assume that (as predicted, for example, in Sturt & Crocker, 1996), the preposition *on* in (10a), is initially attached as a modifier of *mouth*. However, assume also that, for lexical reasons, the processor knows that *onto* cannot be similarly attached (as assumed by Fodor & Inoue, 1994). This means that, in (10a), the processor not only needs to reattach *in her mouth* as a modifier of *candy*, but also to reattach *on the table* as the locative argument of put (both of these count as non-monotonic revisions in Sturt & Crocker, to appear). However, in (10b) only the former of these revisions is necessary. It is fairly natural to assume that a representation-preserving processor would find it more painful to destroy two pieces of its favorite representation rather than just one. If this is the case, then we might expect degree of difficulty in a monotonic parser to correlate with the number of violations of monotonicity.

6.3 Monotonicity Applied to Non-Syntactic Representations

While we have defined conditions for monotonicity that can be applied to representations other than phrase structure, the reader will have noted our implicit assumption that the generator property for each monotonic model will pick out a *subset* of nodes from a phrase structure tree (for example, the set of *thematic nodes* is subset of all the nodes in a phrase structure tree). This means that, according to our definitions, monotonicity is applied to representation types which are, in some sense, *subsumed* by phrase structure trees. We can call such monotonic models *phrase structure based*. Clearly, a phrase structure-based monotonic model cannot 'preserve' representations that are non-isomorphic to phrase structure. One example of a representation which is standardly assumed to be non-isomorphic to phrase structure (though not by everybody—c.f. Steedman, 1991) is intonation structure. On the standard view of constituency, there is no guarantee that a node in a phrase structure tree will correspond to a node in an intonational tree (for example, an intonational phrase may dominate a string of terminals that spans the final half of one phrase structure constituent, and the initial half of a second phrase structure constituent), and so no generator property applied to *phrase structure* trees could be used to define intonational phrases. However, there is no reason why a *non*-phrase structure-based monotonic model cannot be constructed—one could equally well define generator properties and apply them to intonational structure. Thus it would be possible, for example, to construct a model in which a lower level phonological unit could not be 'raised' past its dominating intonational phrase.

7 Concluding Remarks

In this paper, we have been concerned with the notion, common in reanalysis models, that there are certain core aspects of representation which the processor attempts to preserve. In particular, we have considered monotonicity as a useful general framework for the investigation of this question, and have shown how it can be generalized to allow the investigation of *which* representations are treated as the most sacred.

In closing, we would like to make some comments on the place that representation-preserving behavior may occupy with relation to the comprehension system as a whole. In particular, we would like to point out that representation-preservation should not be seen as a global strategy that guides *all* aspects of processing. If this were the case, then we would never expect the processor to make commitments in advance of disambiguation, since there is always a chance that any commitment may be wrong. Yet, thirty years of experimental research on sentence processing have told us that people *do* make commitments in advance of disambiguation. Rather, we think, the global strategy is to make the most sense of the input as it becomes incrementally available. This strategy produces conflicting demands on initial attachment and reanalysis. As far as *initial attachment* is concerned, the strategy implies that interpretable structures should be built quickly, which inevitably requires making commitments that are possibly wrong. As far as *reanalysis* is concerned, however, the strategy implies that the processor should try to make the most of the structure it has already built. The representation- preserving approach to reanalysis is concerned with the question of what is meant by 'making the most' of existing structure, and which aspects of structure this applies to. Generalized monotonicity provides a framework in which such questions can be considered.

Centre for Cognitive Science, University of Edinburgh

References

Adams, B.C. 1995. A model for strategic reanalysis in sentence processing. Unpublished manuscript, University of Virginia, VA.

Bader, M. 1996. On reanalysis: Evidence from German. Unpublished manuscript, Friedrich-Schiller-Universität Jena.

Barker, C. & Pullum, G.K. 1990. A theory of command relations. *Linguistics and Philosophy*, 13, 1, 1-34.

Clifton, C. (to appear). Evaluating models of human sentence processing. In M.W. Crocker, M.J. Pickering, & C.E. Clifton (eds.), *Architectures and Mechanisms for Language Processing*. Cambridge, UK: Cambridge University Press.

Clifton, C., Speer, S., & Abney, S.P. 1991. Parsing arguments: Phrase structure and argument structure as determinants of initial parsing decisions. *Journal of Memory and Language*, 30, 251-271.

Cuetos, F. & Mitchell, D.C. 1988. Cross-linguistic differences in parsing: Restrictions on the use of the Late Closure strategy in Spanish. *Cognition*, 30, 72-105.

De Vincenzi, M. & Job, R. 1993. Some observations on the universality of the Late-Closure strategy. *Journal of Psycholinguistic Research*, 22, 2, 189- 206.

De Vincenzi, M. & Job, R. 1995. An investigation of Late Closure: the role of syntax, thematic structure and pragmatics in initial and final interpretation. *Journal of Experimental Psychology. Learning, Memory and Cognition*, 21, 5, 1303-1321.

Ferreira, F. & Henderson, J.M. 1991. Recovery from misanalyses of garden-path sentences. *Journal of Memory and Language*, 30, 725-745.

Fodor, J.D. & Inoue, A. 1994. The diagnosis and cure of garden pãths. *Journal of Psycholinguistic Research*, 23, 4, 405-432.

Fodor, J.D. & Inoue, A. (this volume). Attach Anyway.

Frazier, L. 1978. *On Comprehending Sentences: Syntactic Parsing Strategies*. Unpublished doctoral dissertation, University of Connecticut, Storrs, CT. Distributed by the Indiana University Linguistics Club, Bloomington, IN.

Frazier, L. 1990a. Identifying structure under X^0. *Yearbook of Morphology*, 3, 87-105.

Frazier, L. 1990b. Parsing modifiers: Special purpose routines in the HPSM? In D.A. Balota, G.B. Flores d'Arcais, & K. Rayner (eds.), *Comprehension Processes in Reading*. Hillsdale, NJ: Lawrence Erlbaum Associates, 303-331.

Frazier, L. & Clifton, C. 1996. *Construal*. Cambridge MA: MIT Press.

Frazier, L. & Clifton, C. (this volume). Sentence reanalysis, and visibility.

Frazier, L. & Rayner, K. 1982. Making and correcting errors during sentence comprehension: Eye movements in the analysis of structurally ambiguous sentences. *Cognitive Psychology*, 14, 178-210.

Gibson, E.A.F. 1991. *A Computational Theory of Human Linguistic Processing: Memory Limitations and Processing breakdown*. Unpublished doctoral dissertation, Carnegie Mellon University, Pittsburgh, PA. Available as Center for Machine Translation Technical Report CMU-CMT-91-125.

Gilboy, E.A.F., Sopena, J.M., Clifton, C., & Frazier, L. 1995. Argument structure and association preferences in Spanish and English compound NPs. *Cognition*, 54, 131-167.

Gorrell, P. 1995. *Syntax and Parsing*. Cambridge, UK: Cambridge University Press.

Inoue, A. & Fodor, J.D. 1995. Information-paced parsing of Japanese. In R. Mazuka & N. Nagai (eds.), *Japanese Sentence Processing*. Hillsdale, NJ: Lawrence Erlbaum Associates, 9-63.

Kamide, Y. & Mitchell, D.C. 1997. Relative clause attachment: Nondeterminism in Japanese parsing. *Journal of Psycholinguistic Research*, 26, 2, 247-254.

Lewis, R. 1993. *An Architecturally-based Theory of Human Sentence Comprehension*. Unpublished doctoral dissertation, Carnegie Mellon University, Pittsburgh, PA. Available as Technical Report CMU-CS-93-226 from reports@cs.cmu.edu.

Lombardo, V. (this volume). A computational model of recovery.

MacDonald, M.C., Pearlmutter, N.J., & Seidenberg, M.S. 1994. The lexical nature of syntactic ambiguity resolution. *Psychological Review*, 101, 4, 676- 703.

Marcus, M., Hindle, D., & Fleck, M. 1983. D-theory: Talking about talking about trees. *Association for Computational Linguistics*, 21, 129-136.

Marslen-Wilson, W.D. 1987. Functional parallelism in spoken word recognition. *Cognition*, 25, 71-102.

Pritchett, B.L. 1988. Garden path phenomena and the grammatical basis of language processing. *Language*, 64, 3, 539-576.

Pritchett, B.L. 1992. *Grammatical Competence and Parsing Performance*. Chicago, IL: University of Chicago Press.

Rayner, K., Carlson, M., & Frazier, L.. 1983. The interaction of syntax and semantics during sentence processing: Eye movements in the analysis of semantically biased sentences. *Journal of Verbal Learning and Verbal Behavior*, 22, 358-374.

Steedman, M.J. 1991. Structure and intonation. *Language*, 67, 2, 260-297.

Stevenson, S. 1994a. Competition and recency in a hybrid network model of syntactic disambiguation. *Journal of Psycholinguistic Research*, 23, 4, 295-321.

Stevenson, S. 1994b. *A Competitive Attachment Model for Resolving Syntactic Ambiguities in Natural Language Parsing*. Unpublished doctoral dissertation, University of Maryland, College Park, MD. Available as Technical Report TR-18 from Rutgers Center for Cognitive Science, Rutgers University.

Sturt, P. (in preparation). *Syntactic Reanalysis in Human Language Processing*. Unpublished doctoral dissertation, Centre for Cognitive Science, University of Edinburgh, Edinburgh, Scotland.

Sturt, P. & Crocker, M.W. 1996. Monotonic syntactic processing: a cross-linguistic study of attachment and reanalysis. *Language and Cognitive Processes*, 11, 5, 449-494.

Sturt, P. & Crocker, M.W. (to appear). Thematic monotonicity. *Journal of Psycholinguistic Research*.

Trueswell, J.C., Tanenhaus, M.K., & Kello, C. 1993. Verb-specific constraints on sentence processing: Separating effects of lexical preference from garden paths. *Journal of Experimental Psychology: Learning, Memory and Cognition*, 19, 3, 528-553.

Wall, R. 1972. *Introduction to Mathematical Linguistics*. Englewood Cliffs, NJ: Prentice Hall.

Warner, J. & Glass, A.L. 1987. Context and distance-to-disambiguation effects in ambiguity resolution: Evidence from grammaticality judgements of garden path sentences. *Journal of Memory and Language*, 26, 714-738.

Weinberg, A. 1993. Parameters in the theory of sentence processing: Minimal committment theory goes East. *Journal of Psycholinguistic Research*, 22, 3, 339-364.

Weinberg, A. 1995. Licensing constraints and the theory of language processing. In R. Mazuka & N. Nagai (eds.), *Japanese Sentence Processing*. Hillsdale, NJ: Lawrence Erlbaum Associates, 235- 255.

AUTHORS INDEX

SUBJECT INDEX

STUDIES IN THEORETICAL PSYCHOLINGUISTICS

1. L. Solan: *Pronominal Reference.* Child Language and the Theory of Grammar. 1983 ISBN 90-277-1495-9
2. B. Lust (ed.): *Studies in the Acquisition of Anaphora.* Volume I: Defining the Constraints. 1986 ISBN 90-277-2121-1; Pb 90-277-2122-X
3. N. M. Hyams: *Language Acquisition and the Theory of Parameters.* 1986 ISBN 90-277-2218-8; Pb 90-277-2219-6
4. T. Roeper and E. Williams (eds.): *Parameter Setting.* 1987 ISBN 90-277-2315-X; Pb 90-277-2316-8
5. S. Flynn: *A Parameter-Setting Model of L2 Acquisition.* Experimental Studies in Anaphora. 1987 ISBN 90-277-2374-5; Pb 90-277-2375-3
6. B. Lust (ed.): *Studies in the Acquisition of Anaphora.* Volume II: Applying the Constraints. 1987 ISBN 1-55608-022-0; Pb 1-55608-023-9
7. G. N. Carlson and M. K. Tanenhaus (eds.): *Linguistic Structure in Language Processing.* 1989 ISBN 1-55608-074-3; Pb 1-55608-075-1
8. S. Flynn and W. O'Neil (eds.): *Linguistic Theory in Second Language Acquisition.* 1988 ISBN 1-55608-084-0; Pb 1-55608-085-9
9. R. J. Matthews and W. Demopoulos (eds.): *Learnability and Linguistic Theory.* 1989 ISBN 0-7923-0247-8; Pb 0-7923-0558-2
10. L. Frazier and J. de Villiers (eds.): *Language Processing and Language Acquisition.* 1990 ISBN 0-7923-0659-7; Pb 0-7923-0660-0
11. J.A. Padilla: *On the Definition of Binding Domains in Spanish.* Evidence from Child Language. 1990 ISBN 0-7923-0744-5
12. M. de Vincenzi: *Syntactic Parsing Strategies in Italian.* The Minimal Chain Principle. 1991 ISBN 0-7923-1274-0; Pb 0-7923-1275-9
13. D.C. Lillo-Martin: *Universal Grammar and American Sign Language.* Setting the Null Argument Parameters. 1991 ISBN 0-7923-1419-0
14. A.E. Pierce: *Language Acquisition and Syntactic Theory.* A Comparative Analysis of French and English Child Grammars. 1992 ISBN 0-7923-1553-7
15. H. Goodluck and M. Rochemont (eds.): *Island Constraints.* Theory, Acquisition and Processing. 1992 ISBN 0-7923-1689-4
16. J.M. Meisel (ed.): *The Acquisition of Verb Placement.* Functional Categories and V2 Phenomena in Language Acquisition. 1992 ISBN 0-7923-1906-0
17. E.C. Klein: *Toward Second Language Acquisition.* A Study of Null-Prep. 1993 ISBN 0-7923-2463-3

STUDIES IN THEORETICAL PSYCHOLINGUISTICS

18. J.L. Packard: *A Linguistic Investigation of Aphasic Chinese Speech.* 1993
ISBN 0-7923-2466-8
19. J. Archibald: *Language Learnability and L2 Phonology:* The Acquisition of Metrical Parameters. 1993
ISBN 0-7923-2486-2
20. M.W. Crocker: *Computational Psycholinguistics.* An Interdisciplinary Approach to the Study of Language. 1996
ISBN 0-7923-3802-2; Pb 0-7923-3806-5
21. J.D. Fodor and F. Ferreira: *Reanalysis in Sentence Processing.* 1998
ISBN 0-7923-5099-5

KLUWER ACADEMIC PUBLISHERS – DORDRECHT / BOSTON / LONDON